INTERNATIONAL PERSPECTIVES ON WOMEN

Edited by Esther Wangari
Towson University

cognella
San Diego, CA

Bassim Hamadeh, CEO and Publisher
Christopher Foster, General Vice President
Michael Simpson, Vice President of Acquisitions
Jessica Knott, Managing Editor
Kevin Fahey, Marketing Manager
Jess Busch, Senior Graphic Designer
Melissa Barcomb, Acquisitions Editor
Sarah Wheeler, Project Editor
Stephanie Sandler, Licensing Associate

First published in the United States of America in 2011 by Cognella, Inc.

15 14 13 12 11   1 2 3 4 5

Printed in the United States of America

ISBN: 978-1-60927-822-9 (pbk)

www.cognella.com 800.200.3908

Contents

Part III: Women and Employment in a Global Economy

Introduction

Goals and Objectives of This Book

This book is interdisciplinary: it takes a global perspective within the contexts of gender relations, class, race, religion, and nationality. These factors are neither static nor biological. They change with economic development, technological advancement, class conflicts, and political actions, as Moghadam (2003) points out in this text. Amott and Matthaei (1991) argue that women's struggle for the right to vote in the 19th century changed gender perceptions and gender relations. In "the 1960s, the transformation of race-ethnic identity into a source of solidarity and pride was essential to movements of people of color such as the Black Power and American Indian Movements." To what extent do the institutionalization and applications of gendered roles, class, race, and religion into social, economic, and political policies impact women in particular, and people in general? These factors shape and differentiate experiences among women and people typically. What are some of the challenges and mechanisms women face and use in their responses to such policies? Although women have diverse differences, locally and internationally, they have been able to organize and participate in socioeconomics and politics around issues that affect all women in their daily lives. Women are instrumental in effecting changes in the areas of policy through legislation, nongovernmental organizations (NGOS), and social movements at the grassroots level. Globally, women bring about changes through international conferences, such as the Beijing International Conference in 1995, the Fourth Conference on Women, and its adoption of the Beijing Platform for Action. These efforts demonstrate some steps taken by international organizations and the United Nations in improving women's working conditions. Furthermore, it offers some recommendations and information on the work done by women and men. The analyses of gender, race, religion, nationality, and class reflect the way socially construed, internalized, and institutionalized terms shape the ways in which people are chosen for different jobs, and how resources are distributed in society. The gendering process of jobs creates a subdivision of labor and hierarchies in the workforce, based on rankings in class, race, religion, and nationality, among other factors. These factors facilitate the understanding of economic restructuring, international economic development, information on global markets, the feminization of labor, including national and international policies that are gendered. The analyses provide some insights in understanding how gendered perspectives are integrated into economics, politics, and global processes. For this, we turn to three major themes of investigation into how these factors are manifested in daily experiences—from local to global.

Part One: The Conceptualization of Gender, Class, Race, Religion, and Nationality

The socialization and construction of gender, race-ethnicity, class, nationality, and religion (among other factors differentiating people and societies) originate from family as an institution, to public institutions. They constitute ideologies, cultural norms, attitudes, and identities that shape most perceptions about gender roles, class, race-ethnicity, nationality, and religious beliefs. At the public level, they are internalized and institutionalized, and become the determinants of policies, distribution, and accessibility to health care, employment, education, environmental safety, and immigration status, among other factors. Rothenberg (2005) points out that in a kinship society, gender relations and hierarchies make up the identity of an individual, and entitlements depend on these hierarchies. Morality, seniority, gender relations, and racial-ethnic privileges and structural arrangements are seen within the context of this culture: a patriarchal culture, in which domination and control are legitimized, and the role of a woman is that of a good mother and wife—an obedient helpmate. According to Waylen (1996) private and public spheres in this type of system seem separate, but they are, in fact, complementary. In various parts of Africa, gender roles overlap, especially in rural communities subject to agricultural production. Women's roles revolve around domestic work, as well as food production. In a capitalist mode of production, patriarchal ideologies filter into the process of production, in which hierarchies are determined on the basis of gender, race-ethnicity, and class. For instance, Hossfeld (Paula Rothenberg 2005) points out that masculinity and femininity are constructed through the gendering of workplace by "reaffirming traditional forms of femininity." Although women work in non-female jobs (especially those in factories), their femininity is affirmed by wearing make-up Such behavior inherently stems from upper-class women, who traditionally did not work. Hossfeld argues that women in the workplace face contradictions, and the "strategy on the part of management serves to devalue women's productive worth." The color-coding by sex—regardless of a woman's occupation—assumes that in every household, there is a man who is the breadwinner. As such, a woman's job is supplementary and temporary, and does not deserve equal pay and benefits compared with that of a man. This generalization is erroneous, since female-headed households are on the rise, according to

Wangari.[1] In her study, she found the impacts of land registration in Mbeere, Kenya, resulted in the disruption of families, which led to an increase in female-headed households.

The expansion of capital in a global market prefers cheap labor in order to minimize the cost of production, thus maximizing profits. The expansion of capital globally, depends on the unskilled labor of women and people of color, particularly in the Third World. Eisenstein[2] points out that "women and girls toil away in maquiladora factories," while the "global village" has been glorified as a key to equality between the core and peripheral countries. The hegemony of political and economic decisions is dominated by the core countries, and those of peripheral nations forming alliances with the international structures of economic power, with race as a determining factor. Likewise, a regional context and global system of states and markets, according to Moghadam, influence each country's social formation, and the roles and status of women. In the Middle East, for instance, women's low status should be seen within the context of economic development and political changes. Islam as a religion alone, she argues, cannot be the determinant of the low status of women, since it is neither more nor less patriarchal than other major religions, such as Judaism and Christianity. The Islamic precepts and the application of legal codes should not be universalized, according to Moghadam.

Part Two: Women and Politics in a Global World

Waylen and Mohanty (1996; 1991) assert that gender-role experiences in Third World women differ, depending on the history and nature of a given state. The experiences of women contrast in terms of class, race, nationality, and religion. Histories—such as colonial, postcolonial, democratic, or authoritarian states—will alter existing gender roles, class, and racial-ethnic social relations. Racial-ethnic and class struggles end up in wars that disrupt whole nations. The presentation of Third World women as the "other" (implying non-Western) is a problematic one, since it constitutes power and domination. The "other" is seen as sharing the same histories of oppression, and that Third World women are powerless, lacking maturity as a group—a group needing to be rescued by Western feminism. Mohanty points out that it is through this construction of the "other" that Western feminists appropriate and colonize the experiences of Third World women. Sisterhood is not universal, Mohanty argues, and she calls for the examination of "concrete histories and political analyses." This image of universalizing also informs economic and political theories, in which women and men share the same policies and economic development. Policies that work in the West are also assumed to work in the Third World and have the same impacts. Economic development policies or political issues are not gender-neutral, nor are they shared by all men. Class, race-ethnicity, nationality, religion, wars, and migration will shape the differences between—and among—women. Waylen (1996; Henderson and Jeydel 2007) dispute theories of generalization and neutrality. They argue that gender roles are not neutral. Women's work is segregated, requires only low skills, and pays less. Western feminists should position their analyses of Third World women on the basis of histories that alter existing gender roles, culture, economic, and political systems. As Staudt[3] points out, "feminist model leadership constitutes commitment of others rather than their subordination. In practice, empowerment means broad responsibilities for all and widely visible decision-making."

Part Three: Women and Employment in a Global Economy

Most of the policies for economic growth implemented in the Third World are based on Western growth models. Such policies are supposed to stimulate growth, and earn a country foreign exchange and investment in the agricultural sector. The cash-crop sector is supposed to be more competitive in the international market, once the devaluation of currency takes effect. Small-scale farmers, most of whom are in rural areas, would benefit in their investment in growing coffee, tea, and other cash crops. Women and men are assumed to share the same experiences. Some of the economic reconstructing consists of land reform through land adjudication, consolidation, and registration and issuing title deeds to the head of the household—a man. The privatization of the agricultural sector excludes women and children from land ownership, thus stripping them of their rights. Land ownership changes from "our land" to "my land," and the owner can sell land without consulting his family or clan. Private ownership results in landlessness and rural–urban migration. The implementation of structural adjustment programs advocated by international financial institutions—such the World Bank and the International Monetary Fund (IMF)—result in budget cuts catering to social services, agricultural subsidy inputs, education, hospitals, employment, the deregulation of commodity prices, and devaluation of the currency, among other factors. Education and hospital institutions demand high costs for their services, and agricultural inputs become more expensive, as will the cost of food. Since some countries do not have social security and insurance, many families will be unable to educate their children or pay hospital bills. Families must then find other alternatives of survival. At a certain level of education, students have to take national examinations for entry into universities and high schools or for further vocational training. Those who fail make up a disadvantaged class of young men and girls; parents must choose between whether a son or a daughter can continue in an education. This will also depend on whether or not parents can afford school fees, books, school uniforms, and building funds—many rural famers cannot. It is likely that a boy will be allocated a parcel of land, while girls will find other alternatives for survival activities: domestic work; prostitution; the informal sector, in which women and (landless) men are involved in various activities. These experiences will also differ, based on gender, class, race, religion, nationality, and other factors. Wichterich and Beneria (2000; 2003) argue that with globalization of the market, feminization and informal labor have increased in Third World countries. Many families find other ways to survive within the informal sector, where the art of recycling, self-employment, and street vending—selling vegetables, fruits, and secondhand clothing in the public domain—are some of activities that thrive in this sector. Governments in these countries are the major employers, and when national policies intersect with international policies through economic reforms, women are more negatively impacted. The cost of living results in economic and political chaos, accompanied by the volunteerism of women in certain activities like soup kitchens and rotating credit, similar to Grameen Bank (in Bangladesh) although at a different set-up. Women groups including men at times contribute to a common fund on monthly basis and rotate credit to members without interest. Where state social services especially in rural areas are not accessible, these groups maintain their communities in monetary as well as in the form of social capital and family cohesiveness. Beneria and Wichterich argue that globalization has resulted in women stepping in to save their families and communities. That is to say, women, with their free labor, end up subsidizing the state for the services eliminated by structural adjustment programs (SAPs). This free labor, though important for the state, is not included in the Gross National Product (GNP). These experiences globally, have facilitated international women's conferences; for instance, the Platform for Action (1995) in Beijing, the Fourth International Conference, demanded better methods for calculating unpaid labor and its inclusion in the GNP. To do so is to recognize women's contributions to the national economy. According to Beneria, Wichterich, and Moghadam, this would also reveal the relationship of women's unpaid work and the domestic sector. In other words, women's unpaid work is integrated with household maintenance, production, and reproduction.

Other nongovernmental organizations (NGOs) and mobilizations of social movements at the grassroots level have emerged as women's labor has become an integral part of the global economy. Moghadam points out that demand changes in the global economy lead to women organizing internationally. For example, the Transnational Feminist Network (TFNS) has been effective in organizing and stating various grievances. The United Nations affords resources toward international conferences for women, in order to challenge some of the local and international policies that do not enhance the well-being of communities. For instance, Beneria, Moghadam, and Wichterich argue that, while labor of women has expanded in the global economy, gender inequalities have persisted. This is especially obvious in garment and electronics factories, as well as in mining industries. Ingrid Macdonald (Lahili-Dutt and Macintyre 2006) asserts that not only are women's rights violated, but also the governments that are supposed to guarantee that the rights of the people are not violated, fail to do so. In the domestic sector, Parreñas[4] argues that domestic work dislocates immigrant women from their countries of origin to countries that marginalize them, with partial rights or no rights.

Notes

1. Gendered Visions for Survival: Semi-Arid Regions in Kenya. 1996 [Eds.]. Dianne Rocheleau, Barbara Thomas-Slayter, and Esther Wangari. *Feminist Political Ecology: Global Issues and Local Experiences*. London: Routledge.
2. Zillah Eisenstein. 2004. *Against Empire: Feminisms, Racism, and the West*. London: Zed Books.
3. Kathleen Staudt. 1990. Ed. *Women, International Development, and Politics*. Temple University Press.
4. Rhacel Salazar Parreñas. 2001. S*ervants of Globalization: Women, Migration, and Domestic Work*. Stanford University Press.

PART I

CONCEPTUALIZING RACE, CLASS, GENDER, RELIGION, AND NATIONALITY

Chapter One

The Foundation of Gender Identity
Garaba, Relational Connectivity, and Patriarchy

Cheryl A. Rubenberg

I've worked since I got married. I love working and I love my job. If I stay at home it's as if I've dropped out of life. Getting out of the house gives me opportunities for different ways of seeing the world. Working is very important for women. It builds character and gives a woman self-esteem. … If my husband told me to stop working I would accept his decision passively and stay at home. I might try to talk with him gently but I wouldn't carry it further than that because I wouldn't want it to reach the stage of divorce. The problem, you see, isn't just between my husband and me; the problem is the whole society. If I were to go to my parents and complain in such a situation, everyone—my father, my brothers, my uncles—would tell me that the issue [of my working] is my husband's responsibility. He is the man of the house. It's his right to make all decisions concerning me, I shouldn't even try to discuss his decision with him, and I should be contented at home. This is not the way I think it should be, but it doesn't matter what I think, it's much bigger than me. Here the norm of male dominance is extremely strong—no matter what class, educational level, social or geographic location, it's the same, and it's overwhelming.
—*Rasha, 28, married with three children, camp resident, "moderately religious" Muslim,* tawjihi *plus two-year diploma*

A battered woman couldn't tell any of her friends or neighbors, much less her children, because of the community. We live with the community. I have a sister who was beaten black and blue every day by her husband. Once he pulled all her hair out and once he punched her eye out. Even I didn't know about any of this for many years—he's an educated man. But she was quiet and patient, and little by little, over the years, he began to appreciate her and to behave better with her. If a woman were to speak about violence outside, the man would react even more violently. And, instead of helping him as she should, she would be damaging him by tarnishing his and his family's reputation. If the man or his family heard about her talk, she would be severely punished by both. Remember, most of the marriages here link families together. So if she hurts her husband and his family, she hurts herself and her family. This means that women must keep their mouths shut. Do I think this is right? It doesn't matter what I think. This is our society. I suffer. I sacrifice. But this is the life God gave me so I accept it.

—Marwa, 45, married with three children, village resident, "very religious"
Christian, tawjihi

Our marriage is very difficult. My husband beats me nearly every day. He doesn't like me—he was forced to marry me as I was forced to marry him. I tried to talk to my family about my problems when we were first married but all that accomplished was creating more problems, especially with his family. So I decided not to tell anyone about my problems—just to keep them to myself … I don't even see my parents anymore … I don't know what God wants from me but to be honest, I don't care anymore. I don't care anything about my husband. All I care about is to have children and to take care of them.

—Nada, 17, married, pregnant with twins, camp resident, "not very religious"
Muslim, completed sixth grade.

Marriage. Work. Violence. Silence. The voices of Rasha, Marwa, and Nada from three different decades, both Muslim and Christian, bring to life the dynamics of women in West Bank society and some of the dilemmas they face.

The Foundation of Gender Identity: *Garaba,* Relational Connectivity, and Patriarchy

In the West Bank (and the Arab world in general), identity signifies something quite different than it does in Western societies. Identity among camp and village women is firmly grounded in *garaba* (kinship) and in the connective web of relations that bonds kin groupings together.[1] In the West, we experience the individuating (separating) process; in

Palestinian society, identity is experienced as "relational connectivity." Palestinians live and conceptualize their lives not as individuals but as members of a family group. Kinship relations give rise to identity through relationality and connectivity within the family group. As Suad Joseph explains, "Relationality is a process by which socially oriented selves are produced under different regimes of political economy. … In the Arab world … various forms of relationality are highly valued and institutionally supported."[2]

Building on the concept of relationality, Joseph further expands our understanding of kinship dynamics by refining it in the concept of "connectivity." Connectivity involves relationships in which a person's personal boundaries are relatively fluid so that the individual understands her "self" to be constituted by "significant others"—overwhelmingly patrilineal agnates—that is, paternal relatives. Connectivity, Joseph argues, should be understood as an activity or intention (rather than a state of being) that acts to reinforce family solidarity.[3] Thus, in the first moment, kinship is deeply inscribed in identity; and relationality is intertwined with patriarchy so that connectivity is structured into a system of domination and subordination.[4]

Apprehending the connection between patriarchy and kinship is crucial to the comprehension of all the relations, roles, and hierarchies growing out of kinship in this particular social environment. Patriarchy involves "the privileging of males and seniors and the mobilization of kin structures, kin morality, and kin idioms to legitimate and institutionalize gendered and aged domination."[5] It gives rise to a group of ideological principles and social relations that privilege the primacy of paternal agnates in all social, economic, and political associations. These principles, in turn, define individual identity, roles (the gendered division of labor), social practices (such as marriage patterns and the preference for sons), and obligations; they also sanction personal connections.[6] Patriarchy is legitimized by the discourse of "honor and shame."[7]

The basic relations in a patriarchal system are control by, and submission to, those who rank higher in terms of age and gender: duties and obligations are strictly defined along these two axes.[8] They are marked by inequality but legitimized through the concept of "complementarity," which means that while roles and responsibilities are dissimilar and unequal, they are idealized as reciprocal and therefore of equal value. The institutionalization of hierarchies of age and gender signifies that older men have more power than do younger men, and men in general have more power than women.

Patriarchy originates in the family and is reflected and reinforced in every social institution. It gives rise to particular "truths" that distinctly position women and signify to them the "reality" of their situation. Several such truths, here expressed in common proverbs, include: "Women are too emotional, they think from their hearts; that is why men should make all the decisions in the house." "Woman's role in life is to be an obedient wife and good mother." "Women's. most important place is in the home—men have the right to go out and do whatever they wish." "Women should not humiliate their husbands by 'talking' outside the home." "Fathers have the right to decide about their daughters' education." "Husbands have the right to determine whether or not their wives may work outside the home." "If a wife disobeys her husband, he has the right to beat her."

Second only to functional hierarchies, "factionalism" is the preeminent dynamic of the *garaba* structure. It involves the fundamental separation of self from other, based on blood ties, and supersedes every other kind of social relation. Factionalism implies that individuals and families will behave differently with relatives than with outsiders *(gharibah)*. Within families, ties are permanent and characterized by mutual support, caring, material assistance, individual sacrifice for the. family good, and trust. Conversely, distrust, exclusion, competitiveness, suspicion, advantage seeking, a balance in obligations, an absence of concern, and frequent conflict typically mark relations among non-kin.[9]

The village women in my research community tended to regard with suspicion and distrust all *gharibah* women—especially those from within their particular village. This division was more blurred, yet clearly present, in the refugee camps. Non-kinswomen were treated formally and were usually contacted only when there was a very specific reason: weddings, wakes, and other formal occasions in which every village family was expected to participate. In terms of general deportment, my observations suggest that while kinswomen can and do laugh and joke together, dance in each other's company, and may even engage in ribaldry on occasion, in the presence of non-kin women, their behavior is proper and constrained. With regard to the inherent distrust, I often heard a woman exclaim to a sister regarding a visit by a non-kin woman: "What did she want?" "Why do you imagine she came by?" The sense of distrust felt by kinswomen toward non-kin women stems, in part, from the fear of the outsider gaining information about the family that could become gossip and then be used against the family. It is also related, at the most basic level, to the binary distinction between self and other—the factionalism inherent in this particular kinship configuration.

Kinship identity among Palestinian camp and village individuals is conceived of in terms of *hamayel* (clans), an ambiguous construction but roughly defined as a semiorganized collection of extended families *('ailah)* based on patrilinality from one eponymous ancestor. *Hamayel* are usually, though not always, geographically contiguous. Historically, some Palestinian hamayel were large, spreading several villages, while many were smaller, forming only part of the population of one village. After the *nakba* in 1948, many *hamayel* were widely dispersed—often to distant countries. However, regardless of size or contiguity, *hamayel* were, and in the main continue to be, the fundamental structure in Palestinian sociopolitical organization and the basis of individuals' most significant social connections. Today, *hamayel* are most clearly observed within village society. In the camps, because the population is usually composed of refugees from more than one pre-1948 village, they are less distinct. Nevertheless, even in the camps, social organization, memory, marriage patterns, and other aspects of social life are organized around enduring clan structures as well as memories of village society that existed prior to 1948. This is apparent in women's everyday conversations about their former lives in their original village, in the hierarchy of their present social relations, and in various other ways.[10] Moreover, even when a *hamulah* is widely geographically dispersed, patrilineal affiliational and social ties remain in force.[11]

The *'ailah,* or functionally extended family, has specific characteristics and broad meaning for individuals in this society. Most significant is that kinship relations supersede every other kind of social relation. Kinship constitutes the dominant social institution through which persons or groups inherit their religious, class, and social affiliations, as well as providing security and support in the face of societal distress. Today loyalty and commitment to the family are the minimum expectations of every family member, while family interests almost always transcend those of individuals. In short, the traditional West Bank family constitutes both an economic and a social unit, and all members are expected to cooperate to ensure its continuation and advancement. It is the primary focus of loyalty, allegiance, and identity.[12] Traditionally, its strength and durability has derived from its ability to provide its members with all their basic needs—material, physical, and psychological. However, as a consequence of changing political and economic circumstances since the *nakba,* the Palestinian *'ailah* has become less and less able to meet the economic and security needs of its members, while at the same time and for the same reasons, many individuals have increasingly needed to rely on their clans.

In West Bank camp and village society, family solidarity has been necessary for social, economic, and political survival. The particular political and economic circumstances that have bounded the West Bank in the past century have reinforced connectivity and have made women's choices—even those that support this dynamic—both rational and functional. Nevertheless, patriarchal kinship, in the particular context of West Bank rural village and refugee camp society, is a system for monopolizing resources, maintaining kinship status, reproducing the patriline, controlling women's sexuality and bodies, legitimating violence, and appropriating women's labor. Two women's stories illustrate some of the ways patriarchal kinship affects women.

Mona grew up in a refugee camp in Jordan and was 18 and living in a refugee camp in the West Bank when I talked with her. Mona's father's family was originally from Ramale. They became refugees in 1948; some family members migrated to West Bank camps while others, like Mona's father, went to Jordanian camps. Mona had completed her secondary education with a 98 percent average, passed the *tawjihi,* and had been accepted at the University of Jordan, where she intended to study medicine. During the summer before she was to start, the wife of one of her father's brothers came to Jordan from the West Bank for a visit. When she saw Mona, she decided Mona would be a perfect bride for her son. Over Mona's objections, the marriage contract was written—without the bride ever having seen her soon-to-be husband. Her aunt promised Mona's father that Mona could continue her education once she married and came to the West Bank. But the promises were not written into the marriage contract since the prospective husband was "family"—he and Mona are patrilateral parallel cousins—and it would have been socially shameful to question the family's word (honor) by requiring such a stipulation. The wedding party was set for two months hence; however, before the appointed time, Mona learned that her husband had been in prison for a violent criminal offense. She wanted to break the engagement but her father refused, insisting that she proceed with the marriage. He argued that since the marriage contract had been signed, if Mona backed out then, she would be considered a divorced woman with all the attendant negative connotations.

Mona had been married for ten months and was three months pregnant when we spoke. She described herself as an "observant" (Muslim) and in a "poor" economic situation. Since she married, she has not seen any of her family in Jordan. She could not even phone them, as there are few telephones in either camp and none in either family's home. Her mother-in-law forced her to leave the nursing school in the camp in which she had enrolled before coming to the West Bank. She did not allow Mona to leave her (the mother-in-law's house where she and her husband lived in one room) without either the mother-in-law or a sister-in-law in accompaniment. Additionally, Mona stated that she had been regularly beaten by her mother-in-law and forced to do all the housework. The physical distance and formalities involved in international travel made a temporary return to her natal home extremely difficult. Divorce was even more out of the question, especially since her husband did not want one. Should she go to court seeking a divorce, a Sharia judge would have inevitably refused her petition because her situation did not fall within any of the legal definitions that allow women to initiate divorce. Further deterrence came from her father's opposition since he did not want the shame that he would incur having agreed to give Mona to his brother's son. Mona cried throughout the interview but ended by saying: "I guess my situation isn't that unique. I simply have to learn to be patient and accept it."

Mona's story is a poignant illustration of the geographically wide-ranging consequences of patriarchal connectivity for women. It is a particularly revealing example of the meaning of the functionally extended family. Felicia's situation is also highly relevant in this context. Though all her paternal relatives reside in one village, her story captures very concisely the dynamics of gender, identity, kinship, and patriarchal connectivity and the negative consequences this matrix of constructs can have on women. Felicia is a 27-year-old mother of three, a village resident who completed *tawjihi*. She is employed as a caregiver in a child daycare center and is an "observant" Muslim, in a "poor" economic situation.

> I was 20 when I got married; I had just completed my first year of university and wanted to continue. My cousin [father's brother's son] was released after four years in prison from the intifada. I didn't know him but I accepted him as a husband—it was a traditional marriage. But I wanted to finish university before I married. My husband wanted to get married right away. He promised to let me finish my education, and my father didn't want to anger his older brother, so he insisted I do what my cousin wanted. I wanted to write in my marriage contract that I could continue my education but my father said no, that it was unnecessary because it was all in the family and it would appear that we didn't trust his word. After we got married—I

got pregnant right away—he told me to leave the university. He said I could choose either to continue studying or to stay with him, but not both. He also said there was no reason for me to go on studying because he would never permit me to work. So I left the university. Then there were serious problems between my father and my husband's father [they are brothers] *over the inheritance my grandfather left them, and their quarrel had a serious negative impact on my relationship with my husband. I also had many problems with my in-laws from the beginning of the marriage. My aunt* [mother-in-law] *used to beat me and shout bad words at me and humiliate me. Many times I went back to my family in despair. My first son was born in my parents' home. Once I stayed with my family for eight months and took a decision not to return to my husband. But the families interfered, especially my father who said I had to go back, because the family problems would get worse if I didn't. ... Yes, my husband beat me frequently when we were first married, but now since I've come back the last time things are a little better. ... I've been working for six years but only because our economic circumstances are so bad and because his mother said yes, and so he said okay. I don't mind the job; the pay isn't much, what I like most is getting out of the house and away from the family problems. My husband is seldom able to find work and we need my income, small as it is, just to feed the family. I do all the housework, child care, cooking, and cleaning. My husband refuses to do anything—he expects me to wait on him totally. My mother-in-law doesn't help me—I have to help her. My father and father-in-law are still quarreling and my mother-in-law still treats me badly, but I've learned to accept things more and to be more patient. All I really care about now are my children. All my hopes and dreams are with them. ... I see the situation of women in this society as quite good, they have freedom, they get their education, they can work, they are in all the professions—even politics. I think the only problem Palestinian women face is their families.*

Neither Mona's or Felicia's story is unusual. Both reveal many of the issues that patriarchal kinship connectivity raises for women: selection of marriage partner, education, employment, in-laws, violence, and limitation of options.

Patriarchal patrilinality affects women in other specific ways. The necessity of producing paternal agnates in the context of patriarchal kinship mandates that women be fertile and bear "fruit," specifically sons. Within West Bank camp and village society, as in all Arab societies, there is a well-known preference for boys over girls that is explained by the importance of patrilinality combined with the son's obligations to his parents and sisters inherent in the relations of patriarchal kinship....

There is great discrimination between boys and girls, and between men and women in our society. When a woman gives birth to a boy, the father and everyone

celebrates. But if she gives birth to a daughter, it's practically a shame—women comfort her and tell her "Inshallah, next time a boy." Yet it is women who give birth, nurture children, provide emotional support—how can they be devalued so much?
     —Jenna, 32, single, village resident, "observant" Muslim, tawjihi

Notes

1. Lila Abu-Lughod, *Veiled Sentiments: Honor and Poetry in a Bedouin Society* (Berkeley: University of California Press, 1986), pp. 39–77, esp. pp. 40–41. Also see Suad Joseph, "Introduction: Theories and Dynamics of Gender, Self, and Identity in Arab Families," Joseph, ed., *Intimate Selving in Arab Families: Gender, Self and Identity* (Syracuse: Syracuse University Press, 1999), p. 12.

2. Joseph, "Introduction," p. 9. Joseph's work in this area has been pioneering. In addition to the sources in note 3, see Joseph, "Family as Security and Bondage: A Political Strategy of the Lebanese Urban Working Class," in Helen I. Safa, ed., *Towards a Political Economy of Urbanization in Third World Countries* (London: Oxford University Press, 1982), pp. 151–174; Joseph, "Gender and Citizenship in Middle Eastern States," *Middle East Report* 26, no. 1 (January–March 1996): 4–10; Joseph, "Elite Strategies for State Building: Women, Family, Religion and the State in Iraq and Lebanon," in Deniz Kandiyoti, ed., *Women, Islam and the State* (Philadelphia: Temple University Press, 1991), pp. 176–200.

3. The concepts of "relationality" and "connectivity" have been specifically articulated and developed by Suad Joseph in many contexts. Here see Joseph, "Introduction," pp. 9–15; Joseph, "Gender and Relationality among Arab Families in Lebanon," *Feminist Studies* 19, no. 3 (Fall 1993): 465–486; Joseph, "Problematizing Gender and Relational Rights: Experiences from Lebanon," *Social Politics* (Fall 1994): 271–272.

4. Abu-Lughod, *Veiled Sentiments*, pp. 39–77.

5. Suad Joseph, "Gender and Relationality," p. 468; Joseph, "Introduction"; Joseph, *Intimate Selving in Arab Families*, p. 12.

6. Abu-Lughod, *Veiled Sentiments*, pp. 39–77.

7. Hisham Sharabi, *Neopatriarchy: A Theory of Distorted Change in Arab Society* (New York: Oxford University Press, 1988), pp. 31–32.

8. Sharabi, *Neopatriarchy*, 1988.

9. Several good analyses of interfamily and intrafamily relations may be found in Lawrence Rosen, *Bargaining for Reality: The Construction of Social Relations in a Muslim Community* (Chicago: University of Chicago Press, 1984), pp. 18–163; Andrea B. Rugh, *Within the Circle: Parents and Children in an Arab Village* (New York: Columbia University Press, 1997), pp. 214–246; and Suad Joseph, *Gender and Family in the Arab World* (Washington, DC: Middle East Research and Information Project, 1994).

10. See, for example, the study by Subhi Jawabreh "Al-Arroub Refugee Camp Case Study: The Pre-'48 Homeland and Social Organization Today," *Jerusalem Times* (Jerusalem, Palestinian weekly, English), May 29, 1998, p. 9.

11. Some observations concerning Palestinian *hamulah* may be found in Kitty Warnock, *Land Before Honor: Palestinian Women in the Occupied Territories* (New York: Monthly Review Press, 1990), pp. 19–32.

12. Halim Barakat, *The Arab World: Society, Culture, and State* (Berkeley: University of California Press, 1993), pp. 97–98.

Chapter Two

Gender, Race, and Class in Silicon Valley

Karen J. Hossfeld

A growing number of historical and contemporary studies illustrate the interconnections between patriarchy and capitalism in defining both the daily lives of working women and the nature of work arrangements in general Sallie Westwood, for example, suggests that on-the-job exploitation of women workers is rooted in part in patriarchal ideology. Westwood states that ideologies "play a vital part in calling forth a sense of self linked to class and gender as well as race. Thus, a patriarchal ideology intervenes on the shopfloor culture to make anew the conditions of work under capitalism" (1985: 6).

One way in which patriarchal ideology affects workplace culture is through the "gendering" of workers—what Westwood refers to as "the social construction of masculinity and femininity on the shop floor" (page 6). The forms of work culture that managers encourage, and that women workers choose to develop, are those that reaffirm traditional forms of femininity. This occurs in spite of the fact that, or more likely because, the women are engaged in roles that are traditionally defined as nonfeminine: factory work and wage earning. My data suggest that although factory work and wage earning are indeed traditions long held by working-class women, the dominant *ideology* that such tasks are "unfeminine" is equally traditional. For example, I asked one Silicon Valley assembler who worked a double shift to support a large family how she found time and finances to obtain elaborate manicures, makeup, and hair stylings. She said that they were priorities because they "restored [her] sense of femininity." Another production worker said that factory work "makes me feel like I'm not a lady, so I have to try to compensate."

This ideology about what constitutes proper identity and behavior for women is multileveled. First, women workers have a clear sense that wage earning and factory work in general are not considered "feminine." This definition of "feminine" derives from an upperclass reality in which women traditionally did not need (and men often did not allow them) to earn incomes. The reality for a production worker who comes from a long line of factory women does not negate the dominant ideology that influences her to say, "At work I feel stripped of my womanhood. I feel like I'm not a lady anymore. It makes me feel ... unattractive and unfeminine."

Second, women may feel "unwomanly" at work because they are away from home and family, which conflicts with ideologies, albeit changing ones, that they should be home. And third, earning wages at all is considered "unwifely" by some women, by their husbands, or both because it strips men of their identity as "breadwinner."

On the shop floor, managers encourage workers to associate "femininity" with something contradictory to factory work. They also encourage women workers to "compensate" for their perceived loss of femininity. This strategy on the part of management serves to devalue women's productive worth. ...

An example of a company policy that divides workers by gender is found in a regulation one large firm has regarding color-coding of smocks that all employees in the manufacturing division are required to wear. While the men's smocks are color-coded according to occupation, the women's are color-coded by sex, regardless of occupation. This is a classic demonstration of management's encouragement of male workers to identify according to job and class and its discouragement of women from doing the same. Regardless of what women do as workers, the underlying message reads, they are nevertheless primarily women. The same company has other practices and programs that convey the same message. Their company newsletter, for example, includes a column entitled "Ladies' Corner," which runs features on cooking and fashion tips for "the working gal." A manager at this plant says that such "gender tactics," as I call them, are designed to "boost morale by reminding the gals that even though they do unfeminine work, they really are still feminine." But although some women workers may value femininity, in the work world, management identifies feminine traits as legitimation for devaluation.

In some places, management offers "refeminization" perks to help women feel "compensated" for their perceived "defeminization" on the job. A prime example is the now well-documented makeup sessions and beauty pageants for young women workers sponsored by multinational electronics corporations at their Southeast Asian plants (Grossman 1979; Ong 1985). While such events are unusual in Silicon Valley, male managers frequently use flirting and dating as "refeminization" strategies. Flirting and dating in and of themselves certainly cannot be construed as capitalist plots to control workers; however, when they are used as false compensation for and to divert women from poor working conditions and workplace alienation, they in effect serve as a form of labor control. In a society where women are taught that their femininity is more important than other aspects of their lives—such as how they relate to their work—flirting can be divisive. And when undesired, flirting can also develop into a form of sexual harassment, which causes further workplace alienation.

One young Chinese production worker told me that she and a coworker avoided filing complaints about illegal and unsafe working conditions because they did not want to annoy their white male supervisor, whom they enjoyed having flirt with them. These two women would never join a union, they told me, because the same supervisor told them that all women who join unions "are a bunch of tough, big-mouthed dykes." Certainly these women have the option of ignoring this man's opinions. But that is not easy, given the one-sided power he has over them not only because he is their supervisor, but because of his age, race, and class.

The women I interviewed rarely pose their womanhood or their self-perceived femininity as attributes meriting higher pay or better treatment. They expect differential treatment because they are women, but "differential" inevitably means lower paid in the work world. The women present their self-defined female attributes as creating additional needs that detract from their financial value. Femininity, although its definition varies among individuals and ethnic groups, is generally viewed as something that subtracts from a woman's market value, even though a majority of women consider it personally desirable.

In general, both the women and men I interviewed believe that women have many needs and skills discernible from those of male workers, but they accept the ideology that such specialness renders them less deserving than men of special treatment, wages, promotions, and status. Conversely, both the men and women viewed men's special needs and skills as rendering men *more* deserving. Two of the classic perceived sex differentials cited by employers in electronics illustrate this point. First, although Silicon Valley employers consistently repeat the old refrain that women are better able than men to perform work requiring manual skills, strong hand-eye coordination, and extreme patience, they nonetheless find it appropriate to pay workers who have these skills (women) less than workers who supposedly do not have them (men). Second, employers say that higher entry-level jobs, wages, and promotions rightly belong to heads of households, but in practice they give such jobs only to men regardless of their household situation, and exclude women, regardless of theirs.

When a man expresses special needs that result from **his** structural position in the family—such as head of household—he is often "compensated," yet when a woman expresses a special need resulting from her traditional structural position in the family—child care or *her* position as head of household—she is told that such issues are not of concern to the employer or, in the case of child care, that it detracts from her focus on her work and thus devalues her productive contribution. This is a clear illustration of Heidi Hartmann's definition of patriarchy: social relationships between men, which, although hierarchical, such as those between employer and worker, have a material base that benefits men and oppresses women (1976). ...

Central to gender-specific capital logic is the assumption that women's paid work is both secondary and temporary. More than 70 percent of the employers and 80 percent of the women workers I interviewed stated that a woman's primary jobs are those of wife, mother, and homemaker, even when she works full time in the paid labor force. Because employers view women's primary job as in the home, and the assume that, prototypically, every women is connected to a man who is bringing in a larger paycheck, they claim that women do not need to earn a full living wage. Employers repeatedly asserted that they believed the low-level jobs were filled only by women because men could not afford to or would not work for such low wages.

Indeed, many of the women would not survive on what they earned unless they pooled resources. For some, especially the nonimmigrants, low wages did mean dependency on men—or at least on family networks and household units. None of the women I interviewed—immigrant or nonimmigrant—lived alone. Yet most of them would be financially better off without their menfolk. For most of the immigrant women, their low wages were the most substantial and steady source of their family's income. *Eighty percent of the immigrant women workers in my study were the largest per annum earners in their households.*

Even when their wages were primary—the main or only family income—the women still considered men to be the major breadwinners. The women considered their waged work as secondary, both in economic value and as a source of identity. Although most agreed that women and men who do exactly the same jobs should be paid the same, they had little expectation that as women they would be eligible for higher-paying "male" jobs. While some of these women—particularly the Asians—believed they could overcome racial and class barriers in the capitalist division of labor, few viewed gender as a division that could be changed. While they may believe that hard work can overcome many obstacles and raise their *families'* socioeconomic class standing, they do not feel that their position in the gender division of labor will change. Many, of course, expect or hope for better jobs for themselves—and others expect or hope to leave the paid labor force altogether—but few wish to enter traditional male jobs or to have jobs that are higher in status or earnings than the men in their families.

The majority of women who are earning more than their male family members view their situation negatively and hope it will change soon. They do not want to earn less than they currently do; rather, they want their menfolk to earn more. This was true of women in all the ethnic groups. The exceptions—a vocal minority—were mainly Mexicanas. Lupe, a high-tech worker in her twenties, explained:

> Some of the girls I work with are ridiculous—they think if they earn more than their husbands it will hurt the men's pride. They play up to the machismo ... I guess it's not entirely ridiculous, because some of them regularly come in with black eyes and bruises, so the men are something they have to reckon with. But, my God, if I had a man like that I would leave. ...

My boyfriend's smart enough to realize that we need my paycheck to feed us and my kids. He usually brings home less than I do, and we're both damn grateful for every cent that either of us makes. When I got a raise he was very happy—I think he feels more relieved, not more resentful. But then, he's not a very typical man, no? Anyway, he'd probably change if we got married and had kids of his own—that's when they start wanting to be the king of their castle.

A Korean immigrant woman in her thirties told how her husband was so adamant that she not earn more than he and that the men in the household be the family's main supporters that each time she cashed her paycheck she gave some of her earnings to her teenaged son to turn over to the father as part of his earnings from his part-time job. She was upset about putting her son in a position of being deceitful to his father, but both mother and son agreed it was the only alternative to the father's otherwise dangerous, violent outbursts.

As in the rest of America, in most cases, the men earned more in those households where both the women and men worked regularly. In many of the families, however, the men tended to work less regularly than the women and to have higher unemployment rates. While most of the families vocally blamed very real socioeconomic conditions for the unemployment, such as declines in "male" industrial sector jobs, many women also felt that their husbands took out their resentment on their families. A young Mexicana, who went to a shelter for battered women after her husband repeatedly beat her, described her extreme situation:

> He knows it's not his fault or my fault that he lost his job: they laid off almost his whole shift. But he acts like I keep my job just to spite him, and it's gotten so I'm so scared of him. Sometimes I think he'd rather kill me or have us starve than watch me go to work and bring home pay. He doesn't want to hurt me, but he is so hurt inside because he feels he has failed as a man.

Certainly not all laid-off married men go to the extreme of beating their wives, but the majority of married women workers whose husbands had gone through periods of unemployment said that the men treated other family members significantly worse when they were out of work. When capitalism rejects male workers, they often use patriarchal channels to vent their anxieties. In a world where men are defined by their control over their environment, losing control in one arena, such as that of the work world, may lead them to tighten control in another arena in which they still have power—the family. This classic cycle is not unique to Third World immigrant communities, but as male unemployment increases in these communities, so may the cycle of male violence.

Even some of the women who recognize the importance of their economic role feel that their status and identity as wage earners are less important than those of men. Many of the women feel that men work not only for income but for respect and dignity. They see their own work as less noble. Although some said they derive satisfaction from their ability to hold a job, none of the women considered her job to be a primary part of her identity or a source of self-esteem. These women see themselves as responsible primarily for the welfare of their families: their main identity is as mother, wife, sister, and daughter, not as worker. Their waged work is seen as an extension of caring for their families. It is not a question of *choosing* to work—they do so out of economic necessity.

When I asked whether their husbands' and fathers' waged work could also be viewed as an extension of familial duties, the women indicated that they definitely perceived a difference. Men's paid labor outside the home was seen as integral both to the men's self-definition and to their responsibility vis-a-vis the family; conversely, women's labor force participation was seen as contradictory both to the women's self-image and to their definitions of female responsibility.

Many immigrant women see their wage contribution to the family's economic survival not only as secondary but as *temporary*, even when they have held their jobs for several years. They expect to quit their production jobs after they have saved enough money to go to school, stay home full time, or open a family business. In actuality, however, most of them barely earn enough to live on, let alone to save, and women who think they are signing on for a brief stint may end up staying in the industry for years.

That these workers view their jobs as temporary has important ramifications for both employers and unions, as well as for the workers themselves. When workers believe they are on board a company for a short time, they are more likely to put up with poor working conditions, because they see them as short term. A Mexican woman who used to work in wafer fabrication reflected on the consequences of such rationalization:

> I worked in that place for four years, and it was really bad—the chemicals knocked you out, and the pay was very low. My friends and me, though, we never made a big deal about it, because we kept thinking we were going to quit soon anyway, so why bother ... We didn't really think of it as our career or anything—just as something we had to do until our fortune changed. It's not exactly the kind of work a girl dreams of herself doing.
>
> My friend was engaged when we started working there, and she thought she was going to get married any day, and then she'd quit. Then, after she was married, she thought she'd quit as soon as she got pregnant ... She has two kids now, and she's still there. Now she's saying she'll quit real soon, because her husband's going to get a better job any time now, and she'll finally get to stay home, like she wants.

Ironically, these women's jobs may turn out to be only temporary, but for different reasons and with different consequences than they planned. Industry analysts predict that within the next decade the majority of Silicon Valley production jobs may well be automated out of existence (Carey 1984). Certainly for some of the immigrant women, their dreams of setting aside money for occupational training or children's schooling or to open a family business or finance relatives' immigration expenses do come true, but not for most. Nonetheless, almost without exception, the women production workers I interviewed—both immigrant and nonimmigrant—saw their present jobs as temporary.

Employers are thus at an advantage in hiring these women at low wages and with little job security. They can play on the women's *own* consciousness as wives and mothers whose primary identities are defined by home and familial roles. While the division of labor prompts the workers to believe that women's waged work is less valuable than men's, the women workers themselves arrive in Silicon Valley with this ideology already internalized.

References

Carey, Pete. 1984. "Tomorrow's Robots: A Revolution at Work." *San Jose Mercury News,* February 8–11.

Grossman, Rachel. 1979. "Women's Place in the Integrated Circuit." *Southeast Asia Chronicle 66—Pacific Research* 9: 2–17.

Hartmann, Heidi. 1976. "Capitalism, Patriarchy, and Job Segregation by Sex." In *Women in the Workplace,* ed. Martha Blaxall and Barbara Reagan, 137–70. Chicago: University of Chicago Press.

Ong, Aihwa. 1985. "Industrialization and Prostitution in Southeast Asia." *Southeast Asia Chronicle* 96: 2–6.

Westwood, Sallie. 1985. *All Day, Every Day: Factory and Family in the Making of Women's Lives.* Champaign: University of Illinois Press.

Chapter Three

Race, Class, Gender, and Women's Works
A Conceptual Framework

Teresa Amott and Julia A. Matthaei

W hat social and economic factors determine and differentiate women's work lives? Why is it, for instance, that the work experiences of African American women are so different from those of European American women? Why have some women worked outside the home for pay, while others have provided for their families through unpaid work in the home? Why are most of the wealthy women in the United States of European descent, and why are so many women of color poor? In this chapter, we lay out a basic conceptual framework for understanding differences in women's works and economic positions.

Throughout U.S. history, economic differences among women (and men) have been constructed and organized along a number of social categories. In our analysis, we focus on the three categories which we see as most central—*gender, race-ethnicity,* and class—with less discussion of others, such as age, sexual preference, and religion. We see these three social categories as interconnected, historical processes of domination and subordination. Thinking about gender, race-ethnicity, and class, then, necessitates thinking historically about power and economic exploitation.

There is a rich and controversial body of literature which examines the ways in which economic exploitation, ideology, and political power create and, in turn, are created by, gender, race-ethnicity, and class; we cannot do justice to the complexity of these issues here.[1] Rather, in this chapter, we develop a basic conceptual framework for thinking about the racial-ethnic histories of women's works which follow in Part II. Then, in the detailed examination of these histories and in the comparison of women across racial-ethnic groups in Part III, we unravel the precise ways in which race-ethnicity, class, and gender have interacted in women's economic lives.

Gender, Race-Ethnicity, and Class Processes: Historical and Interconnected

The concepts of gender, race-ethnicity, and class are neither transhistorical nor independent. Hence, it is artificial to discuss them outside of historical time and place, and separately from one another. At the same time, without such a set of concepts, it is impossible to make sense of women's disparate economic experiences.

Gender, race-ethnicity, and class are not natural or biological categories which are unchanging over time and across cultures. Rather, these categories are socially constructed: they arise and are transformed in history, and themselves transform history. Although societies rationalize them as natural or god-given, ideas of appropriate feminine and masculine behavior vary widely across history and culture. Concepts and practices of race-ethnicity usually justified by religion or biology, also vary over time, reflecting the politics, economics, and ideology of a particular time and, in turn, reinforcing or transforming politics, economics, and ideology. For example, nineteenth century European biologists Louis Agassiz and Count Arthur de Gobineau developed, a taxonomy of race which divided humanity into separate and unequal racial species; this taxonomy was used to rationalize European colonization of Africa and Asia, and slavery in the United States.[2] Class is perhaps the most historically specific category of all, clearly dependent upon the particular economic and social constellation of a society at a point in time. Still, notions of class as inherited or genetic continue to haunt us, harkening back to earlier eras in which lowly birth, was thought to cause low intelgence and a predisposition to criminal activity.

Central to the historical transformation of gender, race-ethnicity and class processes have been the struggles of subordinated groups to redefine or transcend them. For example, throughout the development of capitalism workers' consciousness of themselves as workers and their struggles against class oppression have transformed capitalist-worker relationships, expanding workers' rights and powers. In the nineteenth century, educated white women escaped from the prevailing, domestic view of womanhood by arguing that homemaking work, social homemaking careers, and political organizing. In the 1960s, the transformation of racial-ethnic identity into a source of solidarity and pride was essential to movements of people of color, such as the Black Power and American Indian movements.

Race-ethnicity, gender, and class are interconnected, interdetemining historical processes, rather than separate systems.[3] This is true in two senses, which we will explore in more detail below. First, it is often difficult to determine whether an economic practice constitutes class, race, or gender oppression; for example, slavery in the U.S. South was at the same time a system of class oppression (of slaves by owners) and of racial-ethnic oppression (of Africans by Europeans). Second, a person does not experience these different processes of domination and subordination independently of one another; in philosopher Elizabeth Spelman's metaphor, gender, race-ethnicity, and class are not separate "pop-beads" on a necklace of identity. Hence, there is no generic gender oppression which is experienced by all women regardless of their race-ethnicity or class. As Spelman puts it:

> … in the case of much feminist thought we may get the impression that a woman's identity consists of a sum of parts neatly divisible from one another, parts defined in terms of her race, gender, class, and so on … On this view of personal identity (which might also be called pop-bead metaphysics), my being a woman means the same whether I am white or Black, rich or poor, French or Jamaican, Jewish or Muslim.[4]

The problems of "pop-bead metaphysics" also apply to historical analysis. In our reading of history, there is no common experience of gender across race-ethnicity and class, of race-ethnicity across class and gender lines, or of class across race-ethnicity and gender.

With these caveats in mind, let us examine the processes of gender, class, and race-ethnicity, their importance in the histories of women's works, and some of the ways in which these processes have been intertwined.

Gender

Over the past 20 years, feminist theorists have developed the concept of gender as central to understanding women's lives and oppression. As we will see, while the concept of gender is invaluable, the gender process cannot be understood independently of class and race-ethnicity. Further, there is no common experience of gender oppression among women.

Gender differences in the social lives of men and women are based on, but are not the same thing as, biological differences between the sexes. Gender is rooted in societies' beliefs that the sexes are naturally distinct and opposed social beings. These beliefs are turned into self-fulfilling prophecies through sex-role socialization: the biological sexes are assigned distinct and often unequal work and political positions, and turned into socially distinct genders.

Economists view the sexual division of labor as central to the gender differentiation of the sexes. By assigning the sexes to different and complementary tasks, the sexual division of labor turns them into different and complementary genders. This process is illustrated in Figure 2–1. The work of males is at least partially, if not wholly, different from that of females, making "men" and "women" different economic and social beings. Sexual divisions of labor, not sexual difference alone, create difference and complementarity between "opposite" sexes. These differences, in turn, have been the basis for marriage in most societies.

Anthropologists have found that most societies, across historical periods, have tended to assign females to infant care and to the duties associated with raising children because of their biological ability to bear children. In contrast, men usually concentrate on interfamilial activities, and gain political dominance; hence gender complementarity has usually led to political and economic dominance by men.[5]

The concept of gender certainly helps us understand women's economic histories. As we will see in Part II, each racial-ethnic group has had a sexual division of labor which has barred individuals from the activities of the opposite sex. Gender processes do differentiate women's lives in many ways from those of the men in their own racial-ethnic and class group. Further, gender relations in all groups tend to assign women to the intra-familial work of childrearing, as well as to place women in a subordinate position to the men of their class and racial-ethnic group.

But as soon as we have written these generalizations, exceptions pop into mind. Gender roles do not always correspond to sex. Some American Indian tribes allowed individuals to choose among gender roles: a female, for example, could choose a man's role, do men's work, and marry another female who lived out a woman's role. In the nineteenth century,

Figure 2–1: The Sexual Division of Labor

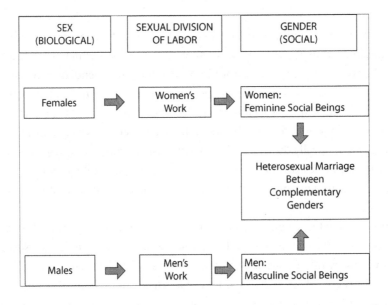

some white females "passed" as men in order to escape the rigid mandates of gender roles. In many of these cases, women lived with and loved other women.

Even though childrearing is women's work in most societies, many women do not have children, and others do not perform their own child care or domestic work. Here, class is an especially important differentiating process. Upper-class women have been able to use their economic power to reassign some of the work of infant care—sometimes even breastfeed-ind—to lower-class women of their own or different racial-ethnic groups. These women, in turn, may have been forced to leave their infants alone or with relatives or friends. Finally, gender complementarity has not always led to social and economic inequality; for example, many American Indian women had real control over the home and benefit from a more egalitarian sharing of power between men and women.

Since the pocesses of sex-role socialization are historically distinct in different times and different cultures, they result in different conceptions of appropriate gender behavior. Both African American and Chicana girls, for instance, learn how to be women—but both must learn the specific gender roles which have developed within their racial-ethnic and class group and historical period. For example, for white middle-class homemakers in the 1950s, adherence to the concept of womanhood discouraged paid employment, while for poor Black women it meant employment as domestic servants for white middle-class women. Since racial-ethnic and class domination have differentiated the experiences of women, one cannot assume, as do many feminist theorists and activists, that all women have the same experience of gender oppression—or even that they will be on the same side of a struggle, not even when some women define that struggle as "feminist."

Not only is gender differentiation and oppression not a universal experience which cre-ates a common "women's oppression," the sexual divisions of labor and family systems of people of color have been systematically disrupted by racial-ethnic and class processes. In the process of invasion and conquest, Europeans imposed their notions of male superior-ity on cultures with more egalitarian forms of gender relations, including many American Indian and African tribes.[6] At the same time, European Americans were quick to abandon their notion of appropriate femininity when it conflicted with profits: for example, slave owners often assigned slave women to backbreaking labor in the fields.

Racial-ethnic and class oppression have also disrupted family life among people of color and the white working class. Europeans interfered with family relations within subordi-nated racial-ethnic communities through rape and forced cohabitation.[7] Sometimes whites encouraged or forced reproduction, as when slaveowners forced slave women into sexual relations. On the other hand, whites have often used their power to curtail reproduction among peoples of color, and aggressive sterilization programs were practiced against Puerto Ricans and American Indians as late as the 1970s. Beginning in the late nineteenth, century, white administrators took American Indian children from their parents to "civilize" them in boarding schools where they were forbidden to speak their own languages or wear their native dress. Slaveowners commonly split up slave families through sale to different and distant new owners. Nevertheless, African Americans were able to maintain strong family ties, and even augmented these with "fictive" or chosen kin,[8] From the mid-nineteenth through the mid-twentieth centuries, many Asians were separated from their spouses or children by hiring policies and restrictions on immigration. Still, they maintained family life within these split households, and eventually succeeded in reuniting, sometimes after generations. Hence, for peoples of color, having children and maintaining families have been an essential part of the struggle against racist oppression. Not surprisingly, many women of color have rejected the white women's movement's view of the family as the center of "women's oppression."

These examples reveal the limitations of gender as a single lens through which to view women's economic lives. Indeed, any attempt to understand women's experiences using gender alone cannot only cause misunderstanding, but can also interfere with the construction of broad-based movements against the oppressions experienced by women.

Race-Ethnicity

Like gender, race-ethnicity is based on a perceived physical difference, and rationalized as "natural" or "god-given." But whereas gender creates difference and inequality according to biological sex, race-ethnicity differentiates individuals according to skin color or other physical features.

In all of human history, individuals have lived in societies with distinct languages, cultures, and economic institutions; these ethnic differences have been perpetuated by intermarriage within, but rarely between, societies. However, ethnic differences can exist independently of a conception of race, and without a practice of racial-ethnic domination such as the Europeans practiced over the last three centuries.

Early European racist thought developed in the seventeenth and eighteenth centuries, embedded in the Christian worldview. Racial theorists argued that people of color were not descended from Adam and Eve as were whites. later, in the nineteenth century, with the growth of Western science and its secular worldview, racial-ethnic differences and inequality were attributed directly to biology. According to the emerging scientific worldview, human beings were divided into biologically distinct and unequal races. Whites were, by nature, on top of this racial hierarchy, with the right and duty to dominate the others ("white man's burden").[9] In this racist typology, some ethnic differences—differences in language, culture, and social practices—were interpreted as racial and hence natural in origin. The different social and economic practices of societies of color were viewed by whites in the nineteenth century as "savage," in need of the "civilizing" influence of white domination. We use the term "race-ethnicity" in this book to grasp the contradictory nature of racial theories and practices, in particular the fact that those people seen as belonging to a particular "race" often lack a shared set of distinct physical characteristics, but rather share a common ethnicity or culture.

European racial theories were used to justify a set of economic and social practices which, in fact, made the "races" socially unequal. In this way, racism and the practices which embody it became self-fulfilling prophecies, as shown in Figure 2–2. Claiming that people of color were inherently inferior, whites segregated and subordinated them socially, economically, and politically. Furthermore, by preventing intenriarriage between people of color and whites, whites perpetuated physical and ethnic differences as well as social and economic inequality between themselves and people of color across the generations. Although few scientists today claim that there are biological factors which create unequal races of human beings, racist practices and institutions have continued to produce both difference and inequality.[10]

Does the concept of race-ethnicity help us understand the economic history of women in the United States? Certainly, for white racial-ethnic domination has been a central force in U.S. history. European colonization of North America entailed the displacement and murder of the continent's indigenous peoples, rationalized by the racist view that American Indians were savage heathens. The economy of the South was based on a racial-ethnic system, in which imported Africans were forced to work for white landowning families as slaves. U.S. military expansion in the nineteenth century brought more lands under U.S. control—the territories of northern Mexico (now the Southwest), the Philippines, and Puerto Rico—incorporating their peoples into the racial-ethnic hierarchy. And from the mid-nineteenth century onward, Asians were brought into Hawaii's plantation system to work for whites as semi-free laborers. In the "twentieth century, racial-ethnic difference and inequality have been perpetuated by the segregation of people of color into different and inferior jobs, living conditions, schools, and political positions, and by the prohibition of intermarriage with whites in some states up until 1967.

Race-ethnicity is a key concept in understanding women's economic histories. But it is not without limitations. First, racial-ethnic processes have never operated independently of class and gender. In the previous section on gender, we saw how racial domination distorted gender and family relations among people of color. Racial domination has also been intricately linked to economic or class domination. As social scientists Michael Omi (Asian American) and Howard Winant (European American) explain, the early European arguments that people of color were without souls had direct economic meaning:

> At stake were not only the prospects for conversion, but the types of treatment to be accorded them. The expropriation of property, the denial of political rights, the introduction of slavery and other forms of coercive labor, as well as outright extermination, all presupposed a worldview which distinguished Europeans— children of God, human beings, etc.—from "others." Such a worldview was

needed to explain why some should be "free" and others enslaved, why some had rights to land and property while others did not.[11]

Indeed, many have argued that racial theories only developed after the economic process of colonization had started, as a justification for white domination of peoples of color.[12]

The essentially economic nature of early racial-ethnic oppression in the United States makes it difficult to isolate whether peoples of color were subordinated in the emerging U.S. economy because of their race-ethnicity or their economic class. Whites displaced American Indians and Mexicans to obtain their land. Whites imported Africans to work as slaves and Asians to work as contract laborers. Puerto Ricans and Filipinas/os were victims of further U.S. expansionism. Race-ethnicity and class intertwined in the patterns of displacement from land, genocide, forced labor, and recruitment from the seventeenth through the twentieth centuries. While it is impossible, in our minds, to determine which came first in these instances—race-ethnicity or class—it is clear that they were intertwined and inseparable.

Privileging racial-ethnic analysis also leads one to deny the existence of class differences, both among whites and among people of color, which complicate and blur the racial-ethnic hierarchy. A racial-ethnic analysis implies that all whites are placed above all peoples of color—as illustrated in the top half of Figure 2–3. In this figure, the pyramid represents the unequal economic structure of the United States, with a small minority of super-rich on the top; the horizontal race line indicates that all whites are economically superior to all peoples of color.

But, in fact, the race line, as European American economist Harold Baron points out, is upward sloping as in the bottom half of Figure 2–3.[13] A minority of the dominated race is allowed some upward mobility and ranks economically above whites. At the same time, however, all whites have some people of color below them. For example, there are upper-class Black, Chicana, and Puerto Rican women who are more economically privileged than poor white women; however, there are always people of color who are less economically privileged than the poorest white woman. Finally, class oppression operates among women of the same racial-ethnic group.

A third problem with the analysis of racial domination is that such domination has not been a homogeneous process. Each subordinated racial-ethnic group has been oppressed and exploited differently by whites: for example, American Indians were killed and displaced, Africans were enslaved, and Filipinas/os and Puerto Ricans were colonized. Whites have also dominated whites; some European immigrant groups, particularly Southern and Eastern Europeans, were subjected to segregation and violence. In some cases, people of color have oppressed and exploited those in another group: some American Indian tribes had African slaves; some Mexicans and Puerto Ricans displaced and murdered Indians and had African slaves. Because of these differences, racial oppression does not automatically bring unity of peoples of color across their own racial-ethnic differences, and feminists of color are not necessarily in solidarity with one another.

Figure 2–2: The Social Construction of Race-Ethnicity

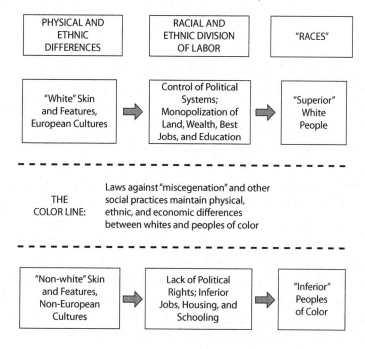

Figure 2–3: Racial Hierarchies

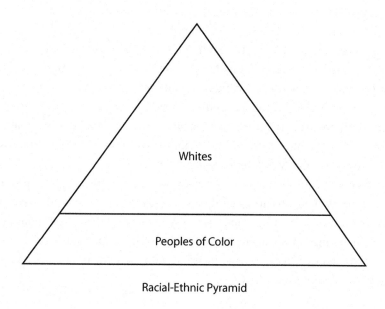

Racial-Ethnic Pyramid

To sum up, we see that, as with gender, the concept of race-ethnicity is essential to our analysis of women's works. However, divorcing this concept from gender and class, again, leads to problems in both theory and practice.

Class

Radical economists stress class as the most important category for understanding economic life. Following Marx, these economists have focused on the ways in which individuals' relationships to the production process are polarized, such that one class reaps the benefits of another class' labor (a process which Marx called "exploitation"). Struggle between the classes over the control of the production process and the distribution of its output, Marx claimed, was the key to economic history. Thus, Marx characterized different societies as involving different "modes of production," each with its own class relations. In the feudal system of medieval Europe, for example, nobles owned the land and serfs were forced to work it, giving over a portion of their product and labor to the leisured nobility. In slavery, slaveowners, by virtue of their property rights in slaves, owned the product of their slaves' labor, living and enriching themselves through their exploitation of the slaves. In capitalism, the owners of the machines and factories are able to live off the labor of the workers, who own nothing but their own labor and hence are forced to work for the owners. In the century since Marx wrote, radical economists have further developed Marx's conception of class, making it into a powerful concept for understanding economies past and present.

We believe that the concepts of class and exploitation are crucial to understanding the work lives of women in early U.S. history, as well as in the modern, capitalist economy. Up through the nineteenth century, different class relations organized production in different regions of the United States. The South was dominated by slave agriculture; the Northeast by emerging industrial capitalism; the Southwest (then part of Mexico) by the *hacienda* system which carried over many elements of the feudal manor into large-scale production for the market; the rural Midwest by independent family farms that produced on a small scale for the market; and the American Indian West by a variety of tribal forms centered in hunting and gathering or agriculture, many characterized by cooperative, egalitarian economic relations, living within these different labor systems, and in different class positions within them, women led very different economic lives.

By the late nineteenth century, however, capitalism had become the dominant form of production, displacing artisans and other small producers along with slave plantations and tribal economies. Today, wage labor accounts for over 90 percent of employment; self employment, including family businesses, accounts for the remaining share.[14] With the rise of capitalism, women were brought into the same labor system, and polarized according to the capitalist-wage laborer hierarchy.

At the same time as the wage labor form specific to capitalism became more prevalent, capitalist class relations became more complex and less transparent. Owners of wealth (stocks and bonds) now rarely direct the production process; instead, salaried managers, who may or may not own stock in the company, take on this function. While the capitalist class may be less Identifiable, it still remains a small and dominant elite. In 1986, the super-rich (the richest one-half of one percent of the households) owned 35 percent of the total wealth in our country, over 70 times the share they would have had if wealth were equally distributed. The richest tenth of all households owned 72 percent of all wealth, over seven times their fair share. This extreme concentration of wealth conveys a concentration of leisure and power over others into the hands of a small number of households, a concentration which is perpetuated through the generations by inheritance laws and customs.[15]

At the other end of the hierarchy, in 1986, the poorest 90 percent of households owned only 28 percent of total wealth, and had to send at least one household member out to work for the household's survival. Among these waged and salaried workers, a complicated hierarchy of segmented labor markets gives some workers greater earnings and power over the production process than others. Indeed, there are many disagreements over how to categorize managers, professionals, and government workers—to name only a few of the jobs which seem to fall outside the two-class model In the chapters to follow, we examine the historical processes by which labor markets became and continue to be segmented.[16]

Class can be a powerful concept in understanding women's economic lives, but there are limits to class analysis if it is kept separate from race-ethnicity and gender. First, as we saw in the race section above, the class relations which characterized the early U.S. economy were also racial-ethnic and gender formations. Slave owners were white and mostly male, slaves were Black. The displaced tribal economies were the societies of indigenous peoples. Independent family farmers were whites who farmed American Indian lands; they organized production in a patriarchal manner, with women and children's work defined by and subordinated to the male household head and property owner. After establishing their dominance in the pre-capitalist period, white men were able to perpetuate and in-stitutionalize this dominance in the emerging capitalist system, particularly through the monopolization of managerial and other high-level jobs.

Second, the sexual division of labor within the family makes the determination of a woman's class complicated—determined not simply by her relationship to the production process, but also by that of her husband or father. For instance, if a woman is not in the labor force but her husband is a capitalist, then we might wish to categorize her as a member of the capitalist class. But what if that same woman worked as a personnel manager for a large corporation, or as a salesperson in an elegant boutique? Clearly, she derives upper-class status and access to income from her husband, but she is also, in her own right, a worker. Conversely, when women lose their husbands through divorce, widowhood, or desertion, they often change their class position in a downward direction. A second gender-related economic process overlooked by class analysis is the unpaid household labor performed by women for their fathers, husbands, and children—or by other women, for pay.[17]

Third, while all workers are exploited by capitalists, they are not equally exploited, and gender and race-ethnicity play important roles in this differentiation. Men and women of the same racial-ethnic group have rarely performed the same jobs—this sex-typing and segregation is the labor market form of the sexual division of labor we studied above. Further, women of different racial-ethnic groups have rarely been employed at the same job, at least not within the same workplace or region. This racial-ethnic-typing and segregation has both reflected and reinforced the racist economic practices upon which the U.S. economy was built.

Thus, jobs in the labor force hierarchy tend to be simultaneously race-typed and gender-typed. Picture in your mind a registered nurse. Most likely, you thought of a white woman. Picture a doctor. Again, you imagined a person of a particular gender (probably a man), and a race (probably a white person). If you think of a railroad porter, it is likely that a Black man comes to mind. Almost all jobs tend to be typed in such a way that stereotypes make it difficult for persons of the "wrong" race and/or gender to train for or obtain the job. Of course, there are regional and historical variations in the typing of jobs. On the West Coast, for example, Asian men performed much of the paid domestic work during the nineteenth century because women were in such short supply. In states where the African American population is very small, such as South Dakota or Vermont, domestic servants and hotel chambermaids are typically white. Nonetheless, the presence of variations in race-gender typing does not contradict the idea that jobs tend to take on racial-ethnic and gender characteristics with profound effects on the labor market opportunities of job-seekers.

The race-sex-typing of jobs makes the effects of class processes inseparable from the effects of race-ethnicity and gender. Not only is the labor market an arena of struggle in which race-ethnicity and gender, as well as class, are reproduced. In addition, the race-sex typing of jobs has been central in determining the job structure itself. For example, secretarial work developed in the late nineteenth century as a white woman's job; hence, in contrast to the white male job of clerk which it replaced, secretarial work cast white women in the role of "office wives" to white men, and involved no path of career advancement into management.

In the chapters of Part II which follow, the operation and maintenance of racism through the labor markets will be made abundantly clear—as will be the fact that white workers, not just white capitalists, helped impose this racial-ethnic hierarchy. White capitalists—wealthy landowners, railroad magnates, factory owners—imported Blacks, Asians, and, later, Puerto Ricans and Mexicans as a low-wage labor supply. The entrance of these workers of color into the labor force was met with hostility and violence by both white workers and small producers such as farmers and craftsmen. Since employers used immigrant workers of color as strikebreakers or low-wage competition, white workers trying to organize for higher wages resisted this immigration. The threat of competition from workers of color and an ideology of white supremacy kept most white workers from recruiting workers of color into their emerging trade unions on equal terms. European immigrants who spoke languages other than English also faced economic and political discrimination. Thus, in an environment of nativism and racial hostility, jobs came to be increasingly segmented along racial-ethnic lines as the result of combined capitalist and worker efforts.[18] Furthermore, as people of different racial-ethnic groups were drawn out of the many different labor systems from which they had come into wage labor, they were also segregated within the developing labor market hierarchy.

The processes which have perpetuated the sex-typing of jobs have, for the most part, been less overt and violent. White male unions, in the late nineteenth century, fought for the passage of "protective legislation" that, by excluding women from dangerous or unhealthy jobs and from overtime work, had the effect of denying them highly paid factory jobs and confining them in lower-paying (and also hazardous) sectors such as apparel and textile manufacture. Women were also confined to low-paid, servile, or care-taking jobs by the sexual division of labor in the home, particularly married women's assignment to the unpaid work of caring for children and serving their husbands. Many employers simply refused to hire married women, with the view that their place was in the home. Domestic responsibilities also limited women's ability to compete for jobs requiring overtime or lengthy training. Professional associations and schools, dominated by white men, restricted the entry of women of all racial-ethnic groups well into the twentieth century. When individual women gained the necessary qualifications and tried to break into jobs monopolized by men of their racial-ethnic group, or into elite, white men's jobs, they were rejected or, if hired, sabotaged, ridiculed, and racially and sexually harassed. These processes have been extremely costly to women in terms of lost wages and job opportunities. This combination of race- and sex-segregation in the labor market meant that, in general, only white men were able to earn a "family wage," adequate to support oneself and a family.

In these ways, the racial-ethnic and gender processes operating in the labor market have transposed white and male domination from pre-capitalist structures into the labor market's class hierarchy. This hierarchy can be described by grouping jobs into different labor market sectors or segments: "primary," "secondary," and "underground." The primary labor market—which has been monopolized by white men—offers high salaries, steady employment, and upward mobility. Its upper tier consists of white-collar salaried or self-employed workers with high status, autonomy, and, often, supervisory capacity. Wealth increases access to this sector, since it purchases elite education and provides helpful job connections. In Part II we investigate at greater length the racial-ethnic, gender, and class barriers erected in the primary sector which have confined most women to other sectors of the labor market and isolated the others in women's professions such as teaching and social work.

The lower tier of the primary sector, which still yields high earnings but involves less autonomy, contains many unionized blue-collar jobs. White working-class men have used union practices, mob violence, and intimidation to monopolize these jobs. By World War

II, however, new ideologies of worker solidarity, embodied in the mass industrial unions, began to overcome the resistance of white male workers to the employment of people of color and white women in these jobs.

In contrast to both these primary tiers, the secondary sector offers low wages, few or no benefits, little opportunity for advancement, and unstable employment. People of color and most white women have been concentrated in these secondary sector jobs, where work is often part-time, temporary, or seasonal, and pay does not rise with increasing education or experience. Jobs in both tiers of the primary labor market have generally yielded family wages, earnings high enough to support a wife and children who are not in the labor force for pay. Men of color in the secondary sector have not been able to earn enough to support their families, and women of color have therefore participated in wage labor to a much higher degree than white women whose husbands held primary sector jobs.

Outside of the formal labor market is the underground sector, where the most marginalized labor force groups, including many people of color, earn their livings from illegal or quasi-legal work. This sector contains a great variety of jobs, including drug trafficking, crime, prostitution, work done by undocumented workers, and sweatshop work which violates labor standards such as minimum wages and job safety regulations.

We will explore these labor markets, and their role in reproducing racial-ethnic and gender inequality, in more detail in the chapters which follow. As they are one of the major mechanisms through which racial-ethnic, gender, and class differences are reproduced, they have been a major arena of struggle against oppression. White women and people of color have waged successful battles to gain admittance to occupations from which they once were barred. Union organizing has succeeded in raising jobs out of the secondary sector by providing higher wages, fringe benefits, a seniority system, and protection from arbitrary firing for workers. Similarly, the boundaries of the underground economy have been changed by struggles to legalize or make illegal acts such as drug use and prostitution—for example, by women's successful struggle to prohibit the sale of alcohol during the early twentieth century—as well as by immigration and labor laws.

Conclusion

Women throughout the United States have not experienced a common oppression as women. The processes of gender, race-ethnicity, and class—intrinsically interconnected— have been central forces determining and differentiating women's work lives in U.S. history. Thus, while the explanatory power of each concept—gender, race-ethnicity, and class—is, in itself, limited, together they form the basis of our analysis of women's works.

As we turn to the economic histories in Part II, a few words of introduction are necessary. These histories are selective and partial, as all histories must be. In these six chapters, we focus on the ways in which racial-ethnic, class, and gender relations have combined to structure women's work lives, and on the transformation of these relations over time with the development of the capitalist economy and the continuing process of struggle against oppression. Many historical events which are not specific to women alone have been central in shaping women's works. For example, Native American women's lives were irrevocably changed by the white takeover of their lands; Puerto Rican women's lives and works have been shaped by the colonial relationship between the United States and Puerto Rico; African American women were freed by the abolition of slavery; poor European immigrant women experienced ethnic and class oppression. Attention to the history of racial-ethnic and class, as well as gender processes is necessary if we are to truly understand women's work lives.

We have chosen to examine each racial-ethnic group of women separately. To avoid repetition, we have purposefully underemphasized the common processes affecting women's lives as a result of the development of U.S. capitalism. Women experienced this development in different ways, filtered through their race-ethnicity and class. In Part III, "Transforming Women's Works," we explore the differential effects of capitalist development on women's lives, and their implications for the future.

The histories we present can evoke strong emotions in the reader: anger that so much injustice has been done, guilt over the complicity of one's ancestors, fear that such injustice might occur again, and pride in the courageous efforts of women and men to survive and to resist. By treating each racial-ethnic group of women separately in Part II, we accentuate the differences and conflicts among women of different racial-ethnic groups. We do this purposefully, for we believe that recognizing these conflicts, and accepting and building on these differences, provides the only solid basis for radical social transformation. As African American lesbian feminist Audre Lorde has written:

> … the strength of women lies in recognizing differences between us as creative, and in standing to those distortions which we inherited without blame but which are now ours to alter. The angers of women can transform differences through insight into power. For anger between peers births change, not destruction, and the discomfort and sense of loss it often causes is not fatal, but a sign of growth.[19]

Chapter Four

Recasting the Middle East, North Africa, and Afghanistan

Valentine Moghadam

> Men are the managers of the affairs of women
> for that God has preferred in bounty
> one of them over another ...
> And those you fear may be rebellious
> admonish; banish them to their couches, and beat them.
> —*Quran, Sura 4, verse 38*

[I]nsofar as all texts are polysemic, they are open to variant readings. We cannot therefore look to a text alone to explain why people have read it in a particular mode or why they tend to favor one reading of it over another. This is especially true of a sacred text like the Qur'an which "has been ripped from its historical, linguistic, literary, and psychological contexts and then been continually re-contextualized in various cultures and according to the ideological needs of various actors" (Arkoun 1994, 5). ... In particular, we need to examine the roles of Muslim interpretive communities and states (the realm of sexual politics) in shaping religious knowledge and authority in ways that enabled patriarchal readings of the Qur'an.

> —*Asma Barlas*

The study of social change has tended to regard certain societal institutions and structures as central and then to examine how these change. Family structure, the organization of markets, the state, religious hierarchies, schools, the ways elites have exploited masses to extract surpluses from them, and the general set of values that governs society's cultural outlook are part of the long list of key institutions. In societies everywhere, cultural institutions and practices, economic processes, and political structures are interactive and relatively autonomous. In the Marxist framework, infrastructures and superstructures are made up of multiple levels, and there are various types of transformations from one level to another. There is also an interactive relationship between structure and agency, inasmuch as structural changes are linked to "consciousness"—whether this be class consciousness (of interest to Marxists) or gender consciousness (of interest to feminists).

Social change and societal development come about principally through technological advancements, class conflict, and political action. Each social formation is located within and subject to the influences of a national class structure, a regional context, and a global system of states and markets. The world-system perspective regards states and national economies as situated within an international capitalist nexus with a division of labor corresponding to its constituent parts—core, periphery, and semiperiphery. As such, no major social change occurs outside of the world context.[1] Thus, to understand the roles and status of women or changes in the structure of the family, for example, it is necessary to examine economic development and political change—which in turn are affected by regional and global developments. As we shall see in the discussion of women's employment, the structural determinants of class location, state legal policy, development strategy, and world-market fluctuations come together to shape the pace and rhythm of women's integration in the labor force and their access to economic resources. Figure 1.1 illustrates the institutions and structures that affect and are affected by social changes in a Marxist-informed world-system perspective. The institutions are embedded within a class structure (the system of production, accumulation, and surplus distribution), a set of gender arrangements and norms (ascribed roles to men and women through custom or law; cultural understandings of feminine and masculine), a regional context (e.g., the Middle East, Europe, Latin America), and a world system of states and markets characterized by asymmetries between core, periphery, and semiperiphery countries.

The study of social change is also often done comparatively. Although it cannot be said that social scientists have a single, universally recognized "comparative method," some of our deepest insights into society and culture are reached in and through comparison. In this book, comparisons among women within the region will be made, and some comparisons will be made between Middle East/North African women and women of other third world regions. Indeed, as a major objective of this book is to show the changing and variable status of women in the Middle East, the most effective method is to study the subject comparatively, emphasizing the factors that best explain the differences in women's status across the region and over time.

Yet such an approach is rarely applied to the Middle East, and even less so to women in Muslim societies in general.[2] Indeed, in the wake of the terrorist assaults on the World Trade Center in New York on September 11, 2001, a new wave of commentary appeared, especially in the United States, that questioned the capacity of Muslim and especially Middle Eastern countries to establish modern, democratic, secular, and gender-egalitarian social systems. One article claimed that Muslim societies have fallen behind Western societies because of the "slow evolution of Islamic societies' treatment of women."[3] Even a disinterested academic study on religion, secularization, and gender equality asserted that countries in the Islamic world are most resistant to the achievement of equality between women and men.[4]

Figure 1.1 Social Structures and Principal Institutions in Contemporary Societies; Their Embeddedness Within Class, Gender, and Regional and Global Relations

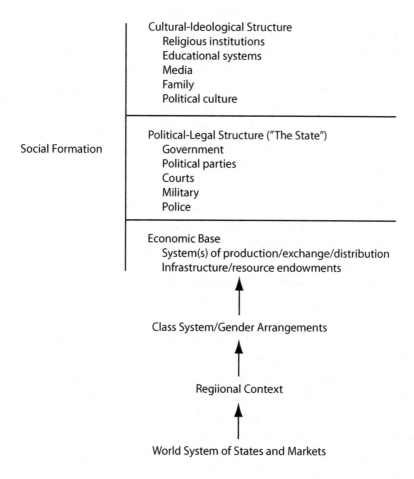

That women's legal status and social positions are worse in Muslim countries than anywhere else is a common view. The prescribed role of women in Islamic theology and law is often argued to be a major determinant of women's status. Women are perceived as wives and mothers, and gender segregation is customary, and sometimes legally required. Whereas economic provision is the responsibility of men, women must marry and reproduce to earn status. Men, unlike women, have the unilateral right of divorce; a woman can work and travel only with the written permission of her male guardian; family honor and good reputation, or the negative consequence of shame, rest most heavily upon the conduct of women. Through the Shari'a, Islam dictates the legal and institutional safeguards of honor, thereby justifying and reinforcing the segregation of society according to sex. Muslim societies are characterized by higher-than-average fertility, higher-than-average mortality, and rapid rates of population growth. It is well known that age at marriage affects fertility. As recently as the late 1980s, an average of 34 percent of all brides in Muslim countries were under twenty years of age, and women in Muslim nations bore an average of six children.

The Muslim countries of the Middle East, North Africa, and South Asia also have a distinct gender disparity in literacy and education, as well as low rates of female labor force participation and labor force shares. In 1980 women's share of the labor force was lowest in the Middle East and North Africa (MENA, 23 percent) and highest in the communist economies of Eastern Europe and the Soviet Union (including Central Asia). In 1997 women's share of the labor force in MENA had increased to about 27 percent, but it was still the lowest of any region in the world economy, including South Asia, where the female share was 33 percent.[5]

High fertility, low literacy, and low labor force participation are commonly linked to the low status of women, which in turn is often attributed to the prevalence of Islamic law and norms in Middle Eastern societies. It is said that because of the continuing importance of values such as family honor and modesty, women's participation in nonagricultural or paid labor carries with it a social stigma, and gainful employment is not perceived as part of their role.[6] Muslim societies, like many others, harbor illusions about immutable gender differences. There is a very strong contention that women are different beings—different often meaning inferior in legal status and rights—which strengthens social barriers to women's achievement. In the realm of education and employment, not only is it believed that women do not have the same interests as men and will therefore avoid men's activities, but also care is exercised to make sure they cannot prepare for roles considered inappropriate. Women's reproductive function or religious norms have been used to justify their segregation in public, their restriction to the home, and their lack of civil and legal rights. As both a reflection of this state of affairs and a contributing factor, those governments of Muslim countries that have signed or ratified the United Nations Convention on the Elimination of All Forms of

Discrimination Against Women (CEDAW) have done so with religiously based reservations that counteract both the spirit and the letter of the convention.[7]

Is the Middle East, then, so different from other regions? Can we understand women's roles and status only in terms of the ubiquity of deference to Islam in the region? In fact, such conceptions are too facile. It is my contention that the position of women in the Middle East cannot be attributed to the presumed intrinsic properties of Islam. It is also my position that Islam is neither more nor less patriarchal than other major religions, especially Hinduism and the other two Abrahamic religions, Judaism and Christianity, all of which share the view of woman as wife and mother. Within Christianity, religious women continue to struggle for a position equal with men, as the ongoing debate over women priests in Catholicism attests. As late as 1998, the Southern Baptist Convention in the United States passed a resolution calling on wives to follow and obey their husbands. In Hinduism a potent female symbol is that of the sati, the self-immolating widow. And the Orthodox Jewish law of personal status bears many similarities to the fundamentals of Islamic law, especially with respect to marriage and divorce.[8] The gender configurations that draw heavily from religion and cultural norms to govern women's work, political praxis, family status, and other aspects of their lives in the Middle East are not unique to Muslim or Middle Eastern countries.

Religious-based law exists in the Middle East, but not exclusively in Muslim countries; it is also present in the Jewish state of Israel. Rabbinical judges are reluctant to grant women divorces, and, as in Saudi Arabia, Israeli women cannot hold public prayer services. The sexual division of labor in the home and in the society is largely shaped by the Halacha, or Jewish law, and by traditions that continue to discriminate against women. Marital relations in Israel, governed by Jewish law, determine that the husband should pay for his wife's maintenance, while she should provide household services. According to one account, "The structure of the arrangement is such that the woman is sheltered from the outside world by her husband and in return she adequately runs the home. The obligations one has toward the other are not equal but rather based on clear gender differentiation."[9]

Neither are the marriage and fertility patterns mentioned above unique to Muslim countries; high fertility rates are found in sub-Saharan African countries today and were common in Western countries in the early stage of industrialization and the demographic transition. The low status accorded women is found in non-Muslim areas as well. In the most patriarchal regions of West and South Asia, especially India, there are marked gender disparities in the delivery of healthcare and access to food, resulting in an excessive mortality rate for women.[10] In northern India and parts of rural China, the preference for boys leads to neglect of baby girls to such extent that infant and child mortality is greater among females; moreover, female feticide has been well documented. As recently as 2002, the female/male sex ratio in China and India was 94: 100. The low status of women and girls, therefore, should be understood not in terms of the intrinsic properties of any one religion but of kin-ordered patriarchal and agrarian structures.

Finally, it should be recalled that in all Western societies women as a group were disadvantaged until relatively recently.[11] Indeed, Islam provided women with property rights for centuries while women in Europe were denied the same rights. In India, Muslim property codes were more progressive than English law until the mid-nineteenth century. It should be stressed, too, that even in the West today there are marked variations in the legal status, economic conditions, and social positions of women. The United States, for example, lags behind northern Europe in terms of social policies and overall security for women. Why Muslim women lag behind Western women in legal rights, mobility, autonomy, and so forth, has more to do with developmental issues—the extent of urbanization, industrialization, and proletarianization, as well as the political ploys of state managers—than with religious and cultural factors.

Gender asymmetry and the status of women in the Muslim world cannot be solely attributed to Islam, because adherence to Islamic precepts and the applications of Islamic legal codes differ throughout the Muslim world. For example, Tunisia and Turkey are secular states, and only Iran has direct clerical rule. Consequently, women's legal and social positions are quite varied, as this book will detail. And within the same Muslim society, social class largely determines the degrees of sex segregation, female autonomy, and mobility. Today upper-class women have more mobility than lower-class women, although in the past it was the reverse: veiling and seclusion were upper-class phenomena. By examining changes over time and variations within societies and by comparing Muslim and non-Muslim gender patterns, one recognizes that the status of women in Muslim societies is neither uniform nor unchanging nor unique.

Assessing Women's Status

Since the 1980s, the subject of women in the Middle East has been tied to the larger issue of Islamic revival, also known as fundamentalism or Islamism, in the region. The rise of Islamist movements in the Middle East has reinforced stereotypes about the region, in particular the idea that Islam is ubiquitous in the culture and politics of the region, that tradition is tenacious, that the clergy have the highest authority, and that women's status is everywhere low. How do we begin to assess the status of women in Islam or in the Middle East? Critics and advocates of Islam hold sharply divergent views on the matter. One author sardonically classified much of the literature on the status of women as representing either "misery research" or "dignity research." The former focuses on the utterly oppressive aspects of Muslim women's lives, while the latter seeks to show the strength of women's positions in their families and communities. In either case, it is the status of women in Islam that is being scrutinized. In some of their writings, secular feminists Juliette Minces, Mai Ghoussoub, Haideh Moghissi, and Haleh Afshar describe adherence to Islamic norms and laws as the main impediment to women's advancement. Leila Ahmed once concluded that Islam is incompatible with feminism—even with the more mainstream/modernist notion of women's rights—because Islam regards women as the weak and inferior sex.[12] Fatima Mernissi, although critical of the existing inequalities, has stressed that the idea of an inferior sex is alien to Islam; it was because of their "strengths" that women had to be subdued and kept under control.[13] Freda Hussein raised counterarguments based on the concept of "complementarity of the sexes" in Islam. Azizah al-Hibri, Riffat Hassan, Asma Barlas, and other Western-based Islamic or Muslim feminists seek to show the genuinely egalitarian and emancipatory content of the Quran, which they maintain has been hijacked by patriarchal interpretations since the early Middle Ages.[14] Finally, those who identify most closely with Islamic law are convinced that Islam provides all the rights necessary for humankind and womankind, and that Islamic states go the furthest in establishing these rights (see Chapter 5 for a discussion of Islamist women activists).

As noted by the Turkish sociologist Yakin Ertürk, these arguments draw attention to interesting and controversial aspects of the problem, but many of them neither provide us with consistent theoretical tools with which to grasp the problem of women's status nor guide us in formulating effective policy for strategy and action. They are either ethnocentric in their critique of Islam or relativistic in stressing cultural specificity. The former approach attributes a conservative role to Islam, assuming that it is an obstacle to progress—whether it be material progress or progress with respect to the status of women. Ertürk argues that overemphasizing the role of Islam not only prevents us from looking at the more fundamental social contradictions that often foster religious requirements but also implies little hope for change, because Islam is regarded by its followers as the literal word of God and therefore absolute. For the Muslim thinkers, a relativist stand is essentially a defensive response and imprisons its advocates in a pseudonationalistic and religious pride. The cultural relativist approach produces a circular argument by uncritically relying on the concept of cultural variability/specificity in justifying Islamic principles.[15] Many Western observers who resort to relativism in their approach to Islam hold liberal worldviews and treat Islamic practices within the context of individual freedom to worship; any interference with that freedom is seen as a violation of human rights. During the 1980s and 1990s, this view underpinned policies of "multiculturalism," "diversity," and "tolerance" in Western Europe and North America, which many feminists came to criticize, arguing that gender differences and inequalities are occluded by this preoccupation with the human rights of cultural groups.[16]

The focus on the status of women in Islam may be important to theologians and to believing women, but it does little to satisfy social science or feminist inquiry. For one thing, Islam is experienced, practiced, and interpreted quite differently over time and space. Tunisian sociologist Abdelwahab Bouhdiba convincingly shows that although the Islamic community may consider itself unified, Islam is fundamentally "plastic," inasmuch as there are various Islams—Tunisian, Iranian, Malay, Afghan, Saudia Arabian, Nigerian, and so on.[17] In order to understand the social implications of Islam, therefore, it is necessary to look at the broader sociopolitical and economic order within which it is exercised. Whether the content of the Quran is inherently conservative and hostile toward women or egalitarian and emancipatory is not irrelevant to social science or feminist inquiry, but it is less central or problematical than it is often made out to be.

Clearly, an alternative is needed to the conceptual trap and political problem created by the devil of ethnocentrism and the deep blue sea of cultural relativism. In this regard it is useful to refer to various "universal declarations" and conventions formulated within the United Nations and agreed upon by the world community. For example, the Universal Declaration on Human Rights (of 1948) provides for both equality between women and men and freedom of religion. The practical meaning of gender equality and means to achieve it have been reflected in the United Nations Convention on the Elimination of All Forms of Discrimination Against Women (CEDAW), adopted on December 10, 1979. The convention entered into force in 1981 and by April 2000 all but twenty-six countries had ratified or acceded to it. Similarly, with the Beijing Declaration and Platform for Action, adopted by the 1995 Fourth World Conference on Women, governments reached a consensus to "seek to promote and protect the full enjoyment of all human rights and the fundamental freedoms of all women throughout the life cycle." The Universal Declaration on Human Rights, CEDAW, and the Platform for Action are all intended to set out universally agreed-upon norms. They were framed by people from diverse cultures, religions, and nationalities and intended to take into account such factors as religion and cultural traditions of countries. For that reason, CEDAW makes no provision whatsoever for differential interpretation based on culture or religion. Instead, it states clearly in Article 2 that "States Parties … undertake … to take all appropriate measures, including legislation, to modify or abolish existing laws, regulations, customs and practices which constitute discrimination against women."[18] All three conventions are thus culturally neutral and universal in their applicability. They provide a solid and legitimate political point of departure for women's rights activists everywhere. In turn, women's rights activists throughout the Middle East seek implementation of CEDAW and the formulation of national action plans for women's advancement based on the Beijing Platform for Action, and are strong proponents of human rights, which they understand to encompass civil, political, and social rights. Many feminists, including Marxist-feminists, would agree with Abdullahi An-Na'im that "human rights are claims we make for the protection of our vital interests in bodily integrity, material well-being, and human dignity."[19]

As for social-scientific research to assess and compare the positions of women in different societies, a sixfold framework of dimensions of women's status adopted from Janet Giele—a framework that is quite consistent with the spirit of CEDAW and the Beijing Platform for Action—can usefully guide concrete investigations of women's positions within and across societies:

> *Political expression.* What righs do women possess, formally and otherwise? Can they own property in their own right? Can they express any dissatisfactions within their own political and social movements?

Work and mobility. How do women fare in the formal labor force? How mobile are they, how well are they paid, how are their jobs ranked, and what leisure do they get?

Family (formation, duration, and size). What is the age of marriage? Do women choose their own partners? Can they divorce them? What is the status of single women and widows? Do women have freedom of movement?

Education. What access do women have, how much can they attain, and is the curriculum the same for them as for men?

Health and sexual control What is women's mortality, to what particular illnesses and stresses (physical and mental) are they exposed, and what control do they have over their own fertility?

Cultural expression. What images of women and their "place" are prevalent, and how far do these reflect or determine reality? What can women do in the cultural field?[20]

This is a useful way of specifying and delineating changes and trends in women's social roles in the economy, the polity, and the cultural sphere. It enables the researcher (and activist) to move from generalities to specificities and to assess the strengths and weaknesses of women's positions. It focuses on women's betterment rather than on culture or religion, and it has wide applicability. At the same time, it draws attention to women as actors. Women are not only the passive targets of policies or the victims of distorted development; they are also shapers and makers of social change—especially Middle Eastern women in the new millennium.

Diversity in the Middle East

To study the Middle East and North Africa is to recognize the diversity within the region and within the female population. Contrary to popular opinion, the Middle East is not a uniform and homogeneous region. Women are themselves stratified by class, ethnicity, education, and age. There is no archetypal Middle Eastern Woman, but rather women inserted in quite diverse socioeconomic and cultural arrangements. The fertility behavior and needs of a poor peasant woman are quite different from those of a professional woman or a wealthy urbanite. The educated Saudi woman who has no need for employment and is chauffeured by a Sri Lankan migrant worker has little in common with the educated Moroccan woman who needs to work to augment the family income and also acquires status with a professional position. There is some overlap in cultural conceptions of gender in Morocco and Saudi Arabia, but there are also profound dissimilarities (and driving is only one of the more trivial ones). Saudi Arabia is far more conservative than Morocco in terms of what is considered appropriate for women.

Women are likewise divided ideologically and politically. Some women activists align themselves with liberal, social democratic, or communist organizations; others support Islamist/fundamentalist groups. Some women reject religion as patriarchal; others wish to reclaim religion for themselves or to identify feminine aspects of it. Some women reject traditions and time-honored customs; others find identity, solace, and strength in them. More research is needed to determine whether social background shapes and can predict political and ideological affiliation, but in general women's social positions have implications for their consciousness and activism.

The countries of the Middle East and North Africa differ in their historical evolution, social composition, economic structures, and state forms. All the countries are Arab except Afghanistan, Iran, Israel, and Turkey. All the countries are predominantly Muslim except Israel. All Muslim countries are predominantly Sunni except Iran, which is predominantly Shi'a, and Iraq, with equal parts Sunni and Shi'a. Some of the countries have Christian populations that were once sizable (Iraq, Egypt, Lebanon, the Palestinians, Syria); others are ethnically diverse (Afghanistan, Iran, Iraq); some have had strong working-class movements and trade unions (Iran, Egypt, Tunisia, Turkey) or large communist organizations (Iran, Egypt, the Palestinians, Sudan). A few still have nomadic and semi-sedentary populations (Afghanistan, Libya, Saudi Arabia). In almost all countries, a considerable part of the middle classes have received Western-style education.

Economically, the countries of the region comprise oil economies poor in other resources, including population (Kuwait, Libya, Oman, Qatar, Saudi Arabia, United Arab Emirates [UAE]); mixed oil economies (Algeria, Iraq, Iran, Egypt, Tunisia, Syria); and non-oil economies (Israel, Jordan, Morocco,

Sudan, Turkey, Yemen). The countries are further divided into the city-states (such as Qatar and the UAE); the "desert states" (for example, Libya and Saudi Arabia); and the "normal states" (Iran, Egypt, Syria, Turkey). The latter have a more diversified structure, and their resources include oil, agricultural land, and large populations. Some MENA countries are rich in capital and import labor (Kuwait, Libya, Saudi Arabia), while others are poor in capital or are middle-income countries that export labor (Algeria, Egypt, Morocco, Tunisia, Turkey, Yemen). Some countries have more-developed class structures than others; the size and significance of the industrial working class, for example, varies across the region. There is variance in the development of skills ("human capital formation"), in the depth and scope of industrialization, in the development of infrastructure, in standards of living and welfare, and in the size of the female labor force.

Politically, the state types range from theocratic monarchism (Saudi Arabia) to secular republicanism (Turkey). Several Gulf states have no constitutions; until 1992 the Kingdom of Saudi Arabia had no formal constitution apart from the Quran and the Shari'a, the Islamic legal code. Many of the states in the Middle East have experienced legitimacy problems, which became acute in the 1980s. Political scientists have used various terms to describe the states in the Middle East: "authoritarian-socialist" (for Algeria, Iraq, Syria), "radical Islamist" (for Iran and Libya), "patriarchal-conservative" (for Jordan, Morocco, Saudi Arabia), and "authoritarian-privatizing" (for Egypt, Tunisia, Turkey). Most of these states have strong capitalistic features, while some retain feudalistic features. In this book

I use "neopatriarchal state," adopted from Hisham Sharabi, as an umbrella term for the various state types in the Middle East.[21] In the neopatriarchal state, unlike liberal or social democratic societies, religion is bound to power and state authority; moreover, the family, rather than the individual, constitutes the universal building block of the community. The neopatriarchal state and the patriarchal family reflect and reinforce each other. For Sharabi, "the most advanced and functional aspect of the neopatriarchal state ... is its internal security apparatus, the mukhabarat. ... In social practice ordinary citizens not only are arbitrarily deprived of some of their basic rights but are the virtual prisoners of the state, the objects of its capricious and ever-present violence. ... It is in many ways no more than a modernized version of the traditional patriarchal sultanate."[22] Although the 1990s saw the beginnings of political liberalization and quasi-democratization, MENA states remain authoritarian and citizen participation limited.

In the Middle East there is a variable mix of religion and politics. Although Turkey is the only country in the region with a constitutional separation of religion and the state, Islam is not a state religion in Syria, whose constitution provides that "freedom of religion shall be preserved, and the state shall respect all religions and guarantee freedom of worship to all, pro vided that public order is not endangered." Syria's Muslim majority coexists with a Christian minority totaling about 12 percent of the population. Christian holidays are recognized in the same way as Muslim holidays. Syria observes Friday rest but also allows time off for Christian civil servants to attend Sunday religious services. The constitution also guarantees women "every opportunity to participate effectively and completely in political, social, economic, and cultural life." In Syria, as in many countries in the region, urban women, especially those who are educated and professional, enjoy a degree of free-dom comparable to their counterparts in, for example, Latin American countries. But it is difficult to reconcile women's rights with Islamic law (Shari'a), which remains unfavorable to women with regard to marriage, divorce, and inheritance. Most of the countries of the Middle East and North Africa are governed to some degree by the Shari'a. This is especially the case in the area of family law, although in some countries the penal code is also based on Islamic law. In the Jewish state of Israel, family law is based on the Halacha and supervised by the rabbinate. Tunisia modernized its family law immediately after independence, and further reforms were adopted in 1993. Turkey's family law was not based on Islam but was quite conservative nonetheless, until the women's movement forced changes in 2001. Elsewhere, family laws based on Islamic texts continue to govern the personal and family status of women, and hence confer on them second-class citizenship.

This second-class citizenship is illustrated in Tables 1.1 and 1.2, which offer economic and political indicators relevant to an understanding of women's legal status and social standing in the region, and compared to other regions.

Table 1.1 Female Economic Activity Rates by Region, 2000

	Rate (%)	Index (1990 = 100)	As % of Male Rate
Arab states	32.9	117	41
East Asia and the Pacific	68.9	99	82
Latin America and the Caribbean	42.0	108	51
South Asia	43.3	106	51
Sub-Saharan Africa	62.3	99	73
Central and Eastern Europe and the CIS (former Soviet Union)	57.8	99	81

Source: *UNDP,* Human Development Report 2002 *(New York: Oxford University Press, 2002), tab. 25, p. 237.*

Note: *The category "Arab states" excludes Iran and Turkey.*

Given the range of socioeconomic and political conditions, it follows that gender is not fixed and unchanging in the Middle East (and neither is culture). As this book will document, there exists intra-regional differentiation in gender norms, as measured by differences in women's legal status, education levels, fertility trends, employment patterns, and political participation. For example, gender segregation in public is the norm and the law in Saudi Arabia but not in Lebanon, Jordan, Morocco, Tunisia, or Syria. Following the Iranian Revolution, the new authorities prohibited abortion, discouraged contraception, and lowered the age of marriage for girls to puberty. Not surprisingly, fertility rates soared in the 1980s (though they dropped in the late 1990s after a policy change). But in Tunisia contraceptive use was widespread in the 1980s and the average age of marriage for women was, and remains, twenty-four. Afghanistan has the highest rate of female illiteracy among Muslim countries, but the state took important steps after the revolution of April 1978 to expand educational facilities and income-generating activities for women (although setbacks occurred when Islamists took power in the early 1990s). Turkish women were given the right to vote in 1930, and in the 1950s and 1960s women began to occupy a large share of high-status occupations such as law, medicine, and university appointments. And, as seen in Table 1.2, women's participation in government as key decisionmakers and as members of parliament varies across the region. In almost all MENA countries, women vote, run for parliament, and are appointed to governmental positions. About 25 percent of judges in Algeria and Tunisia are women, whereas some other MENA countries still ban women from judicial positions.

If all the countries we are studying are predominantly Muslim (save Israel), and if the legal status and social positions of women are variable, then logically Islam and culture are

Table 1.2 Women's Political Participation, MENA in Comparative Perspective

| | % Parliamentary Seats in Single or Lower-Level Chamber Occupied by Women | | | % Women in Decisionmaking Positions in Government | | | |
| | | | | Ministerial Level | | Subministerial Level | |
	1987	1995	1999	1994	1998	1994	1998
MENA							
Algeria	2	7	3	4	0	8	10
Bahrain				0	0	0	1
Egypt	4	2	2	4	6	0	4
Iran	1	3	5	0	0	1	1
Iraq	13	11	6	0	0	0	0
Israel	8	9	12	4	0	5	9
Jordan	0	1	0	3	2	0	0
Kuwait	,0	0	0	0	0	0	7
Lebanon		2		0	0	0	0
Libya				0	0	2	4
Morocco	0	1	1	0	0	0	8
Oman				0	0	2	4
Qatar				0	0	3	0
Saudi Arabia				0	0	0	0
Sudan	8	8	5	0	0	0	0
Syria	9	10	10	7	8	0	0
Tunisia	6	7	7	4	3	14	10
Turkey	1	2	4	5	5	0	17
UAE	0	0	0	0	0	0	0
Yemen		1	1	0	0	0	0
Other							
Argentina	5	22	28	0	8	3	9
Brazil	5	7	6	5	4	11	13
Chile		8	11	13	13	0	8
China	21	21	22	6		4	
Cuba	34	23	28	0	5	9	11
Malaysia	5	8	8	7	16	0	13
Mexico	11	14	17	5	5	5	7

Philippines	9	9	12	8	10	11	19
South Africa	2	25	30	6		2	
Venezuela	4	6	13	11	3	0	7
Vietnam	18	18	26	5	0	0	5

Source: United Nations, *The World's Women: Trends and Statistics 2000* (New York: United Nations), tab. 6A.

Note: *Blank spaces indicate data not available.*

not the principal determinants of their status. Of course, Islam can be stronger in some cases than in others, but what I wish to show in this book is that women's roles and status are structurally determined by state ideology (regime orientation and juridical system), level and type of economic development (extent of industrialization, urbanization, proletarianization, and position in the world system), and class location. A sex/gender system informed by Islam may be identified, but to ascribe principal explanatory power to religion and culture is methodologically deficient, as it exaggerates their influence and renders them timeless and unchanging. Religions and cultural specificities do shape gender systems, but they are not the most significant determinants and are themselves subject to change. The content of gender systems is also subject to change.

A Framework for Analysis: Gender, Class, the State, Development

The theoretical framework that informs this study rests on the premise that stability and change in the status of women are shaped by the following structural determinants: the sex/gender system, class, and economic development and state policies that operate within the capitalist world system.

The Gender System

Marxist-feminists first used the term "sexual division of labor" to refer to the ideological and material ordering of roles, rights, and values in the family, the workplace, and the society that have their origins in male-female sexual difference and especially in women's reproductive capacity. They pointed out that patriarchy, a system of male dominance over women, historically has coexisted with modes of production, and that women's status has been affected by both the sexual division of labor and class divisions corresponding to modes of production. Today the term "gender" is used more broadly to denote the meanings given to masculine and feminine, asymmetrical power relations between the sexes, and the ways that men and women are differently situated in and affected by social processes. Judith Lorber defines gender as "a process of social construction, a system of social stratification, and an institution that structures every aspect of our lives because of its embeddedness in the family, the workplace, and the state, as well as in sexuality, language, and culture."[23] Lorber and other feminists regard gender as a powerful source of social distinctions, while also recognizing that gender differences are elaborated by class and, where relevant, by race and ethnicity.

Combining the Marxist-feminist and sociological perspectives leads to an understanding of the sex/gender system as a cultural construct that is itself constituted by social structure. That is to say, gender systems are differently manifested in kinship-ordered, agrarian, developing, and advanced industrialized settings. Type of political regime and state ideology further influence the gender system. States that are Marxist (for example, Cuba or the former German Democratic Republic), liberal democratic (the United States), social democratic (the Nordic countries), or neopatriarchal (Islamic Republic of Iran) have had quite different laws about women and different policies on the family.[24]

The thesis that women's relative lack of economic power is the most important determinant of gender inequalities, including those of marriage, parenthood, and sexuality, is cogently demonstrated by Rae Blumberg and Janet Chafetz, among others. The division of labor by gender at the macro (societal) level reinforces that of the household. This dynamic is an important source of women's disadvantaged position and of the stability of the gender system. Another important source is juridical and ideological. In most contemporary societal arrangements, "masculine" and "feminine" are defined by law and custom; men and women have unequal access to political power and economic resources, and cultural images and representations of women are fundamentally distinct from those of men—even in societies formally committed to social (including gender) equality. Inequalities are learned and taught, and "the non-perception of disadvantages of a deprived group helps to perpetuate those disadvantages."[25] Many governments do not take an active interest in improving women's status and opportunities, and not all countries have active and autonomous women's organizations to protect and further women's interests and rights. High fertility rates limit women's roles and perpetuate gender inequality. Where official and popular discourses stress sexual differences rather than legal equality, an apparatus exists to create stratification based on gender. The legal system, educational system, and labor market are all sites of the construction and reproduction of gender inequality and the continuing subordination of women.

According to Hanna Papanek, "Gender differences, based on the social construction of biological sex distinctions, are one of the great 'fault lines' of societies—those marks of difference among categories of persons that govern the allocation of power, authority, and resources." Contemporary gender systems are often designed by ideologues and inscribed in law, justified by custom and enforced by policy, sustained by processes of socialization and reinforced through distinct institutions. But gender differences are not the only "fault lines"; they operate within a larger matrix of other socially constructed distinctions, such as class, ethnicity, religion, and age, that give them their specific dynamics in a given time and place. Gender is thus not a homogeneous category. To paraphrase Michael Mann, gender is stratified and stratification is gendered.[26] Nor is the gender system static. In the Middle East, the sex/gender system, while still patriarchal, has undergone change.

Class

Class constitutes a basic unit of social life and thus of social research. Class is here understood in the Marxist sense as determined by ownership or control of the means of production; social classes also have differential access to political power and the state. Class location shapes cultural practices, patterns of consumption, lifestyle, reproduction, and even worldview. As Ralph Miliband put it, class divisions "find expression in terms of power, income, wealth, responsibility, 'life chances,' style and quality of life, and everything else that makes up the texture of existence."[27] Class shapes women's roles in the sphere of production, and it shapes women's choices and behavior in reproduction.

In the highly stratified MENA societies, social-class location, along with state action and economic development, acts upon gender relations and women's social positions. Although state-sponsored education has resulted in a certain amount of upward social mobility and has increased the number of women seeking jobs, women's access to resources, including education, is largely determined by their class location. That a large percentage of urban employed women in the Middle East are found in the services sector or in professional positions can be understood by examining class. As in other third world regions where social disparities are great, upper-middle-class urban women in the Middle East can exercise a greater number of choices and thus become much more "emancipated" than lower-middle-class, working-class, urban poor, or peasant women. In 1971, Constantina Safilios-Rothschild wrote that women could fulfill conflicting professional and marital roles with the help of cheap domestic labor and the extended family network.[28] In 2002 this observation was still true for women from wealthy families, although middle-class women in most of the large Middle Eastern countries are less likely to be able to afford domestic help in these post-oil-boom days and more likely to rely on a mother or mother-in-law. As Margot Badran has noted, whereas some states are committed to women's participation in industrial production (e.g., Egypt, Morocco, Tunisia, Turkey), the system extracts the labor of women in economic need without giving them the social services to coordinate their productive roles in the family and workplace.[29]

Economic development has led to, the growth of the middle class, especially the salaried middle class. The middle class in Middle Eastern countries is internally differentiated; there is a traditional middle class of shopkeepers, small bazaaris, and the self-employed—what Marxists call the traditional petty bourgeoisie. There is also a more modern salaried middle class, persons employed in the government sector or in the private sector as teachers, lawyers, engineers, administrators, secretaries, nurses, doctors, and so on. But this modern salaried middle class is itself differentiated culturally, for many of its members are children of the traditional petty bourgeoisie. The political implications are profound, for Islamist movements evidently have recruited from the more traditional sections of the contemporary middle class: the petty bourgeoisie and the most conservative elements of the professional middle class.

Economic Development and State Policies

Since the 1960s and 1970s the Middle East has been participant in a global process variously called the internationalization of capital, the new (or changing) international division of labor, global Fordism, and globalization. National development plans, domestic industrialization projects, and foreign investment led to significant changes in the structure of the labor force, including an expansion of nonagricultural employment. Oil revenues assisted industrial development projects, which also led to new employment opportunities and changes in the occupational structure. The Middle East has historically been a region with thriving cities, but increased urbanization and rural-urban migration since the 1950s occurred in tandem with changes in the economy and in property relations. Property ownership patterns changed concomitantly from being based almost exclusively on land or merchant capital to being based on the ownership of large-scale industrial units and more complex and international forms of commercial and financial capital. The process of structural transformation and the nearly universal shift toward the non-agrarian urban sector in economic and social terms produced new class actors and undermined (though it did not destroy) the old. Industrial workers, a salaried middle class, and large-scale capitalists are products of and participants in economic development. Mass education and bureaucratic expansion led to prodigious growth in the new middle class; the creation and absorption into the public sector of important productive, commercial, and banking assets spawned a new managerial state bourgeoisie.[30] Other classes and strata affected by economic development and state expansion have been the peasantry, rural landowning class, urban merchant class, and traditional petty bourgeoisie. High population growth rates, coupled with rural-urban migration, concentrated larger numbers of semiproletarians, informal workers, and the unemployed in major urban areas.

In the heyday of economic development, most of the large MENA countries, such as Algeria, Egypt, Iran, and Turkey, embarked on a development strategy of import-substitution industrialization (LSI), where machinery was imported to run local industries producing consumer goods. This strategy was associated with an economic system characterized by central planning and a large public sector. State expansion, economic development, oil wealth, and the region's increased integration within the world system combined to create educational and employment opportunities for women in the Middle East. For about ten years after the oil price increases of the early 1970s, a massive investment program by the oil-producing nations affected the structure of the labor force not only within the relevant countries but throughout the region as a result of labor migration. The urban areas saw an expansion of the female labor force, with women occupying paid positions as workers and professionals. The state played a central role in the development process.

Indeed, between the 1950s and 1980s, the third world state was a major actor in the realization of social and economic development. As such, the state had a principal part in the formulation of social policies, development strategies, and legislation that shaped opportunities for women. Family law; affirmative action-type policies; protective legislation regarding working mothers; policies on education, health, and population; and other components of social policy designed by state managers have affected women's status and gender arrangements. Strong states with the capacity to enforce laws may undermine customary discrimination and patriarchal structures—or they may reinforce them. The state can enable or impede the integration of women citizens in public life. As Jean Pyle found for the Republic of Ireland, state policy can have contradictory goals: development of the economy and expansion of services on one hand, maintenance of the "traditional family" on the other.[31] Such contradictory goals could create role conflicts for women, who may find themselves torn between the economic need or desire to work and the gender ideology that stresses family roles for women. Conversely, economic development and state-sponsored education could have unintended consequences: the ambivalence of neopatriarchal state managers notwithstanding, there is now a generation and stratum of educated women who actively pursue employment and political participation in defiance of cultural norms and gender ideologies.

The positive relationship between women's education and nonagricultural employment is marked throughout the Middle East. Census data reveal that each increase in the level of education is reflected in a corresponding increase in the level of women's nonagricultural employment and a decrease in fertility. Education seems to increase the aspirations of women in certain sectors of society for higher income and better standards of living.[32] Moreover, it has weakened the restrictive barriers of traditions and increased the propensity of women to join the labor force and public life. These social changes have had a positive effect in reducing traditional sex segregation and female seclusion and in producing a generation of middle-class women who have achieved economic independence and no longer depend on family or marriage for survival and status.

At the same time, it is necessary to recognize the limits to change—including those imposed by a country's or a region's location within the economic zones of the capitalist world system. Development strategies and state economic policies are not formulated in a vacuum; they are greatly influenced, for better or for worse, by world-systemic imperatives. Although most of the large MENA countries are semiperiphery countries, the function of the region within the world system thus far has been to guarantee a steady supply of oil for foreign, especially core-country, markets, and to import industrial goods, especially armaments, mainly from core countries. One result has been limited industrialization and manufacturing for export. Another result has been limited employment opportunities for women in the formal industrial sector, as capital-intensive industries and technologies tend to favor male labor. And since the 1980s, socioeconomic problems have bedeviled the region, with wide-ranging implications for women.

The section that follows examines in more detail the gender dynamics of social change in the region—and, by extension, the organization of this book.

Social Changes and Women in the Middle East

One of the ways societies influence each other economically, politically, and culturally is through international labor migration, which also has distinct gender-specific effects. In the Middle East and North Africa, oil-fueled development encouraged labor migration from labor-surplus and capital-poor economies to capital-rich and labor-deficit oil economies. For example, there was substantial Tunisian migrant labor in Libya, Egyptian and Palestinian migrant labor in the Gulf emirates, and Yemeni labor in Saudi Arabia. This migration affected, among other things, the structure of populations, the composition of the households, and the economies of both sending and receiving countries. Many of the oil-rich Gulf states came to have large populations of noncitizens, and female-headed households proliferated in the labor-sending countries. During the years of the oil boom, roughly until the mid-1980s, workers' remittances were an important factor in not only the welfare of families and households but also in the fortunes of economies such as Jordan's and Egypt's. Labor migration to areas outside the Middle East has been undertaken principally by North Africans and Turks. Historically, North Africans have migrated to the cities of France, although large populations of Moroccans have settled in Belgium, the Netherlands, and Spain as well. And in the late 1980s Italy became another destination for North African migrant workers. Turkish "guest workers" have been an important source of labor to (West) German capital since the 1950s.

Labor migration may be functional for the economies of the host country (in that it receives cheap labor) and the sending country (in that unemployment is reduced and capital inflows through workers' remittances are increased); emigration, especially of professionals (the so-called brain drain) also may be advantageous to receiving countries. Like exile, however, labor migration and emigration have other consequences, including social-psychological, cultural, and political effects. In the case of Iran—characterized by the brain drain of Iranian professionals following the 1953 Shah-CIA coup d'etat, the massive exodus of students to the West in the 1960s and 1970s, a second wave of emigration and exile following Islamization, and the proliferation of draft-dodgers in the mid-1980s—the society became fractured and contentious. When, in 1978–1979, tens of thousands of Iranian students in the United States and Europe returned en masse to help construct the new Iran, they brought with them both organizational and leadership skills learned in the anti-Shah student movement and a secular, left-wing political-cultural orientation that put them at odds with the Islamists.[33]

Exile, emigration, and refugee status almost always result in changes in attitudes and behavior, but whether these changes improve or worsen women's lot depends on many intervening factors. In the refugee camps on the Algeria–Morocco border, where 160,000 Sahrawis have lived for some two decades, the women who make up three-quarters of the adult population have played a central role in running the camps from the time of their arrival. They set up committees for health, education, local production, social affairs, and provisions distribution.[34] Janet Bauer informs us that among Algerian Muslim immigrants in France, women have a strong role in maintaining religious rituals and symbolic meanings that are important in preserving cultural identity and adaptation. The same is true for many Turkish residents in Germany. The situation for Iranian refugees, exiles, and immigrants seems to differ, however, as they may be ambivalent about the very traditions and religious rituals from which individuals are said to seek comfort in times of crisis or change. Socioeconomic status and political ideology may also explain differences between Algerian, Turkish, and Iranian immigrants. In her study of Iranian immigrants in France, Vida Nassehy-Behnam states: "Since the initiation of 'theocracy,' Iranian emigration in general has been partly motivated by the pervasiveness of a religious ideology which impinges so dramatically upon individual lifestyles." She then offers two categories of emigrants: (1) political emigrants—that is, those whose exodus began in February 1979, including monarchists, nationalists, communists, and the Iranian Mujahidin; and (2) sociocultural emigrants, defined as those Iranians who were not politically active to any great extent but left the country out of fear over an uncertain future for their children or because of the morose atmosphere that prevailed in Iran, especially for women and youth. In their study of Iranian exiles and immigrants in Los Angeles, Mehdi Bozorgmehr and Georges Sabagh show that some 65 percent of immigrants and 49 percent of exiles had four or more years of college. These findings for Iranians stand in contrast to the figures for many other migration streams. Another difference between Iranian exiles, refugees, and immigrants and those of North Africa and Turkey is the greater preponderance of religious minorities—Christians, Jews, and Baha'is—among Iranians. Such minorities are especially prevalent within the Iranian exile group in Los Angeles. Bozorgmehr and Sabagh offer these religious patterns as an explanation for why the Iranian exiles they surveyed perceived less prejudice than other groups, which may contain a larger share of Muslims.[35]

These factors—socioeconomic status, education, and political ideology—shape the experience of women exiles, immigrants, and refugees. Bauer notes that although women in Middle Eastern Muslim societies are rarely described as migrating alone, many Iranian women do go into exile alone. The women she interviewed in Germany typically had been involved in secular-left political and feminist activities in Iran; many had high school or college educations. She elaborates: "Some married young in traditional marriages; others were single or divorced. Some were working class; others middle or upper middle class … but most of those I interviewed did come into exile with some ideas about increasing personal autonomy and choice."[36]

Can there be emancipation through emigration? Bauer notes the growing feminist consciousness of Iranian exiles and writes that among those she interviewed, there was a general feeling that the traumatic events of 1979–1982 had initiated cross-class feminist cooperation among women and rising consciousness among all Iranians on the issue of gender relations. She adds that larger political goals may be lost, however, as people put aside notions of socialist revolution, social transformation, and political activity and wrap themselves in introspection and their individual lives. Although this was true for the early 1990s, a repoliticization occurred in the latter part of the 1990s, in tandem with the emergence of a movement for political reform within Iran. Expatriate Iranians have regained their political identity and aspirations, with different perspectives on the reform movement, "Islamic feminism," prospects for "Islamic democracy," secularism, and other political alternatives.

The key elements of social change that are usually examined are economic structure and, tied to that, class and property relations. The major source of social change in the Middle East in the post-World War II period has been the dual process of economic development and state expansion. There can be no doubt that over the past fifty years, the economic systems of the region have undergone modernization and growth, with implications for social structure (including the stratification system), the nature and capacity of the state, and the position of women. Much of this economic modernization was based on income from oil, and some came from foreign investment and capital inflows. Economic development alters the status of women in different ways across nations and classes. How women have been involved in and affected by economic development is the subject of Chapter 2. As the state is the manager of economic development in almost all cases, and as state economic and legal policies shape women's access to employment and economic resources, this chapter underscores the government's role in directing development and its impact on women. It also examines shifting state policies in an era of globalization, and their effects on women's employment and economic status.

Another source of social change is revolution, whether large-scale social revolutions or more limited political revolutions. In some Middle Eastern countries, notably Saudi Arabia, change comes about slowly and is carefully orchestrated by the ruling elite. But where revolutions occur, change comes about rapidly and dramatically, with unintended consequences for the masses and the leadership alike. Revolutions have resulted in strong, centralized states whose programs may or may not be in accord with the spirit of the revolutionary coalition (as in the case of the Iranian Revolution). Still, modernizing revolutionary states have been crucial agents in the advancement of women by enacting changes in family law, providing education and employment, and encouraging women's participation in public life. For example, the Iraqi Ba'th regime in its radical phase (1960s and 1970s) undertook social transformation by introducing a land reform program that changed the conditions of the peasantry and by establishing a welfare state for the urban working classes and the poor. In its drive against illiteracy and for free education, the Ba'thist revolution produced one of the best-educated intelligentsias in the Arab world. Even a hostile study of Iraq credited the regime with giving women the right to have careers and participate in civic activities.[37] Such radical measures effected by states and legitimized in political ideologies have been important factors in weakening the hold of traditional kinship systems on women—even though the latter remain resilient. On the other hand, weak states may be unable to implement their ambitious programs for change. The case of Afghanistan is especially illustrative of the formidable social-structural and international hurdles that may confront a revolutionary state and of the implications of these constraints for gender and the status of women. The sociology of revolution has not considered changes in the status of women as a consequence of revolution and has so far been oblivious to the overriding importance of the "woman question" to revolutionaries and reformers. Chapter 3 examines the effect of radical reforms and revolutions in the Middle East on the legal status and social positions of women, including variations in family law. This chapter underscores the gender dynamics of reforms and revolutionary changes, with a view also to correcting an oversight in the sociology of revolution.

Political conflict or war can also bring about social change, including change in the economic and political status of women, a heightened sense of gender awareness, and political activism on the part of women. World War II has been extensively analyzed in terms of gender and social change. Wartime conditions radically transformed the position of women in the work force. Ruth Milkman notes that virtually overnight, the economic mobilization in the United States produced changes that advocates of gender equality both before and since have spent decades struggling for.[38] Postwar demobilization rapidly restored the prewar sexual division of labor, and American culture redefined woman's place in terms of the now famous "feminine mystique." But it is also true that in many Western countries involved in World War II, female labor force participation rose rapidly in the postwar decades. Some authors have begun exploring the complex relationship between gender, consciousness, and social change, suggesting a strong link between the wartime experience and the emergence, two decades later, of the second wave of feminism. The Middle East has encountered numerous wars and political conflicts since the 1950s, with varying implications for societies and for women. In some cases, an unexpected outcome of economic crisis caused by war could be higher education and employment opportunities for women. A study conducted by a professor of education at the Lebanese University suggests that Lebanese parents feel more strongly that educating their daughters is now a good investment, as higher education represents a financial asset. In addition to offering better work opportunities and qualifications for a "better" husband, a degree acts as a safety net should a woman's marriage fail or should she remain single.

In a study I undertook of women's employment patterns in postrevolutionary Iran in 1986, I was surprised to discover that, notwithstanding the exhortations of Islamist ideologues, women had not been driven out of the work force and their participation in government employment had slightly increased relative to 1976. This I attributed to the imperatives of the wartime economy, the manpower needs of the expanding state apparatus, and women's resistance to subordination.[39] A recent study by Maryam Poya confirmed my hypothesis. She found that the mobilization of men at the war front, and the requirements of gender segregation, had resulted in an increased need for female teachers and nurses.[40] In Iraq the mobilization of female labor accelerated during the war with Iran, though this was apparently coupled with the contradictory exhortation to produce more children.[41]

The most obvious case of the impact of political conflict is that of the Palestinians, whose expulsion by Zionists or flight from their villages during periods of strife caused changes in rural Palestinian life and the structure of the family.[42] The prolonged uprising, which has organized and mobilized so many Palestinians, had a positive impact on women's roles, inasmuch as women were able to participate politically in what was once the most secular and democratic movement in the Arab world. Internationally, the best-known Palestinian women have been the guerrilla fighter Leila Khaled and the negotiator and English professor Hanan Ashrawi—two contrasting examples of roles available to Palestinian women in their movement. In the 1970s Palestinian women's political activity and participation in resistance groups expanded, whether in Lebanon, the West Bank, Gaza, universities, or refugee camps. And during the first intifada, or uprising against occupation, which began in 1987, Palestinian women organized themselves into impressive independent political groups and economic cooperatives. A feminist consciousness became more visible among Palestinian women, and some Palestinian women writers. such as Samira Azzam and Fadwa Tuqan, combined a critique of patriarchal structures and a fervent nationalism to produce compelling work. Likewise, the long civil war in Lebanon produced not only suffering and destruction but a remarkable body of literature with strong themes of social and gender consciousness. Miriam Cooke's analysis of the war writings of the "Beirut Decentrists" in the late 1970s and early 1980s shows the emergence of a feminist school of women writers. Indeed, Cooke's argument is that what has been seen as the first Arab women's literary school is in fact feminist.[43]

At the same time, the Palestinian movement has exalted women as mothers and as mothers of martyrs. This emphasis on their reproductive role has created a tension on which a number of authors have commented. During the latter part of the 1980s, another trend emerged among the Palestinians, especially in the impoverished Gaza Strip: Islamist vigilantes who insisted that women cover themselves when appearing in public. The frustrations of daily life, the indignities of occupation, and the inability of the secular and democratic project to materialize may explain this shift. What began as a sophisticated women's movement in the early 1990s that sought feminist interventions in the areas of constitution-writing and social policy experienced setbacks toward the end of the decade, as the West Bank and Gaza faced Islamization and continued Israeli occupation.[44] As noted by Zahira Kamal, a leading figure in the women's movement, "Palestinian women are prisoners of a concept of 'women and the intifada.'"[45]

One important dimension of social change in the region has been the weakening of the patriarchal family and traditional kinship systems. Demographic changes, including patterns of marriage and fertility behavior, have followed from state-sponsored economic development, state-directed legal reforms, and women's educational attainment. Industrialization, urbanization, and proletarianization have disrupted kinship-based structures, with their gender and age hierarchies. In some cases, revolutionary states have undermined patriarchal structures, or attempted to do so, through legislation aimed at weakening traditional rural landlord structures or the power of tribes. Often this type of change comes about coercively. Whether changes to the patriarchal family structures come about gradually and nonviolently or rapidly and coercively, the implications for the status of women within the family and in the society are profound. Yet most MENA states have been ambivalent about transforming women and the family. They have sought the apparently contradictory goals of economic development and strengthening of the family. The latter objective is often a bargain struck with more conservative social elements, such as religious leaders or traditional local communities. Changes in the patriarchal social structure, the contradictory role of the neopatriarchal state, and the profound changes occurring to the structure of the family are examined in Chapter 4.

One of the most vexed issues of the region, with significant implications for the rise of Islamism and the question of women, is the nonresolution of the Palestinian-Israeli conflict. A deep sense of injustice directed at Zionist actions and U.S. imperialism pervades the region. In Iran the 1953 CIA-sponsored coup d'etat against the government of Prime Minister Mohammad Mossadegh and subsequent U.S. support for the second Pahlavi monarch linger in collective memory. That the Shah gave Israel near-diplomatic status in Iran in the 1960s was also used against him during the Iranian Revolution. Significantly, one of the first acts of the new revolutionary regime in Iran in 1979 was to invite Palestine Liberation Organization (PLO) chairman Yasir Arafat to Tehran and hand over the former Israeli legation building to the PLO. Throughout the region—in Lebanon, Iraq, Syria, Algeria—large segments of the population find the displacement of fellow Arabs or Muslims (Palestinians) and the intrigues of Israel and the United States an enormous affront. Although this sense of moral outrage is common to liberals, leftists, and Islamists alike, it is typically strongest among Islamists, who make the elimination of Zionism, the liberation of Jerusalem, humiliation of the United States, and other such aspirations major goals and slogans of their movements—as we saw with Al-Qaida and the events of September 11, 2001.

The implications for women are significant, inasmuch as anti-Zionist, anti-imperialist, and especially Islamist movements are preoccupied with questions of cultural identity and authenticity. As women play a crucial role in the socialization of the next generation, they become symbols of cultural values and traditions. Some Muslim women regard this role as an exalted one, and they gladly assume it, becoming active participants, in some cases ideologues, in Islamist movements. Other women find it an onerous burden; they resent restrictions on their autonomy, individuality, mobility, and range of choices. In some countries, these nonconformist women pursue education, employment, and foreign travel to the extent that they can, joining women's associations or political organizations in opposition to Islamist movements. In Algeria, the Islamist movement spurred a militant feminist movement, something that did not exist before. In other, more authoritarian countries, nonconformist women face legal restrictions on dress, occupation, travel, and encounters with men outside their own families. Their response can take the form of resentful acquiescence, passive resistance, or self-exile. This response was especially strong among middle-class Iranian women during the 1980s, although in the 1990s women began to challenge the gender system and patriarchal Islamist norms more directly. The emergence of Islamist movements and women's varied responses, including feminist responses, is examined in Chapter 5.

To veil or not to veil has been a recurring issue in Muslim countries. Polemics surrounding hijab (modest Islamic dress for women) abound in every country. During the era of early modernization and nation building, national progress and the emancipation of women were considered synonymous. This viewpoint entailed discouragement of the veil and encouragement of schooling for girls. The veil was associated with national backwardness, as well as female illiteracy and subjugation. But a paradox of the 1980s was that more and more educated women, even working women (especially in Egypt), took to the veil. It is true that the veil has been convenient to militants and political activists. For example, in the Algerian war for independence against the French and the Iranian Revolution against the Shah, women used the chador, or all-encompassing veil, to hide political leaflets and arms. But is veiling always a matter of individual choice, or does social pressure also play a part? In the case of compulsory veiling in the Islamic Republic of Iran, Saudi Arabia, or Afghanistan under the Taliban, the answer is clear. But what of the expansion of veiling in Algeria, Egypt, Turkey, and among the Palestinians? Chapter 5 takes up this question as well.

Certainly there are Islamist women activists—as well as secular feminists and Islamic feminists. Much of feminist scholarship over the past twenty years has sought to show that women are not simply passive recipients of the effects of social change. They are agents, too; women as well as men are makers of history and builders of movements and societies. This holds equally true for the Middle East and North Africa. Women are actively involved in movements for social change—revolution, national liberation, human rights, women's rights, and democratization. Besides national groupings, there are regionwide organizations and networks within which women are active, such as the Arab Women's Solidarity Association, the Arab Human Rights Organization, and Women Living Under Muslim Laws, a transnational feminist network. Women are also actively involved in support of and against Islamist/fundamentalist movements. Islamist women are discernible by their dress, the Islamic hijab. Anti-fundamentalist women are likewise discernible by their dress, which is Western, and by their liberal or left-wing political views. In between are Muslim women who may veil but are also opposed to second-class citizenship for women. All in all, women in the Middle East, North Africa, and Afghanistan have participated in political organizations, social movements, and revolutions. Women also have been involved in productive processes and economic development. Whether as peasants, managers of households, factory workers, service workers, street vendors, teachers, nurses, or professionals, MENA women have contributed significantly to economic production and social reproduction—though their contributions are not always acknowledged, valued, or remunerated.

I have said that political conflicts and war are an important part of the process of social change in the Middle East, with implications for women and gender relations. Apart from the long-standing Arab–Israeli tensions, a conflict in the region that influenced women's positions was the Iran–Iraq War, which lasted eight long years (1980–1988). One result of the war in both countries was the ever-increasing allocation of central government expenditure to defense, at the expense of health, education, and services. Also, during the war women in Iran were constantly harassed by zealots if they did not adhere strictly to Islamic dress and manner. Those women who complained about hijab or resisted by showing a little hair or wearing bright-colored socks were admonished to "feel shame before the corpses of the martyrs of Karbala"—a reference to an incident in religious history as well as to the fallen soldiers in the battle with Iraq. However, as mentioned above, an unintended consequence of the war was to override early ideological objections to female employment in the civil service. As the state apparatus proliferated, and as a large proportion of the male population was concentrated at the war front, women found opportunities for employment in the government sector that Islamist ideologues had earlier denied them. Eventually, the war had a deteriorating effect on employment for both men and women. Yet today the Iranian authorities actively encourage women to take up fields of study and employment they deem both socially necessary and appropriate for women, especially medicine and teaching. Meanwhile, Iranian women themselves are making major demands for the modernization of family law and for greater political participation.

Iran constitutes one of the two case studies in this book. The Iranian case deserved further amplification because of its fascinating trajectory from a deeply patriarchal and very repressive theocracy to a parliamentary Islamic republic in which liberals and Islamic feminists are becoming increasingly vocal and visible. (It is also the case of women and social change with which I am most personally involved.) Thus Chapter 6 examines the contradictions of Islamization and the changing status of women in Iran. The subject of Chapter 7 is the prolonged battle over women's rights in Afghanistan. The Afghan case needed its own chapter, too, if only to place the Marxist-inspired reforms of 1978 in proper historical and social context and to show how the subversion of a modernizing state by an Islamist grouping financed by an international coalition of states led straight to the Taliban.46 The elaboration of the Afghan case is necessary to demonstrate its gender dimension—occluded in almost all mainstream accounts—and to show its relevance to the study of social change.

This book, therefore, is an exploration of the causes, nature, and direction of change in the Middle East, North Africa, and Afghanistan, particularly as these have affected women's status and social positions. The economic, political, and cultural dimensions of change will be underscored, and the unintended consequences of state policies as they affect women will be highlighted. The chapters will reveal the contradictions and paradoxes of social change, as well as its more predictable patterns and trends. In particular, the chapters draw attention to the potentially revolutionary role of middle-class Middle Eastern women, especially secular feminists and Muslim feminists using the languages of socialism, liberalism, feminism, and an emancipatory Islam. These women are not simply acting out roles prescribed for them by religion, by culture, or by neopatriarchal states; they are questioning their roles and status, demanding social and political change, participating in movements, and taking sides in ideological battles. In particular, they are at the center of the new social movements for democratization, civil society, and citizenship.

Notes

The opening quote from Asma Barlas is from her book *Believing Women in Islam: Unreading Patriarchal Interpretations of the Qur'an* (Austin: University of Texas Press, 2002), chap. 1.

1. Daniel Chirot, *Social Change in the Modern Era* (San Diego: Harcourt Brace Jovanovich, 1983), p. 3. For an elaboration of the structuralist and Marxist approach, see Christopher Lloyd, *Explanation in Social History* (London: Basil Blackwell, 1986), especially pt. 3. On world-system theory, see Immanuel Wallerstein, *The Modern World-System*, vol. 3 (San Diego: Academic Press, 1989); and Christopher Chase-Dunn, *Global Formation: Structures of the World-Economy*, 2nd ed. (Lanham, Md.: Rowman and Littlefield, 1998).

2. But see Sami G. Hajjar, ed., *The Middle East: From Transition to Development* (Leiden: E. J. Brill, 1985). Although the collection is uneven, especially useful are the introduction by Hajjar, the chapter on demography by Basheer Nijim, and the essay on education and political development in the Middle East by Nancy and Joseph Jabbra. See also Nicholas S. Hopkins and Saad Eddin Ibrahim, eds., *Arab Society: Class, Gender, Power, and Development* (Cairo: American University in Cairo Press, 1997).

3. David S. Landes and Richard A. Landes, "Do Fundamentalists Fear Our Women?" *New Republic*, September 29, 2001. See also Samuel P. Huntington, "The Age of Muslim Wars," *Newsweek*, January 2002; and Francis Fukuyama, "Their Target: The Modern World," *Newsweek*, January 2002.

4. Pippa Norris and Robert Inglehart, "Religion, Secularization and Gender Equality," mimeo, John F. Kennedy School of Government, Harvard University. The paper was a preliminary draft from chap. 3 of their book, *Rising Tide: Gender Equality and Shifts in the Cultural Zeitgeist* (New York: Oxford University Press, 2003).

5. United Nations, *The World's Women 2000: Trends and Statistics* (New York: United Nations, 2000), chart 5.1, p. 110.

6. Nadia Youssef, "The Status and Fertility Patterns of Muslim Women," in Lois Beck and Nikki Keddie, eds., *Women in the Muslim World* (Cambridge: Harvard University Press, 1978), pp. 69–99; John Weeks, "The Demography of Islamic Nations," *Population Bulletin 43* (4)

(December 1988): Fatima Mernissi, *Beyond the Veil: Male-Female Dynamics in Modern Muslim Society*, rev. ed. (Bloomington: Indiana University Press, 1987); Ruth Leger Sivard, *Women ... A World Survey* (Washington, D.C.: World Priorities, 1985); Julinda Abu Nasr, N. Khoury, and H. Azzam, eds., *Women, Employment, and Development in the Arab World* (The Hague: Mouton/ILO, 1985); and Ester Boserup, "Economic Change and the Roles of Women," in Irene Tinker, ed., *Persistent Inequalities: Women and World Development* (New York: Oxford University Press, 1990), pp. 14–24.

7. See *Al-Raida* (quarterly journal of the Institute for Women's Studies in the Arab World, Lebanese American University, Beirut) 15 (80–81) (Winter–Spring 1998), a special issue on Arab countries and CEDAW. See also Jane Connors, "The Women's Convention in the Muslim World," in Mai Yamani, ed., *Feminism and Islam: Legal and Literary Perspectives* (New York University Press, 1996), pp. 351–371.

8. See contributions in V. M. Moghadam, ed., *Identity Politics and Women: Cultural Reassertions and Feminisms in International Perspective* (Boulder: Westview Press, 1994).

9. Pnina Lahav, "Raising the Status of Women Through Law: The Case of Israel," in Wellesley Editorial Committee, ed., *Women and National Development: The Complexities of Change* (Chicago: University of Chicago Press, 1987), p. 199. See also Shulamit Aloni, "Up the Down Escalator," in Robin Morgan, ed., *Sisterhood Is Global* (New York: Anchor Books, 1984), pp. 360–364; and Madeleine Tress, "Halaka, Zionism, and Gender: The Case of Gush Emunim," in *Moghadam, Identity Politics and Women*, pp. 307–328.

10. Urvashi Boutalia, "Indian Women and the New Movement," *Women's Studies International Forum* 8.(2) (1985): 131–133; Barbara Miller, *The Endangered Sex* (Ithaca: Cornell University Press, 1981); and Jean Drèze and Amartya Sen,. *Hunger and Public Action* (Oxford: Clarendon Press, 1989), esp. chap. 4.

11. See Vern Bullough, Brenda Shelton, and Sarah Slavin, *The Subordinated Sex: A History of Attitudes Toward Women* (Athens: University of Georgia Press, 1988).

12. Azar Tabari, "Islam and the Struggle for Emancipation of Iranian Women," and Haleh Afshar, "Khomeini's Teachings and Their Implications for Iranian Women," both in Azar Tabari and Nahid Yeganeh, eds., *In the Shadow of Islam: The Women's Movement in Iran* (London: Zed Books, 1982), pp. 5–25 and 75–90; Mai Ghoussoub, "Feminism—or the Eternal Masculine—in the Arab World," *New Left Review* 161 (January–February 1987): 3–13; Juliette Minces, *The House of Obedience* (London: Zed Books, 1982); and Haideh Moghissi, *Feminism and Islamic Fundamentalism: The Limits of Postmodern Analysis* (London: Zed Books, 1999).

13. Mernissi, *Beyond the Veil*; and Fatna A. Sabbah, *Woman in the Muslim Unconscious* (New York: Pergamon Press, 1985).

14. Freda Hussein distinguishes "authentic Islam" from "pseudo-Islam" and believes that the former is emancipatory. See her introduction in Freda Hussein, ed., *Muslim Women* (London: Croom Helm, 1984). Leila Ahmed once poignantly wrote, "One can perhaps appreciate how excruciating is the plight of the Middle-Eastern feminist caught between those opposing loyalties [sexual and cultural identities] forced almost to choose between betrayal and betrayal." See her essay in *Hussein, Muslim Women*. See also Asma Barlas, *Believing Women in Islam: Unreading Patriarchal Interpretations of the Qur'an* (Austin: University of Texas Press, 2002); Riffat Hassan, "Rights of Women Within Islamic Communities," in John Witte Jr. and Johan D. van der Vyver, eds., *Religious Human Rights in Global Perspective: Religious*

Perspectives (The Hague: Martinus Nijhoff, 1996), pp. 361–386; and Azizah al-Hibri, "Islam, Law and Custom: Redefining Muslim Women's Rights," *American University Journal of International Law & Policy* 12 (1) (1997): 1–43.

15. Yakin Erturk, "Convergence and Divergence in the Status of Muslim Women: The Cases of Turkey and Saudi Arabia," *International Sociology* 6 (1) (September 1991): 307–320. For critiques of the cultural relativist approach, see also Mona Abaza and Georg Stauth, "Occidental Reason, Orientalism, and Islamic Fundamentalism," *International Sociology* 3 (4) (December 1988): 343–364.

16. Multicultural policies were first criticized in the early 1990s by feminists in the UK associated with Women Against Fundamentalism and Southall Black Sisters. See also Joshua Cohen, Matthew Howard, and Martha C. Nussbaum, eds., *Is Multiculturalism Bad for Women?* with Susan Moller Okin (Princeton: Princeton University Press, 1999).

17. Abdelwahab Bouhdiba, *Sexuality in Islam* (London: Routledge and Kegan Paul, 1985).

18. See Division for the Advancement of Women, United Nations Office at Vienna, "International Standards of Equality and Religious Freedom: Implications for the Status of Women," in Moghadam, *Identity Politics and Women*, pp. 425–438.

19. Abdullahi an-Na'im, "Promises We Should Keep in Common Cause," in Cohen, Howard, and Nussbaum, *Is Multiculturalism Bad for Women?* pp. 59–64.

20. Janet Z. Giele, "Introduction: The Status of Women in Comparative Perspective," in Janet Z. Giele and Audrey C. Smock, eds., *Women: Roles and Status in Eight Countries* (New York: John Wiley, 1977), pp. 3–31.

21. Hisham Sharabi, *Neopatriarchy: A Theory of Distorted Change in the Arab World* (New York: Oxford University Press, 1988). Another useful discussion of the state is contained in Alan Richards and John Waterbury, *A Political Economy of the Middle East*, 2nd ed. (Boulder: Westview Press, 1996). And still relevant is Michael Hudson, *Arab Politics: The Search for Legitimacy* (New Haven: Yale University Press, 1977).

22. Sharabi, *Neopatriarchy*, p. 145.

23. Judith Lorber, *Paradoxes of Gender* (New Haven: Yale University Press, 1994), p. 5.

24. For a comparative study of changing family law in Western countries (from patriarchal to egalitarian), see Mary Ann Glendon, *State, Law, and Family: Family Law in Transition in the United States and Western Europe* (Cambridge: Harvard University Press, 1977); and Mary Ann Glendon, *The Transformation of Family Law* (Chicago: University of Chicago Press, 1989).

25. Hanna Papanek, "Socialization for Inequality: Entitlements, the Value of Women, and Domestic Hierarchies" Center for Asian Studies, Boston University 1989. See also Rae Lesser Blumberg, *Stratification: Socio-Economic and Sexual Inequality* (Dubuque, Iowa: W. C. Brown, 1978); and Janet Saltzman Chafetz, *Sex and Advantage* (Totowa, N.J: Rowman and Allanheld, 1984).

26. Michael Mann, "A Crisis in Stratification Theory? Persons, Households/Family/Lineages, Genders, Classes, and Nations," in Rosemary Crompton and Michael Mann, eds., *Gender and Stratification* (Cambridge, UK: Polity Press, 1986), pp. 40–56. The quote by Papanek is from her paper "Socialization for Inequality." On patriarchy, see Chapter 4.

27. Ralph Miliband, *Divided Societies: Class Struggle in Contemporary Capitalism* (Oxford: Clarendon Press, 1989), p. 25.

28. Constantina Safilios-Rothschild, "A Cross-Cultural Examination of Women's Marital, Educational, and Occupational Options," in M. T. S. Mednick et al., eds., *Women and Achievement* (New York: John Wiley and Sons, 1971), pp. 96–113.

29. Margot Badran, "Women and Production in the Middle East and North Africa," Trends in History 2 (3) (1982): 80.

30. Richards and Waterbury, *A Political Economy of the Middle East; and Massoud Karshenas, Oil, State, and Industrialization in Iran* (Cambridge University Press, 1990).

31. Jean Pyle, "Export-Led Development and the Underdevelopment of Women: The Impact of Discriminatory Development Policy in the Republic of Ireland," in Kathryn Ward, ed., *Women Workers and Global Restructuring* (Ithaca: ILR Press, 1990), pp. 85–112.

32. Mary Chamie, *Women of the World: Near East and North Africa* (Washington, D.C.: U.S. Department of Commerce, Bureau of the Census, and U.S. Agency for International Development, Office of Women in Development, 1985); and H. Azzam, Julinda Abu Nasr, and I. Lorfing, "An Overview of Arab Women in Population, Employment, and Economic Development," in Julinda Abu Nasr, A. Khoury, and H. Azzam, eds., *Women, Employment, and Development in the Arab World*, p. 11.

33. The Iranian students abroad were organized in the Confederation of Iranian Students, one of the largest and best-organized student movements anywhere. See Afshin Matin Asgari, *Iranian Student Opposition to the Shah* (Costa Mesa, Calif.: Mazda, 2002). See also Val Moghadam, "Socialism or Anti-Imperialism? The Left and Revolution in Iran," *New Left Review* 166 (November–December 1987): 5–28.

34. Helen O'Connell, *Women and the Family* (London: Zed Books, 1993).

35. Mehdi Bozorgmehr and Georges Sabagh, "Iranian Exiles and Immigrants in Los Angeles," in Asghar Fathi, ed., *Iranian Refugees and Exiles Since Khomeini* (Costa Mesa, Calif: Mazda, 1991), pp. 121–144. In the same volume, see also Janet Bauer, "A Long Way Home: Islam in the Adaptation of Iranian Women Refugees in Turkey and West Germany," pp. 77–101; and Vida Nassehy-Behnam, "Iranian Immigrants in France," pp. 102–119.

36. Bauer, "A Long Way Home," p. 93.

37. Samir al-Khalil, "Iraq and Its Future," *New York Review of Books*, April 11, 1991, p. 12. This does of course raise the question of the impact of the Gulf War and devastation of Iraq on women's status. The paucity of information makes a serious study impossible at this time, but the available evidence suggests that the combination of wars, international sanctions, and Saddam Hussein's own flawed policies and priorities have resulted in the deterioration of women's status and conditions.

38. Ruth Milkman, *Gender at Work: The Dynamics of Job Segregation by Sex During World War II* (Chicago: University of Illinois Press, 1987); and Karen Anderson, *Wartime Women: Sex Roles, Family Relations, and the Status of Women During World War II* (Westport, Conn.: Greenwood Press, 1981).

39. Aisha Harb Zureik, "The Effect of War on University Education," project discussed in Al-Raida (Beirut University College) 9 (52) (Winter 1991): 4–5. See also Val Moghadam, "Women, Work, and Ideology in the Islamic Republic," *International Journal of Middle East Studies* 20 (2) (May 1988): 221–243.

40. Maryam Poya, *Women, Work, and Islamism: Ideology and Resistance in Iran* (London: Zed Books, 1999).

41. Andrea W. Lorenz, "Ishtar Was a Woman," Ms., May–June 1991, pp. 14–15.

42. See Khalil Nakhleh and Elia Zureik, eds., *The Sociology of the Palestinians* (New York: St. Martin's Press, 1980).

43. Miriam Cooke, *War's Other Voices: Women Writers on the Lebanese Civil War* (Cambridge: Cambridge University Press, 1986). See also Margot Badran and Miriam Cooke, eds., *Opening the Gates: A Century of Arab Feminist Writing* (Bloomington: Indiana University Press, 1990), esp. the book's introduction.

44. Julie Peteet, "Authenticity and Gender: The Presentation of Culture," in Judith Tucker, ed., *Arab Women: Old Boundaries, New Frontiers* (Bloomington: Indiana University Press, 1993); Cheryl Rubenberg, *Palestinian Women: Patriarchy and Resistance in the West Bank* (Boulder: Lynne Rienner, 2001); Rema Hammami and Penny Johnson, "Equality with a Difference: Gender and Citizenship in Transition Palestine," *Social Politics* 6 (3) (Fall 1999): 314–343; and Robin Morgan, "Women in the Intifada," in Suha Sabbagh, ed., *Palestinian Women of Gaza and the West Bank* (Bloomington: Indiana University Press, 1998), pp. 153–170.

45. Zahira Kamal, "The Development of the Palestinian Women's Movement in the Occupied Territories: Twenty Years after the Israeli Occupation," in Sabbagh, *Palestinian Women of Gaza and the West Bank*, pp. 78–88; quote appears on p. 88.

46. For a nongendered account, see John K. Cooley, *Unholy Wars: Afghanistan, America, and International Terrorism* (London: Pluto Press, 1999, new edition 2000).

PART II

WOMEN AND POLITICS
IN A GLOBAL WORLD

Chapter Five

The Politics of Gender Equality

Sarah Henderson and Alana S. Jeydel

W hen Gretchen Swan, a part-time employee, was asked by her employer to take on a few more hours of work, she accepted but she asked for something in return—benefits, including a pension. Swan is currently lobbying her company to provide benefits to all part-time employees, the majority of whom are women. In Great Britain, Citigroup recently paid 1.4 million pounds (about 2.8 million dollars) to a former employee, Julie Brower, "whose track record had been described by her manager as 'had cancer, been a pain, now pregnant'" and Deutsche Bank paid 500,000 pounds to Kate Swinburne, "who was described, among other things, as 'hotty totty.'"[2] In Scotland, male government workers recently lodged discrimination complaints because of a dress code that insists that men wear ties at all times, whereas women have no dress code and can show up to work in t-shirts.[3] And in the United States, Wal-Mart is facing a class-action suit from up to 1.6 million present and former employees, who claim they were routinely underpaid and overlooked for promotion because they were women.[4] All of these stories indicate that women and men are still not treated equally in the workforce and that, despite numerous gains, (primarily) women face different, unequal, and, at times, hostile working conditions. Cultural attitudes about women's abilities, gendered divisions of labor within the workforce, and lack of government enforcement of existing legislation are just a few of the variables that stand in the way of women's equal treatment in paid employment.

The economic emergence of women has been one of the most significant developments in the post–World War II era. Between 1970 and 2000, women's participation in the workforce in Organisation For Economic Co-operation and Development (OECD) countries increased from nearly 45 percent to just over 60 percent.[5] Yet, in country after country, women earn substantially less than men.[6] Part of the problem is that women are often segregated into low-paying "female" professions such as secretarial work, sales, teaching, and other service-oriented and caregiver industries. Further, women are less likely to ascend to positions of power and authority and are passed over for promotions more frequently than equally qualified male counterparts are. In addition, women are often clustered in part-time or temporary jobs that offer less financial reward and fewer opportunities for advancement. Nor are working conditions ideal for women. For many decades, employers could discriminate against women because of their reproductive capabilities, and sexual harassment was often a by-product of a predominantly male working environment. By the end of women's lives, these disadvantages take their toll on working women, and, upon retirement, women make up the vast majority of the elderly poor.

How have governments tried to address these inequities in the workforce? The increase in the number of women in the workforce, the emergence of feminist movements in the 1970s, the creation of women's policy machineries, and the increasing numbers of women politicians led many governments to pass equal employment policies to address the barriers that prevented women from participating in employment in the same way that men did. These laws have focused on establishing a more level playing field by mandating equal treatment and equal opportunities for women at work and by criminalizing forms of discrimination such as sexual harassment. The rationale for many of these policies has stressed a liberal, gender-neutral rhetoric. That is, the assumption is that the pathway to better employment conditions lies in stressing women's legal equality with men.

As we shall see, although important, equal employment policies are limited in their impact, for while they can address direct barriers that operate in the job market, they do not address the indirect obstacles, such as gender inequities involved in family life or socialization to gendered divisions of labor, that affect women's abilities to perform equally to men on the job.[7] As one scholar commented, "The design of equal employment policies still needs to recognize that inequities in wage labor are actually a product of forces outside of the labor market."[8] As a result, state activism regarding equal employment legislation has not "solved" the problem of sex discrimination in the workplace. However, equal employment legislation does legitimate the problem of discrimination, demonstrates to society at large that the problem will not be tolerated by the government, and penalizes firms and individuals who engage in blatant acts of prejudicial behavior. It is a necessary tool in the battle for women's equality; however, equal employment legislation in and of itself will not result in economic equality for women.

In this chapter we look an array of equal employment policies that address the following issues: pay; hiring, promotion, and firing; sexual harassment; and retirement income. We use Japan, the United States, and the European Union (EU) as case studies of how states have designed and implemented policy to further women's status in the workforce. Japan has made the least progress in advancing gender equality in the workforce, having implemented equal employment legislation that is merely symbolic in its support for women's equality because it lacks critical enforcement mechanisms. In contrast, the United States has been more successful in implementing a variety of policies to encourage equal employment practices. While government support for this was initially symbolic, a well-mobilized women's movement actively lobbied the state to enforce its own regulations. The European Union provides an interesting example of policy design and implementation at the supranational level, which has, in turn, impacted individual policies adopted by member countries. While the EU has been hospitable to women's demands and lobbying, nonetheless it has been more adept at urging nations to pass equal employment legislation than pressuring them to enforce it. Across our cases, we find that many states are better at advancing the rhetoric of gender equality in the workforce than designing and enforcing policy to ensure a more equitable employment outcome for women.

The Debate Over Equal Employment Policies

One of the most significant demographic trends of the post-World War II era has been the massive influx of women into the paid workforce. As we mentioned previously, in OECD countries in 2000, just over 60 percent of women were employed. Certainly, that broad average masks a number of differences between the thirty member states of the OECD; for example, in Turkey, 26.9 percent of women were working, in comparison to a high of 82.8 percent for women in Iceland. However, most countries are somewhere between these two end points; two OECD countries have female labor participation rates of 40–49 percent, seven are in the 50–59 percent range, twelve are in the 60–69 percent range, seven are in the 70–79 percent range, and one (Iceland) has female labor participation rates at over 80 percent. This 2000 figure is a substantial increase even from the previous decade; for example, from 1990 to 2000, female labor participation rates increased over 12 percent in the United States and almost 6 percent in France. Only the states that already had high employment figures, such as Denmark and Sweden, suffered a slight decrease.[9]

Despite this increase in women's participation, women have often had a separate and unequal experience in the paid labor force. Despite their increasing participation, there are significant employment gaps between men and women. Women are less likely to be employed than men are and are more likely to make less money and advance less quickly when in the workforce; as a result, women are at a higher risk of poverty throughout their lives.[10] For many years, particularly before the passage of antidiscriminatory legislation, these problems could be partially attributed to blatant acts of discrimination. Companies openly refused to hire women, paid them less for identical jobs, and fired them when they got pregnant, often under the rationale that women were less competent, capable, or able to perform their work responsibilities.

Equal employment was one of the early mobilizing issues for feminist movements, and it became one of the earliest targeted areas for state activism in advancing gender equality in the 1960s, 1970s, and 1980s. Equal pay laws were often the first to be legislated, followed by equal treatment laws that criminalized direct discrimination against women in hiring, promotion, and firing.[11] Yet, legislation outlawing direct discrimination did not immediately solve women's experiences in the workforce. While women continued to experience direct discrimination (which was illegal), the larger problem was in designing policy to combat less obvious forms of indirect discrimination.

For example, the vast inequalities between men's and women's salaries are often attributed to women's occupational segregation in careers that are less highly valued and mimic women's "caring" and "nurturing" functions in the household. Various nations' economies are literally divided between "women's jobs" and "men's jobs," in which women are overrepresented in low-paying professions, such as teaching, secretarial work, sales, and domestic services while men predominate in more remunerative careers, such as management, administration, policy, and industry. Such is the case in the member countries of the European Union; 83.7 percent of all employed women are concentrated in the services sector, while men are disproportionately employed in agriculture and industry, which are "male" areas of employment that tend to be more financially rewarding. In the 1990s in the United States, women comprised 98 percent of the nation's preschool teachers, 96 percent of its child-care workers, and 79 percent of its health-care workers. In contrast, 98 percent of the nation's firefighters, 74 percent of its physicians, and 97 percent of its construction workers were male.[12] Women also tend to be overrepresented in low-skilled, low-wage jobs, such as low-tech assembly line production, or in the guise of clerk, service, and shop assistants. At the EU level, 34.4 percent of women work in low-paying occupations compared to 19.9 percent of men.[13] In addition, women are much more likely to work part-time than are men, in part because they still assume primary responsibility for child care, elderly care, and housework. For example, in both Japan and the United States, 70 percent of the part-time workforce is female.[14] In the European Union, 33.5 percent of working women work part-time, while only 6.6 percent of men do so.[15] As a result, women become segregated in jobs that are more disposable and, hence, less well paid. This matters because, as the opening story about Gretchen Swan indicates, part-time workers often do not receive the benefits that their full-time counterparts receive. All of these factors mean that women enter their retirement years in a much more financially precarious situation than men.

Further, a glass ceiling keeps women from ascending the corporate ladder to important management positions. For example, women account for less than 8 percent of top management positions in American corporations, and they comprise only 0.7 percent of chief executives.[16] As we shall discuss in greater detail in the next chapter, women who have children tend to take more time off from work, often at times when they are in the midst of climbing the career ladder, and thus tend to miss out on critical opportunities that could launch them into higher management positions. A study of American graduate managers found that women returning after a break of three years or more lost an average of 37 percent of their earnings.[17] In addition, indirect social barriers continue to impede women's progress. Women for many decades have been shut out of the "old boy's network" and all of the accompanying activities, such as informal lunches, golf games, and trips that mix business and pleasure. As we shall see, it is harder to devise strategies to counter these forms of "indirect" discrimination, for they are not a product of blatant, illegal hiring practices but rather emerge from a variety of societal norms that steer women into occupations, career paths, and work networks that do not advance them as quickly as men.

What are the arguments in support of equal employment policies? Some advocates for women's equal treatment in the workforce frame the issue as one of fairness; as human beings men and women share a common humanity and should treat each other, and be treated by business, government, and social institutions, equally. Second, potential differences in ability are because of socialization patterns, rather than as a result of biological sex, and thus are not valid reasons for discrimination. Women's increased presence in higher education and advanced study demonstrate that, when given the opportunity, women can excel as frequently as men can. Third, discrimination is bad for a nation's economy, for it does not tap the full potential of a nation's citizenry. For example, evidence indicates that hiring women makes good business sense; The Economist reports that research results from America, Britain, and Scandinavia demonstrate a strong correlation between shareholder returns and the proportion of women in high-level executive positions. There are a variety of explanations for this; some posit that women tend to be better at team building and communications, which indirectly can increase profits. Others maintain that a homogenous, white, male executive culture stifles the diversity needed to generate new, innovative ideas.[18] On a more general level, the World Bank notes, "It [gender equality] strengthens countries' abilities to grow, to reduce poverty, and to govern effectively. Promoting gender equality is thus an important part of a development strategy that seeks to enable all people—women and men alike—to escape poverty and improve their standard of living."[19]

However, while many agree on the need for equal employment policies, there is less agreement on potential policy solutions to rectify women's unequal status. States have faced numerous dilemmas in designing equal employment policies. For example, how should equal employment be promoted? Should states simply outlaw discriminatory practices, or should they more proactively ensure that women have equal opportunity to compete in the paid labor force, such as through the use of affirmative action policies? And to what degree should states attempt to correct for gender imbalances in the division of labor in the household, in which women carry the burden of child-rearing and family care? While the next chapter addresses the latter question, in this chapter we address the former ones. Similarly, advocates for women's equality in the workforce also differ on which policies should be implemented under the rubric of equal employment. Does "equal employment" mean that men and women should have similar employment profiles in lifetime work patterns—that is, comparable occupational distributions, job status, salaries, and promotions? Extending this logic, many advocates for women's equality pursue strategies that tend to emphasize men's and women's innate commonalities, rather than their differences, and target abolishing laws that distinguish between men and women based on sex.

Not all proponents of women's advancement believe that focusing on treating women in the workforce equally is an appropriate strategy. For example, difference feminists such as Carol Gilligan argue that men and women are developmentally different.[20] Women's ways of knowing and thinking, and their caring abilities, should be preserved and honored, and difference feminists argue that gender-neutral legislation may dilute differences that should be honored and preserved. Difference feminists argue that policies should not try to treat women and men equally in certain areas, but instead should compensate women for the ways their biology makes them different from men, particularly with regard to their reproductive roles. Further, women's socially constructed roles as nurturers and caretakers further hinder their abilities to participate equally in the workforce, which also should be taken into account. In this view, gender-neutral laws are detrimental since they merely perpetuate and exacerbate inequalities in the household. Difference feminists advocate for differential treatment in the workforce through the passage of protective legislation, specific maternity leave benefits, or affirmative action policies to redress past imbalances. Let us now turn to how states have attempted to rectify inequalities in men's and women's experiences in the workforce.

Policy Areas

Equality in the workplace encompasses a number of topics, among them equal pay; equal treatment in hiring, promotion, and firing; the right to a harassment-free working environment; and equality in retirement benefits. We will now examine each of these four issues in greater depth in our three case studies—Japan, the United States, and the European Union.

Japan has made the least progress in advancing gender equality in the workforce, implementing equal employment legislation that is merely symbolic in its support for women's equality in that it lacks critical enforcement mechanisms. This can be attributed to a variety of factors. For one, Japanese society is, compared to other advanced industrial nations, more accepting of traditional gendered divisions of labor. Women are expected to leave the labor force after marriage, and particularly after having children. In addition, Japan's small women's movement mobilized much later on employment issues and has struggled to gain access to important decision makers in the Japanese state. As a result, the movement has used Japan's participation in international treaties as a pressure point to facilitate domestic reform. In turn, the government has been unwilling to offer more than symbolic policies, which are stronger on rhetorical support for women's equality and much weaker on enforcement mechanisms that could advance that equality. In sum, as Joyce Gelb has argued, legislation to improve women's equality "has produced only limited gains in employment opportunity for a small number of Japanese women and, arguably, has created even worse conditions for many"[21] Larger contextual factors, such as Japan's ongoing economic woes and declining birth rate, have created a backlash against further implementation of equal employment policy.

In contrast, the United States has implemented a variety of policies to encourage equal employment practices. While government support for this was initially symbolic, a well-mobilized women's movement actively lobbied the state to enforce its own regulations. Further, the U.S. system of litigation, in which claimants can sue for substantial monetary damages, has encouraged a number of government agencies and businesses to address the issue of equal employment with proactive policies. While the government has tended to design policy that is gender neutral, it has also introduced various affirmative action policies to promote women, which is still a controversial issue in the United States. Yet, as we shall see, the impact of equal employment policy has been limited in that women still face substantial barriers in breaking the glass ceiling in a number of professions.

Finally, the case of the European Union illustrates efforts to resolve gender inequalities at the supranational level. The European Union is an intergovernmental and supranational union of twenty-five member states (and four candidate countries). Although the EU is not intended to replace the nation-state, its member states have set up common institutions to which they delegate some of their sovereignty so that decisions on specific matters of joint interest can be made democratically at the European level. While enforcement issues are problematic (as they are with all international organizations), the member nations have transferred more sovereignty to the EU than to any other regional organization. Thus, the EU provides an interesting point of comparison with our other two case studies; although it does not act as a traditional nation-state, it has significant and growing influence on the politics of the various countries of Europe.

The European Union repeatedly has advanced a progressive rhetoric regarding equal employment. It has placed pressure on member countries to institutionalize equal opportunity policies, particularly in Mediterranean countries, which lagged behind other member countries in designing policy. However, member states have responded to various directives to improve their legislation with mixed levels of enthusiasm. And while the European Parliament and the European Commission have been hospitable to women's demands and lobbying, nonetheless the European Union has been more adept at urging nations to pass equal employment legislation than at pressuring them to enforce it.[22] We now turn to how our three cases have designed and implemented a range of policies related to equal employment.

Equal Pay

Over the years all advanced industrial nations have enacted legislation designed to eradicate the differentials in pay between men and women, which are substantial. The short-term and long-term impact of this pay gap on women, families, and countries is significant. For example, women's low income increases the incidence of poverty, which often has a female face. In the United States, women's advocates argue that if women received the same pay as men "who work the same number of hours, have the same education, union status, are the same age, and live in the same region of the country, then these women's annual family income would rise by $4,000 and poverty rates would be cut in half."[23] Other issues, such as women's overrepresention in part-time labor and time taken off from work to raise a family, compound this problem. As Britain's Equal Opportunity Commission noted, "taking time off work to bring up children, the average gender-pay gap and the large number of women working in part-time or low-paid jobs all contributed to their poverty."[24] Further, women live longer than men and are increasingly swelling the ranks of the elderly. Since many women who worked did not earn as much as men throughout their lives, their savings and pension benefits tended to be much lower. Thus, the pay gap between men's and women's salaries is a significant policy issue for states. We now turn to how states have tried to legislate equal pay, and the effectiveness of their policies.

Japan

Japan's approach to addressing equal pay has lagged behind that of other industrialized countries. While the Japanese Diet adopted weak equal employment legislation in the 1980s, it did not specifically address the issue of equal pay for equal, or comparable, work. As we shall see, compared to other countries, women's mobilization in Japan has been lower, and much of the pressure to reform Japan's equal employment laws came from external, international pressure. Finally, the government has not been committed to passing and enforcing legislation relating to a wide array of workforce issues that might advance women's equality.

Technically, the Labor Standards Act of 1946 required equal wages for women and men. However, because the equal pay clause only applied to the same type of labor, employers often paid women less by segregating them into separate jobs than men.[25] The passage of the 1985 Equal Employment Opportunity Law (EEOL) prohibited gender discrimination in training, pension allocation, and employee dismissal, but did not specifically address the issue of equal pay. Thus, Japanese policy mandating equal pay for equal work is somewhat murky; although the EEOL does not mention equal pay for equal work, it is the most visible policy that addresses the broader issues of gender equality in employment.

The passage of the equal employment legislation occurred much later in Japan than in other countries and evolved from a combination of international and domestic pressures. While there are organized women's groups in Japan, they did not mobilize as early as those in the United States and Europe. Further, the Japanese government has been slower to respond to their demands and has established relevant women's political machinery much later. In contrast to the U.S. feminist movement, which had developed a well-honed strategy to promote equal opportunity legislation by the 1970s, in contrast, in Japan, the small feminist movement was relatively quiescent until its participation in the 1975 UN Decade for Women. Their participation in this event exposed them to international women's networks and new rhetorical frames and strategies, which in turn acted as a mobilizing force. In addition, the Decade for Women resulted in the establishment of women's political machinery in the Japanese bureaucracy, creating an access point through which women's advocates could lobby for change. Finally, in 1985, Japan ratified the UN Convention on the Elimination of All Forms of Discrimination Against Women (CEDAW), which requires the eradication of all legal, political, social, and cultural structures that prevent women from enjoying full equality with men. According to the provisions of the treaty, the Japanese government is legally obligated to aim for actual, not just formal, equality between men and women. This gave advocates of antidiscriminatory legislation a further weapon; given that government officials had committed themselves to enacting certain policies, activists could now pressure them to honor their commitments. Thus, in Japan, pressure for change came from international influences, which women's organizations exploited for further leverage.

Because of Japan's international obligations, the government was required to take positive action to achieve gender equality, and a coalition of progressive social scientists, sympathetic bureaucrats, and feminist organizations successfully lobbied for the passage of the EEOL in 1985, which prohibits discrimination in hiring and firing, promotion, and pension benefits. Further amendments passed in 1997 provided additional refinements to the law As a result, while Japan has moved to remedy issues of discrimination, the EEOL does not address directly the specific issue of pay equity. In sum, the government's commitment to pay equity has been primarily symbolic, in that it has expressed support for women's equality but has failed to give the legislation substantial "teeth" by supporting it with enforcement mechanisms.

The United States

In contrast, in the United States, women's organizations mobilized in the 1960s on the issue of equal pay. The government responded *with* a series of policy reforms, which initially served a symbolic function, for government agencies were unwilling to enforce the legislation. However, increased pressure from women's movements helped encourage government agencies to enforce existing legislation, creating opportunities for women's progress.

Equal pay for women became a contentious issue in the United States in the early 1960s. Although there were a few government initiatives to address the issue of discrimination, equal pay legislation was not passed at the federal level until 1963, when President Kennedy signed the Equal Pay Act into law, which provides for equal pay for equal work. Although advocates of the bill, such as the Women's Bureau, had wanted the wording to be equal pay for work of comparable worth, they acquiesced to the present wording in order to get the bill passed. The act "provides that when an employer has men and women doing the same or substantially the same job (that is requiring the same or substantially the same skill, effort, and responsibility) at the same location and under similar working conditions, the employees must receive equal pay."[26] However, employers could still base pay differentials on factors such as seniority, merit, and measures related to the quantity and quality of the work. This continued to hurt women who often were segregated in low-prestige jobs, which continued to reinforce pay inequities between men and women.

Improvement upon the Equal Pay Act came the following year, with the passage of the Civil Rights Act of 1964. The initial intent of this act was to end discrimination based on race or religion. However, Representative Howard Smith (D–VA), an opponent of the law, proposed an amendment that he was sure would lead to the act's failure; he added sex to the list of groups protected by the legislation. Much to his chagrin, the amendment passed and so did the act. Thus women attained additional rights in an odd fashion. However, even some women's groups, including the President's Commission on the Status of Women, the Women's Bureau, and the American Association of University Women, also opposed the inclusion of sex in the wording of the act, for they feared that protective legislation barring women from certain occupations would then be declared unconstitutional.

Title VII of the Civil Rights Act, among other things, prohibits discrimination on the basis of race, color, sex, religion, or national origin in determining wages. The act is in many ways stronger than the Equal Pay Act because of its enforcement measures. It created the Equal Employment Opportunity Commission (EEOC) to handle complaints and those found violating its provisions could be subjected to judicially issued cease and desist orders.

However, the impact of the law in its initial decade was limited. First, coverage of legislation was not universal; it did not (and still does not) provide equal opportunity and nondiscrimination protections in pay and benefits for part-time workers.[27] Further, for many years, the EEOC did not respond to complaints. It ignored claims until the National Organization of Women (NOW) formed in 1970s (in part, in reaction to this lack of enforcement) and actively pursued the enforcement of the Equal Pay Act and Title VII.

Women's groups have drawn on strategies used by the civil rights movement and have used the courts actively since the 1960s to advance their interests. One landmark Supreme Court decision, Frontiero v. Richardson, established the precedent that preferential treatment given to military men in pay and benefits was unconstitutional In 1970, Sharon Cohen, then Lt. Sharon Frontiero, opened up her paycheck at Maxwell Airforce Base in Alabama to find that she had not received the expected increase in housing allowance or medical benefits for her new husband. At the time, federal law treated men and women in the military differently. It stipulated that male servicemen could receive an increase in pay for housing costs and health benefits for their wives; however, the same was not the case for women unless they could prove that their husband relied on them for more than half their support. In 1973, the Court ruled that such discrepancies were unconstitutional. While this case specifically pertained to the U.S. military, the decision has been used as precedent in cases arguing for equal pay and benefits for women in the private sector as well.

In sum, while government action on the equal employment issues was initially symbolic, in that it professed support for equal pay, pressure from women's groups eventually led the state to enforce their laws more actively. Women's groups have pursued a predominantly gender-neutral strategy that assumes women and men experience the workforce in similar ways. Later on, we will discuss whether these efforts helped promote equal pay for equal work.

The European Union

The European Union integrated equal employment concerns into its early treaties and has continued to support increased gender equality at all levels with its current policy of gender mainstreaming, which involves the integration of equal opportunity rules into other areas of policy making. In addition, various branches of the EU, such as the European Commission, the European Parliament, and the European Court of Justice, have been responsive to women's mobilization at the national and supranational levels. Yet, many individual member countries were slow to respond with legislation, although they increasingly have recognized, primarily through rhetorical support, the importance of equal rights for women.

Article 119 in the Treaty of Rome (1957), the founding treaty of the European Community (which became the European Union in 1993), provides that women and men should receive equal pay for equal work. In the treaty's words, "Equal pay without discrimination based on sex means: (a) that pay for the same work at piece rates shall be calculated on the basis of the same unit of measurement; (b) that pay for work at time rates shall be the same for the same job."[28] This clause was inserted largely because of French pressure. France had already passed equal pay legislation and wanted to ensure that other member states were required to adhere to a similar standard. However, the initial commitment of member states to equal pay was lukewarm; according to the European Parliament, they showed "little enthusiasm for implementing this provision."[29] Thus, Article 119 was essentially symbolic; it existed on paper, but was not implemented in practice.

However, beginning in 1975 a number of directives were adopted in an attempt to force the issue. A directive is a legally binding joint decision made by the Council of the EU or the Parliament that sets common objectives for member countries. Failure to comply with appropriate legislation or regulations can result in sanctions placed by the European Court of Justice. In 1975, The European Council passed the Equal Pay Directive 75/117, which broadened the definition of pay and equal work. Specifically, the Council clarified that equal work did not have to mean same work, but rather "work to which equal value is attributed." By including equal value in the wording, the council was prohibiting indirect discrimination, such as prejudicial job classification schemes. Further, the directive ordered member states to pass necessary legislation to implement the principle of equal pay for equal work or value and directed states to report on their application of the directive. However, the directive did not define what was meant by "work of equal value," thus limiting the impact of the potential policy.[30] The European Parliament has also issued resolutions backing various commission communications on eradicating pay inequalities.[31]

Further, the EU has taken action on other factors that indirectly address equal pay Further directives issued in the 1970s broadened the principle of equal treatment for men and women.[32] In the 1980s and 1990s, frustrated with the slow pace of reform, the European Commission, the EU's bureaucratic arm, issued four Action Programmes to foster equal opportunity for women in the workforce, which, though not binding, placed pressure on member countries to act more proactively in advancing equal employment policies.[33] And as we shall discuss in greater detail in the following section, in 1999, the Treaty of Amsterdam inserted into the EU treaty the principles of equality and nondiscrimination based on sex or sexual orientation. Finally, the EU Social Charter now guarantees equal rights to part-time workers, and the European Court of Justice has ruled that "unfair treatment of part-time workers can constitute indirect sex-discrimination against women."[34] While these policies do not directly discuss equal pay, they do address issues of discrimination, which often lead to inequality in salaries. Continued pressure from varied offices of women's policy machinery within the EU, such as the Committee on Women's Rights and Gender Equality of the European Parliament, the Equality for Women and Men unit of the European Commission, also kept women's issues on the EU agenda. However, while women's groups were able to access the EU policy machinery by participating in hearings, writing policy briefs, and so forth, it has been harder to translate advocacy into policy gains at the national level. Thus we see that the issue of equal pay in the EU and its member states has received a great deal of legislative attention over the past twenty-five years, even if the member states are not always so keen on following the EU's lead.

Impact

How has all of the above legislation impacted women? Given the vast increase in women's activism, government policy, and corporate efforts to remedy women's often second-class status in the workforce, one might think that the pay gap between men and women is a relic of the past. However, the data indicate otherwise. In no advanced industrial nation do women earn the same as men, even for work in similar or identical occupations.

Equal pay legislation has not been able single-handedly to close the pay gap between men's and women's salaries. This is particularly true in Japan, where working women still earn only 63 percent of the average man's pay.[35] In the United States, according to research done by the General Accounting Office, in 1979 women full-time wage and salary workers earned only 63 percent of their male counterparts; by 2000 this gap had decreased to 76 percent.[36] In 2001, this proportion remained constant; women's median earnings were $29,215, men's were $38,275.[37] Finally, as Table 4.1 indicates, a 2003 survey of the existing fifteen member states of the European Union found that, on average, women's average earnings were 16 percent below those of men. This figure masks large differences between employment patterns in the private and public sectors; while women earned 89 percent of men's salaries in the public sector, the pay differential was 78 percent in the private sector.[38]

Table 4.1 Gender Pay Ratios in the European Union, 2003

COUNTRY	PAY RATIO (BASED ON HOURLY EARNINGS)
European Union members (2003)	.84
Austria	.80
Belgium	.88
Denmark	.85
Finland	.83
France	.87
Germany	.79
Greece	.85
Ireland	.81
Italy	.95
Luxembourg	NA
Portugal	.92
Spain	.85
Sweden	.82
The Netherlands	.79
United Kingdom	.79

Source: Commission of the European Communities, "Gender Pay Gaps in European Labour Markets-Measurement, Analysis, and Policy Implications." Brussels, April 9, 2003, SEC(2003)937.

Some might argue that the pay gap does not mean that women do not have pay equity. They note that the figures used to measure pay inequalities are averages across all work categories and do not take into account important intervening variables, such as years of employment and experience. Yet, even when age, educational background, and years worked are taken into account, there is still a disparity between men and women. For example, in Japan, in the 45–49 age group women earned 82 percent of their male colleagues in 1997.[39] A recent report by the U.S. Census Bureau found that the pay gap persists, even when years of employment and experience are taken into account. The Census Bureau reported that in six major employment categories women still earn less than men do. Further, women working in management, professional, and related fields suffer the biggest gap; the median income in 2000 for men in these categories was $50,034, while women with same jobs and levels of experience received a median income of $35,654.[40] Also, between 1995 and 2000, the earnings gap between full-time female and male managers widened.[41] The 2003 study of EU member nations echoed these findings; even in identical occupations, women made less than their male counterparts, even controlling for years of employment and experience.[42] Thus, the pay gap between men and women, while diminishing, is still significant, despite legislation efforts to correct for it. While it is impossible to determine to what degree antidiscrimination legislation has helped close this gap, nonetheless, it has helped change some of the more obvious prejudicial employment policies against women.

Part of the problem lies in the fact that the persistence of the gender pay gap also can be attributed to indirect discrimination. An EU study linked the pay gap to the pervasive problem of gender segregation in the workforce, women's concentration in low-paying sectors and occupations, and the added responsibilities that women shoulder in child-bearing and child-rearing.[43] Further, women working part-time suffer even greater pay discrimination. Women make up a majority of part-time workers in Japan, the United States, and Europe and often are not paid as well as their full-time female or male colleagues are. Can broader policies that address equality in hiring, promotion, and firing address some of these deeper problems that lead to women's unequal status in the labor market?

Equality in Hiring, Promotion, and Firing

For decades, women have been the last hired and the first fired. Deemed "the weaker sex," women were "protected" from certain occupations because of supposed limitations on their physical capabilities or because the job could potentially interfere with their reproductive health. In fact, it was only recently that Belgium repealed nineteenth-century restrictions on women working at night.[44] Such protective legislation kept women from being hired for many jobs and from advancing if hired. Further, many women remained unhired or were fired after announcing their pregnancies; they were perceived as a threat to profits, and employers assumed that they would "naturally" choose to leave the workforce to devote themselves to motherhood. And while most protective legislation such as this no longer exists, certain barriers still keep women from being hired and promoted. Even when women embark on a career path, they rarely advance far. A glass ceiling still keeps women from achieving the highest positions, with the accompanying prestige, power, and pay. States have responded with legislation that bars employers from discriminating against women. Further, some have more proactively implemented affirmative action policies to promote women's advancement. We now turn to our three case studies. How has each designed policies to combat discrimination, and what has been the impact of these policies?

Japan

As we discussed in the previous section, the UN Convention to End Discrimination Against Women created the international pressure that prompted the Japanese Diet to pass the Equal Employment Opportunity Law in 1985. For the first time; Japanese law prohibited discrimination in termination of employment and encouraged equal treatment in recruitment, hiring, job assignment, and promotion. However, the law, as originally written, was essentially toothless; there were no sanctions for employers who refused to comply.[45] The law "only required that employers 'endeavor' to treat men and women the same in terms of hiring and promotion."[46] Nor were courts given the power to mediate by issuing orders to cease and desist or award punitive damages. And the law did not establish an administrative agency, such as the U.S. EEOC, to enforce compliance. Rather, the Ministry of Labor's Women's Bureau was charged with establishing "administrative guidelines" and "ministerial ordinances" to clarify the legislation. Finally, the legislation established a cumbersome, three-step system of mediation (as opposed to litigation) to attempt resolve disputes. The final third step involved the Equal Opportunity Mediation Commission (EOMC), which would handle the dispute only if one party requested mediation and both parties agreed to it. Yet, at most, mediation bodies could only provide advice, guidance, and recommendations, rather than legal resolution. The law was further amended in 1997 to, among other things, simplify the mediation process and provide for the publication of the names of companies violating the EEOL provisions and the nature of the violation. Nonetheless, the law still lacks significant enforcement mechanisms.[47] In addition to the EEOL, the Japanese Diet passed amendments to the Labor Standards Law, which abolished various protective measures for women related to overtime, late night, and hazardous work.[48] Thus, while the government has become more proactive in making symbolic efforts to advance women's equality, the lack of enforcement mechanisms severely weakens the impact of the law.

The United States

In the United States, until legislation deemed otherwise, employers were permitted to refuse to hire women in a variety of positions, many of them the higher-paying, managerial ones. It was not uncommon for newspaper advertisements to specify men only. Women were often paid less than men even for identical work.[49] The United States began addressing the issue of equality in hiring, firing, and promotion with Title VII of the Civil Rights Act of 1964 as amended in 1972. Title VII states that discrimination on the basis or race, color, religion, sex, or national origin is unlawful in hiring or firing; determining wages (as discussed previously); providing fringe benefits; classifying, referring, assigning, or promoting employees; and more. Most lawsuits concerning discrimination are brought under the auspices of this act. In 1978, the act was further amended; the Pregnancy Discrimination Act declared that classifications based on pregnancy and pregnancy-related disabilities fell within the meaning of "sex" under Title VII.

However, the language of Title VII was open for interpretation. While the law banned discrimination of the basis of an individual's race, color, religion, sex, or national origin, it also specified an important exception, known as the Bona Fide Occupational Qualification (BFOQ), which allowed employers to take factors such as sex into account where it was deemed "a bona fide occupational qualification reasonably necessary to the normal operation of that particular business enterprise."[50] This clause often pulled the courts into the debate, for the wording is open to interpretation. For example, in 1977, the Supreme Court ruled in *Dothard v. Rawlinson* that an Alabama state penitentiary could refuse to hire women as prison guards because, they maintained, women might not be able to maintain order as effectively as men, for women were at risk of assault from inmates "deprived of a normal heterosexual environment."[51] On the other hand, the courts have also found that other employers' policies did not meet BFOQ guidelines and were thus discriminatory. For example, the courts have repeatedly found that employers cannot bar women from holding positions that required lifting more than a certain weight. In addition, men have successfully used the BFOQ clause to take on airlines that pursued a policy of hiring only female flight attendants. The BFOQ clause has been important because courts have often ruled against companies' discriminatory policies under the rationale that limits are often based on stereotypes of women's (and men's) abilities, rather than on factual evidence.

Further, a series of executive orders addressing equality in hiring, firing, and promotion became quite controversial because they sought to not only bar discrimination, but to also remedy past inequalities by taking proactive measures to increase women and minority representation. Executive Order 11246 prohibited discrimination regarding race in hiring, firing, and promotion by contractors and subcontractors with federal or federally funded contracts (this encompasses a massive number of businesses and places of higher learning). This executive order was amended in 1967 by Executive Order 11375 to include sex. These executive orders are often referred to as affirmative action because of the wording of Executive Order 11375, part of which states that "The contractor will take affirmative action to ensure that employees are employed and are treated during employment, without regard to their race, color, religion, sex or national origin."[52] Many people have come to see affirmative action as preferential treatment for women at the expense of men and have been able to frame the policy of affirmative action as one of reverse discrimination. In their interpretation, businesses and places of higher learning use quotas to ensure the promotion of minorities and women, despite their supposed inferior qualifications. The Supreme Court has ruled repeatedly (most recently in the summer of 2003 in a lawsuit against the University of Michigan) that quotas are unconstitutional but that race and sex can be taken into account in hiring and admittance decisions.

A final piece of legislation that might have assisted women in the United States with their claims of equality was the Equal Rights Amendment (ERA). The text of the ERA is as follows: "Equality of rights under the law shall not be denied or abridged by the United States or by any state on account of sex. The Congress shall have the power to enforce, by appropriate legislation, the provisions of this article. This amendment shall take effect two years after the date of ratification."[53] Depending on the design of resulting policy, and the government's willingness to enforce these policies, the ERA potentially also could have been used as an equalizing force in employment. In fact, the ERA passed Congress in 1972 and was sent to the states in search of ratification by three-fourths of the states. However, by 1982 the ERA failed to attain ratification by the requisite number of states and thus did not become an amendment to the U.S. Constitution. Thus, in the United States, litigation has been a successful method of punishing some discriminatory hiring practices; however, more proactive policies, such as affirmative action and constitutional amendments, have been much more controversial.

The European Union

The European Union, as previously discussed, has attempted to integrate equal employment policy into its laws and treaties from its inception. However, the member states have not been too eager to follow the lead of the EU. Throughout the 1970s, the European Community continued to issue directives related to equal opportunity employment issues. As we mentioned in the previous section, a 1976 directive broadened the principle of equal employment for men and women to cover the issues of equal access to employment, which included promotion, as well as job training, and barred discrimination on grounds of sex, particularly with regard to marital and family status.[54] Further, the directive allowed for positive action measures (which in the United States are known as affirmative action policies) to address gender inequalities in the labor force. However, the directive did not contain clear implementation directions for member states, which weakened the directive's force. In addition, the section addressing affirmative action measures were recommendations, and thus were not binding on member nations.

The 1997 Amsterdam Treaty (which took effect on May 1, 1999), extended the EU's abilities to take action on fostering gender equality beyond the issue of equal pay for equal work. The treaty's broader purpose was to update and clarify the conditions of the Maastricht Treaty (which created the European Union), prepare for EU enlargement, and clarify the powers of the European

Parliament and the Council of Ministers on a range of issues, including social policy.[55] In terms of fostering gender equality, Article 13 empowered the Council of Ministers, the executive branch of the EU, to take "appropriate action" to combat discrimination based on sex, racial or ethnic origin, religion or belief, disability, age, or sexual orientation. The Council of Ministers and, to some extent, the European Parliament are vested with the power to design and adopt legislation that goes beyond ensuring equal pay, but also encompasses equal treatment and equal opportunities.

In addition, the European Court of Justice (ECJ), the judicial branch of the EU, has grown more proactive in enforcing the directives and advancing women's equality through its decisions in important cases. Initially, the ECJ was relatively conservative in its approach, issuing two judgments that in essence ruled that affirmative action hiring policies, such as quotas, were contrary to European equal opportunities legislation.[57] However, in the wake of the Amsterdam Treaty, and its expanded definition of gender equality, the court has pursued a more proactive strategy and has recognized that member states can take action to improve women's ability to compete in the labor market so that women with the same qualifications as men can receive preference for promotion in areas in which they are underrepresented.

Thus, equality in hiring, firing, and promotion is protected in various EU treaties, directives, and decisions of the European Court of Justice. Yet, because of the relative youth of the European Union, continuously evolving policies, and changes in leadership style of the European Commission, it is important not to overemphasize the presence of directives, legislation, and court rulings. Certainly, directives oblige all member states to adopt or amend existing legislation to ensure compliance with EU rules. And the rhetorical leadership of the EU on various equal employment policies sets an important example to member nations and can provide further pressure on member countries to implement national-level legislation to meet EU standards. This can also encourage women's organizations at the national level to lobby their governments for prompt legislative initiative, as well as the formation of transnational networks of women's activists. For example, the founding of the European Women's Lobby in 1990 was in response to support from the European Commission and the Committee on Women's Rights of the European Parliament.[58] However, implementation of policy at the national level will be the key challenge.

Impact

What has been the impact of all of this legislation on women? In Japan, despite the EEOL, women still lag behind men in promotions and hiring, in part because of holes in the legislation. For example, the law fails to guard against indirect discrimination. Many companies initially responded to the EEOL by establishing a dual career track system for men and women, with men hired in managerial track positions and women relegated to clerical positions. While managerial positions involve complex judgment, involuntary transfers, and unlimited access to promotion, the clerical track, though often full-time, involves less time, commitment, and thus opportunities for advancement.[59] Given that many Japanese companies operate on an informal policy of "lifelong employment," which offers high job security, demands high worker commitment and involves extensive worker training, this dual model often places women in a long-term, disadvantageous position, from which they are unable to extricate themselves.[60] Further, the lack of strong enforcement measures limits the impact of the EEOL. The Equal Opportunity Mediation Commission can only recommend and encourage parties to resolve their differences, but businesses are under no legal obligation to follow the advice of the commission. In addition, the Ministry of Labor has taken a cautious route and has attempted to appeal to employers' goodwill in complying with the law rather than fighting for greater enforcement mechanisms.[61]

This has not stopped a few women from attempting to fight for more equitable working conditions. Indirectly, the passage of the EEOL, which heightened women's awareness of discrimination issues, led a few to pursue litigation through other means, such as Article 14 of the Constitution, which provides for equality between the sexes, or Article 4 of the Labor Standards Act, which prohibits gender-based discrimination at work.[62] In 1995, four women who worked at Sumitomo Metal Industries Ltd. filed a lawsuit claiming that the company uses a sexually discriminatory employment system that in practice kept women's wages much lower than men's in similar jobs with similar qualifications.[63] Nine and a half years later, the Osaka District Court ruled in their favor and ordered the company to pay compensation. Sumitomo is appealing the ruling.[64] The increased use of lawsuits, even if not under the auspices of the EEOL, point to the greater consciousness surrounding issues of employment.

However, women are still blocked by a very thick glass ceiling. The Japanese government's White Paper on Equal Gender Participation found that women occupy only 8.9 percent of managerial positions, compared to 58.1 percent in the Philippines and 46 percent in the United States.[65] The same White Paper found that 67.7 percent of Japanese women believe that men are given preferential treatment at work.[66] Women's underrepresentation, in part, can be attributed to pervasive cultural attitudes about women and work; women seeking jobs in Japan are described by employers as "too ambitious" and/or "uncooperative" and "too proud to listen to their colleagues' advice."[67] This is coupled with the persistent social belief that "women should be the primary caregivers for children and sick or elderly family members."[68] Given these impediments, women will need more than symbolic policy to change their unequal position in the labor market in Japan.

In the United States, while Title VII and affirmative action policies both have aided women in their quest for equality in hiring, firing, and promotion, their impact is limited. Women slowly are increasing their numbers among the top employees of companies and among chief executive officers. Since 1992, the number of female CEOs of large, nonprofit organizations has increased significantly.[69] And women have clearly increased their numbers among the middle to upper ranks of companies. However, as of October 2003, only six

Fortune 500 companies had female chief executive officers or presidents and 393 of them had no women among their top executives.[70] And a survey conducted by the General Accounting Office found that "women who are full time managers are paid less and advance less often than male managers."[71]

The state of hiring and promotion practices in the EU is also quite poor. In the member states of the European Union, according to the European Parliament, women are still to be found in the basic career grades and "women eligible for promotion are less likely than men to actually get promoted."[72] In fact, women hold only one-third of managerial jobs.[73] Further, according to the European Trade Union Confederation, women remain sequestered in a narrow range of occupations (one in six women works in health and social services) and primarily at the bottom of the ladder.[74] As the EU noted of its own performance, "despite all the efforts of the past decades, complete equality of opportunity has not yet been achieved. … In other words, there is still work to be done in the EU to implement equal opportunities in practice."[75]

Further, as the European Union expands to encompass candidate countries in eastern Europe, its abilities to enforce its rulings will be tested to the limit, as these countries will have to bring their equal opportunity legislation (which is often nonexistent) into line with European standards. Discrimination in hiring is still blatant in eastern Europe, even though some of these nations have recently been admitted to the European Union. Employment advertisements, for instance, still ask for such things as "attractive female receptionist" or "girl under 25," and sometimes women must promise to not get pregnant for five years.[76] For those nations that have recently been admitted to the EU, these practices will need to end because of EU legislation that prohibits such practices.

However, EU policy has affected some countries' domestic policies on equal employment dramatically, which probably could not have changed in the absence of EU pressure. For example, the EU did have an impact on Irish women's equal access to employment. As Julia O'Connor found,

The Community has brought about changes in employment practices which might otherwise have taken decades to achieve. Irish women have the Community to thank for the removal of the marriage bar in employment, the introduction of maternity leave, greater opportunities to train at a skilled trade, protection against dismissal upon pregnancy, the disappearance of advertisements specifying the sex of an applicant for a job and greater equality in the social welfare code.[77]

In this example, the presence of EU directives pushed an individual member country to change its policies to align with European standards.

Sexual Harassment

A third crucial issue for women in the workplace is that of sexual harassment. Sexual harassment is not a new problem; however, it was not seen as an issue for many years because of women's limited participation in the workforce.

Further, for many years, it was treated as an unpleasant working condition to be tolerated. However, beginning in the 1960s and 1970s, women's movements raised the consciousness of many women and many began to question patriarchy and its attendant trappings. By the 1980s women began to believe that sexual harassment was not something they had to accept and they slowly began to work toward changing laws as well as attitudes. Men are certainly subject to sexual harassment as well; however, since it predominantly affects women, women will be our focus here.

Before delving into the topic of sexual harassment it would be helpful to have a working definition of it. What is sexual harassment? One definition, used by the U.S. Equal Employment Opportunity Commission, states that sexual harassment includes

> unwelcome sexual advances, requests for sexual favors, and other verbal or physical conduct of a sexual nature when submission to or rejection of this conduct explicitly or implicitly affects an individual's employment, unreasonably interferes with an individual's work performance, or creates an intimidating, hostile, or offensive work environment.[78]

One problem with sexual harassment has been deciding what actions constitute it. This definition helps but still leaves some people confused. Do dirty jokes told around the water cooler at the workplace constitute sexual harassment? What about statements made regarding one's appearance? The story at the beginning of the chapter about the employee who was called a "hotty totty" by her employer appears today to be a fairly straightforward example of harassment, but other examples are not so clear-cut. However, we adopt the preceding definition because it offers a fairly comprehensive definition that can guide the discussion of this issue.

Another complication is that harassment can be hard to prove, since it often happens in the privacy of someone's office, rather than in public, in front of witnesses. This can make it difficult for women to come forward, as illustrated by the Anita Hill and Clarence Thomas hearings. In 1991 Clarence Thomas was nominated to the U.S. Supreme Court. During the confirmation process allegations arose by his former aide, attorney Anita Hill, that Thomas had sexually harassed her when they worked together at the Department of Education and later at the Equal Employment Opportunity Commission during the early 1980s. Hill underwent grueling cross-examination by the Senate Judiciary Committee, which was made up of all men. They queried her as to why it took so long for her to say something about this harassment and whether she had invented the incidents. Ultimately, the Judiciary Committee confirmed Thomas. The topic of sexual harassment stayed in the public's mind when Paula Jones charged that President Clinton had sexually harassed her when he was governor of Arkansas. And, as the story at the beginning of the chapter illustrates, the problem is certainly not confined to the United States. What laws have been passed to assist women in their quest to end this form of discrimination, and what has been their impact?

Japan

The concept of sexual harassment is still relatively new to Japanese workers. The Japanese language does not even have a word for sexual harassment—the word used, *seku-hara*, has been derived from the English term. And the EEOL, as it was originally written, said nothing specifically about sexual harassment. However, the 1997 amendments to the EEOL make employers responsible for the prevention of sexual harassment. Yet, as we discussed previously, the amendments (and the original law) lack significant punitive measures to enforce compliance. The Ministry of Labor can publicize the names of companies that violate the conditions of the EEOL.[79] In addition, women can use the cumbersome mediation process specified in the EEOL. Thus, as in other areas, the policies are primarily symbolic and lack "teeth" that could enforce new standards of equal employment. Instead, they rely on the Ministry's abilities to cajole good behavior out of companies.

The United States

In the United States, sexual harassment is considered to be a form of gender discrimination that is covered under Title VII of the Civil Rights Act of 1964 as well as under Title IX of the Education Act of 1972. According to the EEOC, sexual harassment includes instances of quid pro quo (e.g., requiring the provision of sexual favors as a term or condition of one's employment) as well as the creation of a hostile working environment. As in many countries, it is often difficult to prove harassment; in the United States, the plaintiff must show that

> (1) she was subjected to unwelcome sexual conduct; (2) these were based on her sex; (3) they were sufficiently pervasive or severe to create an abusive or hostile work environment; and (4) the employer knew or should have known of the harassment and failed to take prompt and appropriate remedial action.[80]

The courts have used a "reasonableness" standard to determine what defines an unwelcome sexual advance and a hostile work environment. That is, under similar circumstances, would a "reasonable person" have identified the behavior as unwelcome? As one can imagine, this does allow for a wide degree of latitude in terms of what constitutes "reasonable." However, the federal courts in the United States have made it clear that companies are financially liable for the actions of their employees. As a result, many employers conduct extensive training and educational outreach with their employees in hopes of halting the problem. Much of this is because of the efforts of the women's movement; NOW and other women's groups litigated and lobbied extensively in the 1970s (and beyond) and as a result were successful in expanding the interpretation of Title VII. Thus, the U.S. system of litigation, the state's willingness to enforce the law, and active women's mobilization have forced many companies and institutions to take the issue of sexual harassment seriously.

The European Union

European countries have been much slower in addressing sexual harassment. However, studies conducted in the 1980s in individual member countries indicated that the problem was severe, and another report published in 1988 revealed that no member state had an express legal prohibition against sexual harassment. In fact, in only two countries—the United Kingdom and Ireland—did courts accept the argument that sexual harassment constituted discrimination. However, the European Commission was divided on whether they needed to issue a directive, which would be legally binding on member states, to address the issue. Some members argued that the 1976 directive on equal treatment, which banned sex discrimination, could be used to sanction harassment. Finally, in 1991, the commission adopted a recommendation (which is not legally binding) on the protection of the dignity of women and men at work and added it to a code of practice on measures to combat harassment. In essence, the commission urged member states to take the matter of sexual harassment seriously, without providing the clarity or enforcement mechanisms that could have made it an effective Europe-wide policy tool. As a result, while member states responded with various legislative acts addressing harassment, the acts are often weak, unclear, or put an undue burden on the woman to prove her case.[81] Thus, while initial efforts heightened awrareness of sexual harassment as a problem and led to initial legislation to address the issue, nonetheless most national-level policies lack strong sanctions against offenders.

The EU raised the issue again, when it amended the 1976 directive on equal treatment in 2002. Currently, "binding legislation defines sexual harassment and outlaws it as a form of discrimination based on sex. It bans any form of unwanted sexual behavior that creates an intimidating or degrading environment and also urges employers to take preventive action against all forms of discrimination and to compile regular equality reports for staff."[82] Under the conditions of the amended directive, when an employee files a sexual harassment claim with an employer, that employer is required to prove that it has done all they could to prevent sexual harassment. Further, employers are financially liable when sexual harassment allegations have been shown to be true. Finally, the directive gives courts a freer hand when awarding financial compensation to victims of sexual harassment. Member states have until 2005 to comply, and some have already passed relevant legislation. For instance, France has made sexual harassment a criminal offense, the only nation in the world to do so. However, not all women's equality advocates have supported this move. Some argue that the criminalization of sexual harassment in France will make it harder for women to bring charges. They argue that a civil law approach, where one uses a lawsuit to threaten a firm, is more successful in getting firms to take the issue seriously. Finally, women in France whose sexual harassment charges against men fail can be hit with a defamation lawsuit by the men and then forced to pay damages.

Impact

What has been the impact of these laws on women's lives? In Japan it appears that sexual harassment is still widespread. A 1997 survey by the Ministry of Labor reported that "62 percent of women claimed to have experienced at least one act of sexual harassment."[83] On a positive note, another survey indicates that some of the more extreme forms of sexual harassment may be on the wane in government workplaces. Female government workers reported a decline in their bosses pressuring them to have a sexual relationship—from 17 percent in 1997 to 2.2 percent by 2000.[84] And there has been a 35 percent increase in the number of women reporting sexual harassment in the workplace since the EEOL revisions went into effect in 1999.[85] Further, as in other areas of equal employment policy, women's disenchantment with the EEOL's mediation process has led women to use other antidiscrimination legislation to press sexual harassment suits. From 1989 to 1997, women brought forward fifty-eight lawsuits related to sexual harassment charges. Thus, the weakness of the EEOL in many ways spurred women on to exploit alternative venues of leverage. While the number of women coming forward pales in comparison to, say, the United States, nonetheless it marks a very small but significant cultural shift in the acceptability of harassment on the job.

In the United States the number of sexual harassment claims to the EEOC more than doubled between 1990 and 1996, from about six thousand to fifteen thousand.[86] While this may be because of the existence of laws allowing women to sue their employers, it also may be, in part, because of the media attention paid to the topic in the 1990s. The Clarence Thomas confirmation hearings were televised, and the allegations by Paula Jones against President Clinton received a great deal of media attention. Some speculate that after these nationally televised events regarding sexual harassment, the cases brought to the EEOC increased dramatically.

The EEOC has also been willing to enforce legislation criminalizing harassment and has charged a number of large corporations with sexual harassment. One of the largest suits it brought was against the Mitsubishi Corporation alleging sexual harassment against more than 350 women. The suit was settled in June 1998 and Mitsubishi was ordered to pay the plaintiffs over 34 million dollars, end sexual harassment in the workplace, and make sure that no retaliation against these women occurred. A team of monitors was established to ensure that Mitsubishi complied. The EEOC has also successfully led a case against the largest lettuce grower in the United States on behalf of female migrant workers who alleged that they had been sexually harassed. The company, while not admitting to any wrongdoing, agreed to pay 1.85 million dollars, fire one manager, reprimand another, and train and monitor all other supervisors and employees. This is an important victory because migrant women have few resources to battle sexual harassment. They often do not know the law, fear losing their jobs, and lack the language fluency to facilitate acting on harassment. The deck is stacked against them even more so than it is for middle-class women.

The number of sexual harassment cases heard in U.S. federal courts has also increased. The Supreme Court has handed down numerous ruling on the topic beginning in the mid-1980s. The first rulings dealt with what behaviors constituted unlawful sexual harassment. More recently, the Court has begun handing down decisions regarding legal responsibility for sexual harassment. In one of the first cases addressing sexual harassment, *Meritor Savings Bank v. Vinson* (1986), the Supreme Court recognized as unlawful both types of sexual harassment defined in the EEOC guidelines. This decision and others, as well as the fact that the Supreme Court is hearing sexual harassment cases, are significant indicators that the courts take the issue of harassment seriously. The Supreme Court can pick and choose which cases it hears, and if it is choosing to hear sexual harassment cases and upholding EEOC guidelines, then this indicates that it views such cases as involving important legal questions, thus granting legitimacy to women's claims.

While sexual harassment persists in the United States, some improvements have occurred. Women are stepping forward to charge their employers with sexual harassment, the EEOC is successfully waging battles against these employers, the Supreme Court has upheld the EEOC guidelines and handed down decisions that assist women alleging sexual harassment, and companies are creating their own guidelines and holding training sessions to educate their employees on the topic. However, sexual harassment does persist. The laws and the legal decisions have assisted women and scared corporations who do not wish to suffer large monetary losses because of the behavior of some of their employees. It will very likely take time and more education to further decrease the incidence of sexual harassment.

The European Union only recently has devoted concerted attention to policy pertaining to sexual harassment, and, as a result, policies still differ significantly at the national level. And sexual harassment is rampant in Europe. One survey indicates that up to 50 percent of European women have experienced some type of sexual harassment (ranging from sexual verbal remarks to assault or rape).[87] However, national estimates vary widely, from 11 percent in Denmark to 54 percent in the United Kingdom to 81 percent in Austria.[88] This discrepancy is largely because of a lack of an agreed-upon idea of what constitutes sexual harassment. In some of the southern European countries women feel sexual harassment is an unfortunate but enduring part of the work environment that must be tolerated. Further, many men do not see their behavior as inappropriate. This is different than in northern Europe, where sexual harassment is recognized more widely and is not condoned by women (and men). So, sexual harassment persists throughout Europe, though in varying degrees from country to country. The attitude of the country, as well as the legal recourse available, have impacted whether or not women have filed suit against harassers and how successful these suits have been. The stories at the beginning of this chapter indicate that women in Europe are bringing suit against their employers for sexual harassment and winning. The EU directive discussed earlier adopts a common definition, which should assist women in identifying what it is and in bringing suit against employers. A common EU policy, accompanied by a public relations campaign designed to educate the populace about the policy, should further assist women by making lawsuits easier to wage and hopefully decreasing the prevalence of sexual harassment in the workplace.

Retirement Income

We now move on to examine our final area of policy in which women have strived to attain equality—retirement income. Retirement income usually refers to income that one receives from the state after one retires, such as Social Security in the United States, pensions that one's employer provides to its workers, and any money that one may have saved over the course of one's life. Retirement income is of crucial concern to all people, but especially to women, in part because women tend to live longer than men and thus need income for a longer period of time than men do. However, for a variety of reasons that we shall discuss in this section, women earn much less than men in retirement income. For example, on average, women's government pensions in Europe are significantly less than men's—the gap between what women and men receive range from a low of 16 percent in the United Kingdom to 45 percent in Austria.[89] And in the United States, at the end of 2003, women's average monthly retirement benefit was $798, compared to $1,039 for men.[90] The result is the feminization of poverty among the elderly. While this is a critical issue for women, there have been fewer efforts to design policy to address this issue. Thus, this final section diverges from the previous ones in the sense that we discuss why retirement is a gender issue rather than discuss the design and impact of policy reforms in our three case studies.

Why is retirement income a women's issue? For one, women who do work often work fewer years than men because they assume the tasks of child care and care of elderly relatives, and the amount of retirement income that one receives from the government is dependent on the number of years that one has participated in the workforce. Thus, women have usually paid less into the government system and get less back upon retirement. As the European Institute for Women's Health finds, "In Italy ... only 20 percent of women have a 30-year contribution record compared to 60 percent of men."[91] In Australia, for the year 2000, men averaged thirty-eight years in the workforce while women averaged only twenty.[92] In countries such as Japan, women's participation in the workforce is perceived as a reason to potentially deny women their benefits, for they have shunned the more valued occupations of wife and mother. For example, a former prime minister of Japan noted in public that women who did not bear children were not worthy of public (government) pensions. He said: "The government takes care of women who have given birth to a lot of children as a way to thank them for their hard work. ... It is wrong for women who haven't had a single child to ask for taxpayer money when they get old, after having enjoyed their freedom and fun (emphasis added)."[93]

The effects of private pension plans on women are similar to government pension plans. One's retirement income from a private pension plan with one's employer is often dependent on the number of years that one has been with a specific employer. Because women move in and out of the workforce more frequently than men (often because of family commitments) they often don't stay long enough in a job to become eligible. Second, women are still relegated to lower-paying jobs than men, and even when they have jobs similar to those of men their income is often less. This means that they often pay less into public and private pension plans and get less back. Finally, many service sector, retail, and part-time jobs—jobs primarily occupied by women—offer no pension plan. In the Netherlands, "of women working part-time and in low paid jobs, more than one-third (37 percent) are not in occupational pension schemes."[94]

The laws governing spousal pension rights in the circumstance of marriage, divorce, and death also often work against women, particularly those who spent their working years caring for their families rather than in the paid labor force. They have accrued little if any retirement income over the course of their lives and thus are often almost entirely dependent on their husband's income. Yet, for example, in the United States, if a couple has been married for less than ten years and they divorce, the ex-wife receives none of her husband's Social Security benefits upon his retirement. Alternatively, if the husband dies, the wife is under sixty, and there are no children under the age of eighteen, the wife receives none of her husband's benefits until she turns sixty. Further, with regard to private pension plans in the United States, for many years men could waive their wife's survivor benefit without her consent. On the positive side, this bolstered a couple's monthly income when the husband retired. However, when the husband died the payments ceased. This was not a problem if the wife died before the husband, but since women often outlive men, this left a great number of women with no retirement income in old age. Thus, women are often placed in a precarious financial situation upon divorce or the death of their husband. Inequality in the distribution of bereavement benefits isn't solely a problem confronting women. In the United Kingdom, until recently men whose wives died were not entitled to a widower benefit; only women could receive benefits when their husbands died. However, the United Kingdom has changed their pension system so that now, should a man outlive his wife, he can receive widower's benefits.

Since women often live longer than men, retirement benefits, particularly those provided by the government, are of crucial importance to their lives. For example, research on elderly women in the United States found that they rely heavily on Social Security for their retirement benefits—only 13 percent of elderly women receive a private pension compared to 33 percent of older men.[95] And, in the United States, "Nearly two-thirds of all women 65 and older receive half or more of their income from Social Security, and for nearly one-third of older women, Social Security is 90 percent or more of their income."[96] Yet, because women receive substantially less in benefits than men do, the result is the feminization of poverty among the elderly. For example, 1994 U.S. Census Bureau figures show that nearly three-quarters of the elderly whho live below the poverty line are women and "two-thirds of women over age 65 have no pension other than social security."[97] In the United Kingdom, one in four pensioner women lives in poverty.[98] According to a report by the Economic and

Social Research Council in the United Kingdom, these inequalities are due in part to gendered divisions of labor at home: "mothers who take career breaks to bring up their children are seven times as likely to face hardship and poverty when they reach their 60s than single women."[99] The United States and the United Kingdom are just two examples in a larger trend affecting all European countries, where, in general, older women are more likely than men to rely on social assistance for their needs.[100] In contrast to our other equal employment policy issues, there have been fewer concentrated efforts to address this imbalance, in part because the inequality in retirement benefits is often the result of indirect forms of discrimination. However, there are a few examples of policy reform that may have a limited impact on women's economic status in their retirement years. In Europe, the European Court of Justice has taken a positive step to improve the lot of part-time workers. They have ruled that part-time workers must be included in private pension schemes on a pro-rata basis. But this still leaves many women without pension plans and so, as the story at the beginning of the chapter regarding Gretchen Swan indicates, women often do not receive pension benefits and must fight for them. The U.S. Retirement Equity Act of 1984 was designed to help widows win more spousal benefits from private pension plans. It "made it mandatory for workers with private pension plans to get the written consent of their spouses in order to waive their survivor benefit."[101] The act also helped divorced women because it requires private pension plans to honor state court orders that divide pension plans in settlements.[102] However, these isolated acts tend to respond to specific issues rather than broadly address issues of gender inequality. As a result, the issue of retirement income is of ongoing concern for women, with few legislative changes in sight.

Advancing Women's Equality

In this chapter we have surveyed the current status of women in their search for equality and examined some of the legal remedies that have been enacted in hopes of attaining equality between the sexes. Despite Improvement in women's working conditions, there is still much room for improvement in all of the areas we have discussed. What are some further suggested reforms? We will briefly examine this question in light of each of the broad areas we have covered in this chapter.

As we discussed earlier, many women are paid less than men because they are segregated into predominantly "female" professions. As a result, they work in different positions than men, and it is thus hard to prove overt discrimination in pay scales when women are paid less for their work. As a result, some women's groups have stressed the importance of "comparable worth," a proposal to pay different job titles the same based on their value. For instance, in a law firm a legal secretary is of vital importance to the firm and in the contracting industry a carpenter is also vital. However, carpenters make significantly more money than legal secretaries even though both jobs may be of comparable importance to their respective employers. As a result, one change that women have fought for is making comparable worth the benchmark for pay. Companies would have to rate the importance of certain jobs; all jobs rated a "5," for example, no matter the description, would receive comparable pay. In this scenario, while factors such as years of experience and performance reviews would affect salary, the gendered divisions with regard to pay inequality would be lessened. However, while women's groups in most advanced industrial nations have lobbied for comparable worth policies, they have been unable to make much legislative progress on the issue.

In our three case studies, women's groups have worked on a variety of specific policy proposals to further the cause of fair pay. In Japan, women's groups have lobbied for the abolition of the "two-track" personnel administration system found in most corporations, in which women form the overwhelming majority of general track (as opposed to management track) jobs, which tend to be lower paying and do not lead to promotions to management positions. Abolition of this system would assist women in gaining equality in the workplace. In the United States, members of the 108th Congress were considering two bills, the Paycheck Fairness Act and the Fair Pay Act. Both of these acts would amend the Fair Labor Standards Act of 1938. The former would amend it to provide for more effective methods of redress for victims of wage discrimination, and the latter would prohibit discrimination in the payment of wages on account of race, sex, national origin, and for other purposes. However, both bills got held up in subcommittees and did not progress any further. Further, women's groups advocate the continued use. of affirmative action policies in hiring and promotion decisions to assist women in achieving equality in the workplace. In the past, affirmative action unquestionably has assisted women in gaining greater access to a variety of jobs and entrance into institutions of higher learning. Finally, the European Union and its member states continue to work toward improving gender equality in pay and hiring and promotion. One improvement for women would be making the European Charter on Human Rights legally binding, which would provide the EU with more tools for ending discrimination.

There are fewer solutions to the ongoing problem of sexual harassment. While many companies are taking necessary steps by educating their workers about what constitutes sexual harassment and methods of communication, broader cultural norms are slower to change. While the U.S. system of litigation has encouraged companies to move more rapidly on implementing harassment policies, there has been less progress on this matter in Europe, where there is less agreement on what constitutes harassment and fewer legislative efforts to combat it.

In terms of retirement benefits, advocates have pushed for a variety of reforms. For example, greater protections for part-time workers in the United States would improve the pay and benefits of part-time workers, the majority of whom are women. Other countries have moved to implement changes that would reward women for their years off from work for raising children. For example, Germany has reformed its pension system to grant women a three-year pension credit if they are the primary caretakers of their children (and thus not employed in the paid labor force). While this amount is more symbolic than significant, it nonetheless acknowledges the contribution of women who are not consistently working outside the home. Further, private pension accounts (worldwide) could be made more female-friendly by shortening the time one has to work until becoming vested. And all retirement schemes would greatly benefit women if women were paid the same as their male colleagues. The pay differential is one of the biggest contributors to women's poverty in their later years.

Conclusion

Despite the strides made with equal employment policies, this chapter also illustrates the limits of equal employment policies in many countries. These policies do not address the fundamental inequalities between men and women outside the workforce; women's caretaking and nurturing responsibilities have a dramatic effect on their abilities to compete in the realm of work, as we shall see in the next chapter. Further, laws can only go so far in ameliorating women's separate and unequal status in the absence of significant cultural change about the acceptability of discriminatory practices. Education is one key to this cultural change, as well as an educational system in which the topic of equality is at the heart of its curriculum and in which women's achievements and contributions are a regular part of the curriculum, not just during Women's History Month in March. Until more cultural change occurs, women will still be fighting an uphill battle for equality. Laws and their enforcement are important, and additional legal changes could assist women in their quest for equality. But societal change must come as well. And while this may be slow in coming, the rewards to individuals and society will be worth the time and effort.

Notes

1. Earn Campbell, "Women Seek Solutions to Pension-System Bias," *Christian Science Monitor,* May 9,1996. Vol. 88, p. 9.
2. Diane Nicol, "Employers Pace Rise in Equal Pay Claims," *The Scotsman,* April 19, 2003, p. 23,
3. Fiona Davidson, "Male Workers Say It's Unfair That Dress Rules Don't Apply to Women; Men Shirty About Ties," *The Express,* July 16, 2003, p. 7.
4. British Broadcasting Corporation News, "Wal-Mart Battles Huge Sexism Claim," September 25, 2003, http://newshbc.co.Uk/l/hi/business/3138188.stm (August 8,2005).
5. OECD Economics Department, "Female Labour Force Participation: Past Trends and Main Determinants in OECD Countries," May 2004, http://www.oecd.org/ dataoecd/25/5/31743836. pdf. (April 22, 2006).
6. United Nations Development Programme, *Human Development Report 2004* (New York: Oxford University Press, 2004), 221–224.

7. Ronnie Steinberg-Ratner, "The Policy and Problem: Overview of Seven Countries," in *Equal Employment Policy for Women*, ed. Ronnie Steinberg-Ratner (Philadelphia: Temple University Press, 1980), 41–42.

8. Amy G. Mazur and Susanne Zwingel, "Comparing Feminist Policy in Politics and at Work in France and Germany: Shared European Union Setting, Divergent National Contexts," *Review of Policy Research* 20, no. 3 (2003): 370.

9. Organization for Economic Co-operation and Development, *OECD in Figures: Statistics for the Member Countries* (Paris: OECD, 2002).

10. European Commission, "Gender Mainstreaming," http://europa.eu.int/comm/ employment_social/gender_equality/gender_mainstreaming/employment/ employment_labour_market_en.html. (October 5, 2003).

11. Amy G. Mazur, *Theorizing Feminist Policy* (New York: Cambridge University Press, 2002), 80–87.

12. Lynne E. Ford, *Women and Politics: The Pursuit of Equality* (New York: Houghton Mifflin Company, 2002), 199.

13. Commission of the European Communities, "Gender Pay Gaps in European Labour Markets—Measurement, Analysis and Policy Implications," Brussels, September 4, 2003.

14. Maggie Jackson, "Study: Part Time Work Is Widespread but Undervalued," The Associated Press, November 20,1997; "Japan: Highlights of Equality Action 2003: Equal Treatment for Part Time Workers," Women's International Network News 29 (Summer 2003): 56.

15. Commission of the European Communities, "Gender Pay Gaps in European Labour Markets—Measurement, Analysis, and Policy Implications," Brussels, April 9, 2003, SEC(2003)937, 22.

16. "The Conundrum of the Glass Ceiling," *Economist*, July 23, 2005.

17. "Helping Women Get to the Top," *Economist*, July 23, 2005.

18. Ibid.

19. World Bank, *Engendering Development: Through Gender Equality in Rights, Resources, and Voice* (New York: Oxford University Press, 2001), 1.

20. Carol Gilligan, *In a Different Voice* (Cambridge: Harvard University Press, 1982).

21. Joyce Gelb, "The Equal Employment Opportunity Law: A Decade of Change for Japanese Women?" *Law & Policy 22* (October 2000): 386.

22. M. Grazia Rossilli, "The European Union's Policy on the Equality of Women," *Feminist Studies* 25 (Spring 1999): 178–180.

23. National Organization for Women, "Facts About Pay Equity," http://www.now .org/issues/economic/factsheet.html (October 6, 2003).

24. Louise Nousratpour, "Hit out over Pay Injustice: Unions Urge Government to Confront Poverty," *Morning Star,* September 18, 2003, p. 1.

25. Hiromi Tanaka, "Equal Employment in Contemporary Japan: A Structural Approach," *Political Science* (January 2004): 66.

26. M. Margaret Conway, David W. Ahern, and Gertrude A. Steuernagel, *Women and Public Policy: A Revolution in Progress* (Washington, DC: Congressional Quarterly Press, 1999), 74.

27. See Eileen Applebaum et al., "Shared Work, Valued Care: New Norms for Organizing Market Work and Unpaid Care Work," Economic Policy Institute, June 2002.

28. "Treaty Establishing the European Community," http://www.hri.org/docs/ Rome57/ Part3Title08.html#Artll9. (April 22, 2006).

29. "European Parliament Fact Sheet 4.8.7. Equality for Men and Women." http://www.europarl. eu.int/factsheets/4_8_7_en.htm (September 30, 2003).

30. M. Grazia Rossilli, "The European Union's Policy on the Equality of Women," *Feminist Studies 25*, no.l (1999): 173.

31. European Union, "Equal Pay," http://europa.eu.int/scadplus/leg/en/cha/ cl0905.htm. (April 22, 2006).

32. Ilona Ostern, "From Equal Pay to Equal Employment: Four Decades of European Gender Politics," in *Gender Policies in the European Union,* ed. Mariagrazia Rossilli (New York: Peter Lang, 2000), 28.

33. Catherine Hoskyns, "Four Action Programmes on Equal Opportunities," in *Gender Policies in the European Union,* 43–47.

34. Scottish Labour, "Women and The Changing European Union," November 4, 2002, http:// www.scottishlabour.org.uk/heleniiddell (September 30, 2003).

35. Hiroyuki Takahashi, "Working Women in Japan: A Look at Historical Trends and Legal Reform," Japan Economic Institute, no. 42, November 6, 1998, http://www.jei.org/Archive/ JEIR98/9842f.htrnl (November 13, 2003).

36. U.S. General Accounting Office, "A New Look Through the Glass Ceiling: Where Are the Women?" January 2002.

37. National Women's Law Center, "The Paycheck Fairness Act: Helping to Close the Women's Wage Gap," May 2003, p. 1, http://www.nwlc.org (October 6, 2003).

38. Commission of the European Communities, "Gender Pay Gaps in European Labour Markets—Measurement, Analysis, and Policy Implications." Brussels, 4.9.2003 SEC(2003)937: 10.

39. Hiroyuki Takahashi, "Working Women in Japan: A Look at Historical Trends and Legal Reform," Japan Economic Institute, no. 42, November 6,1998, http://www.jei.org/ArcMve/ JEIR98/9842f.html (November 13, 2003).

40. Rob Varnon, "Census Report on Earning: Struggling to Bridge the Wage Gap," *Connecticut Post,* August 17, 2003, Your Money section.

41. "Statement by Congresswoman Carolyn B. Maloney: Women's Equality Amendment—11/14/2002," *Women's International Network News* (Winter 2003) 29–1, p. 73.

42. CEC, "Gender Pay Gaps in European Labour Markets," 11–17.

43. Ibid., 15.

44. James Graff et al., "Help Wanted for Europe," *Time,* June 19, 2000, vol. 155, issue 25, p. 18.

45. Ilse Lenz, "Globalization, Gender, and Work: Perspectives on Global Regulation," *Review of Policy Research* 20 (Spring 2003): 35– 38.

46. Dongxiao Liu and Elizabeth Heger Boyle, "Making the Case: The Women's Convention and Equal Employment Opportunity in Japan," *International Journal of Comparative Sociology* 42 (2001):389–390.

47. Tadashi Hanami, "Equal Employment Revisited," *japan Labour Bulletin,* The Japan Institute of Labour 39 (January 1, 2000).

48. Joyce Gelb, "Japan's Equal Employment Opportunity Law: A Decade of Change for Japanese Women?" *Law and Policy* 22 (October 2000): 387.

49. M. Margaret Conway, David W. Ahem, and Gertrude A. Steuernagel, *Women and Public Policy: A Revolution in Progress* (Washington, DC: CQ Press, 2004), 95.

50. As quoted in Lynne E. Ford, *Women and Politics: The Pursuit of Eauality* (New York: Houghton Mifflin, 2002), 211.

51. As quoted in Ibid., 213.

52. Executive Order 11246, 3 C.F.R. 169,1974.

53. "The ERA: A Brief Introduction," http://www.equalrightsamendment.org/ overview.htm. (April 22, 2006).

54. Ostner, "From Equal Pay to Equal Employability," 28.

55. British Broadcasting Corporation, "Amsterdam Treaty," April 30, 2001. http://news.bbc. co.**Uk**/l/hi/m_depth/europe/euro-glossary/1216210.sto

56. Grazia Rossilli, "The European Union's Policy on the Equality of Women," *Feminist Studies* 25, no. 1 (1999): 171–172.

57. European Commission, Directorate-General for Education and Culture, *European Employment and Social Policy: A Policy for People* (Luxembourg: European Communities, 2000): 26.

58. Rossilli, "The European Union's Policy on the Equality of Women," 175.

59. Gelb, "Japan's Equal Employment Opportunity Law," 390–391.

60. Tanaka, "Equal Employment in Contemporary Japan," 66.

61. Gelb, "Japan's Equal Employment Opportunity Law," 394.

62. Ibid., 396–397.

63. Akemi Nakamura, "Four Women Await Outcome of 10-Year Quest for Equal Pay," *The Japan Times,* March 27, 2005; "Four Women Win 63 Million Yen Ruling: Sumitomo Metal Guilty of Gender Bias," *The Japan Times,* March 29, 2005.

64. Ibid.

65. "Only 8.9% of Managerial Positions Taken by Women in Japan," *Deutsche Press–Agentur,* September 13, 2003, Miscellaneous section.

66. Ibid.

67. Takahashi, "Working Women in Japan," p. 11 of 12.

68. Ibid., p. 11 of 12.

69. WomenOf.com, "Non-Profits Improve Numbers of Women CEOs," http://www .womenof. com/News/cn092500.asp (October 6, 2003).

70. Del Jones, "Few Women Hold Top Executive Jobs, Even When CEOs Are Female," *USA Today* January 27, 2003, http://www.usatoday.com/money/jobcenter/2003-01-26-womenceos_x. htm (October 6, 2003).

71. National Organization for Women, "Pay Equity Still a Dream Worth Pursuing: New Report Shows Glass Ceiling Intact," Summer 2002, http://www.now .org/rmt/summer-2002/ payequity.html (October 6, 2003).

72. "The European Parliament Takes Stock," *Women's International Network News* 26, issue 4 (Autumn 2000) p. 59.

73. "EU's gender gap still wide open," *BBC News* March 6, 2006, http:// news.bbc.co.uk/l/hi/ world/europe/4785834.stm (April 22, 2006).

74. "Women and Work: European Situation," http://www.etuc.org.EQUALPAY/ UK./women_ and_work/European-Union/default.cfm (November 11, 2003).

75. European Commission, "European Employment and Social Policy," 24.

76. *Christian Science Monitor,* August 8,1997, vol. 89, issue 178, p. 10.

77. As cited in Heidi Gottfried and Laura Reese, "Gender, Policy, Politics, and Work: Feminist Comparative and Transnational Research," *The Review of Policy Research* 20, no. 1 (2003): 10.

78. Conway, Ahern, and Steuernagel, *Women and Public Policy,* 82.

79. U.S. Department of State, Bureau of Democracy, Human Rights, and Labor, "Japan: Country Reports on Human Rights Practices—2000," February 23, 2001, http://www.state.gOv/g/drl/rls/hrrpt/2000/eap/709pf.htm (November 19, 2003).

80. As quoted in Ford, *Women and Politics,* 218.

81. Jeanne Gregory, "Sexual Harassment: The Impact of EU Law in the Member States," in *Gender Policies in the European Union,* 175–189.

82. Commission of the European Communities, "Report from the Commission to the Council, the European Parliament, the European Economic and Social Committee and the Committee of Regions: Annual Report on Equal Opportunities for Women and Men in the European Union 2002," Brussels, March 5,2003, COM (2003) 98.

83. U.S. Department of State, Bureau of Democracy, Human Rights, and Labor, "Japan."

84. Ibid.

85. Ibid.

86. "Sexual Harassment," Encyclopedia Article from Encarta, http://www.encarta. msn.com/encyclopedia_76i579949/(November 19, 2003).

87. "EU Tightens Sex Harassment Law," CNN.com, April 18, 2002, http://cnn .worldnews. printthis.clickability.com (November 20, 2003).

88. Ibid.

89. Commission of the European Communities, "Report from the Commission to the Council, the European Parliament, the European Economic and Social Committee and the Committee of Regions."

90. Social Security Administration, "Women and Social Security," October 3, 2005, http://www. ssa.gov/pressofnce/factsheets/women.htm. (April 22, 2006).

91. "Women in Europe Towards Healthy Ageing," European Institute of Women's Health (1997), http://www.euroheaim.ie/report/index.htm, Introduction, p. 4 of 5 (September 29, 2003).

92. Ross Clare, "Women and Superannuation," The University of New South Wales, School of Economics and Actuarial Studies, paper presented at the Ninth Annual Colloquium of Superannuation Researchers, July 2001, p. 2.

93. Ayako Doi, "In Other Words," *Foreign Policy: The Magazine of Global Politics, Economics and Ideas* (November/December 20C3), http://www.foreignpolicy .com/story/story. php?storyID=13976 (November 20, 2003).

94. "Women in Europe Towards Healthy Ageing," Introduction, p. 4 of 5.

95. Social Security Network, a Century Foundation Project, "Issue Brief #6: Social Security: A Women's Issue," http://www.socsec.org/facts/Issue_Briefs/ women.htm (October 3, 2003).

96. As quoted in Charles Pope, "Social Security Must Protect Women, Bush Told," *Seattle Post-Intelligencer,* June 13,2001, http://seattlepi.nwsource.com/national/ 27227_socsecl3.shtml (September 29, 2003).

97. Kim Campbell, "Women Seek Solutions to Pension-System Bias," *Christian Science Monitor,* May 9,1996, vol. 88, p. 9.

98. "1 in 5 Women Relying on Partner's Pension," *The Financial Times,* August 16, 2003, Money section, p. 23.

99. "Women Given Unfair Choice of Babies or a Good Pension," *The Western Mail,* July 7, 2003, p. 1.

100. "Women in Europe Towards Healthy Ageing," European Institute of Women's Health, Introduction, p. 4 of 5.

101. Campbell, "Women Seek Solutions to Pension-System Bias," p. 9.

102. Ibid.

Chapter Six

Under Western Eyes
Feminist Scholarship and Colonial Discourses

Chandra Talpade Mohanty

Any discussion of the intellectual and political construction of "third world feminisms" must address itself to two simultaneous projects: the internal critique of hegemonic "Western" feminisms, and the formulation of autonomous, geographically, historically, and culturally grounded feminist concerns and strategies. The first project is one of deconstructing and dismantling; the second, one of building and constructing. While these projects appear to be contradictory, the one working negatively and the other positively, unless these two tasks are addressed simultaneously, "third world" feminisms run the risk of marginalization or ghettoization from both mainstream (right and left) and Western feminist discourses.

It is to the first project that I address myself. What I wish to analyze is specifically the production of the "third world woman" as a singular monolithic subject in some recent (Western) feminist texts. The definition of colonization I wish to invoke here is a predominantly *discursive* one, focusing on a certain mode of appropriation and codification of "scholarship" and "knowledge" about women in the third world by particular analytic categories employed in specific writings on the subject which take as their referent feminist interests as they have been articulated in the U.S. and Western Europe. If one of the tasks of formulating and understanding the locus of "third world feminisms" is delineating the way in which it resists and *works against* what I am referring to as "West ern feminist discourse," an analysis of the discursive construction of "third world women" in Western feminism is an important first step.

Clearly Western feminist discourse and political practice is neither singular nor homogeneous in its goals, interests, or analyses. However, it is possible to trace a coherence of *effects* resulting from the implicit assumption of "the West" (in all its complexities and contradictions) as the primary referent in theory and praxis. My reference to "Western feminism" is by no means intended to imply that it is a monolith. Rather, I am attempting to draw attention to the similar effects of various textual strategies used by writers which codify Others as non-Western and hence themselves as (implicitly) Western. It is in this sense that I use the term *Western feminist*. Similar arguments can be made in terms of middle-class urban African or Asian scholars producing scholarship on or about their rural or working-class sisters which assumes their own middle-class cultures as the norm, and codifies working-class histories and cultures as Other. Thus, while this essay focuses specifically on what I refer to as "Western feminist" discourse on women in the third world, the critiques I offer also pertain to third world scholars writing about their own cultures, which employ identical analytic strategies.

It ought to be of some political significance, at least, that the term *colonization* has come to denote a variety of phenomena in recent feminist and left writings in general. From its analytic value as a category of exploitative economic exchange in both traditional and contemporary Marxisms (cf. particularly contemporary theorists such as Baran 1962, Amin 1977, and Gunder-Frank 1967) to its use by feminist women of color in the U.S. to describe the appropriation of their experiences and struggles by hegemonic white women's movements (cf. especially Moraga and Anzaldúa 1983, Smith 1983, Joseph and Lewis 1981, and Moraga 1984), colonization has been used to characterize everything from the most evident economic and political hierarchies to the production of a particular cultural discourse about what is called the "third world."[1] However sophisticated or problematical its use as an explanatory construct, colonization almost invariably implies a relation of structural domination, and a suppression—often violent—of the heterogeneity of the subject(s) in question.

My concern about such writings derives from my own implication and investment in contemporary debates in feminist theory, and the urgent political necessity (especially in the age of Reagan/Bush) of forming strategic coalitions across class, race, and national boundaries. The analytic principles discussed below serve to distort Western feminist political practices, and limit the possibility of coalitions among (usually white) Western feminists and working-class feminists and feminists of color around the world. These limitations are evident in the construction of the (implicitly consensual) priority of issues around which apparently *all* women are expected to organize. The necessary and integral connection between feminist scholarship and feminist political practice and organizing determines the significance and status of Western feminist writings on women in the third world, for feminist scholarship, like most other kinds of scholarship, is not the mere production of knowledge about a certain subject. It is a directly political and discursive *practice* in that it is purposeful and ideological. It is best seen as a mode of intervention into particular hegemonic discourses (for example, traditional anthropology, sociology, literary criticism, etc.); it is a political praxis which counters and resists the totalizing imperative of age-old "legitimate" and "scientific" bodies of knowledge. Thus, feminist scholarly practices (whether reading, writing, critical, or textual) are inscribed in relations of power—relations which they counter, resist, or even perhaps implicitly support. There can, of course, be no apolitical scholarship.

The relationship between "Woman"—a cultural and ideological composite Other constructed through diverse representational discourses (scientific, literary, juridical, linguistic, cinematic, etc.)—and "women"—real, material subjects of their collective histories—is one of the central questions the practice of feminist scholarship seeks to address. This connection between women as historical subjects and the representation of Woman produced by hegemonic discourses is not a relation of direct identity, or a relation of correspondence or simple implication.[2] It is an arbitrary, relation set up by particular cultures. I would like to suggest that the feminist writings I analyze here discursively colonize the material and historical heterogeneities of the lives of women in the third world, thereby producing/representing a composite, singular "third world woman"—an image which appears arbitrarily constructed, but nevertheless carries with it the authorizing signature of Western humanist discourse.[3]

I argue that assumptions of privilege and ethnocentric universality, on the one hand, and inadequate self-consciousness about the effect of Western scholarship on the "third world" in the context of a world system dominated by the West, on the other, characterize a sizable extent of Western feminist work on women in the third world. An analysis of "sexual difference" in the form of a cross-culturally singular, monolithic notion of patriarchy or male dominance leads to the construction of a similarly reductive and homogeneous notion of what I call the "third world difference"—that stable, ahistorical something that apparently op presses most if not all the women in these countries. And it is in the production of this "third world difference" that Western feminisms appropriate and "colonize" the constitutive complexities which characterize the lives of women in these countries. It is in this process of discursive homogenization and systematization of the oppression of women in the third world that power is exercised in much of recent Western feminist discourse, and this power needs to be defined and named.

In the context of the West's hegemonic position today, of what Anouar Abdel-Malek (1981) calls a struggle for "control over the orientation, regulation and decision of the process of world development on the basis of the advanced sector's monopoly of scientific knowledge and ideal creativity," Western feminist scholarship on the third world must be seen and examined precisely in terms of its inscription in these particular relations of power and struggle. There is, it should be evident, no universal patriarchal framework which this scholarship resist—unless one posits an international male conspiracy or a monolithic, ahistorical power structure. There is, however, a particular world balance of power within which any analysis of culture, ideology, and socioeconomic conditions necessarily has to be situated. Abdel-Malek is useful here, again, in reminding us about the inherence of politics in the discourses of "culture":

> Contemporary imperialism is, in a real sense, a hegemonic imperialism, exercising to a maximum degree a rationalized violence taken to a higher level than ever before—through fire and sword, but also through the attempt to control hearts and minds. For its content is defined by the combined action of the military-industrial complex and the hegemonic cultural centers of the West, all of them founded on the advanced levels of development attained by monopoly and finance capital, and supported by the benefits of both the scientific and technological revolution and the second industrial revolution itself. (145–46)

Western feminist scholarship cannot avoid the challenge of situating itself and examining its role in such a global economic and political frame work. To do any less would be to ignore the complex interconnections between first and third world economies and the profound effect of this on the lives of women in all countries. I do not question the descriptive and informative value of most Western feminist writings on women in the third world. I also do not question the existence of excellent work which does not fall into the analytic traps with which I am concerned. In fact I deal with an example of such work later on. In the context of an overwhelming silence about the experiences of women in these countries, as well as the need to forge international links between women's political struggles, such work is both pathbreaking and absolutely essential. However, it is both to the *explanatory potential* of particular analytic strategies employed by such writing, and to their *political effect* in the context of the hegemony of Western scholarship that I want to draw attention here. While feminist writing in the U.S. is still marginalized (except from the point of view of women of color addressing privileged white women), Western feminist writing on women in the third world must be considered in the context of the global hegemony of Western scholarship—i.e., the production, publication, distribution, and consumption of information and ideas. Marginal or not, this writing has political effects and implications beyond the immediate feminist or disciplinary audience. One such significant effect of the dominant "representations" of Western feminism is its conflation with imperialism in the eyes of particular third world women.[4] Hence the urgent need to examine the *political* implications of our *analytic* strategies and principles.

My critique is directed at three basic analytic principles which are present in (Western) feminist discourse on women in the third world. Since I focus primarily on the Zed Press Women in the Third World series, my comments on Western feminist discourse are circumscribed by my analysis of the texts in this series.[5] This is a way of focusing my critique. However, even though I am dealing with feminists who identify themselves as culturally or geographically from the "West," as mentioned earlier, what I say about these presuppositions or implicit principles holds for anyone who uses these methods, whether third world women in the West, or third world women in the third world writing on these issues and publishing in the West. Thus, I am not making a culturalist argument about ethnocentrism; rather, I am trying to uncover how ethnocentric universalism is produced in certain analyses. As a matter of fact, my argument holds for any discourse that sets up its own authorial subjects as the implicit referent, i.e., the yardstick by which to encode and represent cultural Others. It is in this move that power is exercised in discourse.

The first analytic presupposition I focus on is involved in the strategic location of the category "women" vis-a-vis the context of analysis. The assumption of women as an already constituted, coherent group with identical interests and desires, regardless of class, ethnic or racial location, or contradictions, implies a notion of gender or sexual difference or even patriarchy which can be applied universally and cross-culturally. (The context of analysis can be anything from kinship structures and the organization of labor to media representations.) The second analytical presupposition is evident on the methodological level, in the uncritical way "proof" of universality and cross-cultural validity are provided. The third is a more specifically political presupposition underlying the methodologies and the analytic strategies, i.e., the model of power and struggle they imply and suggest, I argue that as a result of the two modes—or, rather, frames—of analysis described above, a homogeneous notion of the oppression of women as a group is assumed, which, in turn, produces the image of an "average third world woman." This average third world woman leads an essentially truncated life based on her feminine gender (read: sexually constrained) and her being "third world" (read: ignorant, poor, uneducated, tradition-bound, domestic, family-oriented, victimized, etc.). This, I suggest, is in contrast to the (implicit) self-representation of Western women as educated, as modern, as having control over their own bodies and sexualities, and the freedom to make their own decisions.

The distinction between Western feminist representation of women in the third world and Western feminist self-presentation is a distinction of the same order as that made by some Marxists between the "maintenance" function of the housewife and the real "productive" role of wage labor, or the characterization by developmentalists of the third world as being engaged in the lesser production of "raw materials" in contrast to the "real" productive activity of the first world. These distinctions are made on the basis of the privileging of a particular group as the norm or referent. Men involved in wage labor, first world producers, and, I suggest, Western feminists who sometimes cast third world women in terms of "ourselves undressed" (Michelle Rosaldo's [1980] term), all construct themselves as the normative referent in such a binary analytic.

"Women" as Category of Analysis, or: We Are All Sisters in Struggle

By women as a category of analysis, I am referring to the crucial assumption that all of us of the same gender, across classes and cultures, are somehow socially constituted as a homogeneous group identified prior to the process of analysis. This is an assumption which characterizes much feminist discourse. The homogeneity of women as a group is produced not on the basis of biological essentials but rather on the basis of secondary sociological and anthropological universals. Thus, for instance, in any given piece of feminist analysis, women are characterized as a singular group on the basis of a shared oppression. What binds women together is a sociological notion of the "sameness" of their oppression. It is at this point that an elision takes place between "women" as a discursively constructed group and "women" as material subjects of their own history.[6] Thus, the discursively consensual homogeneity of "women" as a group is mistaken for the historically specific material reality of groups of women. This results in an assumption of women as an always already constituted group, one which has been labeled "powerless," "exploited," "sexually harassed," etc., by feminist scientific, economic, legal, and sociological discourses. (Notice that this is quite similar to sexist discourse labeling women weak, emotional, having math anxiety, etc.) This focus is not on uncovering the material and ideological specificities that constitute a particular group of women as "powerless" in a particular context. It is, rather, on finding a variety of cases of "powerless" groups of women to prove the general point that women as a group are powerless.

In this section I focus on five specific ways in which "women" as a category of analysis is used in Western feminist discourse on women in the third world. Each of these examples illustrates the construction of "third world women" as a homogeneous "powerless" group often located as implicit *victims* of particular socioeconomic systems. I have chosen to deal with a variety of writers—from Fran Hosken, who writes primarily about female genital mutilation, to writers from the Women in International Development school, who write about the effect of development policies on third world women for both Western and third world audiences. The similarity of assumptions about "third world women" in all these texts forms the basis of my discussion. This is not to equate all the texts that I analyze, nor is it to equalize their strengths and weaknesses. The authors I deal with write with varying degrees of care and complexity; however, the *effect* of their representation of third world women is a coherent one. In these texts women are defined as victims of male violence (Fran Hosken); victims of the colonial process (Maria Cutrufelli); victims of the Arab familial system (Juliette Minces); victims of the economic development process (Beverley Lindsay and the [liberal] WID School); and finally, victims of the Islamic code (Patricia Jeffery). This mode of defining women primarily in terms of their *object status* (the way in which they are affected or not affected by certain institutions and systems) is what characterizes this particular form of the use of "women" as a category of analysis. In the context of Western women writing/studying women in the third world, such objectification (however benevolently motivated) needs to be both named and challenged. As Valerie Amos and Pratibha Parmar argue quite eloquently, "Feminist theories which examine our cultural practices as 'feudal residues' or label us 'traditional,' also portray us as politically immature women who need to be versed and schooled in the ethos of Western feminism. They need to be continually challenged ..." (1984, 7).

Women as Victims of Male Violence

Fran Hosken, in writing about the relationship between human rights and female genital mutilation in Africa and the Middle East, bases her whole discussion/condemnation of genital mutilation on one privileged premise: that the goal of this practice is "to mutilate the sexual pleasure and satisfaction of woman" (1981, 11). This, in turn, leads her to claim that woman's sexuality is controlled, as is her reproductive potential. According to Hosken, "male sexual politics" in Africa and around the world "share the same political goal: to assure female dependence and subservience by any and all means" (14). Physical violence against women (rape, sexual assault, excision, infibulation, etc.) is thus carried out "with an astonishing consensus among men in the world" (14). Here, women are defined consistently as the *victims* of male control—the "sexually oppressed."[7] Although it is true that the potential of male violence against women circumscribes and elucidates their social position to a certain extent, defining women as archetypal victims freezes them into "objects-who-defend-themselves," men into "subjects-who-perpetrate-violence," and (every) society into powerless (read: women) and powerful (read: men) groups of people. Male violence must be theorized and interpreted *within* specific societies, in order both to understand it better and to effectively organize to change it.[8] Sisterhood cannot be assumed on the basis of gender; it must be forged in concrete historical and political practice and analysis.

Women as Universal Dependents

Beverly Lindsay's conclusion to the book *Comparative Perspectives of Third World Women: The Impact of Race, Sex and Class* (1983, 298, 306) states: "dependency relationships, based upon race, sex and class, are being perpetuated through social, educational, and economic institutions. These are the linkages among Third World Women." Here, as in other places, Lindsay implies that third world women constitute an identifiable group purely on the basis of shared dependencies. If shared dependencies were all that was needed to bind us together as a group, third world women would always be seen as an apolitical group with no subject status. Instead, if anything, it is the *common context* of political struggle against class, race, gender, and imperialist hierarchies that may constitute third world women as a strategic group at this historical juncture. Lindsay also states that linguistic and cultural differences exist between Vietnamese and black American women, but "both groups are victims of race, sex, and class." Again black and Vietnamese women are characterized by their victim status.

Similarly, examine statements such as "My analysis will start by stat ing that all African women are politically and economically dependent" (Cutrufelli 1983, 13), "Nevertheless, either overtly or covertly, prostitution is still the main if not the only source of work for African women" (Cutrufelli 1983, 33). *All* African women are dependent. Prostitution is the only work option for African women as a *group*. Both statements are illustrative of generalizations sprinkled liberally through a recent Zed

Press publication, *Women of Africa: Roots of Oppression,* by Maria Rosa Cutrufelli, who is described on the cover as an Italian writer, sociologist, Marxist, and feminist. In the 1980s, is it possible to imagine writing a book entitled *Women of Europe: Roots of Oppression*? I am not objecting to the use of universal groupings for descriptive purposes. Women from the continent of Africa can be descriptively characterized as "women of Africa." It is when "women of Africa" becomes a homogeneous sociological grouping characterized by common dependencies or powerlessness (or even strengths) that problems arise— we say too little and too much at the same time.

This is because descriptive gender differences are transformed into the division between men and women. Women are constituted as a group via dependency relationships vis-a-vis men, who are implicitly held responsible for these relationships. When "women of Africa" as a group (versus "men of Africa" as a group?) are seen as a group precisely because they are generally dependent and oppressed, the analysis of specific historical differences becomes impossible, because reality is always apparently structured by divisions—two mutually exclusive and jointly exhaustive groups, the victims and the oppressors. Here the sociological is substituted for the biological, in order, however, to create the same—a unity of women. Thus, it is not the descriptive potential of gender difference but the privileged positioning and explanatory potential of gender difference as the *origin* of oppression that I question. In using "women of Africa" (as an already constituted group of oppressed peoples) as a category of analysis, Cutrufelli denies any historical specificity to the location of women as subordinate, powerful, marginal, central, or other wise, vis-a-vis particular social and power networks. Women are taken as a unified "powerless" group prior to the analysis in question. Thus, it is then merely a matter of specifying the context *after the fact.* "Women" are now placed in the context of the family, or in the workplace, or within religious networks, almost as if these systems existed outside the relations of women with other women, and women with men.

The problem with this analytic strategy, let me repeat, is that it as sumes men and women are already constituted as sexual-political subjects prior to their entry into the arena of social relations. Only if we subscribe to this assumption is it possible to undertake analysis which looks at the "effects" of kinship structures, colonialism, organization of labor, etc., on women, who are defined in advance as a group. The crucial point that is forgotten is that women are produced through these very relations as well as being implicated in forming these relations. As Michelle Rosaldo argues, "woman's place in human social life is not in any direct sense a product of the things she does (or even less, a function of what, biologically, she is) but the meaning her activities acquire through concrete social interactions" (1980, 400). That women mother in a variety of societies is not as significant as the value attached to mothering in these societies. The distinction between the act of mothering and the status attached to it is a very important one—one that needs to be stated and analyzed contextually.

Married Women as Victims of the Colonial Process

In Levi-Strauss's theory of kinship structure as a system of the exchange of women, what is significant is that exchange itself is not constitutive of the subordination of women; women are not subordinate be cause of the *fact* of exchange, but because of the *modes* of exchange instituted, and the values attached to these modes. However, in discussing the marriage ritual of the Bemba, a Zambian matrilocal, matrilineal people, Cutrufelli in *Women of Africa* focuses on the fact of the marital exchange of women before and after Western colonization, rather than the value attached to this exchange in this particular context. This leads to her definition of Bemba women as a coherent group affected in a particular way by colonization. Here again, Bemba women are constituted rather unilaterally as victims of the effects of Western colonization.

Cutrufelli cites the marriage ritual of the Bemba as a multistage event "whereby a young man becomes incorporated into his wife's family group as he takes up residence with them and gives his services in return for food and maintenance" (43). This ritual extends over many years, and the sexual relationship varies according to the degree of the girl's physical maturity. It is only after she undergoes an initiation ceremony at puberty that intercourse is sanctioned, and the man acquires legal rights over her. This initiation ceremony is the more important act of the consecration of women's reproductive power, so that the abduction of an uninitiated girl is of no consequence, while heavy penalty is levied for the seduction of an initiated girl. Cutrufelli asserts that the effect of European colonization has changed the whole marriage system. Now the young man is entitled to take his wife away from her people in return for money. The implication is that Bemba women have now lost the protection of tribal laws. However, while it is possible to see how the structure of the traditional marriage contract (versus the postcolonial marriage contract) offered women a certain amount of control over their marital relations, only an analysis of the political significance of the actual practice which privileges an initiated girl over an uninitiated one, indicating a shift in female power relations as a result of this ceremony, can provide an accurate account of whether Bemba women were indeed protected by tribal laws *at all times*.

However, it is not possible to talk about Bemba women as a homogeneous group within the traditional marriage structure. Bemba women *before* the initiation are constituted within a different set or social relations compared to Bemba women *after* the initiation. To treat them as a unified group characterized by the fact of their "exchange" between male kin is to deny the sociohistorical and cultural specificities of their existence, and the differential *value* attached to their exchange before and after their initiation. It is to treat the initiation ceremony as a ritual with no political implications or effects. It is also to assume that in merely describing the *structure* of the marriage contract, the situation of women is exposed. Women as a group are positioned within a given structure, but there is no attempt made to trace the effect of the marriage practice in constituting women within an obviously changing network of power relations. Thus, women are assumed to be sexual-political subjects prior to entry into kinship structures.

Women and Familial Systems

Elizabeth Cowie (1978), in another context, points out the implications of this sort of analysis when she emphasizes the specifically political nature of kinship structures which must be analyzed as ideological practices which designate men and women as father, husband, wife, mother, sister, etc. Thus, Cowie suggests, women as women are not *located* within the family. Rather, it is *in* the family, as an effect of kinship structures, that women as women are *constructed*, defined within and by the group. Thus, for instance, when Juliette Minces (1980) cites *the* patriarchal family as the basis for "an almost identical vision of women" that Arab and Muslim societies have, she falls into this very trap (see especially p. 23). Not only is it problematical to speak of a vision of women shared by Arab and Muslim societies (i.e., over twenty different countries) without addressing the particular historical, material, and ideological power structures that construct such images, but to speak of the patriarchal family or the tribal kinship structure as the origin of the socioeconomic status of women is to again assume that women are sexual-political subjects prior to their entry into the family. So while on the one hand women attain value or status within the family, the assumption of a singular patriarchal kinship system (common to all Arab and Muslim societies) is what apparently structures women as an oppressed group in these societies! This singular, coherent kinship system presumably influences an other separate and given entity, "women." Thus, all women, regardless of class and cultural differences, are affected by this system. Not only are *all* Arab and Muslim women seen to constitute a homogeneous oppressed group, but there is no discussion of the specific *practices* within the family which constitute women as mothers, wives, sisters, etc. Arabs and Muslims, it appears, don't change at all. Their patriarchal family is carried over from the times of the prophet Mohammed. They exist, as it were, outside history.

Women and Religious Ideologies

A further example of the use of "women" as a category of analysis is found in cross-cultural analyses which subscribe to a certain economic reductionism in describing the relationship between the economy and factors such as politics and ideology. Here, in reducing the level of comparison to the economic relations between "developed and developing" countries, any specificity to the question of women is denied. Mina Modares (1981), in a careful analysis of women and Shi'ism in Iran, focuses on this very problem when she criticizes feminist writings which treat Islam as an ideology separate from and outside social relations and practices, rather than a discourse which includes rules for economic, social, and power relations within society. Patricia Jeffery's (1979) otherwise informative work on Pirzada women in purdah considers Islamic ideology a partial explanation for the status of women in that it provides a justification for the purdah. Here, Islamic ideology is reduced to a set of ideas whose internalization by Pirzada women contributes to the stability of the system.

However, the primary explanation for purdah is located in the control that Pirzada men have over economic resources, and the personal security purdah gives to Pirzada women.

By taking a specific version of Islam as *the* Islam, Jeffery attributes a singularity and coherence to it. Modares notes, "'Islamic Theology' then becomes imposed on a separate and given entity called 'women.' A further unification is reached: Women (meaning *all women*), regardless of their differing positions within societies, come to be affected or not affected by Islam. These conceptions provide the right ingredients for an unproblematic possibility of a cross-cultural study of women" (63). Marnia Lazreg makes a similar argument when she addresses the reductionism inherent in scholarship on women in the Middle East and North Africa:

> A ritual is established whereby the writer appeals to religion as *the* cause of gender inequality just as it is made the source of underdevelopment in much of modernization theory. In an uncanny way, feminist discourse on women from the Middle East and North Africa mirrors that of theologians' own interpretation of women in Islam.
>
> The overall effect of this paradigm is to deprive women of self-presence, of being. Because women are subsumed under religion presented in fundamental terms, they are inevitably seen as evolving in nonhistorical time. They virtually have no history. Any analysis of change is therefore foreclosed. (1988, 87)

While Jeffery's analysis does not quite succumb to this kind of unitary notion of religion (Islam), it does collapse all ideological specificities into economic relations, and universalizes on the basis of this comparison.

Women and the Development Process

The best examples of universalization on the basis of economic reductionism can be found in the liberal "Women in Development" literature. Proponents of this school seek to examine the effect of development on third world women, sometimes from self-designated feminist perspectives. At the very least, there is an evident interest in and commitment to improving the lives of women in "developing" countries. Scholars such as Irene Tinker and Michelle Bo Bramsen (1972), Ester Boserup (1970), and Perdita Huston (1979) have all written about the effect of development policies on women in the third world.[9] All three women assume "development" is synonymous with "economic development" or "economic progress." As in the case of Minces's patriarchal family, Hosken's male sexual control, and Cutrufelli's Western colonization, development here becomes the all-time equalizer. Women are affected positively or negatively by economic development policies, and this is the basis for cross-cultural comparison.

For instance, Perdita Huston (1979) states that the purpose of her study is to describe the effect of the development process on the "family unit and its individual members" in Egypt, Kenya, Sudan, Tunisia, Sri Lanka, and Mexico. She states that the "problems" and "needs" expressed by rural and urban women in these countries all center around education and training, work and wages, access to health and other services, political participation, and legal rights. Huston relates all these "needs" to the lack of sensitive development policies which exclude women as a group or category. For her, the solution is simple: implement improved development policies which emphasize training for women fieldworkers, use women trainees, and women rural development officers, encourage women's cooperatives, etc. Here again, women are assumed to be a coherent group or category prior to their entry into "the development process." Huston assumes that all third world women have similar problems and needs. Thus, they must have similar interests and goals. However, the interests of urban, middle-class, educated Egyptian housewives, to take only one instance, could surely not be seen as being the same as those of their uneducated, poor maids. Development policies do not affect both, groups of women in the same way. Practices which characterize women's status and roles vary according to class. Women are constituted as women through the complex interaction between class, culture, religion, and other ideological institutions and frameworks. They are not "women"—a coherent group—solely on the basis of a particular economic system or policy. Such reductive cross-cultural comparisons result in the colonization of the specifics of daily existence and the complexities of political interests which women of different social classes and cultures represent and mobilize.

Thus, it is revealing that for Perdita Huston, women in the third world countries she writes about have "needs" and "problems," but few if any have "choices" or the freedom to act. This is an interesting representation of women in the third world, one which is significant in suggesting a latent self-presentation of Western women which bears looking at. She writes, "What surprised and moved me most as I listened to women in such very different cultural settings was the striking commonality—whether they were educated or illiterate, urban or rural—of their most basic values: the importance they assign to family, dignity, and service to others" (1979, 115). Would Huston consider such values unusual for women in the West?

What is problematical about this kind of use of "women" as a group, as a stable category of analysis, is that it assumes an ahistorical, universal unity between women based on a generalized notion of their subordination. Instead of analytically *demonstrating* the production of women as socioeconomic political groups within particular local contexts, this analytical move limits the definition of the female subject to gender identity, completely bypassing social class and ethnic identities. What characterizes women as a group is their gender (sociologically, not necessarily biologically, defined) over and above everything else, indicating a monolithic notion of sexual difference. Because women are thus constituted as a coherent group, sexual difference becomes coterminous with female subordination, and power is automatically defined in binary terms: people who have it (read: men), and people who do not (read: women). Men exploit, women are exploited. Such simplistic formulations are historically reductive; they are also ineffectual in designing strategies to combat oppressions. All they do is reinforce binary divisions between men and women.

What would an analysis which did not do this look like? Maria Mies's work illustrates the strength of Western feminist work on women in the third world which does not fall into the traps discussed above. Mies's study of the lace makers of Narsapur, India (1982), attempts to carefully analyze a substantial household industry in which "housewives" produce lace doilies for consumption in the world market. Through a detailed analysis of the structure of the lace industry, production and reproduction relations, the sexual division of labor, profits and exploitation, and the overall consequences of defining women as "non-working housewives" and their work as "leisure-time activity," Mies demonstrates the levels of exploitation in this industry and the impact of this production system on the work and living conditions of the women involved in it. In addition, she is able to analyze the "ideology of the housewife," the notion of a woman sitting in the house, as providing the necessary subjective and sociocultural element for the creation and maintenance of a production system that contributes to the increasing pauperization of women, and keeps them totally atomized and disorganized as workers. Mies's analysis shows the effect of a certain historically and culturally specific mode of patriarchal organization, an organization constructed on the basis of the definition of the lace makers as "non-working housewives" at familial, local, regional, statewide, and international levels. The intricacies and the effects of particular power networks not only are emphasized, but they form the basis of Mies's analysis of how this particular group of women is situated at the center of a hegemonic, exploitative world market.

This is a good example of what careful, politically focused, local analyses can accomplish. It illustrates how the category of women is constructed in a variety of political contexts that often exist simultaneously and overlaid on top of one another. There is no easy generalization in the direction of "women" in India, or "women in the third world"; nor is there a reduction of the political construction of the exploitation of the lace makers to cultural explanations about the passivity or obedience that might characterize these women and their situation. Finally, this mode of local, political analysis which generates theoretical categories from within the situation and context being analyzed, also suggests corresponding effective strategies for organizing against the exploitation faced by the lace makers. Narsapur women are not mere victims of the production process, because they resist, challenge, and subvert the process at various junctures. Here is one instance of how Mies delineates the connections between the housewife ideology, the self-consciousness of the lace makers, and their interrelationships as contributing to the latent resistances she perceives among the women:

> The persistence of the housewife ideology, the self-perception of the lace makers as petty commodity producers rather than as workers, is not only upheld by

the structure of the industry as such but also by the deliberate propagation and reinforcement of reactionary patriarchal norms and institutions. Thus, most of the lace makers voiced the same opinion about the rules of *purdah* and seclusion in their communities which were also propagated by the lace exporters. In particular, the *Kapu* women said that they had never gone out of their houses, that women of their community could not do any other work than housework and lace work etc. but in spite of the fact that most of them still subscribed fully to the patriarchal norms of the *gosha* women, there were also contradictory elements in their consciousness. Thus, although they looked down with contempt upon women who were able to work outside the house—like the untouchable *Mala* and *Madiga* women or women of other lower castes, they could not ignore the fact that these women were earning more money precisely because they were *not* respectable house wives but workers. At one discussion, they even admitted that it would be better if they could also go out and do coolie work. And when they were asked whether they would be ready to come out of their houses and work in one place in some sort of a factory, they said they would do that. This shows that the *purdah* and housewife ideology, although still fully internalized, already had some cracks, because it has been confronted with several contradictory realities. (157)

It is only by understanding the *contradictions* inherent in women's location within various structures that effective political action and challenges can be devised. Mies's study goes a long way toward offering such analysis. While there are now an increasing number of Western feminist writings in this tradition,[10] there is also, unfortunately, a large block of writing which succumbs to the cultural reductionism discussed earlier.

Methodological Universalisms, or: Women's Oppression Is a Global Phenomenon

Western feminist writings on women in the third world subscribe to a variety of methodologies to demonstrate the universal cross-cultural operation of male dominance and female exploitation. I summarize and critique three such methods below, moving from the simplest to the most complex.

First, proof of universalism is provided through the use of an arithmetic method. The argument goes like this: the greater the number of women who wear the veil, the more universal is the sexual segregation and control of women (Deardon 1975, 4–5). Similarly, a large number of different, fragmented examples from a variety of countries also apparently add up to a universal fact. For instance, Muslim women in Saudi Arabia, Iran, Pakistan, India, and Egypt all wear some sort of a veil. Hence, this indicates that the sexual control of women is a universal fact in those countries in which the women are veiled (Deardon 1975,

7, 10). Fran Hosken writes, "Rape, forced prostitution, polygamy, genital mutilation, pornography, the beating of girls and women, purdah (segregation of women) are all violations of basic human rights" (1981, 15). By equating purdah with rape, domestic violence, and forced prostitution, Hosken asserts its "sexual control" function as the primary explanation for purdah, whatever the context. Institutions of purdah are thus denied any cultural and historical specificity, and contradictions and potentially subversive aspects are totally ruled out.

In both these examples, the problem is not in asserting that the practice of wearing a veil is widespread. This assertion can be made on the basis of numbers. It is a descriptive generalization. However, it is the analytic leap from the practice of veiling to an assertion of its general significance in controlling women that must be questioned. While there may be a physical similarity in the veils worn by women in. Saudi Arabia and Iran, the specific meaning attached to this practice varies according to the cultural and ideological context. In addition, the symbolic space occupied by the practice of purdah may be similar in certain contexts, but this does not automatically indicate that the practices themselves have identical significance in the social realm. For example, as is well known, Iranian middle-class women veiled themselves during the 1979 revolution to indicate solidarity with their veiled working-class sisters, while in contemporary Iran, mandatory Islamic laws dictate that all Iranian women wear veils. While in both these instances, similar reasons might be offered for the veil (opposition to the Shah and Western cultural colonization in the first case, and the true Islamicization of Iran in the second), the concrete *meanings* attached to Iranian women wearing the veil are clearly different in both historical contexts. In the first case, wearing the veil is both an oppositional and a revolutionary gesture on the part of Iranian middle-class women; in the second case, it is a coercive, institutional mandate (see Tabari 1980 for detailed discussion). It is on the basis of such context-specific differentiated analysis that effective political strategies can be generated. To assume that the mere practice of veiling women in a number of Muslim countries indicates the universal oppression of women through sexual segregation not only is analytically reductive, but also proves quite useless when it comes to the elaboration of oppositional political strategy.

Second, concepts such as reproduction, the sexual division of labor, the family, marriage, household, patriarchy, etc., are often used without their specification in local cultural and historical contexts. Feminists use these concepts in providing explanations for women's subordination, apparently assuming their universal applicability. For instance, how is it possible to refer to "the" sexual division of labor when the *content* of this division changes radically from one environment to the next, and from one historical juncture to another? At its most abstract level, it is the fact of the differential assignation of tasks according to sex that is significant; however, this is quite different from the *meaning* or *value* that the content of this sexual division of labor assumes in different contexts. In most cases the assigning of tasks on the basis of sex has an ideological origin. There is no question that a claim such as "women are concentrated in service-oriented occupations in a large number of countries around the world" is descriptively valid. Descriptively, then, perhaps the existence of a similar sexual division of labor (where women work in service occupations such as nursing, social work, etc., and men in other kinds of occupations) in a variety of different countries can be asserted. However, the concept of the "sexual division of labor" is more than just a descriptive category. It indicates the differential *value* placed on "men's work" versus "women's work."

Often the mere existence of a sexual division of labor is taken to be proof of the oppression of women in various societies. This results from a confusion between and collapsing together of the descriptive and explanatory potential of the concept of the sexual division of labor. Superficially similar situations may have radically different, historically specific explanations, and cannot be treated as identical. For instance, the rise of female-headed households in middle-class America might be construed as a sign of great independence and feminist progress, whereby women are considered to have *chosen* to be single parents, there are increasing numbers of lesbian mothers, etc. However, the recent increase in female-headed households in Latin America,[11] where women might be seen to have more decision-making power, is concentrated among the poorest strata, where life choices are the most constrained economically. A similar argument can be made for the rise of female-headed families among black and Chicana women in the U.S. The positive correlation between this and the level of poverty among women of color and white working-class women in the U.S. has now even acquired a name: the feminization of poverty. Thus, while it is possible to state that there is a rise in female-headed households in the U.S. and in Latin America, this rise cannot be discussed as a universal indicator of women's independence, nor can it be discussed as a universal indicator of women's impoverishment. The *meaning* of and *explanation* for the rise obviously vary according to the sociohistorical context.

Similarly, the existence of a sexual division of labor in most contexts cannot be sufficient explanation for the universal subjugation of women in the work force. That the sexual division of labor does indicate a de valuation of women's work must be shown through analysis of particular local contexts. In addition, devaluation of *women* must also be shown through careful analysis. In other words, the "sexual division of labor" and "women" are not commensurate analytical categories. Concepts such as the sexual division of labor can be useful only if they are generated through local, contextual analyses (see Eldhom, Harris, and Young 1977). If such concepts are assumed to be universally applicable, the resultant homogenization of class, race, religious, and daily material practices of women in the third world can create a false sense of the commonality of oppressions, interests, and struggles between and among women globally. Beyond sisterhood there are still racism, colonialism, and imperialism!

Finally, some writers confuse the use of gender as a superordinate category of organizing analysis with the universalistic proof and instantiation of this category. In other words, empirical studies of gender differences are confused with the analytical organization of cross-cultural work. Beverly Brown's (1983) review of the book *Nature, Culture* and *Gender* (Strathern and McCormack 1980) best illustrates this point. Brown suggests that nature:culture and female:male are superordinate categories which organize and locate lesser categories (such as wild/domestic and biology/technology) within their logic. These categories are universal in the sense that they organize the universe of a system of representations. This relation is totally independent of the universal substantiation of any particular category. Her critique hinges on the fact that rather than clarify the generalizability of nature:culture :: female:male as subordinate organization categories, *Nature, Culture and Gender* construes the universality of this equation to lie at the level of empirical truth, which can be investigated through fieldwork. Thus, the usefulness of the nature:culture :: female:male paradigm as a universal mode of the organization of representation within any particular sociohistorical system is lost. Here, methodological universalism is assumed on the basis of the reduction of the nature:culture :: female:male analytic categories to a demand for empirical proof of its existence in different cultures. Discourses of representation are confused with material realities, and the distinction made earlier between "Woman" and "women" is lost. Feminist work which blurs this distinction (which is, interestingly enough, often present in certain Western feminists' self-representation) eventually ends up constructing monolithic images of "third world women" by ignoring the complex and mobile relationships between their historical materiality on the level of specific oppressions and political choices, on the one hand, and their general discursive representations, on the other.

To summarize: I have discussed three methodological moves identifiable in feminist (and other academic) cross-cultural work which seeks to uncover a universality in women's subordinate position in society. The next and final section pulls together the previous sections, attempting to outline the political effects of the analytical strategies in the context of Western feminist writing on women in the third world. These arguments are not against generalization as much as they are for careful, historically specific generalizations responsive to complex realities. Nor do these arguments deny the necessity of forming strategic political identities and affinities. Thus, while Indian women of different religions, castes, and classes might forge a political unity on the basis of organizing against police brutality toward women (see Kishwar and Vanita 1984), an *analysis* of police brutality must be contextual. Strategic coalitions which construct oppositional political identities for themselves are based on generalization and provisional unities, but the analysis of these group identities cannot be based on universalistic, ahistorical categories.

The Subject(s) of Power

This last section returns to an earlier point about the inherently political nature of feminist scholarship, and attempts to clarify my point about the possibility of detecting a colonialist move in the case of a hegemonic first-third world connection in scholarship. The nine texts in the Zed Press Women in the Third World series that I have discussed[12] focused on the following common areas in examining women's "status" within various societies: religion, family/kinship structures, the legal system, the sexual division of labor, education, and finally, political resistance. A large number of Western feminist writings on women in the third world focus on these themes. Of course the Zed texts have varying emphases. For instance, two of the studies, *Women of Palestine* (Downing 1982) and *Indian Women in Struggle* (Omvedt 1980), focus explicitly on female militance and political involvement, while *Women in Arab Society* (Minces 1980) deals with Arab women's legal, religious, and familial status. In addition, each text evidences a variety of methodologies and degrees of care in making generalizations. Interestingly enough, however, almost all the texts assume "women" as a category of analysis in the manner designated above.

Clearly this is an analytical strategy which is neither limited to these Zed Press publications nor symptomatic of Zed Press publications in general. However, each of the particular texts in question assumes "women" have a coherent group identity within the different cultures discussed, prior to their entry into social relations. Thus, Omvedt can talk about "Indian women" while referring to a particular group of women in the State of Maharashtra, Cutrufelli about "women of Africa," and Minces about "Arab women" as if these groups of women have some sort of obvious cultural coherence, distinct from men in these societies. The "status" or "position" of women is assumed to be self-evident, because women as an already constituted group are *placed* within religious, economic, familial, and legal structures. However, this focus whereby women are seen as a coherent group across contexts, regardless of class or ethnicity, structures the world in ultimately binary, dichotomous terms, where women are always seen in opposition to men, patriarchy is always necessarily male dominance, and the religious, legal, economic, and familial systems are implicitly assumed to be constructed by men. Thus, both men and women are always apparently constituted whole populations, and relations of dominance and exploitation are also posited in terms of whole peoples—wholes coming into exploitative relations. It is only when men and women are seen as different categories or groups possessing different *already constituted* categories of experience, cognition, and interests as *groups* that such a simplistic dichotomy is possible.

What does this imply about the structure and functioning of power relations? The setting up of the commonality of third world women's struggles across classes and cultures against a general notion of oppression (primarily the group in power—i.e., men) necessitates the assumption of what Michel Foucault (1980,135–45) calls the "juridico-discursive" model of power, the principal features of which are "a negative relation" (limit and lack), an "insistence on the rule" (which forms a binary system), a "cycle of prohibition," the "logic of censorship," and a "uniformity" of the apparatus functioning at different levels. Feminist discourse on the third world which assumes a homogeneous category—or group—called women necessarily operates through the setting up of originary power divisions. Power relations are structured in terms of a unilateral and undifferentiated source of power and a cumulative reaction to power. Opposition is a generalized phenomenon created as a response to power—which, in turn, is possessed by certain groups of people.

The major problem with such a definition of power is that it locks all revolutionary struggles into binary structures—possessing power versus being powerless. Women are powerless, unified groups. If the struggle for a just society is seen in terms of the move from powerless to powerful for women as a *group,* and this is the implication in feminist discourse which structures sexual difference in terms of the division between the sexes, then the new society would be structurally identical to the existing organization of power relations, constituting itself as a simple *inversion* of what exists. If relations of domination and exploitation are defined in terms of binary divisions—groups which dominate and groups which are dominated—surely the implication is that the accession to power of women as a group is sufficient to dismantle the existing organization of relations? But women as a group are not in some sense essentially superior or infallible. The crux of the problem lies in that initial assumption of women as a homogeneous group or category ("the oppressed"), a familiar assumption in Western radical and liberal feminisms.[13]

What happens when this assumption of "women as an oppressed group" is situated in the context of Western feminist writing about third world women? It is here that I locate the colonialist move. By contrasting the representation of women in the third world with what I referred to earlier as Western feminisms' self-presentation in the same context, we see how Western feminists alone become the true "subjects" of this counterhistory. Third world women, on the other hand, never rise above the debilitating generality of their "object" status.

While radical and liberal feminist assumptions of women as a sex class might elucidate (however inadequately) the autonomy of particular women's struggles in the West, the application of the notion of women as a homogeneous category to women in the third world colonizes and appropriates the pluralities of the simultaneous location of different groups of women in social class and ethnic frameworks; in doing so it ultimately robs them of their historical and political *agency.* Similarly, many Zed Press authors who ground themselves in the basic analytic strategies of traditional Marxism also implicitly create a "unity" of women by substituting "women's activity" for "labor" as the primary theoretical determinant of women's situation. Here again, women are constituted as a coherent group not on the basis of "natural" qualities or needs but on the basis of the sociological "unity" of their role in domestic production and wage labor (see Haraway 1985, esp. p. 76). In other words, Western feminist discourse, by assuming women as a coherent, already constituted group which is placed in kinship, legal, and other structures, defines third world women as subjects *outside* social relations, instead of looking at the way women are constituted *through* these very structures.

Legal, economic, religious, and familial structures are treated as phenomena to be judged by Western standards. It is here that ethnocentric universality comes into play. When these structures are defined as "underdeveloped" or "developing" and women are placed within them, an implicit image of the "average third world woman" is produced. This is the transformation of the (implicitly Western) "oppressed woman" into the "oppressed third world woman." While the category of "oppressed woman" is generated through an exclusive focus on gender difference, "the oppressed third world woman" category has an additional attribute—the "third world difference." The "third world difference" includes a paternalistic attitude toward women in the third world.[14] Since discussions of the various themes I identified earlier (kinship, education, religion, etc.) are conducted in the context of the relative "underdevelopment" of the third world (which is nothing less than unjustifiably confusing development with the separate path taken by the West in its development, as well as ignoring the directionality of the first-third world power relation ship), third world women as a group or category are automatically and necessarily defined as religious (read "not progressive"), family-oriented (read "traditional"), legal minors (read "they-are-still-not-conscious-of-their-rights"), illiterate (read "ignorant"), domestic (read "backward"), and sometimes revolutionary (read "their-country-is-in-a-state-of-war; they-must-fight!") This is how the "third world difference" is produced.

When the category of "sexually oppressed women" is located within particular systems in the third world which are defined on a scale which is normed through Eurocentric assumptions, not only are third world women defined in a particular way prior to their entry into social relations, but since no connections are made between first and third world power shifts, the assumption is reinforced that the third world just has not evolved to the extent that the West has. This mode of feminist analysis, by homogenizing and systematizing the experiences of different groups of women in these countries, erases all marginal and resistant modes and experiences.[15] It is significant that none of the texts I reviewed in the Zed Press series focuses on lesbian politics or the politics of ethnic and religious marginal organizations in third world women's groups. Resistance can thus be defined only as cumulatively reactive, not as something inherent in the operation of power. If power, as Michel Foucault has argued recently, can really be understood only in the context of resistance,[16] this misconceptualization is both analytically and strategically problematical. It limits theoretical analysis as well as reinforces Western cultural imperialism. For in the context of a first/third world balance of power, feminist analyses which perpetrate and sustain the hegemony of the idea of the superiority of the West produce a corresponding set of universal images of the "third world woman," images such as the veiled woman, the powerful mother, the chaste virgin, the obedient wife, etc. These images exist in universal, ahistorical splendor, setting in motion a colonialist discourse which exercises a very specific power in defining, coding, and maintaining existing first/third world connections.

To conclude, then, let me suggest some disconcerting similarities between the typically authorizing signature of such Western feminist writings on women in the third world, and the authorizing signature of the project of humanism in general—humanism as a Western ideological and political project which involves the necessary recuperation of the "East" and "Woman" as Others. Many contemporary thinkers, including Foucault (1978, 1980), Derrida (1974), Kristeva (1980), Deleuze and Guattari (1977), and Said (1978), have written at length about the underlying anthropomorphism and ethnocentrism which constitute a hegemonic humanistic problematic that repeatedly confirms and legitimates (Western) Man's centrality. Feminist theorists such as Luce Irigaray (1981), Sarah Kofman (see Berg 1982), and Helene Cixous (1981) have also written about the recuperation and absence of woman/women within Western humanism. The focus of the work of all these thinkers can be stated simply as an uncovering of the political *interests* that underlie the binary logic of humanistic discourse and ideology whereby, as a valuable recent essay puts it, "the first (majority) term (Identity, Universality, Culture, Disinterestedness, Truth, Sanity, Justice, etc.), which is, in fact, secondary and derivative (a construction), is privileged over and colonizes the second (minority) term (difference, temporality, anarchy, error, interestedness, insanity, deviance, etc.), which is in fact, primary and originative" (Spanos 1984). In other words, it is only insofar as "Woman/Women" and "the East" are defined as *Others*, or as peripheral, that (Western) Man/Humanism can represent him/itself as the center. It is not the center that determines the periphery, but the periphery that, in its boundedness, determines the center. Just as feminists such as Kristeva and Cixous deconstruct the latent anthropomorphism in Western discourse, I have suggested a parallel strategy in this essay in uncovering a latent ethnocentrism in particular feminist writings on women in the third world.[17]

As discussed earlier, a comparison between Western feminist self-presentation and Western feminist representation of women in the third world yields significant results. Universal images of "the third world woman" (the veiled woman, chaste virgin, etc.), images constructed from adding the "third world difference" to "sexual difference," are predicated upon (and hence obviously bring into sharper focus) assumptions about Western women as secular, liberated, and having control over their own lives. This is not to suggest that Western women *are* secular, liberated, and in control of their own lives. I am referring to a *discursive* self-presentation, not necessarily to material reality. If this were a material reality, there would be no need for political movements in the West. Similarly, only from the vantage point of the West is it possible to define the "third world" as underdeveloped and economically dependent. Without the overdetermined discourse that creates the *third* world, there would be no (singular and privileged) first world. Without the "third world woman," the particular self-presentation of Western women mentioned above would be problematical. I am suggesting, then, that the one enables and sustains the other. This is not to say that the signature of Western feminist writings on the third world has the same authority as the project of Western humanism. However, in the context of the hegemony of the Western scholarly establishment in the production and dissemination of texts, and in the context of the legitimating imperative of humanistic and scientific discourse, the definition of "the third world woman" as a monolith might well tie into the larger economic and ideological praxis of "disinterested" scientific inquiry and pluralism which are the surface manifestations of a latent economic and cultural colonization of the "non-Western" world. It is time to move beyond the Marx who found it possible to say: They cannot represent themselves; they must be represented.

Notes

This essay would not have been possible without S. P. Mohanty's challenging and careful reading. I would also like to thank Biddy Martin for our numerous discussions about feminist theory and politics. They both helped me think through some of the arguments herein.

1. Terms such as *third* and *first world* are very problematical both in suggesting oversimplified similarities between and among countries labeled thus, and in implicitly reinforcing existing economic, cultural, and ideological hierarchies which are conjured up in using such terminology. I use the term *"third world"* with full awareness of its problems, only because this is the terminology available to us at the moment. The use of quotation marks is meant to suggest a continuous questioning of the designation. Even when I do not use quotation marks, I mean to use the term critically.

2. I am indebted to Teresa de Lauretis for this particular formulation of the project of feminist theorizing. See especially her introduction in de Lauretis, *Alice Doesn't: Feminism, Semiotics, Cinema* (Bloomington: Indiana University Press, 1984); see also Sylvia Wynter, "The Politics of Domination" unpublished manuscript.

3. This argument is similar to Homi Bhabha's definition of colonial discourse as strategically creating a space for a subject people through the production of knowledges and the exercise of power. The full quote reads: "[colonial discourse is] an apparatus of power ... an apparatus that turns on the recognition and disavowal of racial/cultural /historical differences. Its predominant strategic function is the creation of a space for a subject people through the production of knowledges in terms of which surveillance is exercised and a complex form of pleasure/unpleasure is incited. It (i.e. colonial discourse) seeks authorization for its strategies by the production of knowledges by coloniser and colonised which are stereotypical but antithetically evaluated" (1983, 23).

4. A number of documents and reports on the UN International Conferences on Women, Mexico City, 1975, and Copenhagen, 1980, as well as the 1976 Wellesley Conference on Women and Development, attest to this. Nawal el Saadawi, Fatima Mernissi, and Mallica Vajarathon (1978) characterize this conference as "American-planned and organized," situating third world participants as passive audiences. They focus especially on the lack of self-consciousness of Western women's implication in the effects of imperialism and racism in their assumption of an "international sisterhood." A recent essay by Valerie Amos and Pratibha Parmar (1984) characterizes as "imperial" Euro-American feminism which seeks to establish itself as the only legitimate feminism.

5. The Zed Press Women in the Third World series is unique in its conception. I choose to focus on it because it is the only contemporary series I have found which assumes that "women in the third world" are a legitimate and separate subject of study and research. Since 1985, when this essay was first written, numerous new titles have appeared in the Women in the Third World series. Thus, I suspect that Zed has come to occupy a rather privileged position in the dissemination and construction of discourses by and about third world women. A number of the books in this series are excellent, especially those which deal directly with women's resistance struggles. In addition, Zed Press consistently publishes progressive feminist,

antiracist, and antiimperialist texts. However, a number of the texts written by feminist sociologists, anthropologists, and journalists are symptomatic of the kind of Western feminist work on women in the third world that concerns me. Thus, an analysis of a few of these particular works in this series can serve as a representative point of entry into the discourse I am attempting to locate and define. My focus on these texts is therefore an attempt at an internal critique: I simply expect and demand more from this series. Needless to say, progressive publishing houses also carry their own authorizing signatures.

6. Elsewhere I have discussed this particular point in detail in a critique of Robin Morgan's construction of "women's herstory" in her introduction to *Sisterhood Is Global: The International Women's Movement Anthology* (New York: An chor Press/Doubleday, 1984). See my "Feminist Encounters: Locating the Politics of Experience," *Copyright* 1, "Fin de Siecle 2000," 30–44, especially 35–37.

7. Another example of this kind of analysis is Mary Daly's (1978) *Gyn/Ecology*. Daly's assumption in this text, that women as a group are sexually victimized, leads to her very problematic comparison between the attitudes toward women witches and healers in the West, Chinese footbinding, and the genital mutilation of women in Africa. According to Daly, women in Europe, China, and Africa constitute a homogeneous group as victims of male power. Not only does this label (sexual victims) eradicate the specific historical and material realities and contradictions which lead to and perpetuate practices such as witch hunting and genital mutilation, but it also obliterates the differences, complexities, and heterogeneities of the lives of, for example, women of different classes, religions, and nations in Africa. As Audre Lorde (1983) pointed out, women in Africa share a long tradition of healers and goddesses that perhaps binds them together more appropriately than their victim status. However, both Daly and Lorde fall prey to universalistic assumptions about "African women" (both negative and positive). What matters is the complex, historical range of power differences, commonalities, and resistances that exist among women in Africa which construct African women as "subjects" of their own politics.

8. See Eldhom, Harris, and Young (1977) for a good discussion of the necessity to theorize male violence within specific societal frameworks, rather than assume it as a universal fact.

9. These views can also be found in differing degrees in collections such as Wellesley Editorial Committee, ed., *Women and National Development: The Complexities of Change* (Chicago: University of Chicago Press, 1977), and *Signs*, Special Issue, "Development and the Sexual Division of Labor," 7, no. 2 (Winter 1981). For an excellent introduction of WID issues, see ISIS, *Women in Development: A Resource Guide for Organization and Action* (Philadelphia: New Society Publishers, 1984). For a politically focused discussion of feminism and development and the stakes for poor third world women, see Gita Sen and Caren Grown, *Development Crises and Alternative Visions: Third World Women's Perspectives* (New York: Monthly Review Press, 1987).

10. See essays by Vanessa Maher, Diane Elson and Ruth Pearson, and Maila Stevens in Kate Young, Carol Walkowitz, and Roslyn McCullagh, eds., *Of Marriage and the Market: Women's Subordination in International Perspective* (London: CSE Books, 1981); and essays by Vivian Mota and Michelle Mattelart in June Nash and Helen I. Safa, *eds., Sex and Class in Latin America: Women's Perspectives on Politics, Economics and the Family in the Third World* (South Hadley, Mass.: Bergin and Garvey, 1980). For examples of excellent, self-conscious work by

feminists writing about women in their own historical and geographical locations, see Marnia Lazreg (1988) on Algerian women, Gayatri Chakravorty Spivak's "A Literary Representation of the Subaltern: A Woman's Text from the Third World," in her *In Other Worlds: Essays in Cultural Politics* (New York: Methuen, 1987), 241–68, and Lata Mani's essay "Contentious Traditions: The Debate on SATI in Colonial India," *Cultural Critique 7* (Fall 1987), 119–56.

11. Olivia Harris, "Latin American Women—An Overview," in Harris, ed., *Latin American Women* (London: Minority Rights Group Report no. 57, 1983), 4–7. Other MRG Reports include Ann Deardon (1975) and Rounaq Jahan (1980).

12. List of Zed Press publications: Patricia Jeffery, *Frogs in a Well: Indian Women in Purdah* (1979); Latin American and Caribbean Women's Collective, *Slaves of Slaves: The Challenge of Latin American Women* (1980); Gail Omvedt, *We Shall Smash This Prison: Indian Women in Struggle* (1980); Juliette Minces, *The House of Obedience: Women in Arab Society* (1980); Bobby Siu, W*omen of China: Imperialism and Women's Resistance, 1900–1949* (1981); Ingeia Bendt and James Downing, *We Shall Return: Women in Palestine* (1982); Maria Rosa Cutrufelli, *Women of Africa: Roots of Oppression* (1983); Maria Mies, *The Lace Makers of Narsapur: Indian House wives Produce for the World Market* (1982); Miranda Davis, ed., *Third World/ Second Sex: Women's Struggles and National Liberation* (1983).

13. For succinct discussions of Western radical and liberal feminisms, see Hester Eisenstein, *Contemporary Feminist Thought* (Boston: G. K. Hall & Co., 1983), and Zillah Eisenstein, *The Radical Future of Liberal Feminism* (New York: Longman, 1981).

14. Amos and Parmar describe the cultural stereotypes present in Euro-American feminist thought: "The image is of the passive Asian woman subject to oppressive practices within the Asian family with an emphasis on wanting to 'help' Asian women liberate themselves from their role. Or there is the strong, dominant Afro-Caribbean woman, who despite her 'strength' is exploited by the 'sexism' which is seen as being a strong feature in relationships between Afro-Caribbean men and women" (9). These images illustrate the extent to which *paternalism* is an essential element of feminist thinking which incorporates the above stereotypes, a paternalism which can lead to the definition of priorities for women of color by Euro-American feminists.

15. I discuss the question of theorizing experience in my "Feminist Encounters" (1987) and in an essay coauthored with Biddy Martin, "Feminist Politics: What's Home Got to Do with It?" in Teresa de Lauretis, ed., *Feminist Studies/Critical Studies* (Bloomington: Indiana University Press, 1986), 191–212.

16. This is one of M. Foucault's (1978, 1980) central points in his reconceptualization of the strategies and workings of power networks.

17. For an argument which demands a *new* conception of humanism in work on third world women, see Marnia Lazreg (1988). While Lazreg's position might appear to be diametrically opposed to mine, I see it as a provocative and potentially positive extension of some of the implications that follow from my arguments. In criticizing the feminist rejection of humanism in the name of "essential Man," Lazreg points to what she calls an "essentialism of difference" within these very feminist projects. She asks: "To what extent can Western feminism dispense with an ethics of responsibility when writing about different women? The point is neither to subsume other women under one's own experience nor to uphold a separate truth for them. Rather, it is to allow them to *be* while recognizing that what they are is just as meaningful,

valid, and comprehensible as what we are … Indeed, when feminists essentially deny other women the humanity they claim for themselves, they dispense with any ethical constraint. They engage in the act of splitting the social universe into us and them, subject and objects" (99–100).

This essay by Lazreg and an essay by S. P. Mohanty (1989) entitled "Us and Them: On the Philosophical Bases of Political Criticism" suggest positive directions for self-conscious cross-cultural analyses, analyses which move beyond the deconstructive to a fundamentally productive mode in designating overlapping areas for cross-cultural comparison. The latter essay calls not for a "humanism" but for a reconsideration of the question of the "human" in a posthumanist context. It argues that (1) there is no necessary "incompatibility between the deconstruction of Western humanism" and such "a positive elaboration" of the human, and moreover that (2) such an elaboration is essential if contemporary political-critical discourse is to avoid the incoherences and weaknesses of a relativist position.

References

Abdel-Malek, Anouar. 1981. *Social Dialectics: Nation and Revolution,* Albany: State University of New York Press. Amin, Samir. 1977, *Imperialism and Unequal Development.* New York: Monthly Review Press.

Amos, Valerie, and Pratibha Parmar. 1984 "Challenging Imperial Feminism." *Feminist Review* 17: 3–19. Baran, Paul A. 1962. *The Political Economy of Growth.* New York: Monthly Review Press.

Berg, Elizabeth. 1982. "The Third Woman." *Diacritics* (Summer): 11–20.

Bhabha, Homi. 1983. "The Other Question—The Stereotype and Colonial Discourse." *Screen* 24, no. 6: 23.

Boserup, Ester. 1970. *Women's Role in Economic Development.* New York: St. Martin's Press; London: Allen and Unwin.

Brown, Beverly. 1983. "Displacing the Difference—Review, *Nature, Culture and Gender.*" *m/f* 8: 79–89.

Cixous, Helene. 1981. "The Laugh of the Medusa." In Marks and De Courtivron (1981).

Cowie, Elizabeth. 1978. "Woman as Sign." *m/f* 1: 49–63.

Cutrufelli, Maria Rosa. 1983. *Women of Africa: Roots of Oppression.* London: Zed Press.

Daly, Mary. 1978. *Gyn/Ecology: The Metaethics of Radical Feminism.* Boston: Beacon Press.

Deardon, Ann, ed. 1975. *Arab Women.* London: Minority Rights Group Report no. 27.

de Lauretis, Teresa. 1984. *Alice Doesn't: Feminism, Semiotics, Cinema.* Bloomington: Indiana University Press.

———. 1986. *Feminist Studies/Critical Studies.* Bloomington: Indiana University Press.

Deleuze, Giles, and Felix Guattari. 1977. *Anti-Oedipus: Capitalism and Schizophrenia.* New York: Viking.

Derrida, Jacques. 1974. *Of Grammatology.* Baltimore. Johns Hopkins University Press.

Eisenstein, Hester. 1983. *Contemporary Feminist Thought.* Boston: G. K. Hall and Co.

Eisenstein, Zillah. 1981. *The Radical Future of Liberal Feminism.* New York: Long man.

Eldhom, Felicity, Olivia Harris, and Kate Young. 1977. "Conceptualising Women." *Critique of Anthropology "Women's Issue,"* no. 3.

el Saadawi, Nawal, Fatima Mernissi, and Mallica Vajarathon. 1978. "A Critical Look at the Wellesley Conference." *Quest* 4, no. 2 (Winter):101–107.

Foucault, Michel. 1978. *History of Sexuality: Volume One.* New York: Random House.. 1980. *Power/Knowledge.* New York: Pantheon.

Gunder-Frank, Audre. 1967. *Capitalism and Underdevelopment in Latin America.* New York: Monthly Review Press.

Haraway, Donna. 1985. "A Manifesto for Cyborgs: Science, Technology and So cialist Feminism in the 1980s." *Socialist Review* 80 (March/April): 65–108.

Harris, Olivia. 1983a. "Latin American Women—An Overview." In Harris (1983b). 1983b. *Latin American Women.* London: Minority Rights Group Report no. 57.

Hosken, Fran. 1981. "Female Genital Mutilation and Human Rights." *Feminist Issues 1,* no. 3.

Huston, Perdita. 1979. *Third World Women Speak Out.* New York: Praeger.

Irigaray, Luce. 1981. "This Sex Which Is Not One" and "When the Goods Get Together." In Marks and De Courtivron (1981). Jahan, Rounaq, ed. 1980. *Women in Asia.* London: Minority Rights Group Report no. 45.

Jeffery, Patricia. 1979. *Frogs in a Well: Indian Women in Purdah.* London: Zed Press.

Joseph, Gloria, and Jill Lewis. 1981. *Common Differences: Conflicts in Black and White Feminist Perspectives.* Boston: Beacon Press.

Kishwar, Madhu, and Ruth Vanita. 1984. *In Search of Answers: Indian Women's Voices from Manushi.* London: Zed Press.

Kristeva, Julia. 1980. *Desire in Language.* New York: Columbia University Press.

Lazreg, Marnia. 1988. "Feminism and Difference: The Perils of Writing as a Woman on Women in Algeria." *Feminist Issues* 14, no. 1 (Spring): 81–107.

Lindsay, Beverley, ed. 1983. *Comparative Perspectives of Third World Women: The Impact of Race, Sex and Class.* New York: Praeger.

Lorde, Audre. 1983. "An Open Letter to Mary Daly." In Moraga and Anzaldua (1983), 94–97.

Marks, Elaine, and Isabel De Courtivron. 1981. *New French Feminisms.* New York: Schocken Books.

Mies, Maria. 1982. *The Lace Makers of Narsapur: Indian Housewives Produce for the World Market.* London: Zed Press.

Minces, Juliette. 1980. *The House of Obedience: Women in Arab Society.* London: Zed Press.

Modares, Mina. 1981. "Women and Shi'ism in Iran." *m/f* 5 and 6: 61–82.

Mohanty, Chandra Talpade. 1987. "Feminist Encounters: Locating the Politics of Experience." *Copyright* 1, "Fin de Siecle 2000," 30–44.

Mohanty, Chandra Talpade, and Biddy Martin. 1986. "Feminist Politics: What's Home Got to Do with It?" In de Lauretis (1986).

Mohanty, S. P. 1989. "Us and Them: On the Philosophical Bases of Political Criticism." *Yale Journal of Criticism* 2 (March): 1–31.

Moraga, Cherríe. 1984. *Loving in the War Years.* Boston: South End Press.

Moraga, Cherríe, and Gloria Anzaldúa, eds. 1983. *This Bridge Called My Back: Writings by Radical Women of Color.* New York: Kitchen Table Press.

Morgan, Robin, ed. 1984. *Sisterhood Is Global: The International Women's Movement Anthology.* New York: Anchor Press/Doubleday; Harmondsworth: Penguin.

Nash, June, and Helen I. Safa, eds. 1980. *Sex and Class in Latin America: Women's Perspectives on Politics, Economics and the Family in the Third World.* South, Hadley, Mass.: Bergin and Garvey.

Rosaldo, M. A. 1980. "The Use and Abuse of Anthropology: Reflections on Fem inism and Cross-Cultural Understanding." *Signs* 53: 389–417.

Said, Edward. 1978. *Orientalism.* New York: Random House.

Sen, Gita, and Caren Grown. 1987. *Development Crises and Alternative Visions: Third World Women's Perspectives.* New York: Monthly Review Press.

Smith, Barbara, ed. 1983. *Home Girls: A Black Feminist Anthology.* New York: Kitchen Table Press.

Spanos, William V. 1984. "Boundary 2 and the Polity of Interest: Humanism, the 'Center Elsewhere' and Power." *Boundary 2* 12, no. 3/13, no. 1 (Spring/Fall).

Spivak, Gayatri Chakravorty. 1987. *In Other Worlds: Essays in Cultural Politics.* London and New York: Methuen.

Strathem, Marilyn, and Carol McCormack, eds. 1980. *Nature, Culture and Gender,* Cambridge: Cambridge University Press.

Tabari, Azar. 1980. "The Enigma of the Veiled Iranian Women." *Feminist Review* 5: 19–32.

Tinker, Irene, and Michelle Be Bramsen, eds. 1972. *Women and World Development.* Washington, D.C.: Overseas Development Council.

Young, Kate, Carol Walkowitz, and Roslyn McCullagh, eds. 1981. *Of Marriage and the Market: Women's Subordination in International Perspective.* London: CSE Books.

Chapter Seven

Common Themes, Different Contexts
Third World Women and Feminism

Cheryl Johnson-Odim

This essay seeks more to explicate issues than to present empirical research or to synthesize theory. However, the basic issues which it raises and endeavors to explain regarding conceptual and practical differences between Third World and Euro-American First World women in relation to feminism will, it is hoped, inform both the generation of research questions and the construction of theory. While it is true that the oppression of impoverished and marginalized Euro-American women is linked to gender *and* class relations, that of Third World women is linked also to race relations and often imperialism. These added dimensions produce a different context in which Third World women's struggles must be understood. Still, while this essay looks at women in these two contexts, it does so primarily to highlight certain historical and contemporary differences that have produced tensions between them, in order to be able to identify underlying misunderstandings and contribute to resolving them.

The term *Third World* is frequently applied in two ways: to refer to "underdeveloped"/ overexploited geopolitical entities, i.e., countries, regions, and even continents; and to refer to oppressed nationalities from these world areas who are now resident in "developed" First World countries. I will be using the term with this dual definition throughout this essay, for despite their great diversity, Third World women seem to have much in common in their relationship to an international women's movement.

While it may be legitimately argued that there is more than one school of thought on feminism among First World feminists—who are not, after all, monolithic—there is still, among Third World women, a widely accepted perception that the feminism emerging from white, middle-class Western women narrowly confines itself to a struggle against gender discrimination. It is also widely felt that this is the "mainstream" feminism of the West and that it holds the most sway and has the most adherents. Joseph (1981), hooks (1981), Moraga and Anzaldúa (1981), Okeyo (1981), Savane (1982), and others have all attested to this perception, and many have defined it as a liberal, bourgeois, or reformist feminism, and criticize it because of its narrow conception of feminist terrain as an almost singularly antisexist struggle.

While it is clear that sexual egalitarianism is a major goal on which all feminists can agree, gender discrimination is neither the sole nor perhaps the primary locus of the oppression of Third World women. Thus, a narrowly defined feminism, taking the eradication of gender discrimination as the route to ending women's oppression, is insufficient to redress the oppression of Third World women, for reasons which I hope this essay will make clear. A number of Third World feminists, including hooks (1981, 1984), Moraga and Anzaldúa (1981), Joseph and Lewis (1981), Okeyo (1981), Hull, Scott, and Smith (1982), Savane (1982), Smith (1983), and many others, have tackled this problem of broadening the definition of feminism and making it relevant (in both philosophy and agenda articulation) to the struggles of Third World women. Still, it remains a challenge at both the national and international levels to construct definitions of feminism that allow for autonomy and that are of immediate relevance in feminist struggles in various places, and yet have the breadth needed for the widest consensus and cooperation.

In reaction to a narrowly defined feminism, some Third World women have elected not to use the term *feminist* at all. Alice Walker, an Afro-American woman writer, has chosen to use the term *womanist* rather than *feminist* Walker (1983) partially describes a womanist as "a Black feminist or feminist of color" and says "womanist is to feminist as purple to lavender" (xi). She further states that a womanist is "committed to survival and wholeness of entire people, male and female" (xi). Walker's comments underscore the feelings among Third World women that their struggle as feminists is connected to the struggles of their communities against racism, economic exploitation, etc. Her desire to coin a new term has nothing to do with a lack of commitment to women's equality and everything to do with her vision of the interconnectedness of her life as a black woman and her perception that "mainstream" (i.e., liberal gender-specific) feminism has been too narrow to encompass it.

Let me take a moment here to say that it is clear that there have always been some radical white feminists who have understood the connections between race, class, and gender in the lives of Third World women. There are even many more who know that, in the United States at least, the greatest periods of feminist struggle have emerged out of the African-American movement against racism. The early radical feminism of the 1960s was, in fact, often broadly defined as being antiracist and antiimperialist, but much of that movement has been displaced by the far more popular liberal feminism which has not sufficiently defined racism and imperialism as major feminist issues. I would agree with Smith (1983), hooks (1984), and others that it is in fact the involvement of Third World women, both within and outside the United States, that has accounted for the broadening definitions of feminism to incorporate race and class analysis.

In any case, I have chosen for the purpose of this essay to remain with the term *feminism* for two reasons: (1) I am more concerned with the participation of Third World women in defining feminism and setting its agenda than with changing the terminology; and (2) the term *feminism* sets this essay in a political context to which women are integral. Since "modern-day" feminism is still in a process of incarnation, especially at the international level, I question whether the coining of a new term simply retreats from the debate, running the risk of losing sight of the fair amount of universality in women's oppression.

In the decade of the 1970s, when attempts at constructing an international feminist movement began to take shape, many women in the Third World were fairly recently emerging from colonialism, and many Third World women in the West were emerging from the most important civil rights movement of the twentieth century. Neither the advent of independence in the former colonies nor the legislation passed as a result of the civil rights movement was to prove immediately victorious in improving the quality of life for the overwhelming majority of Third World women. Undoubtedly, these were factors in shaping Third World women's visions of feminism as a philosophy and a movement for social justice that was inclusive of their entire communities, in which they were equal participants, and which addressed the racism, economic exploitation, and imperialism against which they continued to struggle. Evans (1979), Giddings (1984), and a host of others have argued that the feminism of the 1960s and 1970s in the U.S. emerged from the civil rights movement. They also point out, however, that while many of the women had been involved in antiracist work, this in no way guaranteed a lack of racism in the women's movement or enough attention to the role of racism in the oppression of all women.

At three major international conferences of women held between 1970 and 1980 (Mexico City, 1975; Wellesley, 1976; Copenhagen, 1980), the battle lines were often drawn between First and Third World feminists over what constituted a feminist issue, and therefore what were legitimate feminist foci and goals. Okeyo (1981), Barrow (1985), Cagatay, Grown, and Santiago (1986), and others remark on the tensions between First and Third World women that surfaced at the first two United Nations Decade conferences for women (Mexico City, 1975, and Copenhagen, 1980). The formation of Third World caucuses frequently included women of color who were residents of the First World (though according to Cagatay, Grown, and Santiago, Nairobi was the first at which a significant proportion of attendees from places such as the United States were women of color). These caucuses sought to broaden the agenda and treat feminism as a fundamentally political movement connected as much to the struggle of their communities for liberation and autonomy as to the work against gender discrimination.

Awe (1977) remarked on the same phenomenon at the Women and Development Conference hosted by the Center for Research on Women in Higher Education at Wellesley College in 1976. I was in Nigeria when a number of friends returned from Wellesley. They returned angry, convinced that, in Okeyo's words (1981), "women of the developed world seek to define for themselves a leading role both in academia and through development assistance programs" in defining the needs, aims, and priorities of Third World women. These schisms developed at least partially because Third World women felt First World women were attempting to depoliticize the conferences and implicitly construct a women's movement and a feminism which confined itself to issues of gender discrimination. It was part of the mission, in fact, of the official U.S. delegation to Nairobi to keep "politics" out of the conference, and to instead concentrate on "women's issues" (Okeyo, 1981, 9).

While Cagatay, Grown, and Santiago (1986) maintain that far more of a spirit of coming together among Third and First World women obtained at the NGO [nongovernmental forum] than at the official sessions, and while it is unlikely that the official U.S. delegation (especially of 1985) was representative of even "mainstream" (i.e., liberal gender-specific) U.S. feminists, this tension over "politicization" of the conferences had also arisen at Mexico City and Copenhagen. Okeyo (1981) speaks to this point when she says, "Another assumption that is often voiced by Western feminists in international fora is that women's issues should not be politicized ... [but] for African women the subject of women's advancement is highly political because it is an integral part of our quest for justice not only at the household level but all the way within the local, national and world economic order." Okeyo is describing African women's struggle as taking place equally at the "household level," i.e., within the family including between men and women, and at the international level, where many of the same things which oppress women (i.e., racism, imperialism, economic exploitation) also oppress men, though not, sometimes, without differences. But these differences are usually in the manifestation of the oppression, not in the source.

Third World women resident in the First World also must deal with these issues. Any cursory observation of feminist organizations in the United States, for instance, will reveal that Third World women often prefer to organize separately from Euro-American women. These Third World women's organizations take a critical stance regarding the feminist movement, constantly seeking to inject issues which they see this movement as neglecting. Historically separate organization was often the result of racism in the feminist movement which caused it to exclude women of color, and often poor working-class and white women as well. The discrimination suffered by African-American women in the woman suffrage movement and the Club Women's movement has been well documented by Harley and Terbourg-Penn (1978), Davis (1981), Aptheker (1982), Giddings (1984), and many others, as has the exploitation of Native American, Chicana, Puerto Rican, Asian-American, and other non-European American women.

In the current context, however, separate organization is often the choice of Third World women who know that a gender-based analysis alone, without the factoring in of issues of race and class, can never describe their oppression. And since racism in the current women's movement is one of the issues Third World women seek to raise among feminists, racism also plays its part in contemporary separate organization. Moraga and Anzaldúa

(1981), hooks (1981, 1984), Hull, Scott, and Smith (1982), and Smith (1983), among others, have delineated the need for Third World women to organize separately, and to construct a feminist theory relevant to their needs. Joseph (1981) pointedly states that black women have as much in common, in terms of their oppression, with black men as they do with white women. Understanding African-American women's history for black women in the United States is critical to understanding Joseph's assertion. In her study of black women in slavery, White (1985) documents ways in which the slaveocracy juxtaposed the images of black and white women. Black women were cast as nonwomen, as "unfeminine," as a necessary precondition for exploiting both their productive and reproductive labor to the fullest. But the definition of "femininity" foisted upon white women was that of totally dependent beings. Consequently, for every "Aunt Jemima" who was maligned as a nonwoman, there was a "Miss Ann" imprisoned by the definition of her femininity. Still, it is hard to accept the argument that white women suffered as much from this antagonism as black women. But there is a more important and contemporary question which emerges from the era of slavery which is an analogy of sorts.

Poor whites, it is true, suffered greatly because of slavery. The exploitation and appropriation of black labor (along with the land on which it produced wealth) made paid white labor, even when cheap, nearly superfluous except to help police the black labor force. However, most poor southern whites did not embrace the antislavery struggle; rather, they aspired to be "masters." Thus, their definition of the problem was not that the system of slavery oppressed both them and black people and therefore should be ended, but that they themselves needed the opportunity to be able to benefit from slavery. Black American women sometimes suspect that the movement which purports to represent the interests of "women" is, similarly, the desire of a few white women to enter the corporate boardroom. The metamorphosis which this feat in itself would require in a patriarchal society might slightly better the lives of some women, but would only basically change the sex of the "master."

Thus the fundamental issue for Third World women is not generally whether there is a need for feminism, i.e., a general movement which seeks to redress women's oppression, but rather what the definition and agenda of that feminism will be. The need for feminism arises from the desire to create a world in which women are not oppressed. If there is no term or focus, no movement which incorporates the struggle against sexism, women run the risk of becoming invisible. We do not have to look far to understand why women fear this invisibility. The revolutions in Algeria and Iran raise serious questions about the degree to which women benefited from their participation. Even in socialist revolutions where women's position has been greatly improved and continues solidly toward a goal of equality, such as in Cuba, Nicaragua, Angola, and Mozambique, the changes have required not only the commitment of men but also the constant vigilance and organization of women. The need for feminist theory and organization is clear.

It is also true that Third World women outside the United States find that the source of their oppression cannot be limited or perhaps even primarily attributed to gender alone. Marie Angelique Savane (1982), president of the Association of African Women Organized for Research and Development (AAWORD), has written:

> For although the oppression of women is universal in nature ... It is time to move beyond simple truisms about the situation of women to a more profound analysis of the mechanisms perpetuating the subordination of women in society ... In the Third World, women's demands have been explicitly political, with work, education and health as major issues *per se* and not so linked to their specific impact on women. In addition, women of the Third World perceive imperialism as the main enemy on their continents and especially of women.... (5)

Steady (1985) writes that "in the developing world, equality of women is often viewed as linked to national and economic development" (6). At an October 1984 meeting in Tanzania, in preparation for the U.N. Conference in Nairobi, representatives of twenty-five nongovernmental organizations of women from seventeen African countries affirmed that they recognized that the overriding obstacles to women's progress "lay first in the dual factors of the increasing poverty throughout the African continent and in its unhealthy relation to the inequities of the current world economic order" (Barrow 1985, 10).

In "underdeveloped" societies it is not just a question of internal redistribution of resources, but of their generation and control; not just equal opportunity between men and women, but the creation of opportunity itself; not only the position of women in society, but the position of the societies in which Third World women find themselves. Leacock (1977) comments that the urgency of the need for economic development applies as much to "underdeveloped" national groups in the heart of the "developed" industrialized world as to the so-called developing countries. Thus, Third World women cannot afford to embrace the notion that feminism seeks only to achieve equal treatment of men and women and equal access and opportunity for *women*, which often amounts to a formula for sharing poverty both in the Third World and in Third World communities in the West.

Therefore, gender oppression cannot be the single leg on which feminism rests. It should not be limited to merely achieving equal treatment of women vis-a-vis men. This is where feminism as a philosophy must differ from the shallow notion of "women's rights." Although on a theoretical level, women in the industrialized societies of the West can achieve a semblance of parity with men through legal and moral challenges to patriarchal systems, issues of race and class undermine the potential success of such a movement for all women. In addition, the economic surplus in the West is often directly related to oppression in the Third World. Savane (1982) discusses the "free trade zones" established by transnationals in Third World countries. These zones render special privileges (everything from tax breaks to making labor organization illegal) to corporations in exchange for locating there. The entire August 1983 issue of *Multinational Monitor* is devoted to a series of articles detailing the particular ways that multinationals and the existence of free trade zones operate to oppress Third World women. Seidman (1981) examines the ways in which colonialism marginalized women in Africa and chronicles how generally the independence process barely altered inherited colonial institutions which both excluded women and perpetuated externally dependent political economies and philosophies. These policies, she contends, reinforced an inequitable sexual division of labor in the process of creating a "hospitable investment climate" for multinational corporations. Steady (1985) proposes that the operation of race and class is important in preventing false polarizations between men and women. She states:

> Rather than seeing men as the universal oppressor, women will also be seen as partners in oppression and as having the potential of becoming primary oppressors themselves. Above all, by studying the Black woman we can avoid isolating sexism from the larger political and economic forces operating in many societies to produce internal colonialism and economic dependency—all of which affect both men and women in Africa, the Caribbean, South America and impoverished sections of the United States. (3)

Although certainly the circumstances and status of women differed at various times and places throughout the Third World, it is a totally ahistorical assumption often nourished by contemporary images that women in the Third World have somehow been more oppressed by an indigenous patriarchy than women in the West. Etienne and Leacock (1980) helpfully remind us that "it is critical to clarify the fact that egalitarian relations between women and men are not an imported Western value and that, instead, the reverse is true. Egalitarian relations or at least mutually respectful relations were a living reality in much of the world in precolonial times, which was far from the case in Western culture" (v–vi). The argument is neither that there was no precolonial patriarchy in non-Western societies nor that an analysis of the *degree* of different women's oppression is useful. The point is that factors other than gender figure integrally in the oppression of Third World women and that, even regarding patriarchy, many Third World women labor under indigenous inequitable gender relationships exacerbated by Western patriarchy, racism, and exploitation. For Third World women resident in the West, race and class, along with gender, have been indivisible elements in their oppression.

Third World women can embrace the concept of gender identity, but must reject an ideology based solely on gender. Feminism, therefore, must be a comprehensive and inclusive ideology and movement that incorporates yet transcends gender-specificity. We must create a feminist movement which struggles against those things which can clearly be shown to oppress women, whether based on race, sex, or class or resulting from imperialism. Such a definition of feminism will allow us to isolate the gender-specific element in women's oppression while simultaneously relating it to broader issues, to the totality of what oppresses us as women. If the feminist movement does not address itself also to issues of race, class, and imperialism, it cannot be relevant to alleviating the oppression of most of the women of the world.

In addition to broadening the parameters of feminism, there is the problem of setting a common agenda. One example of this difficulty is the issue of female circumcision, especially in Africa. Cagatay, Grown, and Santiago (1986) discuss the condemnations of female circumcision by First World women at the U.N. Conference in Copenhagen and the ensuing tensions between First and Third World women over how this topic was raised.

Certainly, there are a number of African women who are leading the battle against female circumcision, but many resent what they feel to be the sensationalistic nature of the campaign by many First World feminists. More important, however, is the fact that female circumcision is one issue which can be raised in a manner which is disconnected from the broader struggle. That is, it is tied to an indigenous cultural context which frequently posits an opposition between women and men. In Africa, problems of nutrition, infant mortality, illiteracy, health-care delivery, skill training, etc., are of central importance in women's lives, and many African women have expressed that they wish these issues had the same kind of exposure within the feminist movement in the West as does female circumcision. But to raise these other problems requires feminism to take an antiimperialist position; it necessitates identifying and fighting against the structural elements in many developed countries which participate in the oppression of Third World women. Many Third World women feel that their self-defined needs are not addressed as priority items in the international feminist agenda, which does not address imperialism. Internationally orchestrated exploitation bears on the oppression of women in the Third World as much as patriarchy does in their societies.

Third World women resident in Euro-America also feel neglected in the agenda-setting process. Black American women, for instance, know they must articulate a feminism which has a clear relationship to the general movement of the black community against oppression. Black women recognize that, historically, white women have been no less racist than have white men. They are aware that in the late nineteenth and early twentieth centuries, racism was pervasive in the women's movement (see Davis 1981; hooks 1981; Hull, Scott, and Smith 1982). They wonder, therefore, if white feminists will embrace the struggle against racism as vehemently as they exhort black women to join in the fight against sexism. Moreover, certain feminist issues, such as rape and contraception, are perceived as double-edged swords in the black American community.

While no black feminist would argue anything other than that rape is a violent, inexcusable crime for which the victim is still too often blamed, we know only too well how often racism has excused the rape of black women. We also remember that rape, or even the perceived or concocted threat of rape, has historically posed nearly as great a danger to the safety of black men as to that of black women. For centuries, besides fearing for their own security, black women have feared the maiming, lynching, or jailing of their husbands, brothers, and sons on charges that they were rapists, no matter how unsubstantiated. We are not so far removed from the fraudulent and racist rape or attempted rape charges against the Scottsboro Nine, Emmett Till, Delbert Tibbs, and many others. Every feminist, black and white, should read Davis's (1981) brilliant chapter on "Rape, Racism and the Myth of the Black Rapist," which connects rape not only to racism but to sexism against black *and* white women. This chapter painstakingly documents and makes clear that if we are to combat the treatment rape has received in American society, it must be connected not only to misogyny but to racism as well.

The creeping alliance, in the early twentieth century, between the movement for birth control and eugenics holds lessons (and latent fears) not lost upon the black American community (Davis 1981, 213–16). The fact that surgical sterilization remains free and that federal funding for abortions has been disallowed means that it is poor women to whom the *choice* to abort is denied, and their ranks are disproportionately populated by women of color. The vehement advocacy of contraception and sterilization in the Third World as a method of population control leads to the conclusion that overpopulation is the primary cause of poverty in "underdeveloped" nations. This is a dangerous, false, and simplistic analysis. The testing of contraceptives in the Third World, often before they are approved for distribution in the United States and Europe, is a crime against women. Beneria and Sen (1981) remark on the similarities in the responses of poor Third World women (both in the West and in the Third World) to issues of reproductive freedom. Often they are suspicious about the safety of contraceptive devices and drugs and about the motives of researchers and distributors, even though many feel desperate for safe, effective, affordable, and voluntary birth control. It is not that black or other Third World feminists take a position against contraception, but that they seek to frame the discussion in a context which incorporates the impact of race and class on reproductive issues. The primary responsibility for addressing these questions in this broader context is incumbent on the Third World feminist community, but it is also incumbent on the feminist community as a whole.

The participation of Third World women in defining feminism and setting a feminist agenda is often primarily a question of power. Smith (1983) has discussed the difficulties which black feminists in the West face in being heard, published, and paid attention to. Because Third World women are members of relatively powerless communities, they do not have the same potential for access to resources that First World women have. This calls not only for separate organization to clarify the issues within Third World communities, but also for the development of a working and equal relationship with First World women. We must ensure that the issues that Third World feminists raise become a part of serious discussions of feminist theory and that they are not relegated and ghettoized to a subculture of feminism.

Third World women must articulate needs through the crucial process of constructing a body of relevant feminist theory, which goes beyond mere criticism of First World women.

This is, in fact, happening. Moraga and Anzaldúa (1981), hooks (1981, 1984), Hull, Scott, and Smith (1982), Joseph and Lewis (1981), Smith (1983), and others have all been actively engaged in attempts to define a feminism which is acceptable and relevant to communities of women who suffer as a consequence of racism, sexism, structural poverty, and economic exploitation. In so doing, women of color often labor against suspicions of feminism within their communities, where it is generally perceived as having a white, middle-class agenda—that is, an agenda that creates opportunities for people who are already the most advantageously placed to take advantage of them, and which views gender discrimination as the only fundamental inequality in all women's lives. If this perception describes only bourgeois reformist elements of the feminist community, then it is even more urgent that those among us who have a broader vision articulate it and organize around it.

First World women must constantly challenge the racism of their communities, and acknowledge and struggle against the complicity of their communities in the oppression of Third World women. According to Cagatay, Grown, and Santiago (1986), in analyzing the events at Nairobi, there were several reasons for a greater hopefulness about cooperation between First and Third World women. Conferences during the U.N. International Decade for women, despite tensions within them, have exposed women from around the world to one another. Third World women have been able to have a voice at those conferences normally unavailable to them because of lack of access to financial and media resources. At Nairobi, there were more Third World women from Western nations than at any of the previous conferences. Cagatay, Grown, and Santiago maintain that more First World women were exposed to what it means to be a woman in a Third World setting and that, with that experience, more had moved to a broader definition of feminism:

> Feminism ... constitutes the political expression of the concerns and interests of women from different regions, classes, nationalities, and ethnic backgrounds. There is and must be a diversity of feminisms, responsive to the different needs and concerns of different women, and defined by them for themselves. This diversity builds on common opposition to gender oppression and hierarchy which, however, is only the first step in articulating and acting upon a political agenda. (Cagatay, Grown, and Santiago 1986, 411)

Four years earlier, Marie Angelique Savane, first president of AAWORD, had a similar analysis:

> Feminism is international in defining as its aim the liberation of women from all types of oppression and in providing solidarity among women of all countries; it is national in stating its priorities and strategies in accordance with particular cultural and socioeconomic conditions.

We consider that national and ethnic traditions must be respected and maintained so as to create a genuine sense of nationhood. However, aspects of our culture which discriminate, restrict and devalue women's physical, psychological and political development must be eliminated. To achieve this, women must be mobilized politically for action.

In order to create an alternative culture, responsive to national needs and open to international solidarity, we women defend our right to speak from a woman's perspective and to express this in writings and through action. We demand that society give and maintain value and respect for women's contributions in their roles within the labour force, in the family and culturally. At the same time, as individuals, as citizens, as mothers, and as wives, we women deplore the loss of resources and of lives in the present senseless resistance to change towards a more equal and just society. Equally, we condemn discrimination and injustice based on race or ethnicity just as much as that based on gender. We believe our hope lies in joining with those progressive forces which will achieve a future human society in harmony with the environment and free of discrimination and inequality between men and women, black and white, believer and unbeliever. (Savane 1982, 15)

But there is a broad base on which First and Third World feminists must agree if feminism is truly to be concerned about redressing the oppression of women. This broad base must at least recognize that racism and economic exploitation are primary forces in the oppression of most women in the world. It must acknowledge that while gender is a potential bond, women participate in the oppression of other women all over the world. It must respect different cultures, and it must agree that women in various places are perfectly capable of having their own voice. This can be a beginning. It must also strive to see the world through noncolonial eyes. For example, I remember a few years ago being asked to give a paper (during Women's History Week) on African women in Africa.

This was at a major university in the Midwest. I arrived to discover that the paper had been assigned to a panel on minority women. Since African women are not a minority in Africa, I felt the assignment of the paper to that panel (rather than the creation of an international panel) reflected an ahistorical Eurocentric mindset in which all non-Europeans are somehow viewed as minorities. We must stop reproducing pictures of the world only from the inside out, and try to look from the outside in. If we view the world in raw numbers rather than power relationships, most people are non-European.

We must discontinue reproducing our own oppression in the ways we treat one another, in the ways we raise our children, in our misdiagnosis or half-definition of the problem. Based on the things we have in common as women, which are greater in number through space and time when we make the right connections between them, we must view women's oppression in the context of all oppression. We must challenge a feminist perspective to envisage a human-centered world, in which the satisfaction of human needs, justly met, is a primary goal.

References

Aptheker, Bettina. 1982. *Woman's Legacy*. Amherst, Mass.: University of Massachusetts Press.

Awe, Bolanle. 1977. "Reflections on the Conference on Women in Development: 1." *Signs* 3, no. 1: 314–16. Barrow, Nita. 1985. "The Decade NGO Forum." *Africa Report* (March/April): 9–12.

Beneria, Lourdes, and Gita Sen. 1981. "Accumulation, Reproduction, and Women's Role in Economic Development: Boserup Revisited." *Signs* 7, no. 2: 279–98.

Cagatay, Nilufer, Caren Grown, and Aida Santiago. 1986. "Nairobi Women's Conference: Toward a Global Feminism?" *Feminist Studies* 12, no. 2 (Summer): 401–12.

Davis, Angela. 1981. *Women, Race and Class*. New York: Random House.

Etienne, Mona, and Eleanor Leacock, eds. 1980. *Women and Colonization: Anthropological Perspectives*. New York: Praeger.

Evans, Sara. 1979. *Personal Politics: The Roots of Women's Liberation in the Civil Rights Movement and the New Left*. New York: Vintage.

Giddings, Paula. 1984. *When and Where I Enter: The Impact of Black Women on Race and Sex in America*. New York: William Morrow.

Harley, Sharon, and Rosalyn Terborg-Penn, eds. 1978. *The Afro-American Woman*. Port Washington, N.Y.: Kennikat Press. hooks, bell. 1981. *Ain't I a Woman?* Boston: South End Press.

_____. 1984. *Feminist Theory: Prom Margin to Center*. Boston: South End Press.

Hull, G., P. Scott, and B. Smith, eds. 1982. *But Some of Us Are Brave*. Old Westbury, N.Y.: The Feminist Press.

Joseph, Gloria. 1981. "The Incompatible Menage a Trois: Marxism, Feminism and Racism." In Lydia Sargent, ed., *Women and Revolution*. Boston: South End Press. 91–107.

Joseph, Gloria, and Jill Lewis. 1981. *Common Differences: Conflicts in Black and White Feminist Perspectives*. New York: Anchor Books.

Leacock, Eleanor. 1977. "Reflections on the Conference on Women and Development: III." *Signs* 3, no. 1: 320–22.

Moraga, C., and G. Anzaldúa, eds. 1981. *This Bridge Called My Back: Writings by Radical Women of Color*. Watertown, Mass.: Persephone Press.

Okeyo, Achola Pala. 1981. "Reflection on Development Myths." *Africa Report* (March/April): 7–10.

Savane, Marie Angelique. 1982. "Another Development with Women." *Development Dialogue* 1, no. 2: 8–16.

Seidman, Ann. 1981. "Women and the Development of Underdevelopment." In R. Dauber and M. Cain, eds., *Women and Technological Change in Developing Countries.* Boulder, Colo.: Westview Press.

Smith, Barbara, ed. 1983. *Home Girls: A Black Feminist Anthology.* New York: Kitchen Table: Women of Color Press.

Steady, Filomina Chioma. 1985. "African Women at the End of the Decade." *Africa Report* (March/April): 4–8.

Walker, Alice. 1983. *In Search of Our Mother's Gardens.* New York: Harcourt, Brace, Jovanovich.

White, Deborah. 1985. *Ar'n't I a Woman: Female Slaves in the Plantation South.* New York: W. W. Norton.

Chapter Eight

Analysing Gender in the Politics of the Third World

Georgina Waylen

Introduction

This chapter will outline some of the issues involved in the analysis of gender in Third World politics. The inadequacy of the conventional politics literature indicates that several things have to be done. First, women have to be put back into the study of formal politics. But gender should not be 'added in' to the analysis of political process at the expense of other forms of social relations such as class and ethnicity. Second, it is necessary to make clear how ostensibly neutral political processes and concepts such as nationalism, citizenship and the state, are fundamentally gendered. Third, it is not enough simply to reintegrate women as actors in the study of conventional politics. Those activities women are typically involved in outside the male dominated institutional sphere must also be included in any analyses. This challenge to the conventional construction of the political is crucially important, as without it much of women's political activity can be dismissed or marginalized as it does not fit easily into conventional categories and, as a result, the important role it plays in the political process will be ignored. Before doing this, it is useful to consider the development of gender as an analytic category.

Feminist academics have debated whether to focus primarily on 'women' or on 'gender'. This debate has encompassed both intellectual and political arguments and raises more complex issues than might at first appear. Those advocating a focus on 'women' have argued that a book about gender will inevitably be predominantly about women, rather than gender as an analytic category, and that a reluctance to make this explicit is due to a desire to sound 'academic', that is more respectable, less political and therefore more acceptable within the academy. There are several strong counter arguments to this position. First, as we will see, there are so many difficulties associated with the use of the term 'woman' that it cannot be used as a catch-all category, disregarding difference in terms of race, class and sexuality, in any simplistic way. Second, focusing on 'women' can result in women being 'added in' without any fundamental transformation of disciplines occurring. Third and most importantly, using the term 'gender' demonstrates the interconnectedness of relations between men and women, which might be lost in a focus on women alone. This book will not just have women as its subject matter, although inevitably this will provide a large focus, but will also analyse the nature of the social relations between men and women.

The term 'gender' has been used widely over the past two decades. Initially it was utilized, particularly by social scientists, to describe a fundamental axis of social differentiation, alongside class and race. Many sociologists and psychologists used gender in a simplistic way almost synonymous with socialization. The construction of gender difference was seen in terms of boys and girls being socialized into different roles. Of particular importance was the notion that gender was a social construct, and therefore observed gender differences were seen as the product of social relations. This problematizing of gender had a huge significance (Flax 1987: 627). Within this framework, many characteristics which had been considered the result of inherent biological differences and as such natural, of social relations. If gender differences are historically and culturally specific and what it means to be a man or a women varies over place and time, then the variations need to be investigated and, if desired, political programmes can be instituted to alter gender differences.

The understanding of gender has become more sophisticated and complex. More recently, the influence of other disciplines and deconstructive and psychoanalytic theories has moved the emphasis towards an analysis of the construction of gendered subjectivities. The influence of Freud, Lacan and Derrida has been important as well as French feminists such as Kristeva and Irigaray (Butler 1989). As a result, attention has been focused on the ways in which masculinity and femininity are constructed in the individual subject rather than seeing gender as a set of roles into which people are socialized.

Much of the interest in gender relations is due to feminism. Feminists of all descriptions have characterized gender relations as relations of inequality and subordination. There have, however, been important developments in the ways in which these relations have been theorized and understood. The 1970s was dominated by feminist academics searching for origins of unequal gender relations and trying to find explanations and causes for these relations of subordination (Barrett and Phillips 1992: 2–3). As we will see in succeeding chapters, much of the work on gender in the Third World has been influenced by liberal feminism and socialist feminism, two of the three strands which were important in this period.

It is radical feminism and socialist feminism which formed the two major analytical camps dominant in the 1970s. Both strands believe that societies are fundamentally structured around profound inequalities in gender relations and both use the term 'patriarchy' to describe such systems of male dominance. However they differ as to the causes and solutions. Radical feminists argue that gender divisions are the most profound division within society and that all societies are patriarchal. They believe that men as a group oppress women, and that men benefit from that oppression. Put simply, men are the problem. As a result the radical feminist analysis highlighted certain issues which hitherto had been neglected They directed attention towards The control exercised by men over women's sexuality, their reproductive capacity and its role in their oppression (Firestone 1970; Brownmiller 1975). In political terms this resulted in campaigns centring around sexual violence and pornography. Radical feminists have been criticized for being essentialist and biologically reductionist; that is, that their approach is rooted in the belief that men are somehow destined to oppress women and that they are unable to provide a non-biological explanation of why this should be the case.

Socialist feminists, while sharing a structural analysis of women's oppression and using the term patriarchy, differ from radical feminists on several important points. They are influenced by Marxism, but believe that it has strong limitations, due primarily to its concentration on class differences, which makes it 'sex-blind' (Hartmann 1981) and therefore unable to provide an adequate analysis of women's subordination. But socialist feminists often use the work of Engels, examining gender relations in the spheres of production that is paid employment, and reproduction that is the reproduction of the labour force in the domestic sphere, and the links between them. Socialist feminists therefore believe that capitalism plays a role in the oppression of women but that this is not the only factor. In capitalist patriarchy, while capitalism did not create women's oppression it has often used and transformed it (Barrett 1981).

Liberal feminism is the third and perhaps the most diverse strand. It is less concerned with finding structural explanations for women's subordination than either socialist or radical feminism. Instead it sees the socialization of men and women into different roles, reinforced by discrimination, prejudice and irrationality, as responsible for women's unequal position in society. The solutions to inequality are changes which will give women a better deal within the existing system such as legal changes and the promotion of equal opportunities, allowing women access to things on the same terms as men. Liberal feminism has been criticized for its overly individualistic approach and its lack of a coherent analysis of women's oppression.

These feminist approaches, dominant in the 1970s, came in for profound criticism in the 1980s. They had often taken for granted the notion of 'woman' as a unitary and a historical category. Some had treated women as one homogeneous group, making the assumption that it was both possible and unproblematic to generalize about all women and their interests. This often meant that the experience of white, middle-class and Western women was generalized to black, working-class and Third World women. As part of a sea change in theoretical debates, the different ways in which the category 'woman' has been constructed historically have been explored (Riley 1988). The notion of a 'women's interest' shared by all women regardless of race, class and sexuality became highly contested. It is impossible to say, in any uncomplicated way, that all women are oppressed by all men. As a result the need to forge commonality across difference through alliances and coalitions becomes a key issue within feminism.

This critique had particular implications for analyses of Third World women made by First World feminists and academics (Spivak 1987). First, many analyses were informed by notions, paralleling ideas about the common oppression of women, that 'sisterhood is global,' i.e. that there was more uniting women of different races, classes and sexualities than dividing them. This was often expressed in various cross-cultural analyses of patriarchy. Second, when difference was actually acknowledged it was often done by turning all Third World women into a non-Western 'other.' As we will see in Chapter 2, the 'women in development' literature, in particular, is often marked out for displaying these characteristics—treating all Third World women as the same, whether they were, for example, upper-class urban educated professionals or lower-class rural peasant women and advocating general 'solutions' to various perceived problems which affected them from the framework of a universal homogenizing feminism. This had the effect of removing agency from Third World women, by seeing them as *objects* rather than subjects and as passive victims of barbaric and primitive practices (Lazreg 1988; Mohanty 1988, 1991; Ong 1988).

Three major elements have contributed to the breakdown of this kind of universal theorizing (Barrett and Phillips 1992). First, black women have provided a powerful challenge to much of the work of white feminists, arguing that their analyses were imbued with racist and ethnocentric assumptions, again generalizing the experience of white feminists to black women (Moraga and Anzaldua 1983; hooks 1984). Second, the re-emergence of the 'equality versus difference' debate broke down the confident distinctions between sex as a biological category and gender as a social construct. In some quarters (often women-centred or radical feminist) sexual difference came to be celebrated rather than denied (Scott 1988). Debates moved on to ask how to deal with embodiment, arguing that it is not difference that is the problem, but how it is constructed and dealt with (Bock and James 1992). Third, the feminist challenge to mainstream theorizing has been paralleled by the post-structuralist and postmodern critiques of the universal grand frameworks which characterized enlightenment thought and have heralded the end of the metanarrative (Nicholson 1990). There has been a shift from 'things,' that is an emphasis on structures so favoured by a social science approach, to 'words,' an emphasis on language and discourse derived from literary and critical theory (Barrett 1992). Form and representation become much more important if language is no longer seen as transparently and directly reflecting 'reality' but as playing a significant role in the construction of that reality.

Interest in notions of identity and the ways in which subjects are constructed has therefore increased. This has been accompanied by the fracturing of the Cartesian unitary human subject and the self so beloved of rationalist enlightenment thought to be replaced by multiple subject identities, notions of difference, plurality and multiplicity. Identity is seen as complex and a combination of different elements such as class, race, gender and sexuality, rather than simply one factor (Butler and Scott 1992). Therefore a plurality of identities exist in the single subject. At the same time, there is also a greater recognition of diversity and difference between women. According to Scott (1992), the task becomes one of seeing how subjects' identities are constructed through 'experience' and discourse without essentializing them. Subject's identities are created through agency, and this agency is 'created through situations and statuses conferred upon them' (Scott 1992: 34). Within this kind of framework, politics becomes a discourse by which people 'determine who they are and who they shall become as social beings' (Schild 1991: 140).

As a consequence of these theoretical developments, the study of gender relations has become complex. Jane Flax (1987: 630) argues that it entails two levels of analysis: gender as construct or category that helps us make sense out of particular social worlds and histories, and gender as a social relation that enters into and partially constitutes all other social relations and activities. Uniting several analytical strands, the historian Joan Scott (1986) also argues for the adoption of gender as an analytic category. In the past, she claims there has been a tendency for gender to be used either descriptively, as a substitute for women, or causally, in the quest for origins of women's subordination. Scott (1986) too, wants a two part but interrelated definition of gender, which she claims, must remain analytically distinct. First, gender is a constitutive element of social relationships based on perceived differences between the sexes, for example through the representation of cultural symbols and their interpretation; subjective identities and the construction of gender not just in the kinship system but also in the polity and economy. Second, gender is a primary way of signifying relations of power.

It is in her second proposition that gender is a primary way of signifying relationships of power that Scott (1986) believes the theorization of gender can be developed. Clearly influenced by Foucauldian notions of power, gender becomes implicated in the way power is constructed. Power, its construction and legitimation, is obviously crucial to the study of politics. Foucault advocates a radically different way of conceptualizing power to that used by the majority of political scientists. He believes that modern power is 'capillary,' in that it is exercised 'strategically' at all levels of society right down to the level of 'micropractices,' that is everyday social practices. Foucault is therefore arguing for a 'politics of everyday life' in a way that gives potential for a politics of resistance. This conceptualization of power:

finds some resonance with those who argue for wider definitions of the political. As part of his interest in the way in which power is exercised, Foucault argues that knowledge and the ability to construct knowledge equals power to define 'subjects' (Fraser 1989; Barrett 1991). Oppositional political activity can therefore play an important role in subverting dominant discourses and representations.

While it has often been obscured and overlooked, the contextually specific ways in which politics constructs gender and gender constructs politics become an important subject of enquiry. Scott (1986) outlines some of the ways in which gender can be used, both explicitly and implicitly, in the study of politics. Gender has been used explicitly in political theory to justify or criticize rulers and to express the relationship between ruler and ruled. Changes in gender relationships can be initiated by views of the needs of the state. According to Scott, these actions can only be understood as part of an analysis of the construction and consolidation of power. Gender has also been used implicitly as a crucial part of the organization of equality or inequality. As we will see in Chapter 3, it formed part of the British project of colonialism where the empire was constructed around a specifically white masculine self. Where does this leave the study of gender in Third World politics? New developments in feminist theorizing have meant that, if universalistic discourses of patriarchy and women's oppression can no longer be used uncritically by a white Western and predominantly middle-class feminism, new forms of analysis must be found which can accommodate specificity, diversity and heterogeneity. This would make possible an approach which can look at the complexity of gender in the Third World from a perspective of the multiplicity of difference rather than 'otherness.'

Conventional Politics

While conventional politics is largely seen as synonymous with electoral politics in the First World, this correlation doesn't hold so clearly in the Third World where authoritarian and military regimes and even the revolutionary overthrow of the state have been more commonplace. But it is now well documented that men and women participate differently in all forms of formal politics in both the First and Third Worlds, whether getting issues on the political agendas, or in policy making and implementation (Ackelsberg 1992). In the past men's political behaviour has been seen as the norm by political scientists, and women's analysed in terms of its deviation from this male norm. As part of this, many myths and stereotypes about women's political participation have grown up, for example that women are passive, apolitical and conservative, which feminist political scientists have endeavoured to dispel. It has been widely observed, that initially on gaining the vote, women don't vote with the same frequency as men in either the developed or developing world. However, this gap closes rapidly and once voting rates are controlled for age, class, education, etc., these differences disappear. It is clear that women's 'tendency to vote less' is not inherent but transient and contingent, for example it declines with increasing urbanization (Randall 1987).

There is, however, a marked tendency for women to participate less than men in formal politics as one ascends higher up the echelons of power (Peterson and Runyan 1993). At the grassroots level women on the whole make up a smaller percentage of the members of political parties than men. In the late 1960s women made up between only 15 and 20 per cent of party members in Chile and Peru. There was no greater number in the socialist bloc; in 1980 women formed only 19 per cent of ordinary Cuban communist party members. Women have often been marginalized in women's sections. Many one party states in the Third World, particularly in Africa, created women's organizations or co-opted already existing ones which became part of the dominant political party. These organizations have been more vehicles for the state to control women's participation, mobilizing them on its own terms and providing the regime with a base, rather than ways for women to gain representation within the system (Staudt 1986: 208). In Zimbabwe, for example, the ZANU women's organization was headed by Sally Mugabe, the president's wife. However, as we will see in Chapter 6, in parts of Latin America, with democratization many women activists have set up more autonomous women's sections in parties of the centre and centre left with distinctly feminist agendas (Waylen, 1994).

Inevitably, given the low numbers of women members of political parties, the numbers elected to representative bodies are also low. While women tend to participate in greater numbers in local level politics, the average percentage of women in national legislatures globally in 1987 was 10. This number hides wide diversity. In 1987 the proportion of women legislators in sub-Saharan Africa was approximately 7.5 per cent; Latin America 7 per cent; South Asia 5 per cent and Southeast Asia 12 per cent, but the proportions had increased all regions since 1975 (United Nations 1991: 32). It appears that women fare better in systems with proportional representation.

There tend to be even fewer women found in the executives of governments whether they are authoritarian, elected, state socialist or revolutionary. Often, the very, small number of women are appointed to posts which reflect the role that women so often play in the private sphere, e.g. women are often given resposibility for health, education, welfare and women's affairs (where this portfolio exists). In 1987–8 an average of only 3.5 per cent of the world's cabinet ministers were women and 93 countries, including 31 from Africa, 24 from Latin America and the Caribbean and 30 from Asia and the Pacific had no women ministers at all. Women are largely excluded from key areas such as economic policy, defence and political affairs. Even in the 'social' areas, women formed only 9 per cent of the ministers in Africa and 6 per cent or less in the rest of the Third World (United Nations 1991: 31).

There are several explanations for this pattern of participation in conventional politics. In Africa, the low political representation of women is attributed, amongst other factors, to low levels of literacy and formal sector employment among women and the operation of the legal system, particularly laws concerning property and land (Parpart 1988). Many women are constrained by their roles in the private sphere, which prevent them from participating in the public sphere on the same terms as men and gaining the experience deemed necessary for a career in politics. However, it has been suggested that this affects middle- and upper-class women to a lesser extent in much of the Third World, because they can utilize the labour of female servants to free them from their domestic responsibilities (Richter 1990–1: 530). Shirin Rai (1995) found that in 1994 the majority of the 48 women representatives in the Indian parliament were highly educated and came from high caste and elite backgrounds. Almost universally, middle-class and élite women, because of factors such as economic resources and employment, levels of education and confidence, find it easier than poorer women to participate in the upper echelons of conventional politics. However, it is not only the nature of many women's lives which prevents them from participating, but also the structures of formal politics. This ranges from the timing of meetings, the combative style and machismo (often commented on in left-wing parties), and more widespread discrimination against women, for example in selection procedures, which prevents them from rising in political parties (Caldeira 1986).

One phenomenon which has been noted particularly in Asia and appears to go against these trends, is the relatively. high number of women leaders in the Third World, such as Indira Gandhi in India, Benazir Bhutto in Pakistan, Corazon Aquino in the Philippines and Violetta Chamorro in Nicaragua amongst others (Genovese 1993). There are particular explanations for this which do not contradict the basic pattern. Mary Fainsod Katzenstein (1978) has claimed that in India there is a link between the degree to which politics is institutionalized and the participation of women, as the permeability of institutions allows women to achieve political prominence. Also in the Asian context, Linda Richter (1990–1) has argued that, among the factors which enable women to reach leadership positions are elite status, high levels of female participation in the movements struggling for independence, and crucially, links to politically prominent male relatives, often accompanied by their martyrdom, e.g. their assassination. However, Wolkowitz (1987), in her study of women politicians in Andhra Pradesh, argues that it is misleading to place too much emphasis on the significance. of the family ties of female politicians.

Richter (1990–1) claims that women leaders suffer important disadvantages over their male counterparts; they do not generally have an institutional base, a regional constituency, an administrative track record or a military niche; they are often seen as temporary leaders, making them vulnerable to coup attempts. Women leaders are sometimes seen as conciliators who can bring the country together after a period of profound conflict and dislocation. Elsa Chaney (1979) has argued that, in Latin America, women in politics have often played the role of the 'supermadre', the mother of the people. The social welfare activities of Eva, the wife of Argentinian president Juan Perón, dispensing help to the poor and sick are often cited as an example of this role.

While women are, on the whole, underrepresented in formal politics, this does not mean of course that the policies made and implemented in the political process do not have a huge impact on the lives of different groups of women and on gender relations in general. When examining policy making and its outcomes, the gendered nature of the state becomes an important focus. There are often large numbers of women employed in state bureaucracies, but few are found at the top of the state hierarchies in all types of political system whether electoral, authoritarian or state socialist (Staudt 1989a). In the 1980s the highest proportion of female public sector administrative and managerial workers was found in Latin America at 20 per cent, with 13 percent in Africa and 10 per cent in Asia. While these figures had increased significantly in all areas since 1970, women are found only rarely in positions in central banks, or foreign trade (United Nations 1991: 35). The state therefore is a gendered hierarchy, with women having an uneven representation in the bureaucracy (Franzwav *et al.* 1989: 30). Some analysts have gone on to focus not simply on the lack of women but also on the embedded masculine style and organization of state bureaucracies, epitomized for example by the Weberian rational model (Ferguson 1984). It has been suggested, however, that in some Third World states, middle-class educated women are in a good position to play a strategic role in the bureaucracy (Charlton *et al.* 1989: 13). Indeed Alvarez, after examining Brazil, has suggested that state-led development increases employment opportunities for female professionals and technocrats within the state. (Alvarez 1990a: 261).

When examining links between state action and gender relations, policies and their impact can be divided into three major categories (Charlton *et al* 1989) The first category consists of policies which are aimed particularly at women. These often focus around so-called protective legislation and reproduction, for example abortion and laws surrounding childbirth such as the provision of maternity leave. A second category is those policies which deal with relations between men and women, particularly property rights, sexuality, family relations, areas where power relations between men and women and therefore sets of gender relations are often institutionalized. As we will see in Chapter 3 the laws and regulations surrounding these issues frequently become an area of contestation when attempts are made to alter the existing pattern of power relations, as occurred with the enforcement of colonial rule in Africa when marriage, divorce and women's mobility became highly contested (Channock 1982; Barnes 1992; Manicom 1992).

The third category, general policies, are supposedly gender neutral but have a different impact on men and women. These can be further subdivided into those policy areas linked to the public sphere and somehow seen as 'masculine,' such as state-defined politics war, foreign policy, international trade, resources extraction and long distance communication, and those connected with welfare and reproduction. Women have traditionally been excluded from the so-called masculine areas of policy. The most extreme example of this has been war, where women have, until very recently, participated on a very different basis to men. As we will see in Chapter 4, while recent national liberation struggles and revolutionary mobilizations have incorporated women as fighters, this too has often happened in gender specific ways, i.e. the image of the woman fighter as mother with a rifle in one arm and a baby in the other (Reif 1986). Those policy areas more intimately connected to the private sphere and reproduction, for example, housing, health and education, fall under the general rubric of welfare and the welfare state. In contrast to the 'masculine' policies of the public sphere, welfare states have, for some time, been the subject of feminist analyses, particularly in the First World, looking at how they were established assuming particular patterns of gender relations or with the effect of creating or maintaining particular gender roles, and emphasizing issues of control and empowerment for women (Wilson 1977).

Even in much of the Third World where welfare states are far less developed and comprehensive, women are, on the whole, in the majority among providers of state welfare services. The state sector provides employment opportunities for different groups of women. Middle-class professional women are more likely to be employed by the state than the private sector, for example as teachers, social workers and nurses in sex-segregated employment (Seager and Olson 1986). Women also form the majority of consumers of welfare services. This is because of the role traditionally ascribed to many women in the domestic sphere as mothers and household managers that it is women within the household who often liaise with welfare services on behalf of other members of the household, for example the young and old. It is women who often make up the majority of the poor and are the major recipients of whatever welfare services exist. Any cuts in welfare services have particular implications for many women, both as providers and consumers of state welfare services, as has been seen in the impact of adjustment policies in the Third World (Afshar and Dennis 1992): Welfare states therefore have a differential impact on particular groups of women such as women in female headed households. Poor women, as the recipients of welfare services whether chosen or imposed, experience the welfare state very differently to the middle-class professional women who are employed to provide these services. This brings us to consider the gendered nature of the state, citizenship and nationalism.

Citizenship, Nationalism and the State

These three categories are linked together. Citizenship, for example, is an important way in which the relationship between the individual and the nation state has been theorized. It is not gender neutral. Men and women have been incorporated into citizenship in Western states in very different ways. Initially citizenship was restricted to men (for long periods excluding working-class men and men of different races such as black slaves in the United States, for example) and incorporated them as soldiers and wage earners, that is through activities in the public sphere, and only later women were incorporated, often as mothers, that is through their activities in the private sphere. So despite formal equality as voters, men and women have been differentially incorporated as citizens by the state.

This raises the question of links to the nation and nationalism, as citizens are citizens of a nation state. Clearly in the study of Third World politics, an analysis of nationalism and the processes surrounding the creation of ethnic identities and the nation state is crucial. Nationalism also is not constructed in a gender neutral fashion (Parker *et al.* 1992; McClintock 1993). While recognizing the lack of a unitary category woman, Nira Yuval-Davis and Floya Anthias (1989) have located five major ways in which women have tended to participate in ethnic and national processes and state practices on different terms to men. These are:

1. as biological reproducers of members of ethnic collectivities, as 'mothers of the nation';
2. as reproducers of the boundaries of ethnic/national groups, for example by accepting or refusing sexual intercourse or marriage with prescribed groups of men;
3. as central participants in the ideological reproduction of the collectivity and transmitters of its culture, for example as mothers or teachers;
4. as signifiers of ethnic/national differences—as a focus and symbol in ideological discourses used in the construction, reproduction and transformation of ethnic/national categories, expressed for example in the advertising slogan 'Singapore girl—You're a great way to fly';
5. as participants in national, economic, political and military struggles. (Yuval-Davis and Anthias 1989: 7)

The control of women and their sexuality is central to these processes. Kandiyoti (1991) has argued that this identification of women as bearers of cultural identity and boundary markers will have a negative effect on their emergence as full-fledged citizens. In the post-colonial context, as we will see in Chapter 3, many nationalist movements and nationalist projects equated the emancipation of women with 'modernity,' for example through battles over 'women's souls' (seen in conflicts over education for women) and over women's bodies (exemplified in battles over fertility control). Some successor states have then appeared to reverse reforms, for example women's civil rights, when the previous secularist projects appear to break down (Kandiyoti 1991).

It is clear that a gendered analysis of the nation state is also necessary here. The conventional literature on the state is of little use. Both the more recent work on the state in the First World (including the statist literature inspired in part by Skocpol (1985) and her colleagues) and the now quite large body of work on the Third World has paid very little attention to questions of gender when examining the state. With the exception of the Rothchild and Chazan volume (1988) which focuses on different aspects of societies,' including women's disengagement from the state in Africa, this omission is the same, regardless of the analytical approach adopted. Alavi's (1972) structuralist approach to the postcolonial state inspired by Marxist and underdevelopment theory is as gender blind as the more recent strong/weak state literature exemplified by Migdal (1988).

At the same time the analysis of the state has not been a priority for feminist academics. Many writers tended to concentrate on either the macro, e.g. overarching theoretical studies analysing the relationship between capitalism and patriarchy, seeing the state as a mechanism to reconcile the two systems, or the micro, for example detailed empirical studies, with very little in between (Alvarez 1990a). Others focused on women as the *objects* of state policy, seeing the state as something external and 'out there' which affects women's lives but over which women have very little control. Those who did look at women's struggles with the state often used a 'them and us' framework.

Few feminist analyses have gone beyond seeing the state as either somehow essentially good or essentially bad for women in general. In the First World context, some feminist academics more identified with radical feminism such as Mackinnon (1983) and Ferguson (1984), argued that the state is inherently patriarchal in that it simply reflects society outside the state. Indeed it is an agent of control over women and feminists are well advised to steer clear of any involvement with it, as it will inevitably act to uphold patriarchy. Other feminists writing about the First World and Scandinavia in particular, were more enthusiastic about the potential of the state to further the interests of women in general (Hemes 1987). This enthusiasm resulted in a benign analysis of the welfare state arguing that, because they can get resources from the state, women can escape dependence on individual men.

A new literature on women and the state in the Third World has begun to develop but much of it replicates the general characteristics outlined above (for example Parpart and Staudt 1990). Most studies do not conceptualize the state in a very sophisticated manner and partly as a result of this lack, concentrate on women as the objects of policy (for example Charlton *et al* 1989). They have replicated the tendency either to see the state as essentially good, that is as potentially a modernizing force which will bring benefits for women, or as essentially bad, inevitably representing men's interests to the detriment of some notion of women's interests (see Kandiyoti 1991 for some discussion of this tendency).

It is too simplistic to portray the state as essentially good or bad. It has no necessary relationship to gender relations, but this is evolving, dialectic and dynamic. 'The State' can rarely if ever be seen as a homogeneous category. It is not a unitary structure but a differentiated set of institutions and agencies, the product of a particular historical and political conjuncture. It is far better to see the state as a site of struggle, not lying outside of society and social processes, but having, on the one hand, a degree of autonomy from these which varies under particular circumstances, and on the other, being permeated by them. Gender (and racial and class) inequalities are therefore relations are also partly constituted through the state (Pringle and Watson 1992).The state therefore partly reflects and partly helps to create particular forms of gender relations and gender inequality. State practices construct and legitimate gender divisions and gendered identities are in part constructed by the law and public discourses which emanate (Sassoon 1987). Manicom (1992), among others, highlights the gendered nature of these processes in colonial Africa. Manicom (1992: 456) argues that the naming and recording of 'the native' as head of household in the administration of urban townships in southern Africa early in the twentieth century was 'a moment of moral regulation and gendered state formation and an example of the way in which an apparently neutral, regulatory process inscribed gender and authorized a particular social form. "The Native" as a category of rule was a masculine one.' Manicom (1992: 456) goes on to stress that, as part of the process in which categories are defined within practices of rule, 'state policy and practices are also constructing "women" as objects of rule, reproducing or restructuring normative gender meanings and subordinate social and political identities in the same process.'

Because the relationship between the state and gender relations is not fixed and immutable, battles can be fought out in the arena of the state. Consequently, while the state has for the most part acted to reinforce female ordination, the space can exist within the state, to act to change gender relations (Alvarez 1989a; Charlton et al. 1989). At different times and within different regimes, opportunity spaces can be used to alter the existing pattern of gender relations. Women's relationship to the state, particularly its welfare element, can also be seen as a site of contestation which provides the context for mobilization, and the welfare state can function as a locus of resistance. The actions of the state can also become a focus for political activity by groups outside the state, for example poor women campaigning for an extension of services. Alvarez, for example, has argued that the extension of the remit of the state into the realm of the private has the effect of politicizing the private, for example through issues such as abortion, rape and domestic violence. This politicization then gives women's movements a handle to campaign around and influence the political agenda. Shifting the boundary between the public and the private then becomes an important point of influence (Alvarez 1990a).

Different groups of women therefore interact with the state in different ways, and can have some influence over the way in which the state acts. Feminist analyses relation to men, to examining the ways in which particular divide in different contexts. As part of the process of engagement with the state, interests and identities can also be constructed. It is therefore important to analyse under what conditions and with what strategies women's movements can influence the state and policy agendas. Debate has centred around whether women's movements should attempt to work with the state and political parties. Australian 'femocrats' argue that it is a potential agent of empowerment and feminist strategies should involve winning gains from the state (Watson 1990). As we will see in Chapter 6, 'state feminism' has emerged as an issue in the context of democratization with the return to civilian governments in some Latin American countries. The point at issue here is whether feminist movements can enter the state and achieve their own agendas or whether incorporation means co-optation (Waylen 1993). This brings us to look at 'women's political activity.'

Once the definition of the 'political' is widened, whole new areas of activity, many of them involving women, come under scrutiny. Why do women undertake political activity under certain circumstances, what form does this activity take and how can women's movements be analysed in the Third World context? If identities are complex, comprising multiple intersections of class, race, gender and sexuality, leading individuals to react in different ways at different times, women will act politically, not simply on the basis of gender, but race, class and sexuality as well, in a complex interaction. In the same way as it is difficult to talk of a unitary category 'woman' and women's interests, it is impossible, therefore, to talk of a women's movement. There is not one movement, but a diversity of different movements of which feminist movements are one part. Broad generalizations are therefore not possible.

It is important not to fall into the trap of essentialism by attributing specific qualities to all women. Some scholars, for example, have analysed women's activities in terms of an 'ethic of care' and maternal thinking, arguing, in positive and perhaps rather romantic terms, that women bring to activities in the public sphere supposedly 'female' values of caring, mothering and peacefulness (Gilligan 1983; Ruddick 1989). They have been criticized for both essentialism and universalism: looking at gender to the exclusion of other forms of difference such as race and class, and trying to create grand universal frameworks.

Recently attention has also focused on the form that women's political activities take, including whether women find new ways of 'doing politics' (Waylen 1992a). Using approaches influenced by postmodernism and poststructuralism, political action is seen, in part, as a struggle over dominant meanings, including dominant ideas of woman, and aiming to change those meanings. Foucault has been influential here with the suggestion that knowledge and the ability to construct knowledge equals power. Much greater emphasis is therefore placed on the form of political protests: on their use of the body and symbols and metaphors and how far they subvert dominant discourses of womanhood. One of the most powerful symbolic and subversive acts carried out by women protesting at the disappearance of their relatives, for example in Argentina, has been the takeover of public space not normally seen as part of their domain for their protests. This has been accompanied by other metaphorical and symbolic devices, leading some to highlight the importance of staging and performance in political action, for example, contrary to an essentialist interpretation, that the Madres are 'performing' as mothers (Franco 1994). In Chile women protesting about human rights abuses danced the Cueca, the national dance. It is usually danced by a man and woman, but they danced it alone to powerfully emphasize that their men were missing.

What is needed, therefore, is some exploration of the bases on which women come together as women. This would also focus on, for example, the ways in which women use their socially prescribed roles to act politically, and, without ignoring class and racial identities, explore both the relationship between gendered identities and political activity and the form that this activity takes. Increasingly, the politicization of women's social roles has been analysed, for example the ways in which women have used their roles as mothers or household managers as the basis of protests or to make demands (Kaplan 1982). Most of the activities involve entering either making demands on acting collectively, local or Community based level. This kind of action therefore entails the politicization of the private sphere and entry into the public sphere on that basis. The participant's gender therefore becomes a fundamental part of this type of political activity, as the fact of their being women is a central part of the action. This can involve using 'traditional' social roles for oppositional purposes and also challenging and subverting these roles. Often women involved in 'the politics of everyday life' do not see their activities as political (Caldeira 1990). However, in some contexts, for example, under authoritarian rule, such activities are defined by the regime as oppositional, subversive and therefore come to be seen by both protagonists and others as political.

Women's movements are organized in a variety of different ways around a variety of different issues. One fundamental division that can be made is between those activities which defend the status quo, that is try to preserve the existing social order, and those which attempt to change the status quo, that is broadly defined as oppositional.

Activities which seek to defend the status quo have sometimes caused anxiety to feminists. Often this has been framed in the following terms: why should groups of women mobilize in defence of something that is not seen as being in their long term interests (which are defined as some kind of a feminist project of emancipation and liberation) and organize to uphold and continue a system that is seen as oppressing them? In the past, this has been explained as being due to women's naivety, and by political scientists as due to women's inherently reactionary political beliefs. Debates have also centred around how far women have either shown complicity with or been victimized by certain regimes. None of these approaches is terribly helpful. The examples of women mobilized by the Right show that the women involved often found their activities empowering, enabling them to be active and mobilized in the public sphere, often doing things in the name of motherhood and womanhood using very 'unfeminine methods' (Waylen 1992a). Valentine Moghadam (1994: 19), discussing female support for Islamist movements, uses the concept of identity politics arguing that they promise women of different classes security and meaning, offering stability in part through clearly defined sex roles, family life and a religious orientation.

Deniz Kandiyoti (1988) has supplied a potentially useful way of explaining and analysing the apparently contradictory reasons for and strategies behind women's political activities in defence of the status quo, in the form of the patriarchal bargain. According to Kandiyoti (1988: 277), 'different systems may represent different kinds of "patriarchal bargain" for women with different rules of the game and differing strategies for maximising security and optimising their life options.' Kandiyoti believes that this formulation helps to explain why women act in certain ways which may superficially seem to be in conflict with their long term interests. Women pay the price of a particular bargain and in return get a degree of protection. If a particular bargain looks as if it might be breaking down, women may mobilize to hold on to rule which appear to worsen their situation, because it is part of the strategy of maximizing security by gaining and keeping the protection of men. This if likely to occur in the absence of other more empowering alternatives for women. Kandiyoti cites the case of the United States where one response to some men opting out from the breadwinner role has been attempts to bolster the family in order to reinstate the patriarchal bargain in a society which has very little to offer women on their own. Other examples might be female support for arranged marriages and women binding the feet of their daughters. This notion of the patriarchal bargain can provide a framework with which to analyse, for example, the activities of middle-class women on behalf of the Right against Popular Unity in Chile in the face of their elevation of women's 'traditional' roles and the apparent attempts of the Left to undermine them (Waylen 1992a).

The most documented form of activity undertaken by women's movements is oppositional. There is great diversity in those movements and activities which can be seen as oppositional and attempting to alter the status quo. First, there are those activities which attempt to influence the state and political parties, and therefore interact with the conventional political arena. This can be through protest or lobbying, for example the human rights campaigns of the Madres of the Plaza de Mayo. The demands made can either be specifically concerning women, for example abortion, or more general demands relevant to their roles as household managers, for example around food subsidies and prices. Second, there are autonomous activities which don't attempt to pressurize the state, e.g. autonomous women's organizations and community organizations organizing around economic survival,

Important question therefore arise: first, how can these movements be dissaggregated, for example in terms of the sorts of women involved and their aims and objectives; second, what are the links between different types of women's movement, particularly between feminist and other women's movement, and third, what is the relationship of these movements to other oppositional movements.

One widely used way of disaggregating these questions has been to utilize Maxine Molyneux's (1985a) notion of practical and strategic gender interests. According to Molyneux, women's interests do not exist in any general sense, but she argues for a notion of gender interests, which can be divided into practical and strategic gender interests.

Practical gender interests arise from actual situations and are formulated by the women in those situations, and will vary from situation to situation. A number of analyses have used this notion to explain female collective action arising in response to an immediate perceived need, e.g. the leading role often played by women in food riots, and the examples of miner's wives mobilizing to defend the jobs and interests of their male partners. Practical gender interests therefore are generally expressed as social and economic dermands. These sorts of activities correspond to the category 'the politics of everyday life.' They can take the form, of spontaneous protests, protests, the most obvious being food riots of the sort which occurred in many Third World countries in the 1980s, sparked off by the imposition of harsh structural adjustment packages. They can also take the form of more organized campaigns and activities (Radcliffe and Westwood 1993). These are often not exclusively women-only but women frequently make up the majority of the members. Movements organizing around practical gender interests frequently focus around consumption issues, often organizing in a particular location or community. Some activities which can be characterized in this way involve the pressurizing of the state or political parties, for example campaigns in poor areas to get the state, whether on a local or national level, to provide services such as water, electricity and improved health care. Other activities operate more autonomously, often focusing around collective survival strategies, for example communal kitchens providing food on a collective basis, setting up workshops to produce goods for sale as part of income generating schemes such as bakeries, craft workshops, and credits unions like SEWA in India (Everett 1989). Other examples include women's centres which offer crèches, advice and meeting rooms. While these sorts of activities are often based in poor urban areas, there are examples of women's movements operating in rural areas, particularly among peasant and landless women (Fisher 1993, 75–102). The tradition of women's informal or voluntary associations in Africa can be fitted into this category (Wipper 1984).

It is clear from the examples of women organizing to protect the livelihoods of their families that class and gender are closely linked in this case. Many of these movements can be categorized as 'popular' or working-class, although this is not always so. Argentina's housewives' movement can be seen as an exception; it was middle- and lower middle-class based as the middle class had been very badly hit by economic crisis (Fisher 1993: 145–50). This kind of activity typically involves the politicization of women's social roles, as their roles as mothers and household managers form the basis of their political activities and entry into the public sphere. According to Molyneux, movements operating around practical gender interests do not necessarily act to reduce gender inequality, nor are they often intended to.

In contrast, strategic gender interests are those interests which can be derived deductively from an analysis of women's subordination and from the formulation of a more satisfactory set of arrangements (Molyneux 1985a). It is these strategic gender interests are often called 'feminist' or women's 'real' interests, and according to Molyneux, require a feminist level of consciousness to struggle for them. Feminist movements can therefore be seen as movements of women coming together autonomously and self-consciously as women, pressing gender based demands. They do not, on the whole, rely on the politicization of women's social roles. Different types of feminist movements have appeared in the Third World as well as in the First World. Some middle-class based feminist movements emerged at the same time as nationalist movements campaigning for independence from colonial powers, for example in India, and middle-class based movements campaigning for female suffrage appeared in Latin America in the early part of the twentieth century (Jayawardena 1986; Miller 1991). A variety of feminist movements have (re) emerged in the last two decades (Saporta *et al* 1992).

However, there is a need to explore the links between 'feminism' and popular women's movements. Many studies have shown that groups of women involved in campaigns around practical gender interests have become increasingly focussed on issues around women's subordination and come to see themselves as increasingly feminist (Fisher 1993: 177–200). They often see this as a form of 'popular feminism,' however, that is it is not the same as either feminism from the First World, nor often the feminist movements active within the Third World countries themselves. The difference is often expressed in terms of movements, which do not prioritize gender issues over and above the issues which surround class and imperialism. As Mohanty argues, 'feminist movements have been on the grounds of cultural imperialism, and of short-sightedness in defining the meaning of gender in middle-class, white experiences, and in terms of internal racism, classism and homophobia' (Mohanty 1991: 7). Some contemporary feminist movements, for example in many parts of Latin America, are seen by many as predominantly middle-class movements, and for example in Brazil, as predominantly white. A rigid analytical dichotomy between movements active around practical and strategic gender interests is overly simplistic as there is considerable overlap between the two.

Conclusion

It is clear when looking at gender in Third World politics that Third World women do not constitute an 'automatic unitary group,' but that the term Third World women can be used as it designates a political constituency (Mohanty 1991: 7). Mohanty believes what constitutes 'Third World women' as an oppositional alliance is a *common context of struggle*. She wants to get away from analyses which see Third World women as victims, focusing instead on a dynamic oppositional agency of women. Mohanty uses Benedict Anderson's notion of 'imagined communities' to move away from essentialist notions of potential alliances, substituting 'imagined communities of women with divergent histories and social locations, woven together by the *political* threads of opposition to forms of domination that are not only pervasive but systemic' (1991: 4). She therefore believes that it is possible to 'retain the idea of multiple fluid structures of domination which intersect to locate women differently at particular historical conjunctures, while at the same time insisting on the dynamic oppositional agency of individuals and their engagement in "daily life"' (1991: 13). The notion of an imagined community of struggle can be extended to Third World oppositional struggles in general. It therefore becomes difficult to see women's oppositional activities as discrete entities somehow separate from other struggles, for example against colonialism, imperialism and for national liberation.

It is important, however, that the analysis of the political activities of women's movements does not occur separately from the analysis of formal politics. The use of wider definitions of the political means that the two must be integrated. In particular, there is a need to explore the interaction between the two in terms of the state and political parties. This will allow for more sophisticated understandings of concepts such as citizenship which play such an important role in the analysis of political processes.

Now that we have examined some of the key issues, such as what is meant by gender, and unpicked some of the concepts involved in a gendered approach to Third World politics, it is possible to outline a loose framework with which to examine key political formations. Combining some of the themes and questions which emerge from the structural analyses of socialist feminists developed in the 1970s together with some of the new insights of the 1980s, we will focus on three key areas in each formation. In each case, we must consider first the role played by different groups of women in conventional political arenas. Second, we have to make a gendered analysis of the state and policy making in that context, examining the impact of particular policies in constructing and changing existing patterns of gender relations. Third, it is necessary to examine the political activities undertaken by different groups of women outside of the conventional political arena, and their interaction with the state and the policy making process in each formation.

Before it is possible to focus primarily on the domestic political arena, we must consider what is meant by the term the Third World, look at the position of Third World countries in the international economic and political system and examine the relationship between the national and the international context. This inevitably leads us also to consider the nature of 'development' and the impact of diverse processes of social and economic change on women and gender relations. It is to this topic that we move in the next chapter.

Chapter Nine

Hierarchy and Class in
Women's Organizations
A Case from Northern Mexico

Gay Young

T he case against separate women's development organizations is widely known:
women become further marginalized because separate is not equal, especially since
such organizations focus more often on women's reproductive activities than on their
contributions to production. Just as well known is the critique of "integrated" programs
as not integrated but instead male-dominated, with women's interests either subsumed
under men's or assumed to be the same as men's. However, even if women were integrated
as equals into mainstream development projects, that would not eliminate the need for
separate women's development organizations.[1]

Separate women's organizations "offer ... the opportunity to develop self-confidence
and skills within a supportive framework ... and enable women to gain access to resources
and ... to take greater economic and political responsibility."[2] Moreover, women's rationale
for such organizations—self-management and respect for their productive activities—challenges their "proper" roles.[3]

Given that women's organizations are a legitimate part of the development landscape,
how they function becomes a key question for investigation. The analysis herein reveals how
issues of internal structure (hierarchy) and the socioeconomic position of participants (class
relations) in women's development organizations influence organizational functioning.
Concepts from feminist organization theory and from development literature on women
illuminate a case from northern Mexico. It is a case fraught with paradoxes—for example, a

Gay Young; Kathleen Staudt, ed., "Hierarchy and Class in Women's Organizations," *Women,
International Development, and Politics: The Bureaucratic Mire*, pp. 79–97. Copyright © 1990 by
Temple University Press. Reprinted with permission.

commitment to "democracy" in the midst of a *mystified* hierarchy—due, in part, to the lack of models for avoiding the reproduction of traditional (male) inequality in organizations.

A Feminist Theoretical Analysis of Social Organizations

Women's organizations in the United States have struggled with issues of both hierarchy and class. Four ideas or themes in feminist theory that developed in the context of the women's movement merit particular attention. Three of them address the phenomenon of hierarchy—bureaucratization, structurelessness, and leadership; the fourth comprises questions about the intersection of gender issues and class divisions. Some years ago Boulding summarized the antihierarchy position of feminists in the statement: women are nurturers, and nurturance is nonhierarchical.[4] This assertion undergirds the belief (as well as the wish, Boulding suggests) that women can develop organizational techniques that do not require the exercise of dominance. Yet, feminists still seek to elaborate nonhierarchical patterns for working in large-scale organizations. *Bureaucratization,* as the typical response to scale, has been recognized as antithetical to women's interests.[5] Simply staffing bureaucratic organizations with women will not alter them, for relations of hierarchical domination in bureaucracy serve to perpetuate social inequalities. Specifically, bureaucracy systematizes male preference and limits discussion of change in gender relations.[6]

One of Ferguson's central arguments is that embedded in women's traditional experience as caregivers is the outline of a nonbureaucratic vision of collective life.[7] Others assert that the anchoring effect of children has left women closer to and more aware of nurturance needs of their families as well as sensitized to such needs among their neighbors; thus, community redistribution systems became the business of women. These traditional networking skills present an alternative to hierarchical organizational patterns.[8] However, Ferguson suggests that the values coming out of the experience of mothering also lead women to avoid risk and conflict—that is, the "clash of will that authentic nonbureaucratic [organizational] politics requires."[9]

Ferguson's own analysis of organizational class structure—in which all but the elite undergo a process she identifies as "feminization" in order to function in a subordinate status in the bureaucracy—implies a more general source of these attributes. Within the context of male organizational patterns, the feminized are industrial and clerical workers, marginal workers in secondary labor market jobs, clients of service bureaucracies, and even the so-called new working class made up of white-collar professionals and technicians. That is, all embody traits that women have adopted to accommodate to the power of men.

It is noteworthy that a similar process (unlikely to be called feminization, however) appears to be working in Smith's discussion of the rationale for success in the Mexican political system since the 1940s.[10] He elaborates a set of "rules" (most obvious when they are broken) for surviving and achieving within the bureaucratic authoritarian state structure. Examples include: study the system and make lots of friends; don't make enemies but do demonstrate loyalty to your superior; don't rock the boat; avoid mistakes by staying in line, following orders, and keeping quiet; pass difficult decisions on to your superior. No provisions exist for "clashes of will." Rather, these are guidelines for subordinates, for only the president, an office few among the elite will achieve, is not in a subordinate relation to someone higher in the Mexican system of politics and government. Viewed another way, the rules provide an outline for socialization into the male dominance system.

Thus, bureaucracy contributes to social inequality, and doubts exist regarding its capacity to offer solutions to the problems created by social inequalities. Indeed, Ferguson asserts that organizations representing women's interests—even those that routinely work with bureaucracies—cannot themselves become bureaucratic or they cease to be representative of their constituents. In a study of women's international nongovernmental organizations (NGOs), Boulding concludes that these NGOs' activities have been limited because women have accepted male organizational patterns, bureaucratic hierarchy, in particular.[11] However, she also notes that that system of status gave the NGO women the little recognition they were getting.

If women's experience as caregivers leads to an identity of connection and an ethic of responsibility, women still must extract this experience from the many others in their daily lives that are linked to the survival of subordination.[12] Only in this way can they act on the integrity of those virtues and change society. Do women have rooted in their nurturing relations the capacity to solve the persistent problems facing egalitarian and participatory, nonbureaucratic organizations?

Hierarchical structure is an issue with which the contemporary women's movement in the United States has had to struggle. Freeman asserts that among the consequences of the movement idea that all hierarchy is bad ("because it gives some people power over other people and does not allow everyone's full talents to develop") have been problems created by *structurelessness*.[13] Although structurelessness is not a necessary result of horizontal leadership, in practice, antihierarchy has meant antileadership more often than shared leadership.[14] The consequence has been the limitation of task efficiency and political effectiveness because of the time devoted to group process rather than group ends, according to Freeman. In addition, there was loss of control of movement leadership (to the media, in part), and the performance of leadership functions by thousands of other women had to be "hidden," as Bunch puts it.

Although attention to process may have the potential to humanize bureaucracy, it does not necessarily lead to outcomes in women's interest.[15] Moreover, in the women's movement emphasis on process in the absence of any structural framework forced "leaders" to put extra energy into maintaining good personal relations and maintaining a personable environment. Besides its balance against instrumental action, Freeman contends, participation that is aimed at maintaining good interpersonal relations is not conducive to confronting and resolving conflict, which is part of the democratic process.

The structurelessness resulting from antihierarchical sentiments contains contradictory Implications for *leadership* in women's organizations. For example, Bunch describes one double bind experienced through the 1970s: women identified as leaders in the women's rights sector, often working in hierarchical organizations, were judged in the movement by the collectivist norms of the liberation sector and condemned as elitist.[16] As another example, highly visible women were vilified as "media stars," but there was no mechanism to "remove" them. Nonetheless, even in situations that are antihierarchical, women have performed leadership functions. But they must then hide their leadership activities, and they cannot be supported—or held accountable.[17] Relations of leadership in the women's movement have produced persistent problems and thus generated theoretical analyses.

In a special collection of *Quest* on feminist theory, St. Joan presents an "ideal type" of feminist leadership.[18] She asserts that a leader's authority comes from the quality of her relationships with constituents; the group empowers the leader with certain responsibilities. Also critical to her typification is the notion of "shifting leadership." She sees in the empowering aspects of mothering a model or analog for feminist leadership: the relations of letting go of power, on the one hand, and of accepting responsibility, on the other. This is akin to Bunch's understanding of power identified with "energy, strength, and effective interaction, rather then with manipulation, domination, and control."[19] The feminist model of leadership, then, contains commitment to the empowerment of others rather than their subordination. In practice, empowerment means broad responsibilities for all and widely visible decision-making power. It is not the same as structurelessness—indeed, it requires clear delineation of participants' tasks.[20]

Freeman's account of experience in the women's movement reveals that the ironic result of the antihierarchy (antileadership) position was only a slight variation on the kind of discriminatory and exclusive system of leadership women historically have fought. The criteria, used to select leaders were similar to those people use to select friends (background and personality), not those an organization uses to be politically effective (competence and potential contribution to the movement).[21] Moreover, with no structure in place to enhance participation, consensus was built through homogeneity, which, in turn, served to exclude women who did not match the white middle-class norm—for whatever reason—and deprived the movement of these women's leadership, energy, and strength.[22]

Yet another style (if one is willing to take antileadership as a style) of leadership, noteworthy because it has been observed in women's organizations, is charismatic leadership. Charisma stands against bureaucratic hierarchy in ways that are different from feminism's opposition to it.[23] People submit to charismatic leadership because of their belief In the extraordinary qualities of the specific person: the image of the leader verges on the divine. The charismatic leader derives her right not from selection by the people but rather from followers' conviction that it is their *duty* to recognize her as their leader by virtue of her mission. Duty to obey is implied; compliance with the leader's directives creates a particular hierarchical relationship between leader and followers.

Recognition and response to charismatic leadership are distinctive in yet other ways.[24] It is a nonformal style of leadership: relations between the followers and the leader are conducted on a personal basis that is not formalized in positions; thus followers respond to the leader by internalizing her ideas and definitions of reality. It is an inherently unstable style of leadership largely because of the intensity and quality of the emotional commitment by followers that involves devotion, awe, and reverence for the leader. Among the relations of charismatic leadership, there are no mechanisms for resolving conflict, which thus appears personal or "heretical."

In her study of five women's organizations in Latin America and the Caribbean, Yudelman reviews the pros and cons of charismatic leadership. Charismatic leaders represent their organizations effectively and they often have political clout. However, an organization can become identified with its charismatic leader, which impedes institutionalization. In addition to strong, emotional commitment on the part of organization members, charismatic leadership engenders informal management styles that lack "procedures for internal reporting, role definition, personnel evaluation and staff training." Such leadership also creates relationships within the organization that appear "personal rather than professional," and it unintentionally may give rise to "dependency, resentment, and internal conflict."[25]

In sum, Yudelman observes that women seem to have real difficulty creating and maintaining organizations that are "participatory, conflict-free *and* functional."[26] She suggests that underlying this problem is the high level of emotional commitment organization members feel toward charismatic leaders, making them demanding of themselves and critical of others. In contrast, Ferguson and Boulding root the apparent problem in obstacles to women's drawing on the relevant values arising from their caregiver relations, and Freeman identifies it as part of the so-called tyranny of structurelessness.

Feminists have begun to analyze the ways in which internal organizational structure, particularly the issue of hierarchy, can present obstacles to the pursuit of women's interests. Feminists have also struggled with the issue of how women's subordination connects to class inequalities.

In order to portray the complexity of women's lives and of social organization, feminist analysis must take fully into account the interplay of gender, race, and class. All women experience gender subordination, but gender relations have "race-specific" and "class-specific" dimensions as well.[27] The various inequalities interact to condition the particulars of women's lives. For example, a working-class, lesbian *mestiza* experiences female oppression in specific ways.

Although wide recognition exists of women's experience of oppression other than gender subordination, the relations among them have not been thoroughly elaborated. For example, feminists acknowledge class divisions, but, in Bunch's view, they have little understanding of the significance or the consequences of class for feminist activism.[28] As another example, it appears to be easier to reveal the exclusion of women of color from women's studies than to demonstrate how working-class women have been marginalized in the discipline.[29]

Class distinctions are in a mutually reinforcing relationship with male-domination. Class relations structure the concrete meaning gender has for women, and male-female relations condition women's experience of productive activities. Moreover, the class system puts some women in positions of power relative to other women and thereby weakens all women in their struggle against domination.[30] How can feminists act on common interests as well as embrace a diversity of actors?

First, women do share interests that transcend class lines (and color lines) around which they can organize and which can inform the agenda of women's organizations. These include the gender-based division of labor, patriarchal authority, personal aspirations, and the need for self-respect.[31] Yet, in women's diverse experiences feminists gain a more complete understanding of complex systems of domination and of obstacles to be overcome for treatment as equals.[32] Historically, however, those people in the most privileged positions in society have presented difference as a threat to the situation—even survival—of the group. That is, they transformed diversity into a tool for maintaining domination.

Middle-class women clearly benefit from the class system. Through struggles against their own oppressive behavior as well as against oppression in society, they can relieve their responsibility for their class privilege. This can begin with the recognition that one does not need a college degree to "see political solutions to personally experienced problems." Class supremacy views working-class women as less personally "evolved" or politically "savvy" because they do not act and talk the way middle-class women do.[33]

A diverse and inclusive feminism that forgoes the security of familiarity will allow women to see how the individual's struggle links to a wider struggle shared with women who are different. Personal experience is political, and it is shaped by the sociocultural system. It alone does not suffice as a basis for feminist analysis and action, however. Pushing beyond the limits of personal experience and learning from the diversity of women's lives is crucial to the struggle against domination.[34]

The Women in Development (WID) literature adds the dimension of nation to relations of class and race when studying women's situation. Attending to inequalities other than female subordination illuminates the reality that women share various experiences based on gender. Analyses inspired by the U.N. Decade for Women, especially those by Third World women, illustrate both women's differences and the common interests among them.

Development Organizations and Development Strategy

Writing at the close of the women's decade, Sen assesses the beginnings of the process of empowering women In developing countries and empowering women's development organizations to oppose gender oppression as well as the oppression of class, race, and nationality.[35] She, as well as Staudt, argues that the nature of the task involves both an ongoing process of self-empowerment among women *and* their making demands collectively on governments and other bureaucracies for wider changes.[36] Thus, to create effective change organizations, women must tie together a process orientation and values from their daily experience with knowledge and skill development and leadership formation.

Sen outlines issues that continue to challenge women's development organizations: reluctance to propose development programs for society from women's perspective; an unrealized potential of allying with other grassroots organizations; the problematic nature of relations with bureaucratic structures (agencies and governments) that are vital to effecting gender redistribution; innovative ways of delegating authority and responsibility that do not perpetuate relations of dominance and subordination; developing styles of conflict management and resolution within a democratic process.[37]

The last point—conflict in women's organizations—remains a central challenge. However, in her analysis of what five women's development organizations do well, Yudelman illustrates how they are meeting some of the other challenges Sen presents.[38] That they organize and mobilize women and enhance their self-worth and capacity for self-help is clear. They are also attempting to connect with larger frames of reference—that is, to see the "big" picture. Indeed, women's organizations have used political clout to bring about policy changes and are beginning to network with other organizations.

Yet, women's organizations remain constrained in ways that hinder their responses to certain challenges. Two constraints Yudelman identifies are the sometimes hostile cultural climate in which women's development organizations operate, especially regarding women's proper role, as well as their pervasive need for funds. As these organizations have grown, their loose structures and informal management styles (once strengths) now present problems as well—among them difficulties in dealing with donor agencies.[39] Finally, relations of leadership and power remain ambiguous as women struggle to create new forms for organizing for change.

Against this backdrop" I examine a women's development organization in northern Mexico in terms of the ways in which issues of class relations and hierarchical structures arose in the organization and influenced its functioning. A few comments about Mexico's development strategy provide the larger context for this analysis.

One troubling aspect of many Third World state development strategies has been the use of women's low-cost labor to transform the economy.[40] In a comparative analysis of development strategies and the status of women, Leahy concludes that, although Mexican women could offer an abundant source of cheap labor, "the political and economic costs of fully utilizing this labor would be great."[41] In Mexico's northern border region, tens of thousands of women have been drawn into the new international division of labor as low-cost assembly workers for transnational corporations. No thoroughgoing account of the consequences of this process yet exists.[42]

The *maquiladoras*, export-oriented assembly plants of Mexico's industrialization program, constitute a key element in the nation's development strategy.[43] Approximately 1,000 plants with close to 250,000 assembly workers (and about another 50,000 administrators and technicians) are currently operating.[44] For twenty years the *maquiladoras* have been employing predominantly female labor to work in factories assembling garments and electric or electronic components for subsidiaries of (mainly) U.S.-based corporations,. The vast majority (90 percent) of these plants have been located in the northern border regions. By the mid-1980s the *maquiladora* industry had become Mexico's second most important producer of foreign exchange after oil, although still only about 5 percent of the total.

The organization that is the empirical case in this analysis emerged in response to perceived problems arising from,the influx of women into the wage labor market created by the *maquiladoras*. The problems raised most often with the *maquiladoras* are the absence of significant linkages to the Mexican economy, vulnerability to and dependency on swings in the U.S. economy, and the exploitation of women's labor and the consequent disruption of traditional Mexican family relations. The Women's Center arose out of the last concern.

Egalitarianism and Participation in a Mexican Women's Organization

The Women's Center is a grassroots development organization concerned with equality and democratic participation. The analysis presented here is based on systematic observation of the organization over a period of about twenty months—from the fall of 1982 through the spring of 1984.[45] In what follows I examine how class, absence of hierarchy, and charismatic leadership (which characterized the center in earlier years) affect organizational functioning.

Inequalities of Class and Egalitarianism

Class relations have been a factor at the Women's Center since its inception in the late 1960s. A group of relatively privileged women, acting on their sense of social responsibility toward those less fortunate, formed a small philanthropic institution to assist the growing number of women in the *maquiladoras* who were confronting the dual roles of wage earner and family member. Their initial concern was with the morality of women swept up in the rapid industrialization created by the establishment of export-oriented assembly plants in Cd. Juarez. In their view, these young factory workers needed guidance to maintain the high moral standards of the traditional Mexican women's role.[46]

To the founders' credit, as they become more directly involved with women workers and listened to the concerns those women expressed—about the loss of sense of self that results from being an appendage of a machine and the need to rediscover dignity and value—they moved toward collaboration with the *maquiladora* women to create a center responsive to workers' own perceived needs.

Nonetheless, the nature of the center's genesis was such that little impetus existed for organizing women to force change in the conditions of the workplace; instead, the broad project of the center has been more ameliorative: to enable women to cope constructively with the fact of *maquiladoras* in their lives and to develop and channel women's potential as community change agents. Such a project is more in line with the upper middle-class location of its founders, which is not to imply, however, that the organization's activities do not speak to real needs of working-class women. Evidence that they have is discussed below.

The center's objectives, articulated in 1978 in a proposal to a U.S. donor agency for funding, included: providing counsel to the *mujer obrera* about her changing role as a woman and an employee; helping her resolve personal, family, and work-related problems; helping her understand her reality and her potential role in society; promoting solidarity, participation, social responsibility, and openness to change; and channeling the working woman's *inquietudes* (anxieties) toward community-related activities.

The activities of the center's twenty-two staff members—seventeen of whom were women and half of whom had previously worked in the *maquiladoras* themselves—operationalized these objectives. A general understanding of the center's purpose—education and development of women, especially factory women—guided their daily work. Staff members believed they had a clear sense of the needs of women to which the center should respond. But this was not a unified sense: some advocated preparing women workers for better jobs, and others, taking a more abstract view, emphasized enhancing women's understanding of the world.

Without benefit of formal input from factory women regarding the center's programming, the legitimacy of the staff's assessment of women's needs as well as the center's claim to be a workers' organization rested on the members' own working-class experience. Some viewed this as the only valid experience on which to base the creation and carrying out the center's project. This extreme position created a climate of "anti-intellectualism"—intellectuals being those who had no direct experience in the *maquiladoras* but who studied the situation in other ways—and gave rise to contradictions for some of the "workers-turned-intellectuals" on the staff.

The upper middle-class, graduate school-educated director ably deflected criticism of her own background by emphasizing to the staff the weight their experience carried in defining and implementing the center's activities. The result was further support for the anti-intellectual position. However, more problematic was the hint of paternalism it revealed, for practical manifestation of this position is an orientation, common among staff members, focused on helping factory women rather than on empowering them.

Although it is reasonable to raise the issue of the degree to which staff members themselves were empowered in their relations at the center, their helping orientation can also be traced to the institution's origin, which has been a continuing influence on the center's fundamental project.

Analysis of the formalized curriculum offered by the center reveals more about this issue of women's empowerment. It also illustrates that women's concerns do, indeed, cut across class lines. The process of *concientización*, embedded in Paulo Freire's approach to education and adopted by the center, leads factory women to question their situation as women.

The curriculum in use contained some radicalizing material, but the scenario most often presented was not one where class-conscious *maquiladora* workers act on their common interest against the dominant interests. Rather, it was a reformist scenario in which socially conscious women organize themselves to ameliorate the conditions of their lives and their communities. Reform and radical messages were both conveyed in the curriculum, but the course neither purposefully promoted ideologically inspired activism nor detailed strategies for effective reform—in terms of what does and does not "work" and how women can organize to influence the system.[47]

With only a fragile, newly found sense of empowerment, the women found that the result of the course was frustration, at times, and, in the extreme, immobilization, as they were presented with a complex reality they possessed few tools to change. Yet, personal transformation of women who participated in the center's courses has always been evident.

Through experiences at the center, factory women have gleaned an awareness of their rights as women and thereby begun to undermine the patriarchal relations within which they live. They have developed a more self-assured style based on enhanced self-respect. They aspire to be autonomous, equal actors having an effect on their world. Though male dominance, the devaluing of women, and artificial limitations on women's potential are all conditioned by class position, it is also the case that all women share these gendered experiences. The center's programs enabled working women to analyze their situation as women and start to grasp how the "personal is political."[48]

Factory women came away from the center with a foundation for the ongoing process of self-empowerment. However, strategies for making demands for wider changes in the institutions that shape their lives, such as government bureaucracies or work organizations, remained obscure to them. This was due, in part, to the nature of the center's fundamentally ameliorative project. It was also an outcome of problems with the center's own organizational structure and style of management.

Participation and the Consequences of Charisma

The center's organizational structure was characterized by the absence of hierarchy, an expression of its democratic and participatory ideals. The structure was simple: a director assisted by a relatively undifferentiated staff; an advisory board existed but played no significant role. Beneficiaries compose an additional element of the organizational structure, but to begin with, this analysis pays attention primarily to center staff.

By definition, the informal management style that accompanied this organizational structure lacked specific procedures. Nonetheless, staff members did make internal reports: over half the staff reported on an almost daily basis to the director—verbally, not in writing. And though staff members did learn new skills, the most valuable training experiences were limited to the privileged few with whom the director worked very closely. Because organizational role definitions were not precise and no formal procedures existed, personnel evaluations were fated to be personalistic.

The primary basis for relations in the organization, then, was personal rather than positional—as exemplified by the informal management style. At one time this had been a strength, and there is no intent in this critique to suggest that staff members should be reduced to instruments merely for the use of the organization. However, as the center increased its dealings not only with the bureaucracies of the state and of industry but also international donor agencies, elements of the informal management style became liabilities.[49] The organization grew, and its tasks became more complex. This intensified the need for precise specification of tasks and responsibilities so that operations were rationalized rather than based solely on "good" personal relations.

Problems arose in the organization because job descriptions were vague and did not really reflect what staff members were doing. Thus, structurelessness, in the sense of little clear delineation of tasks, meant *not* that nobody was responsible for anything but that everyone became responsible for everything. That, in turn, led to serious overextension of some staff members and to their inevitable exhaustion. However, no mechanism existed to address the personal inequities resulting from organization structure, and the frustrations felt were further complicated by the importance of maintaining good personal relations in the organization. It does not seem an overstatement to assert that staff members were often victims of the tyranny of structurelessness.

The center's management style, which led to many of the problems of structurelessness, was conditioned by the nature of organizational leadership. Among the founders was a charismatic woman who became the organization's director and remained in that position until 1984. As a person with extraordinary qualities, she elicited strong commitment from the staff, who internalized her definition of the situation of women in the *maquiladoras*. She was illustrative of the leader who derives her right from people's conviction that they must follow her dutifully because of her mission. Her nearness to divinity in the eyes of the others was revealed when she suffered an apparently life-threatening illness that was followed by a medically inexplicable recovery, an episode that occurred toward the end of the evaluation on which this analysis is based.

Charismatic leadership is both a nonformal and an inherently unstable leadership style. For example, as happened at the center, the strong emotional commitment elicited by a charismatic leader made organization members more demanding of themselves and more critical of their colleagues, which led to internal conflict.[50] Complicating matters in this case was the importance of maintaining a personable work environment: in contrast to the *maquiladoras,* where workers were merely cogs in the wheel, relations between the director and the staff and among staff members were highly personalistic. Such a situation is not conducive to confronting and resolving conflict. Thus, not only was internal conflict very likely, it was also devastating, for the organizational relations associated with charismatic leadership contain no provisions for the constructive handling of conflict.

The case examined here contributes little to a comparative analysis of whether women's organizations have greater difficulty resolving conflict than do men's organizations. However, what observation of the center did demonstrate is that "it is as difficult to *remain* a democratic organization as it is to *create* one."[51] Without models for participatory and egalitarian organizational forms that operate through processes other than maintaining "good" relations (nothing in the hierarchical Mexican patronage system offers guidance), the charismatic director and the staff "ad hoced" an organizational form and process that limited effectiveness and ultimately exacerbated conflict.

In a change-oriented workers' organization such as the center, empowerment should be an ongoing and deliberate process. However, charismatic leadership comprises few of the elements of empowering leadership. Although charismatic leaders can articulate issues and mobilize people around goals (certainly true in this case), organizations, in turn, become identified with and dependent upon their charismatic leaders.[52] Leadership succession at the center became an ambiguous and highly charged issue.

The male pattern of the leader's choosing his successor, as in the succession to the Mexican presidency, provided the most visible model.[53] Though rejecting that process but still groping for a way to transfer power, the center never confronted the issue thoroughly. It was typically met with dismissive statements to the effect that "of course others are capable—the workers can run the center." Ultimately, the charismatic director departed and the organization experienced a diaspora.[54]

The dynamics of the center offer a lesson in the difficulties of empowerment and moving with others in self-empowerment. Specific aspects of the center's structure and processes acted as obstacles to actualizing the image of a nonhierarchical and participatory organization that empowers women.

Formal staff meetings were not scheduled regularly, and when they were held, they were more often reactive to some crisis rather than proactive. As center activities became more complex, the informal management style exacerbated problems already existing because information was centralized in the head of the director. Thus, because the director was the primary source of staff information about the center's ongoing work and she called meetings irregularly, staff members experienced considerable fragmentation of knowledge regarding organizational activities.

Few of them were able to articulate an integrated overall picture. In a sense, the anti-intellectual climate, with its emphasis on knowledge through direct experience, also limited the "sources" on which staff members could draw to explain the ways in which more recent projects were linked to the center's basic project of working with factory women or to elaborate the role of the center in the broader process of social change in the city or the region. This suggests the limits on the degree of empowerment experienced by staff members.

Yet, despite the irregularity of staff meetings, staff members did believe that they had a say in the organization. Unstructured observation and observation of center meetings revealed that the most influential and active participants from the staff were those people who had greater personal resources, such as more education, and who worked on a daily basis with the director. Meetings were periodically called to brainstorm about the organization and its activities, but little evidence exists of a fundamental role for staff members in defining the basic project of the organization. On the other hand, all center activities were undertaken by staff consensus. However, giving approval is not the same as empowerment.

The center's informal management style, based on charismatic leadership, engendered two interrelated problems: internal conflict became destructive in the absence of rules or strategies for confronting dissent, and without specific provisions for staff development, staff members were not empowered in their relations in the organization. Few staff members were prepared practically to take on responsibility and authority, and we must ask whether greater staff empowerment might have enhanced members' ability to advance the self-empowerment of the women the center served. Finally, with neither a forum, nor any creative means available to the staff for managing and resolving conflict, high expectations and emotions contributed importantly to the center's virtual dissolution in 1984.

The director now heads an organization that carries out research. She has little formal contact with the center where, during the last few years, a core of staff members has undertaken various activities. Their organization will doubtless comprise a new form and processes. What can be extracted from earlier experiences that should inform the center's re-emergence?

Conclusions

Organizations opposed to hierarchy, especially those that strive to be egalitarian and participatory, struggle with particular problems. This study reveals that the issues of leadership and conflict resolution emerge as critical challenges confronting women's organizations as they attempt to create alternatives to bureaucratic domination. Although the center did not reproduce a "gendered" form, women's empowerment was limited because the organization did not find—in the maintaining of good relations under the wing of a charismatic leader— a workable alternative to dominance. Some aspects of organizational relations still reflected politics as men play it in the Mexican bureaucracy. Is it possible that rooted in women's experience are keys to resolving these difficulties and to creating democratic organizations?

Linking concepts and observations, I first draw out insights into hierarchy and empowerment to be taken from this analysis.

Structurelessness has been one response by women's organizations to the negative assessment of hierarchy. Although structurelessness implies attention to process, the process in which organization members get involved seems to be one of personal accommodation rather than conflict resolution. Avoidance of risk and conflict—that is, accommodation—is rooted in values associated with women's subordination, not in the values of the caregiver/mother who empowers. (This is not to deny the obvious, that gender subordination conditions mothering just as class and race or nation do.) Although both are part of female experience, they have different implications for women's organizing. Women need to develop tools for negotiating as equals. Accommodation has not facilitated conflict management and resolution; empowerment holds out more promise for fulfilling the democratic process in women's organizations.

Leadership by women can also be understood over against bureaucratic hierarchy. Any power the bureaucrat possesses is conditioned by her position in the bureaucracy. In contrast, the charismatic leader (common in women's organizations) exercises power because people feel a duty to follow her. Women's organizations have rejected hierarchy as perpetuating inequalities and limiting potential, but charisma engenders crisis management and highly emotional commitment, which have proven to be organizational liabilities of a different nature.

An alternative conceptualization of leadership is the ideal of the reciprocal (group to leader and vice versa) empowerment of rotating feminist leadership. Part of women's organizing project must be to develop ways of delegating authority and responsibility that do not involve relations of dominance and subordination and that do allow efficient accomplishment of tasks and effective promotion of women's interests.

Class divisions form part of the basis for bureaucratic hierarchy and organizational inequality, and the argument is compelling that equality in organizations, including women's organizations, cannot be achieved without more equality and the end of class divisions in society. Nonetheless, women's capacity to reform organizations that are change oriented can be enhanced. And in working on that task, we can clarify the connections between gender subordination and inequalities that are due to class position (as well as race and level of national development).

All women as women share common interests around which to organize and mobilize, but women of relative privilege, especially, must guard against constricting the meaning of women's empowerment to gender relations alone. The other inequalities women experience condition the concrete meaning of gender. Development organizations enabling women's empowerment must confront all sources of women's subordination, for they are interconnected. To do that will require tremendous resources, but only then will women be treated as equals in society.

Notes

1. This is a premise of Sally Yudelman, *Hopeful Openings: A Study of Five Women's Development Organizations in Latin America and the Caribbean* (Hartford, Conn.: Kumarian Press, 1987).
2. Ibid., p. 3.
3. Ibid.
4. Elise Boulding, "Female Alternatives to Hierarchical Systems, Past and Present: A Critique of Women's NGOs in the Light of History," *Women in the Twentieth Century World* (New York: Sage, 1977).
5. Argued most notably by Kathy Ferguson, *The Feminist Case Against Bureaucracy* (Philadelphia: Temple University Press, 1984).
6. Within the context of an analysis of the U.S. Agency for International Development, this is argued by Kathleen Staudt, *Women, Foreign Assistance, and Advocacy Administration* (New York: Praeger, 1985).
7. Ferguson, *The Feminist Case.*
8. Boulding, "Female Alternatives."
9. Ferguson, *The Feminist Case,* p. 25.
10. Recent political events in Mexico notwithstanding, "the rules of the game" are elaborated in Peter Smith, *Labyrinths of Power* (Princeton, N.J.: Princeton University Press, 1979), esp. pp. 242–78.
11. Boulding, "Female Alternatives."
12. While recognizing that mothering is "implicated" in the creation and maintenance of male domination—see Nancy Chodorow, *Mothering* (Berkeley: University of California Press, 1978)—we must remember that the relations of mothering also comprise other attributes, as discussed below.
13. Jo Freeman, *The Politics of Women's Liberation* (New York: David McKay, 1975), esp. p. 105.
14. Charlotte Bunch, "Woman Power and the Leadership Crisis," *Passionate Politics* (New York: St. Martin's, 1987), pp. 122–33.
15. Staudt, *Women, Foreign Assistance and Advocacy Administration.*
16. Bunch, "Woman Power."
17. Sources of more elaborate discussions include ibid, and Freeman, *The Politics of Women's Liberation.*
18. Jackie St. Joan, "Female Leaders: Who Was Rembrandt's Mother?" In *Building Feminist Theory: Essays from Quest,* ed. Charlotte Bunch (New York and London: Longman, 1981).
19. Bunch, "Woman Power," p. 128.
20. More on shared leadership can be found in ibid.
21. Freeman, *The Politics of Women's Liberation,* p. 123.
22. Bunch, "Woman Power," p. 125.
23. The analysis by Max Weber on which this discussion is based appears in H. H. Gerth and C. Wright Mills, *From Max Weber* (New York: Oxford University Press, 1946), esp. pp. 245–52.

24. Ann Ruth Willner, *The Spellbinders: Charismatic Political Leadership* (New Haven: Yale University Press, 1984).

25. Yudelman, *Hopeful Openings,* pp. 98–99.

26. Ibid., p. 100.

27. Maxine Baca Zinn, Lynn Weber Cannon, Elizabeth Higginbotham, and Bonnie Thornton Dill, "The Costs of Exclusionary Practices in Women's Studies," *Signs* 11, no. 2 (1986): 290–303.

28. Charlotte Bunch, "Class and Feminism," *Passionate Politics* (New York: St. Martin's, 1987), pp. 94–102.

29. Baca Zinn et al., "The Costs of Exclusionary Practices."

30. Bunch, "Class and Feminism," pp. 94–95.

31. Myra Marx Feree, "The Women's Movement in the Working Class," *Sex Roles* 9, no. 4 (1983): 493–505.

32. Baca Zinn et al., "The Costs of Exclusionary Practices."

33. For more examples, see Bunch, "Class and Feminism," and Feree, "The Women's Movement in the Working Class."

34. The significance of diversity is presented in Charlotte Bunch, "Making Common Cause: Diversity and Coalitions," *Passionate Politics* (New York: St. Martin's, 1987), pp. 149–157, and Baca Zinn et al, "The Costs of Exclusionary Practices."

35. Gita Sen, *Development, Crisis, and Alternative Visions: Third World Women's Perspectives* (New Delhi: Development Alternatives with Women for a New Era, 1985).

36. Staudt, *Women, Foreign Assistance, and Advocacy Administration.*

37. Sen, *Development, Crisis, and Alternative Visions.*

38. Yudelman, *Hopeful Openings.*

39. Ibid.

40. Kathleen Staudt, "Women, Development and the State: On the Theoretical Impasse," *Development and Change* 17 (1986): 325–33.

41. Margaret E. Leahy, *Development Strategies and the Status of Women* (Boulder, Colo.: Lynne Rienner, 1986).

42. The most up-to-date bibliography is Leslie Sklair, *Maquiladoras: Annotated Bibliography and Research Guide to Mexico's In-Bond Industry, 1980–1988,* monograph series, vol. 24, Center for U.S.-Mexican Studies (La Jolla, Calif.: University of California at San Diego, 1988).

43. Gay Young, "The Development of Ciudad Juarez: Urbanization, Migration, Industrialization," in Gay Young, ed., *The Social Ecology and Economic Development of Ciudad Juarez* (Boulder, Colo.: Westview, 1986).

44. These estimates are projected from data provided by the Direction de Investigation Económica, Banco de México, Serie Documentos Intemos, "La Industria Maquiladora de Exportation (1980–1986)."

45. Chosen by the center's director, a Mexican counterpart and I took the lead in an evaluation of center activities funded by one of the center's donor agencies. In addition to offering

programming for approximately 100 women workers—a program that included the "basic course," training in areas of paraprofessional employment, and community service/action research—the center also administered three cooperatives and four basic education centers (for school dropouts eleven to fourteen years old) during the period covered by the evaluation.

Nonetheless, almost every staff member was involved in the Women's Program in some way, either as her or his main job or in addition to the main job. The course director drew on other staff members (as well as the center director) as lecturers, discussion leaders, instructors in the areas of specialization, leaders of action research teams, and more. She even called on members of the small office staff, who beyond their typical clerical duties also had the task of assisting the many visitors (practitioners and scholars) attracted to the center. Staff members assigned to coordinate the workings of the various coops as well as to ran the basic education program also played roles in the program for women workers. Finally, a group of staff (varying from two to four members), generally referred to as the Research Department, carried out descriptive analysis of data collected from program participants and clipped newspapers stories bearing on the *maquiladoras in* addition to their responsibilities in the Women's Program; two of them were given the job of working with us on the evaluation.

This analysis relies on all of the observational strategies employed in the evaluation— relatively unstructured observation of day-to-day activities, a field experiment comparing women in the course with other women in terms of course aims, and hours of interviews about the center with community and labor leaders, direct beneficiaries of the center's work, and with the staff and director. At the risk of oversimplification, the emphasis of this work, in contrast to the larger evaluation per se, is on how the organization operated rather than what it was doing and how well.

46. This is taken from Maria Patricia Fernandez Kelly, "COMO: A New Frontier in Popular Education" (unpublished manuscript, 1985).

47. Kathleen Staudt, "Programming Women's Empowerment," in Vicki Ruiz and Susan Tiano, eds., *Women on the U.S.-Mexico Border: Responses to Change* (Boston: Allen & Unwin, 1987).

48. Gay Young, "Gender Identification and Working Class Solidarity Among Maquila Workers in Ciudad Juarez," in Riuz and Tiano, eds., *Women on the U.S.Mexico Border.*

49. A position also articulated in Yudelman, *Hopeful Openings.*

50. Observed as well by ibid.

51. Robert Wasserstrom, *Grassroots Development in Latin America* (New York: Praeger, 1985), p. 12.

52. Yudelman, *Hopeful Openings.*

53. Admittedly, the process may no longer be as clear-cut as presented in Alan Riding, *Distant Neighbors* (New York: Alfred A. Knopf, 1984), pp. 94–134.

54. This concept is used by Yudelman, *Hopeful Openings.*

PART III

WOMEN AND EMPLOYMENT
IN A GLOBAL ECONOMY

Chapter Ten

The Sweeper Women of Structural Adjustment, or the Feminization of Social Security

Christa Wichterich

Unpayable Labour

For years economists, ergonomists and publicists have been predicting that we will soon run out of work—even as a jobs miracle is celebrated in the USA or Holland. Far from being accidental, it makes theoretical and practical sense that it should be men who are striking up the requiem for the work society. When Jeremy Rifkin speaks of a coming 'world without work,'[1] he closes his eyes to the fact that nearly 70 per cent of work performed on this planet is unpaid: work, that is, in personal care and relationships, child-rearing and education, in homes, gardens and fields. This blindness to everything outside the market and money is the reflex of a totally earnings-centred economy.

The paid labour about which gentlemen speak, and which is treated in classical economics as the only productive and valuable form of work, is for women only part of a larger whole. For only a third of the work performed by women is paid; two-thirds is unpaid and left out of the economic statistics. In the case of men, the proportion is almost exactly the reverse. It is the merit of the United Nations Development Programme to have globally quantified unpaid female labour for the first time, in both time and money It is estimated at $11 billion a year—nearly half the total of world production, which is thought to be around $23 billion a year.[2]

These findings are confirmed by a time-budgeting study conducted by the German Statistical Office for the constituent states of the old Federal Republic. In 1992, it concluded, 77 billion hours of work were unpaid and only 47 billion paid. If every hour of housework had attracted DM 11.70, a total of nearly DM900 billion marks would have had to be paid out. Inge Rowhani-Ennemoser has calculated for Austria that, if all housekeeping and child-rearing work were converted into salaried positions, it would create more than the existing total of jobs held by women on the formal labour market.[3]

The Platform of Action adopted by governments in 1995 in Beijing, at the Fourth World Conference on the Status of Women, recommended that unpaid labour should be calculated in parallel to gross national product, so that its true extent could be made known and economically evaluated. The Women's Ministry in Bonn immediately stated that the money was lacking for another time-budgeting study.

The bulk of unpaid labour is assigned to women as if there were a natural law which said that it should be so. The economist Ingrid Palmer calls this the 'reproductive tax' that societies impose upon women.[4] The market economy externalizes the costs of its own reproduction by entrusting this to women as a labour of pure love. With their free labour, usually without Sundays or holidays off, women subsidize a market economy which itself operates according to quite different principles. For their 'care economy' is geared not to turnover, profits and growth, but to well-being and social security, living and survival. As the sociologists Veronika Bennholdt-Thomsen, Maria Mies and Claudia von Werlhof have argued, it is literally life-creating and life-preserving and oriented to subsistence. The market economy is bolstered and nurtured by the altruistic principles of this 'love economy' (Hazel Henderson) in which it is embedded.[5]

For decades, two tendencies seemed to be reducing the amount of unpaid female labour: the introduction of technology into the home, especially in the industrialized countries; and the public assumption of socially necessary tasks, both by the Western welfare state and by the socialist state in the planned regimes. The care-work thus transferred from private households was integrated into the labour market: unpaid labour was transformed into paid work.

Now this trend is being reversed. Rationalization is converting paid labour into unpaid labour. In the service sector, 'presumption' work, i.e. consumption-related work, increases: supermarket customers weigh their own vegetables and begin to scan the prices of their goods, bank customers take money from their account via automatic machines. New activities tend to cancel out the time saved through household appliances: parents are expected to help children more with their homework, and mothers to chauffeur them around between tennis clubs, piano lessons and visits to friends. The Freiburg Ecology Institute calculates that, despite the technological revolution in washing, no less time is spent on it today in German homes than in the 1950s—simply because there is far more washing to be done. Societies are falling back on unpaid work as on a natural raw material that can be appropriated free of charge.

The advances that women made towards equality in the former GDR and other 'actually existing socialist countries' mainly rested upon the extensive daytime facilities provided for children by the state. If 90 per cent of women could go out to work, this was only because workplace crèches and day-centres socialized childcare and released women for paid employment. The great difficulty of combining a job and a family is something new for women in Eastern Germany and elsewhere in Eastern Europe. When day-nurseries that used to be virtually free now cost DM500 a month and private lessons or holidays for children are also expensive, childcare inevitably wends its way back into the home. This, together with the waves of redundancies, is forcing many East German women into becoming full-time mothers and housewives. Their 'propensity to outside employment' has not changed—indeed, a mere 4 per cent consider a life only as mother and housewife to be desirable. Abstinence from child-bearing was the first reaction of women in the new states of the Federal Republic to this female variant of the 'unification shock,' birth rates falling by almost two-thirds. It was not that they had ceased to want children, only that they considered living conditions with children to have become much more difficult.[6]

The number of European women in paid work is highest in the countries where public childcare support is best: that is, in Scandinavia. In Denmark, where the government provides the most facilities for mothers and children, the proportion of childless women in paid work is almost as high as that of mothers with several children: 79 per cent.[7]

The state is 'a girl's best friend,' more dependable than diamonds and men. That, anyway, is what women thought for a few decades in the welfare systems of Scandinavia. Pre-school nurseries as well as midday meals for children of school age really made it possible for women to choose between staying at home and going out to work. As a result, Swedish and Finnish women could afford to have the highest birth rates in Europe.

Sweden is the only country in the world which takes the idea of equality so seriously that it tries to get fathers to spend a month full-time looking after their child. This month of childcare 'leave' can be taken only by the father, not the mother—otherwise the entitlement lapses.

The German concept of childcare 'leave' for pocket-money of DM600 a month effectively removes any burden from the father and drives the mother out of the jobs market. The father's prospects of career advancement and higher income, as well as the still widespread acceptance of gender roles, mean that 99 per cent of those taking childcare leave are women and only a derisory 1 per cent are men, and that even these often have to pay the price of employers' ill-will and career sanctions. This is in keeping with an economy that still operates under the model of one breadwinner and one supporting income. The woman's work at home among the family ensures that the husband is not troubled by anything other than his paid employment.

The financial crisis facing local authorities in Germany has so far prevented all parents from taking up their legal right to nursery provision.

And now the tighter labour market makes it more difficult for mothers to return to work after a break of a number of years. Every child is a 'labour market risk' unevenly distributed between mother and father.[8] It reduces the opportunities for women to get out of their full-time activity as unpaid reproductive workers. The gender division of labour remains in place.

Honour Where Honour is Due

The futurological visions to which we referred at the beginning of this chapter have one striking feature in common. Starting from the fact that there will never again be full employment for all, the experts turn their eyes on the unpaid labour they never previously noticed and call for a new distribution of paid and unpaid activities.

The Olympian 'Club of Rome', for example, in its report 'The Employment Dilemma and the Future of Work', proposes the division of work into three spheres: one provided and subsidized by the state; one comprising a private market completely free of government regulation; and one located within an unpaid non-profit-making sector. Each and every one of us would be expected to take part in 'voluntary' activities, but the examples given by the Club of Rome are all of typically female tasks. In order to reduce hospital expenditure, relatives or friends of patients would take responsibility for tasks that have up to now carried a monetary remuneration. Similarly, 'grandparents' would be expected to step in and help out with childcare.[9]

Jeremy Rifkin imagines that, alongside the public and private sectors, both the unemployed and people on reduced working hours could fit into a 'third sector' of useful and publicly minded voluntary work. This emphasis on the value of unpaid work in the community, as well as on the associated redistribution of tasks, takes up a key feminist demand that has been around for several decades. What male futurologists leave out of account, however, is the whole issue of power between the sexes. Feminist theorists have constantly criticized the gender division between paid employment and the work of caring for the home and other people, and have seen a fairer distribution of paid and unpaid work between men and women as a way of overcoming inequalities of power.

As the communitarian eulogization of family and civil duties gained popularity in the United States, the conservative parties in Germany again put personal responsibility and public spirit at the centre of moral-political debate, at the precise moment when the state was abandoning the public interest and eroding the principles of the social-welfare state. Claudia Nolte, formerly the Christian Democrat minister for family and women's issues, rejoiced that more and more people in Germany—17 per cent of the total population—were willing to engage in some kind of voluntary work. In July 1997 she even brought to life a so-called Citizens for Citizens Foundation, whose use of the male form Bürger für Bürger in German ignored the fact that women make up two-thirds of 'volunteers' in the sphere of welfare activity and the churches, in homes and community care for the elderly, in hospices for the dying, in self-managed women's projects and cafés, and in self-run crèches.

To make voluntary work more visible and presentable, the Catholic Women's Community of Germany has introduced a certification booklet. Women can be found giving words of comfort or doing shopping for sick people in clinics, saving an old neighbour a trip to the city council or collecting fruit and vegetables and distributing them to homeless people after the supermarkets shut on Saturday. Whereas the women doing voluntary activity used to be mainly in the forty to sixty age group, more and more are now still at an age when they have young children to look after. 'Volunteers' step in and help out when local councils try to economize by reducing library staff, or when public baths are threatened with closure. The traditional male volunteers have been in the fire brigade, sports clubs and local community activities.

The media and education, as well as research, science and culture, are greatly subsidized by unpaid work. Many authors never see a penny for articles they publish in magazines and books. Numerous seminars, lectures and cultural performances depend upon work that is done for nothing or the merest pittance. Academics sometimes run teaching programmes without payment, for the sake of their reputation and for something to show on their c.v.

Many women do a spell of voluntary work on a project, then are given a job for a couple of years under some job-creation programme, and end up again doing unpaid work on it when the job-creation funding runs out. Such practices are widely regarded as a necessary preparation for a proper job or contract. In hospitals, for example, young doctors work a huge amount of unpaid overtime in order to obtain their specialist qualification.

An especially precarious field is the care of the elderly and chronically sick. In Germany, 1,125,000 people come under this category in private homes, and more than a million of them are looked after by friends or relatives—women providing the main care in 83 per cent of cases. A report by the Ministry for Family and Senior Citizen Affairs in 1992 showed that most carers of this kind did not have formal employment, 27 per cent had given up their job, and another 12 per cent had limited the number of hours they worked.

Public nursing insurance is far from being sufficient to cover the costs and relies upon family members or volunteers to fill the gaps, as Gerhild Frasch of Evangelical Women's Aid critically points out. For grade three of care need, assessed at DM 1300 a month, all a carer can obtain from monthly pension entitlements is DM34. Clearly we are not talking, then, either of wage compensation or of adequate old age insurance. Moreover, those who have to look after somebody for a long period often suffer from intense psychological pressure, social isolation and even psychosomatic disorders. Many women, Frasch remarks, have a whole 'life's history of care': first they bring up their children, then they care for their parents and parents-in-law and finally for their husband. All the time they are unable to save enough money to pay for care when their own health finally gives out.[10]

When the social system supposedly grows too expensive for the state, calls are heard for it to be 'democratized.' All parties aim to mobilize the hidden labour reserves of civil society in order to guarantee peace and order. The more holes appear in the social safety-net, the more volunteers (mostly women) are brought in as a stopgap to manage the crisis. 'Less state, more market'—the two pillars of neoliberalism—are supplemented with 'more work on one's own account' as a way of dampening potential causes of friction. A combination of voluntary work and cuts in social services appears as the integrated political model.

The Social State Discharges Its Children

Ronald Reagan and Margaret Thatcher must have been a dream couple for the theorists of free trade and privatization. Their programme of ridding the state of all costly ballast became the accepted credo in the industrial heartlands of the West. One government after another terminated the characteristic 'New Deal' combination of social-market economy and Keynesian welfare state. The state had proven to be an unreliable ally for women.

The Democrat Clinton completed the social reform started by the Republican Reagan. A living example of what this has meant is Martha, a seventeen-year-old black from Harlem who is pregnant for the second time, without a job, without an income and without a husband. All she has are $430 a month in welfare, two sisters, an aunt and a few friends and neighbours in a similar situation. Martha must feel really great now that, as the social reformers put it, she has been shaken out of her lethargy and freed of her dependence on the state. After two years on welfare she will have to take any job offered her—otherwise she will not get another penny. The state thus sets the limits of poverty by defining how long a person is allowed to be poor—a maximum of five years in a lifetime. When that time is up, there is no longer any right to public assistance.

Once again the United States is proving to be the land of unlimited opportunities—only this time it is opportunities for social downsizing. In the past two decades, poverty and social inequality have grown as social expenditure has been reduced. Twenty years ago, more than 80 per cent of the economically active population had a right to unemployment benefit; now it is only a quarter. This is mainly due to the transformation of stable employ- ment into insecure employer-employee relations. But the main reason why only 30 per cent of the unemployed actually draw benefit is the state strategy of 'chumming', the systematic practice of bureaucratic discouragement and bloody-mindedness. In this way the govern- ment escapes having to bear the social costs of its policies.

Women are hit twice over by the crisis in public spending: on the one hand, they make up the majority of welfare recipients; on the other, they have fewer job opportunities as a result of the cut in social services. For the state is one of their largest employers, and social or educational activities are their main fields of employment.

Since the 1970s young single mothers—mostly blacks and chicanas—have been the thorn in the side of those carrying out forced cutbacks. Treated as a national disgrace, they are supposed to go out to work and, for heaven's sake, not to burden the state with any more children. In 1991, shortly after the five-year contraceptive implant Norplant was approved for use, it was being discussed in the media whether it could serve as a means of 'combating black poverty' and 'reducing the number of social misfits.' In the state of Maryland, where such experiments were carried out in 1993 at schools for teenage mothers, the governor proposed to link welfare payments to acceptance of the contraceptive implant.

The governor was ahead of his time in thus making welfare conditional, but since 1 July 1997 it has been common practice throughout the country. On that day the federal system of social welfare, which dated back sixty-two years to the time of Roosevelt and the New Deal, was brought to an end by an act of legislation. In its place was to be a decentralized system in which the keyword was Work. This, above all, would bring about the necessary social discipline. Anyone who wouldn't play ball would no longer get any money; at most they'd be given food coupons and a bit of poverty relief. The French sociologist Loic Wacquant calls this a turn 'from the benevolent state to the punitive state.'[11]

The responsibility for welfare has thus been transferred from the federal government to the fifty individual states. Each one receives a derisory sum from Washington and itself decides who shall be entitled to benefits. 'The result' notes the *New York Times,* 'is a system evolving from a national safety-net into a series of state trampolines: They are better equipped to lift the needy into the job market.'[12] As welfare recipients are forced to perform low-paid work, the competition in that sector is expected to become considerably fiercer and to cause a further drop in wages. More money is not planned for vocational training.

Martha is afraid that she will only be offered the most menial jobs: sweeping the streets, or 'taking some big shot's dog for a walk,' or 'cleaning out their john.' For although she sat out a few years at school, she is practically illiterate. And without some educational qualifications she does not stand much of a chance. The state will take care of one thing for her: she can leave her kids at a day-centre when she finds a job. But there remains the question of health cover, which used to be provided by the Medicaid system. If she gets a job, she will hardly be able to pay for insurance out of her meagre earnings, and the employer's contribution has recently been reduced. So she and her children will join the 40 million Americans who currently have no health insurance.

In future, under-age people like Martha will be required to live with their parents on pain of having their benefit cut. But Martha has not seen her dad for more than ten years, and her mother, who does not have a grip on her own life, threw her out when she had her first child.

If Martha's children go to school in Harlem, they too will most likely end up only half-literate. For schools in the U.S. are mainly funded out of property taxes, and whereas rich districts and regions can afford to spend a lot per child, Harlem or other poor areas of the country do not raise enough in taxes to pay teachers well and to provide a good education. Social inequality and educational differences are thus reproduced at a higher level.

The street in Harlem where Martha lives is an expanse of not only social rubble. Every third house is unoccupied and completely dilapidated, with the windows boarded or walled up. In the last two decades, public housing funds have shrunk to less than a third of what they used to be, while spending on criminal justice has risen fivefold and on prisons twelvefold. The battle against violence and drug addiction—both of which increase with poverty and marginalization—has driven the number of prison inmates up to one-hundredth of the total population. Every third young black has been or is currently in jail, or is serving a suspended sentence on probation.

When the state has abandoned the goal of social justice and redistribution, forces in civil society are mobilized for damage limitation. Thus Bill Clinton called for an 'Alliance for Youth' and rang in a new 'era of community spirit'; two million young people are supposed to need voluntary 'mentors' to take them under their wing and stop them sliding into crime and violence.[13]

The demolition of the old social security system by the Clinton administration has been taking place alongside the deregulation of markets and the neoliberal withdrawal of the state from the economy. Both were precipitated by soaring public debt and massive pressure from capital for far-reaching liberalization. Governments loosened the reins that financial and social policy had fastened to market forces, and again disclaimed responsibility for social equality or for the creation of buffers between the strong and the weak in the highly competitive market regime. Deregulation does not mean that the global market functions without rules. Trade restrictions on goods and financial services may be overcome, but governments are introducing more and more rules to improve the free operation of business forces. This entails a long goodbye to the state's role as guarantor of social security and cohesion. More and more governments are becoming little more than backers of the private sector.

The growing power of 'global players' weakens the power of individual states for political or financial action, resulting in a general decline in the effectiveness of financial and social security policy. Huge fiscal holes appear in the coffers of the home states of transnational corporations, both because these companies transfer their profits in e-mail time to low-tax countries and because there are fewer people employed to pay income tax.[14] To make their country a more attractive location for investors, governments also offer sweetheart deals with juicy tax and subsidy breaks. Mass unemployment and rising pension payments meanwhile exert upward pressure on social transfer benefits.

Save, save, save is thus the guiding maxim of statecraft. Public assets are converted into money, public corporations are privatized, and public administrations are slimmed down. The state sheds responsibility for public welfare and wards off claims for redistribution; society is handed over to the market mechanism. As the elements of personal security are gradually privatized and commercialized, an exit from the social welfare state is presented as a necessary adjustment to altered market conditions.

In the industrialized countries, the scrapping of benefits is directed first of all against the unemployed and the elderly. For their numbers are growing as a result of mass unemployment and demographic changes respectively.

In Germany the policy of spending reductions is such that women are especially hard hit. Childcare time will no longer be covered by unemployment insurance. The long-term unemployed (70 per cent of whom are women in the new states of the Federal Republic) have to accept a three-hours travelling time to reach the workplace—an absurd proposition for mothers. At the same time, measures are being taken to ensure that women can be more easily kicked out of the labour market. There will no longer be protection against wrongful dismissal in firms with fewer than ten employees, and it is overwhelmingly women who are employed in such firms.

After the pensions 'reform', the level of pensions is due to decline proportionately, years spent in full-time education will count for less, and the retirement age for women will rise from sixty to sixty-three years. For women with a record of oscillation between family labour and outside employment, this could mean a halving of their eventual pension. In the old states of the Federal Republic, the average pension is currently DM 1800 a month for men but DM1000 less for women. Only 18 per cent of women, compared with 93 per cent of men, receive a pension above social welfare level.[15] The old demands of the women's movement—that every woman needs her own protection for old age, that basic pensions should no longer be linked to time in employment, and that women's paid and unpaid labour should be taken into account—have not been given a hearing in the current pension reform.

In 1995 figures produced by the Senate of Berlin showed that nearly forty thousand people over sixty-five in the city had to live on less than DM600 a month, and that nine out of ten of these were women. Not even a fifth of them were in receipt of social assistance.[16] This is what is commonly known as bashful old-age poverty. The 'reformed' future of pensions will mean that still more women experience old age as a time of shame and need.

Ursula Sottong of the National Council of German Women's Organizations raised the alarm that the welfare cutbacks are affecting women's health three times over: as patients, as employees and as carers in the family. In rehabilitation, for example, 40,000 new breast cancer patients each year fail to be given necessary aftercare and therapy. The planned closure of 200 rehabilitation clinics now endangers 25,000 jobs, 86 per cent of them held by women. The rehabilitation work in question will be taken over, if at all, by other women in the family, mainly on an unpaid basis.[17]

In many EU countries, the convergence criteria for the Euro currency act are acting as a lever for structural adjustment. In order to plug their budget gaps, governments are further cutting spending on the elderly and the unemployed, on health and childcare; economic stability is being prioritized at the expense of social security.

In this situation, those who can afford it try to minimize their risks by all manner of individual commercial protection: from insurance for legal costs through private security services to personal pension funds. In the United States, one and a half times more is spent on private than on public security services. The massive speculation of pension funds on the stock exchange has been prototypical of the marketization of social security. They float free, instead of being part of a social contract that redistributes social costs and benefits.

Farewell to Arab Socialism

Mokattam lies at the point where the capital city has been wrested from the desert. Hoda sits with her daughters outside her front door, among heaps of bulging plastic bags. She tears open one refuse bag of the wealthy after another, and the two girls help her to sort organic from non-organic waste. It is a binary system operated without gloves or masks, amid swarms of flies. The crumbs from the tables of Cairo's middle classes stink to high heaven.

In Mokattam, 25,000 people live off the waste of a metropolis of 11 million souls. With perfect organization, 30 per cent of Cairo's household refuse is transported here on donkey carts to be sorted by women. Men collect paper into towering balls, stuff tins and boxes into sacks to be resold, and use simple machines to shred plastic into pieces that can be recycled.

This small town, which is really a transit camp for urban refuse, is part of Cairo's informal sector. Hoda and her daughters appear in statistics as 'family helpers,' because the trade in refuse is in the hands of their husbands, as are the earnings from it.

There are no reliable figures for the number of women 'self-employed' or 'helping' in the informal sector. But one thing is beyond doubt. The sector is booming like no other, in every corner of Egypt.

Maisa El-Gamal, speaking for the International Centre for Economic Growth in Cairo, sees the future for women in the informal sector. 'Macro-economically, Egypt is already a near-miracle,' she enthuses in her elegant offices in Dokki, a top bourgeois district, as she refers to the country's annual growth-rate of 4.9 per cent. Then she adds with cooler objectivity, as if answering a questionnaire: 'Has the section living in poverty grown? Yes! Have many people lost their jobs? Yes! Is there hope that they will find other employment? Very little, because they don't have any qualifications.' By way of conclusion, the eloquent Harvard graduate coolly notes: 'Every problem should be multiplied with a high multiplier for women, because their starting point is much worse than that of men.'

So, in the short term, Maisa does not see any positive effects of privatization for women in Egypt. Nor in the medium term, she fears. But in the long term? Well, then the opportunities for women will improve thanks to the boom in the informal sector and small-scale industry—so long as more has been invested in 'human capital,' or, in other words, so long as women are better qualified.

The farewell to Gamal Abdel Nasser's 'Arab socialism' has not been made in gung-ho fashion. President Hosni Mubarak announced a 'cautious' programme designed to avoid social injustices and harmful effects on 'people with limited incomes.' His government has been pursuing privatization and liberalization in small steps, often in a zig-zag course. One of these steps is the adjustment of labour legislation to the needs of the free market.

Two proposals currently on the table are not exactly cautious as far as women are concerned; they would mean a straightforward loss of legal protection. The first would limit maternity rights to a maximum of two children, so that a woman having a third child would not be entitled to fifty days at home on full pay. The aim of this is evidently to reduce secondary wage-costs. The second measure, involving an offer of limited redundancy payments, is supposed to make early retirement at forty-five attractive to women, and would serve to slim down the public sector workforce. The government has committed itself, under the terms of an IMF structural adjustment programme, to slash the number of public employees by 2 per cent a year through early retirement and redundancies—after many years in which there has been a freeze on new employment.

As CAPMAS, the Egyptian Statistical Bureau, tersely puts it: 'Job opportunities are becoming fewer and fewer for both men and women, but especially for women. As usually happens in times of rampant unemployment, the answer that seems to offer itself most readily is to send women back to their homes.' Already in 1992, when the jobless rate was 17 per cent, four out of five of the registered unemployed were women.[18]

Since the 1950s the state has been the largest employer of women, 43 per cent of all 'economically active' women working in public administration and services or in state-run textile, leather, food and pharmaceuticals enterprises. Now the government wants little by little to offer most of its three hundred enterprises for sale on the stock exchange.

Only 14 per cent of economically active women work in the private sector, and as everywhere else they are concentrated in low-paid labour-intensive jobs that offer no further training or chances of promotion. Private employers do not stand on ceremony: they treat maternity leave and childcare as an 'occupational hazard' that makes female labour more expensive in the end.[19] This is why, according to a recent study, only 17 per cent of job offers in the daily papers are directed at women.

In agriculture, too, less work is available for women. Traditionally they have served as stopgaps to be used in emergencies. Thus, when a lot of men emigrated to the Gulf states in the 1970s, women and children replaced their absent husbands and brothers in the fields. But when the men returned in the 1980s, female employment fell back once more. Mechanization—in cotton farming, for example—is currently the major threat to women's chances of finding work.

As Maisa baldly states, the poor section of society has grown as a result of a shrinking labour market, declining real wages and rising costs of living. There is a clear correlation between poverty and gender in female-run households: 65 per cent of their members live below the poverty threshold, compared with only half that number in male-run households.[20] Poverty forces such women into a desperate search for ways to make ends meet. Paid labour is for them pure compulsion, not an opportunity; bitter toil, not self-fulfillment.

Domestic service, street trading or outwork—that is the range of possibilities open to them in the urban informal sector.

Only every third poor household has any kind of health insurance. In the 1980s the state's per capita expenditure on health fell by a third as structural adjustment programmes demanded an end to subsidies and a move to cost-cover principles. The quality of public health care dramatically worsened, while private doctors and clinics remained beyond the reach of the poor. Much better value, sometimes even free, are the small health centres attached to the mosques.

Poor women also turn to the religious community whenever the mutual aid system in their family or neighbourhood is too weak to bear the strain of an emergency. They are helped over the hurdles of everyday life—such as the purchase of school books or kitchen utensils, clothing or wedding festivities—by the informal credit system known as *gamaiyas*. For the public safety-net does not cover them, and non-governmental organizations reach only a few.

Just when the labour market is dumping women as so much ballast, when the public sector workforce is threatened with redundancy, and when cuts in social services and ensuing impoverishment drive people into the arms of religion, the conservative Islamist leadership pushes itself to the fore. 'The first, holiest and most important task of women is to be a wife and a mother. They should not disregard this priority. Only if they have free time left over should they then take part in public activities,' says finger-wagging Zeinab El-Ghazali, founder of the Muslim Women's Union. The Islamist agitator Youssef El-Badri is of the view that Islam permits women to engage in paid labour provided they do not compete with men, who should always take precedence as the family 'breadwinners.'

A survey of female college students from the lower middle classes showed a third who believed that women should go out to work only in cases of extreme need, and 21 per cent who would in principle not like to see women employed outside the home. Many regarded their own education mainly as a preparation for their future roles as wife and mother. Male students from this social layer also spoke in favour of women's education, but against their going out to work. Clearly there is a dilemma, then, between economic compulsion and religious values. For the more that middle-class living standards are squeezed, the greater is the pressure on women to make life more secure by combining paid with unpaid labour.

Adjusting to Adjustment

The 8th of August 1990 went down in Peruvian history as the day of the 'Fuji shock.' That evening, President Alberto Fujimori officially proclaimed a tough new economic policy of structural adjustment. Overnight the price of food and kerosene tripled, and petrol became thirty times more expensive.

It is estimated that by mid–1991 as much as 83 per cent of the population was no longer getting enough calories and proteins. More than 38 per cent of children suffered from malnutrition. Every fourth child in the countryside, and every sixth in Lima, died before reaching the age of five. The proportion of poor people in the population as a whole had risen from 40 per cent to 60 per cent.[21]

Not only was health spending massively reduced; now everyone had to pay for medical care, which used to be free. Public employees, doctors, nurses and teachers all went on strike, because they were unable either to live or to die on the little that remained of their previous salary. Vaccination programmes came to a standstill for lack of funds. And in the cholera epidemic of 1992, 2000 people paid with their lives—and hundreds of thousands more with severe illness—for the government's shock therapy. Tuberculosis also took on epidemic proportions, and there was an alarming spread of both malaria and dengue fever.

What saved the impoverished masses from famine, especially in Lima, and what saved the government from an insurrection, was the people's food kitchens organized by an estimated 100,000 women. In mid–1991 there were 800 such kitchens in the poor district of Villa El Salvador alone. An average of thirty women took it in turns to shop and cook, often supplying food from their own vegetable gardens. They also organized milk distribution to ensure that children had basic nourishment.

The more the state pulls out of social services, the more community tasks are taken over by groups within civil society, especially women doing voluntary work. They collect refuse, keep their neighbourhood clean and organize basic health care. For Virginia Vargas, founder of the Flora Tristan women's group in Lima, the increased significance of NGOs in recent years is a result of the state crisis in a context of unbearable social need. She sees women's NGOs as counteracting social fragmentation through impoverishment, and as constituting the most important 'subversive force' against an undemocratic state.

In the last few years, however, more and more women from the food kitchens in Peru have been forced to hunt for some source of income in the informal sector, because men have been losing their jobs and the number of women living alone has also been on the increase. The number of group members has thus declined, individual women have had to take on heavier workloads and the costs of retail purchases have shot up. The people's kitchens movement has become noticeably thinner on the ground.

The only possible source of income for women is in the already chock-a-block informal sector. Apart from the 10 per cent unemployed, 77 per cent of the Lima population capable of work in 1993 was active in the informal sector. What they earn there is usually below the subsistence minimum. The ILO calculates that 84 per cent of the 'new jobs' created between 1990 and 1995 in Latin America and the Caribbean were informal activities—and, it must be added, not enough to provide a living.[22]

Not only mothers but children as well have to contribute their mite towards the family's upkeep, mostly within the informal sector. School attendance—no way! Many girls have been working since the age of ten as helps in middle-class homes, usually twelve hours a day for next to nothing.

UNICEF already noted in 1983 that women and children in particular were paying a huge social price for structural adjustment programmes. World Bank and IMF loans, taken up by governments when their debt-ridden economy is already in acute crisis, act as a lever for this drastic treatment. Since the early 1980s they have followed a stereotyped pattern: devaluation of the national currency plus trade deregulation plus cuts in public expenditure. This is supposed to put the state's finances in order so that it can repay its debts on time, and to promote private sector structures more compatible with the world market.

In macroeconomic terms, structural adjustment has quite often been a success. Economic growth has been given a boost, most of all in Asia and least of all in sub-Saharan Africa. Microeconomically, however, at the level of the private household, the medicine has been bitter indeed for most of the population. Women have paid for the upturn with longer and more arduous workdays, by accepting the transfer of functions from the wider economy into their unpaid subsistence-oriented economy.[23]

To meet strong criticism of these social costs, the World Bank designed a second, 1990s generation of adjustment programmes 'with a human face' and a 'social dimension.' Social funds and action programmes were supposed to pick up and relieve the most severe cases of hardship. Nevertheless, 1990s–style structural adjustment is for many still without a safety-net to soften the overnight social collapse.

For Argentinian pensioners the shock came at the beginning of 1992. In the 1980s they had enjoyed advantageous state pensions, but pressure from the World Bank, IMF and international creditors led the government of President Carlos Menem suddenly to apply the guillotine. Nearly two-thirds of the three million or more pensioners had their income cut to only $150 a month. With a cost of living roughly the same as in the United States, this meant that they could not meet even half of their monthly food and housing expenses. People who had all their lives considered themselves middle-class, as teachers, government employees but also private sector workers, suddenly found themselves in the ranks of the 'new poor.' Pensions were now equivalent to just 10 per cent of real wages. 'They were having to discover how their life's plans could go up in smoke,' commented Nélinda Redondo, an expert on the problems of old age.[24]

Paula Duarte was one of many in Buenos Aires whose life's plans were destroyed. Instead of an old age spent in security, she had to look for a job to make ends meet. Life below the subsistence threshold was a humiliation that she escaped with the help of a nylon cord; twenty-two desperate older women followed her example. The President, however, does not feel qualified to comment on the rash of suicides; he is, as he puts it, 'not a psychologist.'

Poverty, the World Bank never tires of pointing out, is a 'transitional phenomenon.' In the FAO's sober diagnosis, however, adjustment has led to the creation of a 'new class' of poor people.[25]

Meanwhile the Argentinian economy has been growing, inflation has been brought under control, and stability is attracting foreign investors to the country. The jobless rate fluctuates around 17 per cent. Labour legislation has been made more flexible, so that companies can employ for two years without any secondary wage costs (a) women in any age group, (b) workers over the age of forty, and (c) disabled people and war veterans. Today's public services employ a total of 300,000, compared with a million in 1991. Women teachers, whose income has been cut by half, declared a hunger strike in May 1997. Of the 1.3 million people who receive social benefits, 77 per cent are women. The rift between rich and poor is widening; the old middle class has been impoverished. According to a joke doing the rounds in Buenos Aires, when the magician David Copperfield came to Argentina, he was full of envy and asked President Menem to teach him how a whole middle class could be made to disappear.

The Acrobatics of Survival

In 1992 Margaret lost her secretarial job at the Ministry of Agriculture in Nairobi. She had not exactly been overworked there, and her office had not been a model of efficiency, but that was how things were run. After she had been shown the door with a small pay-off, she was unable to find another office job and had no alternative but to plunge into the informal sector as a 'self-employed' worker.

Once a month she and two friends travel to the border with Tanzania to buy a few bundles of old clothes, more expensive than the rest because they contain a high component of jeans. The three then hire a taxi and, several times on their way to Nairobi, have to grease the palms of policemen who supplement their meagre pay with a special kind of road toll. For it is illegal to bring second-hand clothing into the country, at least for small fish like these three women with their six bundles. Such laws do not apply to the son of President Daniel arap Moi, for example, who has his own fleet of lorries to carry yesterday's European fashions to the farthest corner of Kenya and into neighbouring countries.

Back in Nairobi Margaret picks out all the denim shirts, dresses and trousers and sells the less valuable remainder to women in the small markets on the outskirts of the city. She charges US$1.50 for a girl's skirt, $2 for a shirt, $4 for a pair of trousers. You have to be highly specialized, Margaret says, or else you go under. But however specialized, she will never be rich. Her customers are students who have to think twice about every shilling they spend, for a short while ago their grants were reduced yet again. The problem of selling their goods is even greater for the group of women in her neighbourhood who, with the church's help, have bought themselves a couple of sewing-machines and now stitch together children's clothing. The cheap second-hand and third-hand competition means that they hardly stand a chance.

They, like Margaret, groan under the rising cost of living. Worst of all are the soaring prices for basic foods and transport. The cost of a matatu or shared taxi has been rising by 50 per cent a year, and the cost of unga (corn meal) and sugar by 20 per cent.

The capital city, to which Margaret came ten years ago from Siaya District near the Ugandan border, has been changing at breakneck speed. Traffic in the city centre forms one continual jam in which a growing number of BMWs and Mercedes are to be seen. Office towers and shopping malls have also been shooting up all around, with high-class shops full of imported goods and restaurants boasting international cuisine. A skyline mirror-glazed by property speculators towers over poor districts peopled by street children, corruption and crime.

Sociologists use the term 'dual city' to refer to this side-by-side proximity of rich and poor, yuppies and homeless, growth and decay, all marked by both globalization and localization. Banks, shopping centres and foreign corporations occupy the inner city. But the ghettoes are also growing denser through constant inflow from the countryside. Space is the valuable commodity: street traders are driven off the pavement; 'illegal settlements' suddenly catch fire and burn down during the night; the police close off an area of land that is shortly afterwards sold to the city council; apartment blocks rise up from nowhere.

'I hate the city,' Margaret says, but there is no way back to the country. For only here can she earn the money she needs to send her two daughters to school. And the girls' education is enormously important to her.

Recently Margaret again had the hope that one of her male acquaintances might just lead the long-awaited march to the altar. Wrong message. For her friends, too, she notices that it is more and more difficult to maintain a relationship or a marriage. First the mass migration from country to town, now the permanent economic crisis, have had a corrosive effect on social and family relations. It looks as if men are more than ever roving in a network of girlfriends, which is what takes the place of polygamy in the cities. Social certainties, just as much as material ones, are constantly breaking down. In the slums of Nairobi it is an ordinary daily event for someone to 'go missing.' A husband or lover leaves the shack one morning without saying a word and never comes back. He tries to find happiness somewhere else with another woman and another casual job. Children also 'disappear' in a world full of drugs, prostitution and crime, living in street gangs and perhaps turning up again a few months later in their mother's shack. Or perhaps not.

Brutalization of relationships, decay of the social fabric, impoverishment of emotions and the psyche: these costs of the spiral pulling down more than a third of the population are never picked up in the statistics. Charities and church organizations lament the growth of domestic violence in the slums of Nairobi, the accumulated frustration with life to which it gives vent, and the ever larger number of single mothers. The more that men shirk family responsibilities through migration and multiple relationships with women, the more important for the safeguarding of society are ties among female relatives and among women in the same neighbourhood. The break-up of the social fabric goes hand in hand with a feminization of social responsibilities for provision within the family.

The idea of a neighbourhood, in which women help one another, is itself a female concept. Men also have friends, but for them the crucial bond is the drinking of alcohol together, rather than mutual aid in everyday life.

What drives Margaret to despair are the rising costs of her daughters' education. They both live with their grandmother in the Siaya District, as Nairobi is too expensive. Fees, uniforms, reading material, exercise books, school maintenance contributions: they all cost more and more since the government introduced the 'cost cover' principle into health and education in 1989. Kenya is now one of seventeen African countries where a declining percentage of children ever start school and a rising percentage leave before the end. Despite this, schools are bursting at the seams because of the high birth rate in earlier years. New teaching staff are not being taken on, nor are new equipment and teaching material being acquired.

Last year Margaret could not get the fees together, even though she has a few sources of income apart from the trade in clothing. Fortunately her mother in Siaya could make up the deficit, by supplying the headmaster with maize from her own field in lieu of cash. She also has living with her, three children of a sister who died from AIDS. The children did not know where to turn, so she took them in. As in neighbouring Uganda, it is mainly the older women who try to pick up the pieces when a sister or brother or children die a tragic death of this kind.

To fall ill in Siaya is a catastrophe. At the district hospital all that is left is a skeleton staff of doctors and nurses to handle emergencies. Anyone who can keeps well away. The laboratory equipment is ancient and ramshackle. There are hardly any drugs, and no generator to take over during the frequent power cuts. Thus, it may happen that the medical staff is thrown into darkness in the middle of an appendix operation or a complicated birth.

As real incomes and the level of education and medical care all relentlessly decline, women mobilize all their reserves to make a little extra in the informal sector, whether by cooking beans for the building workers at a nearby site or by serving them at a bar in the evening. Women also cut costs in ways that make their unpaid labour more intensive: for example, they walk instead of catching the bus, or they cook with environmentally damaging charcoal instead of the more convenient, but also more expensive, kerosene. And women cushion their hardships in neighbourhood groups, where they try to make collective savings by careful management, to cultivate their fields in common, to sell their crops and put the proceeds into a pool from which each draws in turn. Since malnutrition became more widespread among the young children of Siaya District, women's voluntary groups have been organizing twice-monthly sessions in the villages to weigh babies and to give new mothers advice about breastfeeding. More and more often, women's groups also provide assistance at burials. For AIDS means there are young people dying in every family, and other members have to bear the considerable expense of a funeral ceremony. It is well known that not even death is free.

Women's groups are the nurses of society, the Sisyphean toilers on behalf of the community—literally from cradle to grave. Their self-help and neighbourly assistance is a collective response to impoverishment that is social as much as material. Although their damage limitation and poverty management is often unprofessional enough on the ground, they remain an expression of solidarity in an age when existing social structures are being taken apart. Cooperation takes place in immediate local surroundings, but it also goes beyond the limits of geographical proximity. Women living in the city take food from their mother's field and send money back to the country. If they have themselves become middle-class, they will often form support committees for their region of origin and provide the funds for a kindergarten, a health centre or a funeral service.

This collective everyday assistance shows that the welfare of society can be achieved only through multiple strategies which combine paid and unpaid, market and communal labour, publicly and privately funded, monetary and non-monetary services.[26]

Women's groups are part of an armada of forces within civil society that are seeking to fill the gaps in care left by the failure and withdrawal of the state. These forces range from unpaid informal groupings active in villages and slums through to major NGOs and charities which receive money from foreign public or private donors and which, in some cases, carry out extensive operations in a professional manner.

Patricia McFadden, a feminist from Zimbabwe, criticizes governments for seeking to convert women's groups into a 'charitable movement' that would take some of the burden off their own shoulders. Women who have already internalized responsibility are thus called upon to invest their 'natural' capacity for welfare activity as a public resource. Florence Butegwa of the WILDAF women's rights network in Zimbabwe hopes that women's groups will more and more come forward regardless as 'political actors and leading advocates of women's rights.'[27]

The activities of NGOs thus tend to be ambivalent: on the one hand, they are instrumentalized in ways that are self-exploitative and let the state off the hook; on the other hand, they are forces for autonomous action and greater democracy. The growing corruption of state regimes, together with their loss of significance as agencies of social equality and provision, have led to the hyping up of NGOs in recent years as the great hope for developments towards social justice. The creativity and improvisation characteristic of women's groups has thus given rise to a myth about women's supposedly inexhaustible power of survival. As well as failing to appreciate that structurally adjusted women also have limited time and energy, this myth falsely romanticizes the feminization of responsibility.

Voluminous bridal clothes swing surreally in the autumn sky between the branches of a tree. At the next stand, leather jackets and fur hats hang on scaffolding five metres high, and next to them a tower has been built of boots and padded shoes. The pitches are small in Moscow's Luzhniki Park, so it is only logical that the traders should build their displays skywards. A pitch costs 100,000 rubles (currently $15) a day, plus protection money. Luzhniki is one of the central trans-shipment points for imported goods, from cosmetics through clothing to food. Masses of people jostle one another in the narrow spaces between the stands, constantly squeezed aside by handcarts brimful of huge chequered plastic bags.

Chelnoki are a new type of trader who first appeared with perestroika. Commuting on jet flights to and from Turkey, Poland, India, China or Thailand, they may buy 200 kilos of goods, grease the palms of officials and customs officers, and then resell them at a fat profit. Seventy per cent of the chelnoki are women. Why? Natalya, who has been one for five years, does not bat an eyelid: women are simply cleverer and more supple in dealing with traders abroad and the authorities at home. Men could not handle money so well and would spend too much of it on booze. So Natalya's division of labour is that she commutes and he manages the selling at Luzhniki, with her help.

Those who, like Natalya, have developed good business contacts can also earn quite a lot. But their life is not without its dangers. Some of Moscow's thirty mafia circles are also involved in this commuter economy. And apart from women like Natalya who commute on their own account, others work on a commission basis for big merchants. Most of these women were originally victims of Russia's sea-change and the cull in public sector employment; they were among the 60 per cent of all economically active women who lost their job during the 'collapse.' But they anticipated which way the wind would blow and went into the lucrative import business. Highly skilled women engineers and technicians are also to be found in it.

The trading women who buy at Luzhniki commute at a national level. They transport the goods to small markets in Moscow, or by bus and train to more distant Russian cities. Throughout Russia the conspicuous chequered bags hold out a promise of imported goods and the expensive fragrance of the big wide world.

The third category of women traders stand guard at the metro entrance in front of Luzhniki Park; they are Muscovites who offer a dress, a child's snow-suit or a pair of socks as a bargain. They trade in what they have just snapped up at a favourable price, whether as a single item or by the dozen. For most of them it is a second or third job, coming after they have spent the early morning hours cleaning buses, or helped out with the mail, or put in a few hours as a secretary, telephonist or door-keeper. In the time of actually existing socialism, women earned on average 70 per cent of a man's income; today they pick up no more than 40 per cent at the end of the month.

There are also illegal traders; for example, the women who appear with shopping bags full of beer, cola and vodka, after the street kiosks with their ample supply of alcohol have closed for the day. They have no licence to sell and take to their heels as soon as they glimpse someone in uniform.

All these women are looking in the informal sector for ways to 'adapt' to the newly privatized conditions of market economy. According to official statistics, 39 per cent of those who obtain a licence to trade are women. 'The older the women are, the harder it is for them to adapt'; this was the rule of thumb discovered by Marina Malysheva, an expert at the Institute for Gender Studies. 'Those who don't adapt, sink into poverty.'

One who has not managed to adapt is Lena Lokteva. For thirty years she managed a club for amateur film-makers together with her husband, built a film library and travelled through the various republics of the Soviet Union organizing film festivals. 'My work was just everything to me, much more important than keeping house or consuming things. I was completely happy with the life we had.'

Perestroika brought a new way of judging her work: it had to be economically viable. And since the club had always existed to promote culture, not to make a profit, Lena and her husband were made redundant. At first she worked as a book-keeper, then got a job in a kindergarten for the equivalent of US$40 a month. In addition there was her mother's pension of $60. So there were $100 for four people, with $25 going on the rent and electricity.

In 1997 her mother died, and then quite suddenly her own husband. The funerals were expensive. Previously she had gone on holiday every year with her husband and son to the Black Sea; now she did not even have enough money to ring her friends there and tell them of her husband's death. How do they get by at all, in a country where most things cost as much as in Germany? Most of the time they eat bread and potatoes. 'We make the spuds nice and tasty.' She looks skinny and care-worn. What affects her the most is the fact that no one appreciates her thirty years of work. Cultural activity, her real specialism, is no longer in demand. She feels worthless.

Yulia and Tamara, on the other hand, are still young and would be quite happy to adapt. But Tamara's husband left her when he learnt that their second child was severely handicapped. Yulia has two children, a disabled husband, and a father-in-law in need of care. During the Soviet period, her husband worked as a restorer in the historical museum and sent letters critical of the regime to U.S. radio and television stations. As a result, he disappeared into a psychiatric clinic and was treated with mind-altering drugs. He has been severely depressed ever since. Yulia gave up her teaching job when the second child came along. But she is certainly not lacking in energy. 'I am the horse that pulls the cart in which my family sits,' she laughs. She wants to return to her profession when the young ones are a little older.

Russian society no longer has any shock-absorbers for women like Lena, Yulia and Tamara, who have to live in the direst poverty. The number of poor people in Moscow is estimated at 50 to 60 per cent of the population. Single mothers, because of the collapse of state childcare facilities, are clear losers in the new Russia.

However, it is old people who have paid the highest price for the transformation. 'What society has done to them is criminal. No one can forgive and forget it,' says Marina Malysheva. They saved all their lives and then lost everything in the hyperinflation. The measly pension of $60 a month is not enough to live or die on. It is a cheated and deceived generation. Old people used to have power in the family, and enough money to help out the younger generation. Now they depend on the support of the young adapters.

The resulting loss of authority and respect, and therefore of self-respect, is a traumatic experience. Women are a considerable majority in the older generation, since the doubling of alcohol consumption has dramatically cut male life expectancy to just fifty-seven years, compared with seventy-one years for women. The size of this difference is unique in the world.

Often the pension does not arrive for two or three months at a time. Many female pensioners clean eight hours a day for $40 a month, so long as their bent backs allow it. In the metro a partially sighted woman is begging for alms, led by her granddaughter; on the Arbat, the old commercial street, a babushka sings a melancholy popular song; and everywhere in markets and metro entrances, one sees old women offering a kilo of apples, two bunches of flowers, or a saucepan looking much the worse for wear. Gradually all their household goods are fetched out for sale—plate by plate, sheet by sheet.

The bitterness on their faces is nothing other than the shame of having to beg. For years many have not been able to afford any new clothes or shoes. Every winter not only hunger but also illness, and particularly toothache, hang suspended over them like the sword of Damocles. Public health care is lamentable, private facilities far too expensive. Old women in need of dentures have to wait two years to be treated in the state dental clinic.

'Shock therapy from above' is how university lecturer Olga Vershinskaya describes the passage from the age of provision to the age of private initiative. Formerly the state was 'father and mother rolled into one'—an unsustainable system, she says in retrospect. But today those who, for whatever reason, cannot fend for themselves in the market economy are mercilessly excluded.[29] 'It is like a postwar period, like the period after the Third World War,' suggests Elena Balayeva, who has also been made redundant and cast aside. She used to be a researcher at the Academy of Sciences, but the state no longer has the money for research. Now she is self-employed in the global academic market, and happy to have got a study grant from the Ford Foundation.

The amount of unpaid labour done by women has been sharply increasing, both at home and in society at large. 'We used to have a double burden with state support; now we have it without state support,' complains Marina Liborakina from the Independent Women's Forum in Moscow. Marina has herself cleaned floors at the hospital where her children were being treated. She calls this extra women's burden 'compulsory volunteering.' 'We are slowly catching on that the rundown in social services is not a passing trend,' for it is part of the deal negotiated between the Russian government and the World Bank.

This unpaid feminization of social provision is accompanied by the rebirth of a conservative image of women. In a general swing away from the values of actually existing socialism—against its collectivism, against the compulsion to work, and against the breakdown of family bonds—the media and the restrengthened Orthodox Church celebrate woman as mother and protectress of the home, as a stable pole in the midst of turmoil and collapse.

The penalty that women make society pay for the general loss of security is the falling birth rate, down by a half in the last fifteen years. Instead of 2.6 children, the statistically average woman now bears only 1.3. The number of abortions is twice as high as the number of births.

Men react to the new insecurity with growing violence against women in the family. At the workplace, sexual harassment is so common that many women seeking employment add to their small ads in the paper: 'No intimacies!' The daily hotline operated by the Institute for Gender Studies between 9.00 a.m. and 9.00 p.m. is never quiet for a moment. Women's groups are building a network of advice services throughout Moscow and in other Russian cities.

All these silent tragedies in every corner of the country—this erosion of old generational ties, this shrinking population, this increase in divorce, violence and crime—are known in the official rhetoric as 'unforeseen consequences of the transition to market economy.'

The growth of social inequality counts as another 'unforeseen consequence.' Ten per cent is the estimate commonly given for the dollarized class of 'new Russians.' This includes those businessmen who, in the days of perestroika, made the leap into the market economy by buying raw materials cheap in the state sector and selling them dear on the free market —in the United States, for example—one of the raw materials on offer being women. The new economy was reflected in the growth of corruption, and in those mafia circles which now control city politics and dictate prices. While every old woman is ashamed of her undeserved poverty, this new bazaar bourgeoisie shamelessly puts its power and affluence on display. The way in which drivers of the latest limos ignore red lights is a symbol of this demise of the old laws and regulations. The women of the globalization profiteers live in gilded cages, able to go out only with a bodyguard. They shop with dollars at Pierre Cardin in the outrageously expensive art nouveau GUM department store on Red Square, buy children's clothes with deutschmarks at Karstadt's, and fly off on holiday to five-star hotels in Tunisia or Spain, if they do not already have a house of their own in the South of France.

Between the impoverished majority and the obscenely rich New Russians, only a relatively small middle layer has come into being. The social architecture is thus completely different from that which has characterized most European countries in recent decades.

Typical of the new middle layer are the class of traders like Natalya, who have achieved a certain routine of life together with high profit margins, but also the class of book-keepers, bank staff and secretaries earning three to five times more than a public employee. Foreign companies are especially valued as employers: that is, they pay in dollars or marks. This 'generation of book-keepers' is both achievement-motivated and consumption-oriented.

How people feel about their future prospects in the market economy is directly proportional to age: the younger, the more optimistic. Marina Malysheva feels quite sure: 'The market system offers women greater choice in education, jobs and travel. They have good prospects—but only if they are young, mobile and energetic.'[30]

One woman who has successfully adapted to the market is Tatyana Andrejeva. She is boss and part-owner of Iltis, a firm specializing in computer software, management training and marketing advice. There is currently a lot of demand for such services, and the competition is intense. The young businesswoman has five permanent employees and ten contract workers. She studied physics and specialized in laser technology at Moscow's prestigious Technical University, which did research for the space programme and cooperated with the military-industrial complex. In addition, she completed a professional course in patent law. Highly qualified, highly motivated and still in her youth, she could sense the change in the air and applied for a grant from the German Carl Duisberg Society. She finished her practical training at various German corporations and at the medium-sized Iltis consultancy firm in Rothenburg. Then in 1993 she founded Iltis, Moscow. The business is doing well.

Tatyana is well thought of as a businesswoman, 'because everyone knows that a woman has to be especially good.' She and fifteen other businesswomen in Moscow have formed an association to exchange views about their special problems. Most of these other women are active in typically female areas, producing such things as cosmetics or educational videos for schools.

Nearly everyone who was a fellow-student of Tatyana's is today without a job, for neither space travel nor the military-industrial complex is in good shape. The men cling much more than the women to their prestige and fear that they will have to take a humbler position. 'Add some alcohol, and his personality is finished.' The women, on the other hand, feel responsible for their family and accept deskilling in order to put some food on the table. When asked who have been the losers from Russia's sea-change, they are in no doubt: 'Men.'

Winner Takes All, or the Splitting of Society

'Investments in women's health are undergoing a tragic decline in an age of growing wealth,' complains Patricia Giles from the Commission on Women's Health appointed by the World Health Organization. One indicator of this is the worldwide increase in childbirth mortality. Not so long ago the WHO estimated that half a million women died each year from complications in pregnancy, childbirth or unsafe abortions, but now it seems that the figure needs to be revised upward, to nearly 600,000 a year. 'Many of these deaths are easily avoidable,' says WHO chief Hiroshi Nakajima, 'it is poverty and powerlessness that make the women ill.' Russia, China, India and Cuba today have higher childbirth mortality rates than in 1990, and the situation has not improved at all in a further fifty-one countries.[31]

As a result of ongoing privatization, concludes the Women's Global Network for Reproductive Rights, health is no longer considered a human right, but rather a commodity to be bought and sold on the market.

In African countries, cuts in the public health and education systems have led to two classes of provision. Those who can afford it send their children to private schools and foreign universities, go to a private doctor and a private hospital. Staff in the public system work without enthusiasm in wretched conditions, constantly driven by rock-bottom wages to look for additional income on the side. In the private sector, the earnings are higher, the motivation greater, and the equipment more modern. It is a dual system, which inscribes social polarization in people's bodies and heads.

Take Zimbabwe, for example. In the 1980s the country set itself the goal of significantly improving its schools and medical facilities. After fees were introduced between 1991 and 1993 as part of a structural adjustment programme, 40 per cent fewer X-rays were taken, 20–30 per cent of hospital beds were empty, childbirth mortality doubled in Harare, tuberculosis control broke down, average life expectancy fell by five years, 26 per cent of all school-age children stayed away from school, and doctors and teachers emigrated in droves to neighbouring countries that offered higher pay.[32]

It is true that a 'social development fund' in Zimbabwe is supposed to target poor people in special need, to relieve them of school and hospital charges, and, since the elimination of food subsidies, to support them with the princely sum of 75 cents a month. But it is so complicated to prove one's entitlement and to fill in the necessary forms that the approval procedure has become impossibly expensive and arbitrary. Fewer and fewer claims are made, and anyway there is not enough to go round for everyone. Oxfam explained: 'The experience of Zimbabwe calls into question the seriousness with which the World Bank has attempted to integrate poverty-reduction mechanisms into structural adjustment.'[33]

A take-up analysis of the social measures supposedly accompanying structural adjustment has established that it is mainly men who benefit from support. The largest wad of money goes into employment programmes for public sector workers who have been made redundant. In Bolivia 99 per cent of the beneficiaries were men, in India 84 per cent, in Honduras three-quarters. Only one of the thirty projects to promote small business in Zimbabwe has been directed at women. Food aid is the most that is still made available to them.[34]

It is generally the case that money from social assistance funds seldom reaches the poorest layers. One reason for this is the way that it is supposed to be demand-driven. Those in need, or an NGO acting on their behalf, must first make an application and often even submit a proposal for a project. The demand thus steers the supply in accordance with principles of market behaviour and individual responsibility. Often the necessary information does not even get through to the poorest people in remote regions. But if an NGO takes up a case, it usually does so in the interests of male applicants. At best, an accompanying social programme can limit the damage for a few poor women; it can by no means keep them out of poverty.

The fact that people are no longer seen as having a human right to life's necessities means a splitting of society between the rich (for whom they are an ordinary consumption good) and the poor (for whom they are an unattainable luxury). In Orissa, which in 1997 became the first Indian state to privatize its energy supply, the elimination of subsidies has led to a fivefold increase in electricity prices for private households, together with a 23 per cent reduction for industrial users. In the cities of India, poor people often filch a little juice for a light-bulb from their better-off neighbours. But when electricity suddenly becomes noticeably more expensive, the rich become more tight-fisted and put a stop to this informal subsidy.

The advantages given to big over small users are also apparent in credit dealings. The tiny sums borrowed by poor women in slums, or the loans taken out by small farmers for subsistence production, are charged at a higher rate of interest than large business loans. Small but expensive, is the law of the market.[35]

Water, too, is everywhere supposed to fetch its market price. For it is running dangerously short, mainly because of its use in agricultural irrigation and various industrial processes. Pricing policy is meant to check wastefulness. But most people in the rural regions of the South would never even dream of wasting water. Since time immemorial, women there have been the living aqueducts, carrying buckets and containers over long distances on their heads and shoulders. When a price is put on water—whether on a tap in an urban slum, or on the supply drawn by small farmers from the spring or tank of a landowning 'waterlord'—the women are the first to make a move by walking still further to fill their cans in a pond or a brook; without purification or filtering, of course.

The commercialization of essential supplies and social services raises the importance of money in countries where a large part of the economy has not previously been monetized. The poor are excluded from the new markets for lack of purchasing power. But, in a self-reinforcing circle of poverty and exclusion, their access to money or purchasing power is in turn limited by their lack of purchasing power to invest in their own 'human capital.'

UNDP, the United Nations Development Programme, has recently made a distinction between income poverty and 'capability poverty,' the latter measured by undernourishment of young children, deficient medical care during childbirth, and the illiteracy rate among women. Accordingly, 21 per cent of the population in the South live below the income-related poverty threshold, but 37 per cent suffer poverty in human capabilities.[36] The World Bank defines any annual income below $370 as absolute poverty, and it is true that the percentage of people in the world with less than a dollar a day to live on has been declining. Yet the absolute numbers of the poor still grew between 1987 and 1993 from 1.2 billion to 1.3 billion, a quarter of humanity. Poverty and wealth go together; they are two sides of the same coin.

Seventy per cent of the world's poor are women; they are, in the development jargon, more 'vulnerable' than men. Traditional disadvantages, combined with marginalization through new forms of development, have been increasing the risk of poverty for women. Where food and employment, health and education facilities are all in short supply, cultural norms of selection and distribution work against women. The main cause of the feminization of poverty is the contrast between heavy work burdens and low earnings. This disparity is most blatant in the case of 'female heads of household' (accounting for 35 per cent of households around the world), where it directly triggers the slide into poverty. Single mothers, with no ifs and buts, have to perform a balancing act between care for their children and the need to earn a wage for the family. Constant stress and chronic overwork make them especially prone to illness. Their 'unprotected' social status increases the risk of violence.

According to UNDP figures, the shape of poverty has been rapidly changing since the 1980s. Women, children and old people are more at risk of poverty than men, people in towns more than in the countryside, and people in Africa more than in Asia.[37] The UNDP has had the merit in recent years of ruthlessly exposing the wealth gap that has opened up between rich and poor. In 1960 the wealthiest 20 per cent of the world's population disposed of 70 per cent of world income, but by 1994 the figure had risen to 86 per cent. The share going to the poorest fifth fell over the same period from 2.3 per cent to 1.1 per cent. In other words, those at the top owned thirty times more in 1960 and seventy-eight times more in 1994.

'Globalization has not so much reduced wages in developed countries and made people unemployed, as led to greater prosperity in large parts of the world.' This is how Martin Wolf, financial editor of the *Financial Times*, changes the angle of vision.[38] Clearly his absolute measure of prosperity takes no account of the extremely unequal distribution of that prosperity.

Assets are concentrated mainly in the accounts of transnational corporations. According to *Fortune*, the profits of the world's 500 largest companies rose in 1996 by an average of 25 per cent. Leading the pack was General Motors, with an annual turnover higher than the gross national product of Denmark. Ford's yearly business is greater than South Africa's, and Norway cannot keep pace with Toyota. So do the relations of power change between states and private corporations.

The UNDP remarks: 'As trade and foreign investment have expanded, the developing world has seen a widening gap between winners and losers.' Apart from the richest bracket, everyone else saw their income decline, so that by 1991 85 per cent of the world's population disposed of only 15 per cent of world income. The assets of the 358 richest people in the world are equal to the income of 2.3 billion people, 45 per cent of all those living on earth. In short: 'The greatest benefits of globalization have been garnered by a fortunate few.'[39]

Social polarization has intensified within many countries. The gap between rich and poor is widest in Brazil, Guatemala, Guinea-Bissau and the United States.[40] But recently poverty has also been increasing in the industrialized countries, where unemployment has reached record levels and income differentials are greater than at any time in the last hundred years. Everywhere the scale of poverty is headed by single parents and the elderly. More than a hundred million people in the 'rich' countries live below the poverty threshold: nearly 14 per cent of the population in the USA, 11 per cent in Germany. Portugal and Britain head the poverty tables in Europe.

A quarter of the British population is poor, 60 per cent of them women. Why is this? Seventy per cent of women who go out to work are in the low-pay category; four out of five women have a part-time job. 'Thatcher's children' is the name given to those who fell into the social holes dug by Thatcherite cuts in social services: a low level of education, a casual job here and there, no proper roof over their head. At the same time, the British economy is experiencing an upturn; here, more than anywhere else, poverty is a phenomenon of growth. Gone are the times when growth brought prosperity for all and social integration. Now it is the engine driving social distinction and exclusion.[41]

In Germany, the society where everyone was supposed to be middle-class has more recently been drifting apart. Less than half the population earns roughly the average income, while the proportion of incomes less than 75 per cent of the average has been steadily rising. The number of people on income support has grown by 50 per cent in the last decade and now stands at 2.8 million. Over the same period, however, the numbers earning more than DM 10,000 a month have increased more than sixfold.[42] The meltdown of the middle layers signals the end of the Fordist social contract, which based itself upon the consumption and purchasing power of a broad section of the population. For the French sociologist Alain Touraine, what looms ahead is a 30:30:40 society in which no more than 40 per cent of the population live at a relatively high level of social security and prosperity. Others fear that the tendency to social inequality is more likely to result in a two-thirds or even a 20:80 society.[43]

One echo of these economic trends is the social democracy of Tony Blair, in which neoliberalized politics aims at most to produce equal opportunities but no longer equal results. True, it has become easier for women to take part in the social competition, through education and training, flexible forms of work, and even special advancement programmes. But when it comes to distribution, the results are little changed. In the split society, women are not so often found in the ranks of the triumphant wealthy elite; but there are many indeed in the growing group of losers, of the redundant, excluded and poor.

Notes

1. Jeremy Rifkin (1995), *The End of Work. The Decline of the Global Labor Force and the Dawn of the Post-Market Era*, New York.
2. UNDP (1995), pp. 87–98.
3. *Frankfurter Rundschau*, 16 November 1995; Inge Rowhani-Ennemoser (1997), 'Die Folgen sind für Frauen katastrophal und existenzbedrohend', *Frankfurter Rundschau*, 7 April.

4. Ingrid Palmer, 'Gender Equity and Economic Efficiency in Adjustment Programmes,' in Afshar and Carolyne Dennis (eds) (1992), pp. 69–83.

5. Diane Elson in *WIDE* (1995), pp. 13ff.; Veronika Bennholdt-Thomsen, Maria Mies and Claudia von Werlhof (1988), *Women: the Last Colony*, London, pp. 83; Hazel Henderson, 'Building a Win-Win World: Life beyond Global Economic Warfare,' address to the Grenzenlos conference, Wuppertal, 21–22 November 1996.

6. Ursula Schröter (1992), 'Ostdeutsche Frauen im Transformationsprozeß,' *Rund-brief des Deutschen Frauenbunds*, February, 1992, pp. 6–12.

7. DGB (1995b), p. 8.

8. Gunhild Gutschmidt (1997), 'Die gerechte Verteilung des "Arbeitsmarktrisikos Kind,"' *Frankfurter Rundschau*, 4 August.

9. Patrick Liedtke, 'Some Keynote Issues of the Report to the Club of Rome,' in HVBG (1997), pp. 37f.

10. Gerhild Frasch, report to the Frauenbündnis für Arbeit und gegen Sozialabbau, Bonn, 7 March 1996.

11. Loic J. D. Wacquant (1997), 'Vom wohltätigen Staat zum strafenden Staat,' *Frankfurter Rundschau*, 12 July 1997.

12. *New York Times*, 30 June 1997.

13. Konrad Ege (1997), 'Wenn Drachentöter helfen wollen,' *Freitag*, 16 May.

14. See Martin and Schumann (1997), pp. 61ff.

15. Deutscher Frauenrat, press statement, 7 May 1997.

16. *Frankfurter Rundschau*, 26 July 1995.

17. Deutscher Frauenrat, press statement, 7 May 1997.

18. Faiza Rady (1997), 'An Egyptian Feminine Mystique,' *Al-Ahram*, 20–26 February.

19. Heba Nassar (1996), 'The Employment Status of Women in Egypt,' American University Cairo and Friedrich Ebert Stiftung, December.

20. Heba El Laithy (1996), 'The Economic Status of Women in Egypt,' American University Cairo and Friedrich Ebert Stiftung, December.

21. Chossudovsky (1997), pp. 191–214; Bea and Jules Rampini Stadelmann (1994), 'Auswirkungen des Neoliberalismus in Peru,' *Finanzplatz Schweiz* 2.

22. IPS, 25 February 1997.

23. Gabriele Zdunnek, 'Strukturanpassung und geschlechtsspezifische Differenzier-ungen am Beispiel Nigerias und Ghanas,' in M. Braig, U. Ferdinand and M. Zapata (eds) (1997), *Begegnungen und Einmischungen*, Stuttgart, pp. 160f.

24. See James and Susanne Paul (1994), 'Die Zerstörung der Altersversorgung,' *Informationsbrief WEED*, 5 December.

25. FAO (1995), *World Agriculture: Towards 2010*, Chichester, p. 272.

26. Gudrun Lachenmann (1994), 'Ansätze der Transformation und Kreativen Fortentwicklung Traditioneller und Informeller Sozialer Sicherungssysteme in Afrika,' *Nord-Süd aktuell* 2, pp. 283–94.

27. Wichterich (1996), pp. 74ff.

28. *Matrioshki* are the dolls within dolls that symbolize the unfathomable Russian soul.

29. Olga Vershinskaya, 'Gender Aspects of Socio-Economic Transformation in Russia,' manuscript of a talk given to the conference on Employment and Women, ICRW, The Hague, 18–19 September 1996.

30. Marina Malysheva (1995), 'Gender Identity in Russia,' *Canadian Women's Studies* 16/1, pp. 22–7.

31. IPS, 28 February 1997.

32. Thomas Siebold (1995), 'Die soziale Dimension der Strukturanpassung eine Zwischenbilanz,' *INEF Report,* vol. 13, Duisburg, pp. 37ff.

33. Jean Lennock (1994), *Paying for Health,* Oxford, p. 35.

34. Jessica Vivian (1994), 'Social Safety-Nets and Adjustment in Developing Countries,' UNRISD, Geneva, pp. uff.

35. Claudia v. Braunmühl, 'Thesen zum Umgang der Entwicklungszusammenarbeit mit den Herausforderungen von zukunftsfähiger Entwicklungspolitik,' in Germanwatch (1997), *Zukunftsfähige Entivicklungspolitik—Vision oder Illusion?,* Bonn, p. 43.

36. UNDP (1996).

37. UNDP (1997), pp. 53ff.

38. Quoted in *Le Monde Diplomatique,* June 1997.

39. UNDP (1996), pp. 2ff; UNDP (1997), p. 9.

40. UNDP (1996), pp. 16–17.

41. Werner Schiffauer (1997), 'Kulturdynamik und Selbstinszenierung,' *Tageszeitung,* 4 March.

42. *Tageszeitung,* 1–2 November 1997; *Berliner Zeitung,* 17 September 1997; Uwe Jeans Heuser (1997), 'Wohlstand für wenige,' *Die Zeit,* 24 October.

43. See Martin and Schumann (1997), pp. 1–11.

Chapter Eleven

Paid and Unpaid Labor
Meanings and Debates

Lourdes Beneria

One of the defining movements of the 20th century has been the relentless struggle
for gender equality. When this struggle finally succeeds—as it must—it will mark a
great milestone in human progress. And along the way it will change most of today's
premises for social, economic and political life
—UNDP, Human Development Report, 1995: 1

This chapter shifts our attention from the wider issues of development, globalization, and labor markets to the debates around paid and unpaid labor. It is centered around what I have called the "accounting for women's work project." Its central theme is the analysis of how conceptual and theoretical conventions are at the root of statistical biases leading to the underestimation of women's work in labor force and national accounting statistics across countries. Initially viewed as a way of making women's work more visible, the project has gradually evolved to include all unpaid work, mostly performed by women but also by men, although to a smaller extent. In addition, this project presents an illustration of how the questions raised by feminists have a relevance that transcends feminism and challenges basic tenets in conventional economic thinking. Finally it is also a project with domestic and global dimensions.

For me, this challenge first surfaced when I witnessed what I have come to call "the paradox of Cheshaouen," named after the picturesque town in Northern Morocco, which I visited in 1978 while working at the ILO. Preparing for the trip, I had looked at statistics showing that the labor force participation rate for men and women in Morocco differed widely—over 75 percent for men and less than 10 percent for women. However, what I saw in the streets of Cheshaouen the morning after my arrival told me a very different story from that reflected in these statistics. I saw many women moving about the busy streets, some carrying dough on their heads to bake bread in public ovens, others carrying wood on their backs or clothes to be washed in the brook bordering the town; still other women were carrying baskets or bags on their way to shopping, often with children at their side. The men were less busy; many of them were sitting outside their shops, idle and chatting, perhaps waiting for the tourist season to increase the demand for the beautiful crafts sold in many stores. I immediately thought that there was something wrong in the statistics I had seen. It was the first time I had paid attention to this type of discrepancy, but I soon learned how prevalent it was across countries and regions.

Others had been concerned about this issue as well. Ester Boserup had pointed out that "the subsistence activities usually omitted in the statistics of production and income are largely women's work" (p. 163). Boserup was a pioneer in emphasizing the time-consuming character of these activities, which, in rural economies, included physically demanding tasks such as fetching wood and carrying water as well as food production and the "crude processing of basic foods"—with great variations across countries in the time taken. Earlier in the United States, Margaret Reid, in her book *Economics of Household Production*, published in 1934, had been concerned about the exclusion of domestic production in national income accounts and had designed a method to estimate the value of housework.

Since the late 1960s, the international women's movement and the debates among feminists had prepared the ground for a new look at this topic. Many in the movement saw this issue as symbolic of society's undervaluation of women and of their contribution to social well-being. The various UN World Decade of Women Conferences were instrumental in including the issue in their agendas and in subsequent plans of action. Individual authors, research institutions, and governments also contributed to the effort. Marylin Waring's book *If Women Counted,* published in 1988, made a significant contribution by making the analysis of this issue and of its implication for action more readily accessible to a larger audience. Finally, during the past two decades, an increasing number of governments and individual researchers and activist groups took up this project and prioritized it in their agendas.

This process unfolded gradually, despite initial skepticism and even hostile reactions to the overall project. Its objective was officially sanctioned and summarized in the Platform of Action adopted in 1995 at the Fourth World Conference on Women in Beijing which called for the design and implementation of

> suitable statistical means to recognize and make visible the full extent of the work of women and all their contributions to the national economy including their contribution in the unremunerated and domestic sectors, and to examine the relationship of women's unremunerated work to the incidence of vulnerability to poverty. (UN 2001: 93)

In the past and over the years, an important body of literature not necessarily imbued with feminist goals has developed, addressing time allocation data that includes unpaid work. In fact, the first systematic collection of this data goes back to 1924 and is from the USSR, with the objective of obtaining information about variables such as leisure time and community-oriented work (Juster and Stafford 1991). Since the 1960s, national and comparative studies of time use have been carried out for a variety of purposes, such as the expansion of national accounting statistics and the analysis of household behavior. This work has taken place both in industrialized and developing countries.[1] However, although useful and often with parallel objectives to those of the "accounting project," these studies do not contain a specific feminist concern regarding their implications for women and for gender equality. This chapter presents a summary of some of the theoretical and practical issues involved in this project as they have evolved during the past two decades.

The Accounting Project

The underestimation of unpaid work in national and international statistics is reflected in labor force as well as GNP and national income data. Labor force statistics and national income accounts were designed primarily to gather information about the level of economic activity and changes over time, and to provide a basis for economic policy and planning. Given that, in capitalist economies, the market has been considered the core of economic activity, participation in the labor market was historically defined as engagement in work "for pay or profit" (as defined by the International Conference of Labor Force Statisticians in 1954). Likewise, the inclusion of production in national income accounts was defined by its connection to the market. The typical story about the decrease in GNP when a man marries his housekeeper is well known by readers of introductory economics textbooks even if, as a wife, her household activities might not have changed or might, in fact, have increased. This is because the wife, unlike the housekeeper, is not paid a wage and her work is not part of the market, therefore her work is not considered economically significant.

Thus, the problem of undercounting springs from the way "work" has been defined, in theory and in conventional statistics, as a paid economic activity linked to the market. Until World War II, statistics on the economically active population were gathered through population censuses, but the unemployment problems derived from the Great Depression generated a growing interest in the collection of reliable labor statistics. In 1938 the Committee of Statistical Experts of the League of Nations recommended a definition of the concepts "gainfully occupied" and "unemployed," and drew up proposals to standardize census data with the purpose of facilitating international comparisons. As a result, many countries expanded the collection of what, from then on, would be called "the labor force" (League of Nations 1938; ILO 1976). In 1966, the UN Statistical Commission updated the earlier definitions for the purpose of providing not only a measure of the unemployed but of labor availability. The adopted definition of "economically active population" referred *to all persons of either sex who furnish the supply of labor for the production of economic goods and services*. The objective of this definition was to facilitate not only estimates of employment and unemployment but of underemployment as well.[2]

Another aspect of this definition was the link assumed between the labor force and the national product—active labor being defined as that which contributes to the national product plus the unemployed. This definition leads to questionable measurements of work. Family members working part time can be classified as employed or underemployed when working in unremunerated agricultural activities but not when engaged in household production. A large proportion of unpaid work was therefore excluded from national product and income accounting as well as from labor force statistics under this definition. However, the problem of underestimation of unpaid work and the reasons behind it differ for each of the four sectors in which it predominates—namely, subsistence production, the household economy, the informal sector, and volunteer work.

The Subsistence Sector

Despite considerable efforts made since 1938 to improve labor force and national accounting statistics, the basic concepts remained essentially untouched until the past two decades. One important exception was the effort to include estimates of subsistence production in GNP accounts. As early as 1947, Kuznets had warned about the need to improve the then-still young system of national income accounts and argued for the inclusion of subsistence production in the accounts. Methods to estimate the value of this type of production and the proportion of the population engaged in it were recommended in the UN system of national accounts during the 1950s, particularly for countries in which this sector had a relatively important weight. Thus, countries such as Nepal, Papua New Guinea, Tanzania, and others developed methods of estimating the contributions of this sector to GNP. By 1960 a working party of African statisticians recommended) that estimates of rural household activities, such as the cultivation of backyard vegetables, could and should be added to those of subsistence production in agriculture, forestry, and fishing (Waring 1988). However, the recommendation was not accompanied with an implementation effort.

This process was consolidated with the 1966 definition of labor force recommended by the International Conference of Labor Statisticians, which referred to (ILO 1976). Whether this supply was furnished through the market was irrelevant in this case. Thus, although what constituted "economic goods and services" was not clear, the new definition introduced an exception to the market criterion—justified by the notion that subsistence production represents "marketable goods." As a result, it seemed logical to view the labor engaged in the sector as part of the labor force, including "family labor." Thus, despite the practical difficulties in estimating the market value of subsistence production, it became an accepted practice without important theoretical or conceptual objections. The objective was to arrive at more accurate estimates of GNP and of economic growth. To quote Ester Boserup,

> [T]he present system of under-reporting subsistence activities not only makes the underdeveloped countries seem poorer than they really are in comparison with the more developed countries, but it also makes their rate of economic growth appear in a more favorable light than the facts warrant, since economic development entails a gradual replacement of the omitted subsistence activities by the creation of income in the non-subsistence sector which is recorded more correctly. (Boserup 1970: 163)

In practice, however, the participation of women in subsistence production was not fully accounted for, given that the boundaries between agricultural and domestic work can be difficult to trace, particularly for women. To the extent that women's unpaid agricultural labor is highly integrated with domestic activities—such as with food cultivation, the fetching of wood, care of animals and many others—the line between the conventional classifications of family labor (in agriculture) and domestic work becomes thin and difficult to draw unless some clear-cut convention is established. The result has been a tendency to underestimate women's work in subsistence production, particularly whenever it is classified as domestic work.

The same problem appeared when censuses classified workers according to their "main occupation." In such cases, the tendency to underreport women family workers in agriculture or any other type of nondomestic production has been prevalent. Historically, such underreporting has been observed across countries and it was already pointed out by the ILO in 1977, referring in particular to North Africa and Southwest Asia where "... the female unpaid family workers were, to a large extent, not recorded" (ILO 1977, vol VI: 11). Since then, there have been efforts to include this category of workers in many countries' labor force statistics. Even so, there are still reasons to believe that underreporting continues to be a problem; they range from the relative irregularity of wormen's work in agriculture—for example in cases when it is mostly seasonal or marginal—to the deeply ingrained view, subject to multiple cultural and historical variations, that women's place is in the household. The result of these problems has been the nonexistence or the unreliability of national statistics regarding women's work and the difficulties in making meaningful comparisons across countries.[3]

The Informal Sector

A different type of problem is represented by the sparse statistical information on the informal sector at least until recently. This sector comprises a wide array of activities ranging from underground production of goods and services, to street vendors, to officially sanctioned micro-enterprises in all sorts of industries, including construction, garment, toys, and even shoes. In this case, the measurement problem is not one of conceptualization, given that it represents largely paid activities and therefore it falls within conventional definitions of work; the problem has to do with the difficulties of obtaining reliable statistics.

The absence of appropriate and systematic data collection on the informal sector becomes a significant problem given the large (and growing) proportion of its workforce in many countries.[4] For women, the informal sector often provides a primary, even if precarious, source of income. Informal activities range from homework (industrial piecework) to preparing and selling street foods, to self-employment and work in micro-enterprises. As analyzed in chapter 4, rather than being gradually replaced by formal sector activities as the earlier literature had expected, the tendency in many countries has been the opposite—the size of the informal sector has been growing, and it has absorbed the largest numbers of people who have remained marginal to the "modern economy" or expelled from it when unemployment has increased. To be sure, many case studies and efforts of data collection of informal activities have been undertaken, but the difficulties of gathering systematic, sectoral information are enormous; they derive from the invisible and even underground character of significant parts of this sector—illegal activities or at the borderline of illegality—and from its unstable, precarious, and unregulated nature.

Periodic and systematic country surveys, however, can realistically be elaborated to provide estimates of the sector's weight in the labor force and GNP estimates—as it has already been done in many cases. In the early 1990s, several branches within the UN prepared conceptual and methodological guidelines for the measurement of women's work in this sector—including industry, trade, and services—and carried out useful pilot studies, such as in Burkina Faso, Congo, the Gambia, and Zambia (UN Statistical Office/ECA/INSTRAW 1991a and 1991b; INSTRAW 1991). In each case, microeconomic survey data—for example for individuals and households—was combined with macroeconomic information, depending on data availability for each country. Similar efforts have been undertaken by other organizations, governments, and individual authors (Charmes 2000; De Soto 2001). This information-gathering effort is key to facilitate policy design and actions to improve the working conditions of those who participate in the sector.

Domestic Work

In the case of domestic production and related activities, the problem is not so much one of underestimation as of total exclusion because it has been conceptualized as falling outside of the conventional definition of work. Historically, even authors who have been open to the possibility of defining domestic work as "production," did not give much priority to the project. As stated by Blades (1975), "the production boundary should encompass non-monetary activities *which are likely to he replaced by monetary activities as an economy becomes more specialized*." But he concluded that "Because of the practical difficulties of measurement *the case for including housewives' general services is considerably weaker"* (emphasis mine).

As mentioned earlier, with few exceptions such as Margaret Reid's, this exclusion of domestic work from labor force statistics was not much questioned until the late 1970s. Boserup argued strongly for the inclusion in national accounts "of food items obtained by collecting and hunting, of output of home crafts such as clothing, footwear, sleeping and sitting mats, baskets, clay pots, calabashes, fuel collected by women, funeral services, hair cuts, entertainment, and traditional administrative and medical services," together with "pounding, husking and grinding of foodstuffs and the slaughtering of animals" (pp. 162–63). However, she saw these activities as subsistence production—"marketable goods," not as domestic work. Although Boserup mentioned the omission of "domestic services of housewives" from national accounts, she was less vociferous about it than in the case of subsistence production. Yet, she did emphasize the need to include production for own consumption, which she pointed out was larger in the economically less-developed and agricultural countries than in the more industrialized ones.

To some degree, a reversal in the historical trend for domestic work to shift from the household to the market as countries develop has been observed. As labor costs have increased in the high-income countries, self-help activities such as home construction, carpentry, and repairs, often performed by men, have also increased significantly. This has been added to the bulk of unpaid work at the household level, a trend reinforced by the decreasing tendency in the hiring of domestic workers as countries develop (Langfeldt 1987; Chadeau 1989; UNDP 1995).[5] In the United States, for example, some authors have estimated that the time allocated to unpaid work by men and women converged between the 1960s and 1980s (Bittman and Pixley 1997). The same tendency has been observed in other industrialized countries.[6] However, this convergence thesis ignores the extent to which multiple tasks are performed simultaneously. As Floro (1995) has argued, there is growing evidence that the performance of overlapping activities over prolonged periods especially by women is not an isolated phenomenon. Her conclusion is that, as women's participation in market work has increased, work intensification resulting from overlapping activities requires a revision of the convergence thesis.

To sum, production tends to shift out of the household at some stages in the development process while at Least part of it might return at later stages, regardless of whether it is performed by women or men. If household production is not accounted for, growth rates are likely to be overestimated when this production shifts to the market; on the contrary, they are likely to be underestimated when paid activities are taken up by (unpaid) household members. Given the predominant division of labor and women's role in the domestic sphere, the exclusion affects mostly—but not exclusively—women's work. This takes into consideration the fact that some tasks are often carried out simultaneously—such as when a housewife is cooking, doing the wash, and caring for the children at the same time.

Volunteer Work

Like in the case of domestic work, the wide range of tasks in the volunteer sector creates both conceptual and methodological problems for measurement because it is not directly linked to the market. Conceptually, volunteer work refers to work whose beneficiaries must not be members of the immediate family. In addition, there cannot be any direct payment—it's unpaid work by definition, and the work must be part of an organized program. That is, volunteer work is clearly different from domestic work even though there are close connections between the two—as when volunteer work takes place in one's neighborhood or community—which can make the boundaries difficult to draw in some cases. In addition, while some volunteer tasks can easily be defined as production, such as in the case of job training and home-building organizations, others are more difficult to classify, such as some of the activities associated with charitable or church-related work. Yet even in the latter case, some accounting of these tasks seems important if they provide free substitutes for what otherwise would be paid market work. To illustrate, in the United States, reliable data on volunteer work has existed since 1987. Estimates for 1995 indicate that 93 million Americans volunteered an average of 4.2 hours per week per person, with a total of 15.7 billion hours of formal volunteering and 4.6 billion hours of informal volunteering.[7] The 15.7 billion hours of formal volunteer time were estimated to represent the equivalent of 9.2 million full-time, private-sector employees. At a wage of $12.84 (the average hourly wage of a nonagricultural worker in 1995), the monetary equivalent for volunteer work is $201.5 billion. This work is often of a professional nature, as in the case of the relatively high number of volunteers in the health sector (Gora and Nemerowicz 1991).

Many factors influence the extent to which people engage in volunteer work—gender being one them since gender asymmetries in this type of work are abundant. Thus, in the U.S., women are more likely than men to engage in volunteer activities, particularly women who are married and relatively well-educated with children under eighteen.[8] These gendered disparities have many dimensions. For example, in 1984 New Zealand women mobilized around the notion that, while monetary contributions (often male) to charity are tax-deductible, time contributions (often female) are not. The result of this mobilization was the inclusion of a question about time dedicated to volunteer work in the 1986 Census of Population, a pioneer effort to New Zealand's credit (Waring 1988).

Similarly, volunteer work varies according to social characteristics. In the United States, a survey conducted in 1996 showed that volunteering correlated with income: the highest proportion (62 percent) of volunteering was among people with income above $75,000 and the lowest among those with income below $20,000 (AARP 1997). However, these differences might be misleading since much remains to be done to document volunteer work worldwide. Among the poor, volunteering can represent very significant individual and collective actions in times of crises. A well-known example was provided by the collective soup kitchens in the Andean countries during the 1980s and 1990s. Organized and run mostly by women, soup kitchens functioned as survival strategies to deal with the drastic deterioration of living standards that resulted from structural adjustment policies and increasing urban poverty. It has been estimated that in Lima, Peru, 40,000 low-income women formally organized a federation of self-managed communal kitchens, located in 2,000 sites in Lima's poor neighborhoods, and pooled their resources to feed about 200,000 people as often as five times a week (Barrig 1996; Lind 1997). Managing such an impressive endeavor requires a wide range of skills—from contacting food providers to handling money and dealing with charitable institutions and other funding sources—some of which were acquired by women as they engaged in survival work for their families and neighbors.

Collective food kitchens, in fact, raise questions about the conventional definition of volunteer work, since the beneficiaries often include both the immediate family *and* the community/neighborhood. Hence, these workers perform both domestic and volunteer work. Food kitchen volunteering also raises questions about the extent to which participation in volunteer work results from choice or lack of it; participation springs from the urgent needs of survival and from the inability of individual households to meet their needs on their own. Collective soup kitchens are clearly not exclusive to the Andean region. They take different forms and can also be found in high-income countries. For example, in the United States, soup kitchens that serve the poor, unemployed, and homeless are often run by women,[9] again pointing to the importance of documenting and analyzing the significance of this type of unpaid work.

To sum, the project of accounting for women's work was twofold from its beginning. First, it required the refinement of categories and improvement of data collection in the areas of paid work that were, in theory at least, included in conventional statistics. Second, it resulted from the need to rethink and redefine the concept of work and to develop ways to measure unpaid activities involving mostly domestic and volunteer work. In what follows, I will concentrate largely on domestic work.

The Contributions of Two Decades

Although questions and objections about the extent to which unpaid work should be measured still remain, much progress on the practical issues involved has been made since the 1980s. This progress has proceeded mainly on three fronts: conceptual, theoretical, and methodological. On the *conceptual front* and as a result of the initial Nairobi conference recommendation, the International Research and Training Institute for the Advancement of Women (INSTRAW) and the Statistical Office of the UN Secretariat took the lead to review and promote the revision of national accounts and other statistical information on women's work, with several meetings held for this purpose since 1986. A significant consensus has been built on the need to measure unpaid domestic work on the basis that it makes an important contribution to welfare. Most recommendations have opted for the development of separate or supplementary accounts that would permit the generation of "augmented" estimates of GNP (UN Office of Vienna 1989).

The purpose of such "satellite accounts" is to measure unpaid production of goods and services by households and to provide indicators of their contribution to welfare. This can be done by using time as a form of measurement—as done in time-use surveys—or by imputing a monetary value to time inputs or to the goods and services produced. Given the numerous and varied tasks being performed in the home, the question of which tasks to include or exclude has been an important focus of the discussion. The most accepted operational criterion is still Margaret Reid's *third-person principle,* according to which domestic production should refer to unpaid activities that can also be performed by a third person in a paid form. While tasks such as shopping, cleaning, food preparation, and child care are included under this criterion, watching television and getting dressed are not. This still leaves some ambiguities (the very rich or the ill might have a paid person to help them dress) but as a whole it represents an important step in setting a standard of definition that can allow, for example, comparisons between countries.

The third-party principle has been criticized for assuming the market as the model of economic activity and therefore precluding "the existence of economic activity unique to the household, since anything that does not, or does not yet, have a commodity equivalent cannot be considered economic" (Wood 1997: 50). However, although the principle does assume market production as the point of reference, it does not follow that a domestic activity without a market equivalent cannot be included; it can, as long as a third person can perform it. Wood goes further in criticizing the principle for its exclusion of personal activities such as "emotional care-taking, sex and childbirth from definitions of economic activity" (Wood 1997: 52). This argument, however, takes up the discussion of what should be considered as "work" to a level of ambiguity that makes it difficult to define. In any case, what needs to be emphasized here is that, overall, a significant shift has taken place in the conceptualization of economic activity toward the inclusion of tasks that contribute to social reproduction and the maintenance of the labor force and which are not directly connected with the market.

At the *theoretical* front, significant changes preceded or were parallel to the conceptual and practical work of the last two decades, particularly in terms of a greater understanding of the nature of domestic production. Since the 1950s and even more so since the 1960s, economic analysis focused increasingly on the household—within the framework of different theoretical paradigms and with different objectives. As pointed out in chapter 2, the neoclassical literature, particularly the New Household Economics, analyzed household production as a way to understand the gender division of labor and the participation of men and women in the paid labor force. Feminist versions of this analysis have pointed out some of its shortcomings and have placed greater emphasis on the social construction of gender roles and the extent to which it results in gender discrimination (Blau and Ferber 1986). On the other hand, within the Marxian paradigm, the domestic labor debate of the 1970s emphasized the importance of domestic work for the daily maintenance and reproduction of the labor force. The emphasis was on understanding the nature of domestic work, its links to the market and the economic and social power relations established between paid and unpaid domestic work and between men and women (Gardiner 1985; Molyneux 1979; Deere 1990). As mentioned earlier, questions about the application of the notion of exploitation to domestic work were also raised (Folbre 1982).

From a feminist perspective, neither of these two approaches placed enough attention to gender and power relations within the household. However, they were useful to enhance our understanding of the economic significance of domestic work and the need to develop methods to evaluate its contribution to production and welfare. In addition, the more strictly feminist analyses further contributed to elaborate the theoretical dimensions of domestic work as well as its political implications (Hartmann 1976a; Folbre 1994; Bergmann 1995).[10]

A different debate has centered around one of the main obstacles to measuring household production and volunteer work, namely, the difficulty of comparing them with market production: can this comparison be made given that they take place under very different conditions and norms of behavior? In particular, domestic work is not subject to the competitive pressures of the market and therefore productivity levels might be very different in the two sectors. Likewise, the quality of outputs can differ substantially, according to whether these are performed at home or in the market, such as in the case of childcare, meals, nurturing services, and many other activities. Similar arguments can be applied to volunteer work. Could we then be comparing apples and oranges? We will return to this issue below in more detail, but we should keep in mind that *there are several purposes to the project of measuring and documenting unpaid work.*

First, an important objective has been to make household work more visible and socially appreciated. Second, it facilitates the establishment of indicators to evaluate its contribution to social well-being and the reproduction of human resources, and it provides the basis for revising GNP and labor force statistics. Third, its measurement is crucial to analyzing the extent to which total work (paid and unpaid) is shared equally at the household and society level. Fourth, both at the micro and macro levels, measurement can provide information on how time is allocated between work (paid/unpaid) and leisure. Fifth, it is a crucial input for the project of "engendering budgets" in order to make explicit that they are not neutral tools of resource allocation (Bakker and Elson 1998). Sixth, measurement of unpaid domestic work has other practical uses such as in litigation and in estimating monetary compensation in divorce cases (Cassels 1993; Collins 1993). Seventh, even if productivity levels are not comparable, time-use indicators can be used to analyze tendencies and trends in the share of paid/unpaid work overtime. Finally, this information can help governments and other entities to design policy and action more effectively.

At the *methodological* level, substantial progress has been made on two fronts. One is the revisions of data-gathering methods to capture with greater accuracy the contributions to GNP made by the various types of unpaid work. The other is the progress in dealing with the complex task of designing different methods to measure its value. Here, I will refer mostly to domestic work, differentiating between input and output-related methods and showing the difficulties and advantages of each. Time budget studies and surveys carried out in many countries have provided the empirical base for such a task, often with large samples. In addition, empirical studies have been useful in analyzing the actual content and complexities of domestic work and household dynamics. Two main approaches to measuring the value of domestic work have been introduced: one based on the imputation of value to labor time (i.e., an *input-related method*) and another based on the imputation of market prices to goods and services produced in the domestic sphere (i.e., *an output-related method*).

For each approach, different estimation methods have been used. For the input-related method, a key problem is which value to impute to labor time. Three main methods have been identified:[11]

- The *global substitute* method uses the cost of a hired domestic worker, assumed to be paid to carry out all types of household tasks.
- The *specialized substitute* method uses the average wage of a specialist with skills for each specific household task.
- The *opportunity cost* method is based on the wage that the person performing domestic work could receive in the market.[12]

Each method has some advantages and disadvantages. The global substitute method tends to yield very low estimates given that domestic workers are at the lower end of the wage hierarchy. Also, a domestic worker is not likely to perform all of the work of the household. Therefore, unless the full contribution of all household members is estimated and added up, this approach will further reinforce the tendency toward low estimates. On the contrary, the specialized substitute method tends to generate high estimates, even though it is more indicative of the market value of household production. One practical problem associated with this method is the need to desegregate each task, with the corresponding problems, mentioned earlier, of comparing unpaid and paid work.

The opportunity cost method yields the widest range of estimates, depending on the skills and opportunity wage of the individual involved. This can result in rather absurd estimates since, for example, a meal produced by a doctor will be imputed a higher value than an identical meal prepared by an unskilled worker, even if the latter is a better cook. Another problem in this case has been pointed out repeatedly: the tautology suggested by the fact that, if the cook is a full-time housewife, her opportunity costs (i.e., the income she would get in the paid labor force) are, in turn, correlated to her condition as a full-time housewife. To quote Ferber and Birbaum (1980), "a person who has been out of the labor market, especially when it has been a long time, will not have reliable information about how much s/he could earn …" (p. 389).

As for output-related estimates, they require methods of imputing value to domestic production and deducting the cost of inputs from it. The problem again is to determine which market goods and services are equivalent to those produced at home, and what price to impute to inputs such as labor and raw materials not purchased in the market (for example, wood gathered by family members or home-made utensils). A different problem, again, is the disparities in the quality of goods and services produced, which in the case of nonmarket work can not be captured by an imputed price. At the empirical level, it is a tedious method requiring time-budgets data, hourly wages, and a relatively high number of input and output prices. While a proportion of such data can be obtained from existing censuses, most have to be generated through surveys. This is precisely the type of information that satellite accounts could provide periodically. How often they should be elaborated depends on available resources and projected needs. They could be obtained every few years instead of annually.

Input vs. output methods raise other issues with respect to their usefulness. For example, if the time needed to fetch water increases, input-related accounting will show an increase in time input while there is no increase in output. This suggests that, in terms of welfare, an output-related method is superior since it shows more accurately changes in welfare. Yet, from the perspective of documenting the time needed for domestic work, the input-related method is more explicit. In addition, the institutional and social dimensions of time complicate this issue. As Floro (1997) has argued, the notion of time and its uses is different across countries and cultures, and, in some cases, activities that Westerners might see as recreational—such as traditional festivities and gift exchange—can, in fact, represent unpaid work in other societies.

Although real, these difficulties are not insurmountable. The practical progress made so far and the guidelines provided by international organizations have laid a foundation from which to proceed. At the practical level, the efforts to measure unpaid work have been on the increase. Although they can be costly, in the last resort it is a question of priorities and political will. Table 5.1 presents an illustration of some of the attempts carried out at the country-level during the past two decades. It shows that the large majority of measurements are based on time-use data although input-output methods have been used in some countries. As can be observed, the proportion of childcare time provided by women across the countries included in the table ranges from 64 percent (Denmark) to 88 percent (Japan).

At the international level, special mention should be made of the pioneer effort that UNDP undertook in preparing its annual *Human Development Report* in view of the 1995 UN Conference in Beijing. The report included estimates of the share of paid and unpaid work across a variety of countries. Based on time-use data for different years, it showed that, for both developing and industrial countries, on average women work more hours than men—their work representing 53 percent of total time in developing countries and 51 percent in industrial countries. In both groups of countries, only 34 percent of women's work was included in national income accounts; the corresponding figure for men was 76 percent for developing countries and 66 percent for industrial countries.

However, as tables 5.2 and 5.3 illustrate, country data vary widely and the rural-urban differences within countries are significant. Among selected developing countries, the urban difference between women's work burden and that of men's (table 5.2) ranges from 3 percent (Kenya) to 12 percent (Colombia); in the rural context, the range is between 10 percent (Bangladesh) and 35 percent (Kenya). Among selected industrial countries, table 5.3 shows that the corresponding figures for the country as a whole range between –2.0 percent (Denmark) and 21.1 percent (Italy). Although a good proportion of the data used for the report relied on the "third-person criterion" for its estimates, these figures were based on studies that varied in data collection methods—raising methodological questions about comparability.[13] Recognizing this problem, the report points out that, in the absence of better data, these estimates provide "a valuable glimpse of the general pattern of time use by women and men" across countries.

Table 5.1 Measuring Unpaid Work

COUNTRY	SCOPE OF MEASUREMENT (AND AGENCY RESPONSIBLE)	YEARS SURVEY UNDERTAKEN	MEASURE-MENT METHODS USED	SOME HIGH-LIGHTS AND PERCENTAGE OF CHILD CARE TIME PROVIDED BY WOMEN
Australia	National (every 5 years) (Australian Bureau of Statistics)	1987 (pilot), 1992, 1997	time-use	78%
Austria	National (Vienna, Austrian Central Sta-tistical Office)	1981, 1992	time-use	76%
Bangladesh	National	1989, 1992	time-use	Average hours per week of house-work: Women = 31, Men = 5[a]

COUNTRY	SCOPE OF MEASUREMENT (AND AGENCY RESPONSIBLE)	YEARS SURVEY UNDERTAKEN	MEASURE-MENT METHODS USED	SOME HIGH-LIGHTS AND PERCENTAGE OF CHILD CARE TIME PROVIDED BY WOMEN
Bulgaria	Multinational Comparative (Bulgarian Academy of Science—1965) National (Sofia, Central Statistical Office—1988)	1965, 1988	time-use	81%
Canada	National (Ottawa, Statistics Canada)	1961, 1971, 1981, 1986, 1992	-time-use –input/output also for 1981,1986[c]	71%
Denmark	National (Copenhagen, Danish National Institute of Social Research)	1987	time-use	64%
European Union	EUROSTAT (European Union, Statistical Office)	1996 (pilot), 1997	time-use	A harmonized time use survey for countries in the EU is proposed for 1997 with the pilot in 1996[b]
Finland	National (Helsinki, Central] Statistical Office of Finland)	1979, 1987, 1990	–time-use –input/output also for 1990[c]	75%
Former USSR	Multinational Comparative (1965—Academy of Sciences of the USSR) Joint US–USSR Project (1986—Russian Academy of Sciences)	1965, 1986	time-use	75%

COUNTRY	SCOPE OF MEASUREMENT (AND AGENCY RESPONSIBLE)	YEARS SURVEY UNDERTAKEN	MEASURE-MENT METHODS USED	SOME HIGH-LIGHTS AND PERCENTAGE OF CHILD CARE TIME PROVIDED BY WOMEN
Germany, Federal Republic	National (Germany, Staticher Bundesamt)	1965, 1991, 1992	time-use	71%
Hungary	National Way of Life Survey (Budapest, Central Statistics Office)	1976, 1986	time-use	64%
India	National	1989,1992	time-use	Average hours per week of house-work: Women=34, Men=10[a]
Israel	National Time-Budget Survey (Israel, Central Bureau of Statistics)	1991,1992	time-use	75%
Italy	National (Rome, National Statistical Institute of Italy)	1988,1989	time-use	
Japan	National (5 yearly) (Tokyo, Bureau of Statistics)	1976,1981, 1986,1991	time-use	–88% –Women work 9 times the amount of unpaid times as men do[a]
Korea, Republic of	National (Seoul, Korean Broadcasting System)	1987,1990	time-use	80%
Latvia	National (Riga, Institute of Econom-ics)	1972,1987	time-use	69%
Lithuania	National (Helsinki, Central Statistical Office of Finland)	1974,1988	time-use	75%

COUNTRY	SCOPE OF MEASUREMENT (AND AGENCY RESPONSIBLE)	YEARS SURVEY UNDERTAKEN	MEASURE-MENT METHODS USED	SOME HIGH-LIGHTS AND PERCENTAGE OF CHILD CARE TIME PROVIDED BY WOMEN
Nepal	National	1989,1992	time-use	Average hours per week of housework: Women = 42, Men = 15a
Norway	National (Oslo, Norweigian Central Bureau of Statistics)	1980,1981,1990	time-use	71%
Poland	Time Budget Survey of Working People (Warsaw, Cent. Stat. Office)	1984	time-use	69%
Spain	–National (Madrid, Instituto de Economia y Geografia)	1991	time-use	86%
	–Catalonia, Institute Catalâ de la Dona	2001	time-use	% increase in GNP contrib-uted by domes¬tic production 66%d
Sweden	National (Stockholm, Statistics Sweden)	1990,1991	time-use	72%
United Kingdom	Daily Life Survey	1984	time-use	76%
United States	National (Univ. of Michigan–1996) (Univ. of Mary-land—1986)	1965,1986	time-use	72%

Sources:[a] United Nations: The World's Women 1995: Trends and Statistics; [b] Luisella Goldschmidt-Clermont and Elisabetta Pagnossin-Aligisakis (1995), "Measures of Unrecorded Economic Activities in Fourteen Countries," Human Development Report Occasional Papers; [c] Duncan Ironmonger, "Counting outputs, capital inputs and caring labor: estimating gross household product"; [d] Comajuncosa et al. (2001).

Table 5.2 Burden of Work by Gender, Selected Developing Countries

COUNTRY	YEAR	WORK TIME (MINUTES A DAY)			WOMEN'S WORK BURDEN COMPARED WITHMEN'S (% DIFFERENCE)
		AVERAGE	WOMEN	MEN	
Urban					
Colombia	1983	378	399	356	12
Indonesia	1992	382	398	366	9
Kenya	1986	581	590	572	3
Nepal	1978	567	579	554	5
Venezuela	1983	428	440	416	6
Average		471	481	453	6
Percentage share			51	49	
Rural					
Bangladesh	1990	521	545	496	10
Guatemala	1977	629	678	579	17
Kenya	1988	588	676	500	35
Nepal:	1978	594	641	547	17
–Highlands	1978	639	692	586	18
–Mountains	1978	592	649	534	22
–Rural hills	1978	552	583	520	12
Philippines	1975–77	499	546	452	21
Average		566	617	515	20
Percentage share			55	45	
National					
Korea, Republic of	1990	479	488	480	2
Average for sample countries		514	544	483	13
Percentage share			53	47	

Source: UNDP, *Human Development Report,* 1995, Table 4.1.

Indeed, although these are rough estimates, they provide an indication upon which it is possible to construct more accurate measures.

Overall, these figures illustrate several basic facts. First, unpaid domestic work is important in relation to total work time. Second, women bear a larger burden of total work time. Third, a disproportionate amount of women's work is not included in national income accounts. There is much, however, that these figures cannot capture, given that they are based on averages. For example, working time for men and women vary across social class. Likewise, there are areas of activity, such as shopping and driving the children to school—consumption and reproduction tasks—that could be considered "work" but conventionally are not. We will return to these issues below.

The Emergence of New Issues

The accounting project continues to be important as current labor market trends have raised new questions about the links between paid and unpaid work and about their distribution and boundaries. We are witnessing a significant transition in the ways this distribution is affecting individuals, households, and communities across countries. Several developments are contributing to these trends.

First, the increasing participation of women in the paid labor force has reinforced the importance of how paid and unpaid work are shared among family members. Together with changing constructions of gender roles and of women's positioning in society, it is likely to decrease women's tolerance for gender inequality in the distribution of working time and to increase their autonomy and bargaining power. Hence the "crisis of care" already being felt in many countries is intensified by the fact that, as Mary Daly (2001) has argued, "care work tends to be squeezed to the margins of many people's lives" (p. 6). Estimates of the extent and requirements of unpaid work will be necessary whether the solution to the crisis of care is worked out through the market, the provision of public services, or through more equal sharing of those activities between men and women.

Table 5.3 Burden of Work by Gender, Selected Industrial Countries

| COUNTRY | YEAR | WORK TIME (MINUTES A DAY) | | | WOMEN'S WORK BURDEN COMPARED WITH MEN'S (% DIFFERENCE) |
		AVERAGE	WOMEN	MEN	
Australia	1992	443	443	443	0
Austria	1992	416	438	393	11.5
Canada	1992	430	429	430	−0.2
Denmark	1987	454	449	458	−2
Finland	1987/88	420	430	410	4.9
France	1985/86	409	429	388	10.6
Germany	1991/92	441	440	441	−0.2
Israel	1991/92	376	375	377	−0.5
Italy	1988/89	419	470	367	28.1
Netherlands	1987	361	377	345	9.3
Norway	1990/91	429	445	412	8
United Kingdom	1985	412	413	411	0.5
USA	1985	441	453	428	5.8
Average for sample countries		419	430	408	5.8
Percentage share			51	49	

Source: UNDP, *Human Development Report,* 1995, Table 4.3.

Second, in high-income countries those who are unemployed and marginalized from mainstream economic life have to negotiate survival strategies involving a shifting reliance on unpaid work, including forms of labor exchange that are not captured in conventional statistics.[14] The same can be said for developing countries undergoing structural adjustment or the consequences of financial policies leading to the intensification of unpaid work in the household and in communities; as argued in previous chapters, they tend to increase the number of activities that are not included in conventional statistics.

Third, high incidence of underemployment and of part-time work results in cyclical or fluid combinations of paid and unpaid activities related to changes in the economy and affecting women and men in different ways. As will be argued below, measuring the extent of these changes is important in assessing variations in living standards and contributions to social well-being. Similarly, discussions about the thirty-five-hour week that have taken place, particularly in Western Europe, have many gender implications regarding the distribution of paid/unpaid work. These discussions are carried out under the assumption that a reduction in working time will be helpful in dealing with unemployment. But as Figart and Mutari (1998) have argued, the underlying assumption is that "full time, year-round employment is a social norm constructed around gendered assumptions," such as that "a full-time worker, presumably male, faces limited demands from unpaid work and family life" (p. 2). A different assumption, they argue, is that the concentration of women in part-time work will continue, regardless of their choice. This suggests that statistics documenting who performs unpaid work can be useful to understanding the distribution of working time. In the same way, households with multiple earners need to address this question if they are concerned about gender equality and about the fair distribution of caring work among household members.

Finally, given that unpaid work represents roughly 25 percent to 50 percent of economic activity, depending on the country and methods of estimation, its exclusion from national accounts is difficult to justify. In terms of domestic work, there is some evidence showing that unpaid labor is increasing more rapidly than market production. Australian data, for example, indicate that between 1974 and 1992 household work grew at a rate of 2.4 percent per year, while the corresponding rate for market production was 1.2 percent (Ironmonger 1996). The increase in domestic work can be attributed to a variety of reasons: rapid rise in the number of small size households—resulting in a loss in economies of scale—to the aging of the population and the changing preferences of more affluent societies. Ironmonger notes that this increase in unpaid labor has happened despite raising women's labor force participation rates and despite the diffusion of new household technologies that are labor-saving.

All of these factors explain why there has been an increasing awareness of the extent to which paid and unpaid work are unequally distributed among men and women. The quote from the *Human Development Report* that heads this chapter underlines this point clearly. Likewise, the 1996 report of the Independent Commission on Population and the Duality of Life, *Caring for the Future,* includes a call for the redefinition of work and for equality in the distribution of its output:

> The Commission proposes ... to redefine work in a broad sense that encompasses both employment and unpaid activities benefiting society as a whole, families as well as individuals, and ensuring an equitable distribution of the wealth generated. (p. 147)

To sum, the project of redefining and measuring unpaid work has gained much support in recent decades. However, and as expected given that we are dealing with a complex issue, there is also opposition to it. The following section discusses the various arguments casting doubts on the project.

The Continuing Debate

At least three types of objections to the accounting for unpaid work project have emerged. Two of them actually derive from feminist circles, while the third springs out from the core of orthodox economics.

Useless Effort

We may call this objection "the waste-of-time argument." It results from the fear that the effort and use of resources necessary to generate statistics on unpaid work will not make any difference to those engaged in it, particularly women. To what extent, for example, can the information be used to decrease the burden of poor women who toil many hours a day or to empower the urban housewife with no income of her own? Could it be used to increase their bargaining power at some level? Can it *really* make a difference to those individuals engaged in unpaid activities? On the contrary, this argument goes, greater social recognition of the importance of domestic work might, in fact, reinforce a division of labor that relegates women to activities providing no financial autonomy and little control over the resources they need. This would therefore not contribute to gender equality; it would instead perpetuate women's dependency on men.

I call this type of argument "the post-Nairobi blues," reflecting the doubts some of us felt after the 1985 UN Conference on Women, which took place in Nairobi, Kenya. For the first time, the official report of the conference, *Forward-Looking Strategies for the Advancement of Women*, strongly recommended appropriate efforts to measure the contribution of women's paid and unpaid work "to all aspects and sectors of development." The report significantly moved the action forward and, in doing so, it also raised questions and doubts about whether setting this agenda would make any difference to women.

A similar version of this argument has been offered by Barbara Bergmann who, although not objecting to the effort itself, thinks too much energy is spent on it. Feminists, she argues, should emphasize the need for women to engage in paid work in order to reduce their dependency on men and increase their bargaining power in and outside of the home. Thus, she believes that feminists should first place their efforts on the design and implementation of policies that facilitate the incorporation of women into the paid labor force, such as child care provision and maternity leave. Likewise, they should work on policy and action leading to the enforcement of gender equality in the labor market such as pay equity, affirmative action, and comparable worth. Bergmann is skeptical about the possibility that better information on unpaid work "can help a single woman," in the same way that "the inclusion in the GNP of food produced in the subsistence sector does not make any difference to farmers."[15] She also fears that statistics on housework are likely to be used by those who want "to glorify the housewife," as in the case of some right-wing groups in the United States, which "can argue that housework is irreplaceable because it performs crucial services to society." Hence, she concludes that "there is an anti-feminist implication in valorizing housework."

This type of objection ignores the fact that action, policy design, and implementation of projects affecting those engaged in unpaid work requires as much systematic information as possible in order to make optimal estimates. We should remember the problems created by lack of information. In the words of Indian feminist Devaki Jain, "One of the greatest difficulties in assisting women has been the absence of any reliable data regarding their number, problems and achievements" (Jain 1975). This applies not only to obvious problems requiring urgent solutions such as violence against women or wage discrimination; the weight and distribution of unpaid work can be important in many ways. For example, high estimates of time spent in fetching water by women in any country might prevent authorities from giving low priority to the installation of running water on the grounds that fetching water does not take much of women's time. Likewise, time-use information about time spent on traveling with children can be an important input for transportation policies.

To elaborate with another example, it is important to know the extent to which an economic slowdown that increases unemployment and reduces household income results in unpaid labor picking up the slack, for example through the intensification of domestic work or subsistence production. We do know that the financial crises and adjustment policies of the past two decades led to coping strategies that required the intensification of unpaid work, with a disproportionate burden for women. In such cases, a decrease in real income may or may not result in a corresponding decline in family welfare—depending on the extent to which unpaid work makes up for the reduced income. An evaluation of these shifts cannot be done without systematic statistical information on unpaid work. As Floro (1996) has argued, a more precise information on people's daily activities helps us to assess the quality of their lives more accurately and develop indicators of work intensity, performance of multiple tasks, stress, individual health, and even of child neglect. This is because varied dimensions of work—such as work intensity and the length of the working day—have been shown to be related to stress and health of workers and their families (Floro 1996).

Thus, the accounting project must be viewed, on the one hand, not as an end in itself but as a means to understand who contributes to human welfare and human development—and to what extent. The symbolic value of estimations of unpaid work should not be underestimated. As a male economist who participated in the first attempt to calculate the value of domestic activities in Catalonia, Spain, stated in his presentation of the report, it was not so much the specific figures arrived at but what he had learned about the significance of this work that changed his views about it (Comajuncosa et al 2001). On the other hand, these estimates can provide information for the design of policies to distribute the pains and pleasures of *work* in a more egalitarian fashion. The fear that some political groups might use the information for their own purpose must be weighted with the fact that it can also be used for a variety of positive outcomes, including the more accurate design of social policies as in the case of social security payments, pensions, and other forms of social insurance.

The Importance of "Difference"

A second objection, concerning mostly domestic and unpaid caring work, is perhaps more difficult to deal with since it springs from the notion that this type of activity includes personal and relational aspects that make it qualitatively very different from market work. Sue Himmelweit (1995) has argued that, although recognizing unpaid labor as "work" is an important way to make it visible and to validate women's contributions in the home, something is lost in the process. She questions "whether the best way for women's contribution to be appreciated [is] to force it into a pre-existing category of work,' borrowed from an economics which inherently failed to value most of what made women's domestic contribution distinctive" (p. 2).

As an example, Himmelweit argues that "caring" is an ambiguous notion that can stretch from physical to emotional care; while the first "might to some extent be independent of the relation between the career and the person cared for," the second requires that "the person doing the caring is inseparable from the care given" (p. 8). She points out a second characteristic of caring work—namely, its self-fulfilling quality. Hence, Himmelweit is reluctant to view as conventional "work" the time spent on activities that provide emotional care and support, which, in addition, are also very difficult to quantify.

Himmelweit concludes that not everything needs to be seen as "work" or "nonwork," particularly since this may lead to the social undervaluation of activities that do not fit into the first category:

> By insisting that domestic activities gain recognition by conforming to an unchallenged category of work, the significance of caring and self-fulfilling activities remains unrecognized, (p. 14)

This argument, although interesting, seems problematic for different reasons. First, greater visibility and documentation of these unpaid activities is likely to increase the recognition of their significance for human welfare, particularly if their nature is well understood and emphasized. As we have seen, recent history demonstrates that this is exactly what the theoretical, methodological, and practical efforts of the last three decades have accomplished. The shift of a significant proportion of caring work from the unpaid reproductive sphere to the market has not always taken away some of its basic characteristics. For example, work motives associated with solidarity, altruism, and caring can be found in the market as well as in unpaid work. Second, many unpaid activities are not caring and self-fulfilling while some paid activities are. Hence, it is difficult to argue that there is no personal and relational aspects in some of the paid services offered through the market, even though the service is offered in exchange for a monetary reward.

To be sure, some market-oriented caring services are not likely to provide the same quality of care and emotional support that a loving family member can offer—whether or not the caring work might be based on motives such as love and affection, a sense of responsibility, respect, intrinsic enjoyment, altruism, or informal *quid pro quo* expectations. However, it is not difficult to find exceptions to these cases. To illustrate, there can be market-based care providing selfless emotional support beyond the exchange contract. On the other hand, there can be family care based on selfish expectations (an inheritance) or on some form of coercion (as in the topical case of a wife having to take care of her inlaws even when there might not exist much affection between them). As for Himmelweit's argument that something is lost in the process of evaluating unpaid caring work, it needs to be contrasted with the fact that something is also won.

Third, there is a dialectical relationship between market and nonmarket work, in such a way that, to some extent, the skills used in one sphere can be used in the other and vice versa.[16] Thus, a paid nanny or nurse might provide a high quality of personal care with skills learned at home; and managerial skills learned in the labor market might be used as a way to reduce unpaid working time in the household. This means that it is difficult to draw a clearly defined dividing line between the two.

Fourth, in addition to caring labor, unpaid work includes other types of activities that are only indirectly related to caring, such as gathering wood, taking care of domestic animals, cleaning the house, and participating in community activities. These tasks vary by country, cultural factors, and social background of participants. In this sense, Himmelweit's argument has a built-in bias—reflecting the activities of an urban nuclear family rather than those typical of rural settings.

Overall, this is not to dismiss Himmelweit's important arguments. They raise the question of the extent to which the self-less, caring work that is conventionally attributed to domestic labor can be projected on to other activities outside of the household, including market activity, a subject further discussed below.

Theoretically Misguided

The third type of objection to the project of measuring unpaid work is related to theoretical and methodological questions that spring from more conventional value theory in economics. Despite criticisms emanating from these circles, very few have been expressed in writing.[17] The discussion that follows is based on a paper by economist Sujai Shivakumar (1996), which represents a pioneering effort and in many ways captures many of the unwritten criticisms. In what follows, I will focus exclusively on this paper.

One of Shivakumar's objectives is to show that the *monetary imputation* of unpaid work "is not consistent with present conceptions of the theory of value in economics" and that this imputation is merely a "rhetorical effort" without theoretical foundation or a "dubious game of statistical football" (p. 374). To elaborate this argument, he includes a historical account of the development of value theory in economics leading to three main criticisms. First, he claims that the accounting project is a socialist-feminist effort in terms of its rhetoric, forms of analysis, and policy prescriptions—using gender as the central "tool of analysis," presenting alternative visions of economic processes, and centering economics around the notion of "provisioning of human life." Second, he argues that the project is based on Ricardian-Marxian notions of value based on the labor theory of value instead of the "modern" orthodox value theory based on subjective preferences and expressed through market prices; as such, he views the project as theoretically unacceptable:

> Modern economic theory does not support time-use analysis as a basis for im- puting the monetary value of work. ... The labor theory of value on which this type of analysis is based has roots in Ricardian-Marxian theory of value that is no longer recognized in economics, (p. 333)

In this sense, Shivakumar states that the money value estimates, such as those included in UNDP's 1995 *Human Development Report,* are meaningless because they are based on time-use data.

Third, Shivakumar criticizes the methods used to estimate the value of unpaid work. In doing so, he repeats many of the methodological objections that have previously been recognized and addressed by different authors, including those involved in the project. However, rather than pointing out the ways in which methodologies might be improved, he does not see much redeeming value in the attempt to do so. Thus, comparing the account- ing effort with that of the environmentalists who want to take environmental costs into consideration in national accounting statistics, he writes:

> With no theoretical guideline on how to choose among alternative ways of conducting the valuation, the selection among alternative ways of imputation in environmental accounting then comes to reflect on the relative strengths of competing political interests.... (p. 405)

Hence, Shivakumar views the value estimates such as those of the 1995 *Human Development Report* as "meaningless" Although the estimates present problems, as men- tioned earlier, due to poor or insufficient data, a more constructive approach is to see them as a pioneering but nevertheless important effort in need of improvement. Shivakumar points out the problem of comparability between market and nonmarket time. However, he does not mention the fact that most advocates of including unpaid work in national income accounts recognize this problem (hence, the use of satellite accounts referred to earlier, to avoid the mixing of apples and oranges).

Shivakumar's critique is more fundamentalist in his insistence on the issue that any monetary evaluation "displays an ignorance of the concept of value *as something realized through the exchange process*" (p. 27, emphasis added). That is, he views the exchange process as the only source of value, despite the fact that the value of nonmarket goods in subsistence production has been estimated for many years, and that many economists make use of "shadow prices" in their work. As argued above, this practice has been supported by the notion that subsistence production represents "marketable goods." Yet, a good proportion of domestic work is marketable and, with economic growth, increasing portions of it are taken up by paid work, including, food production, cleaning services, and childcare.

Thus, there is a double standard in Shivakumar's critique since he does not make reference to these facts. Within neoclassical economics, the imputing of market prices to household production is a standard practice. Shivakumar does not make any reference to the fact that, in many ways, the New Household Economics pioneered the application of "modern" human capital theory to household production and decisionmaking and that other economists have also taken seriously the task of analyzing household production (Fraumeni 1998). It would be ironic to categorize the work of human capital theorists like Jacob Mincer, Gary Becker, and many other neoclassical economists as socialist-feminist and based on the labor theory of value.

In associating the effort to measure unpaid work to Ricardo and Marx, Shivakumar ignores the fact that orthodox Marxist theory would agree with his insistence on seeing value as originated only through the exchange process. In addition, it is far from clear that Marxian value theory is based on labor inputs without regard to the weight of demand to determine market value (Itoh and Yokokawa 1979; Elson 1979). Although he is right in affirming that gender as an analytical category and "the provisioning of human life" are central to feminist economics, this is not specific to any branch of feminism. Feminist economists of different persuasions would probably agree with his statement. He also ignores that the actual work toward measuring unpaid labor includes a large number of feminists and professional men and women with diverse theoretical approaches and practical politics.

Beyond these basic points, some of Shivakumar's criticisms are not well informed, as with his statement that feminists "have not spelled out any particular policy prescription other than to seek to better inform policy makers" (p. 394). Feminists *have* called for and suggested gender-aware policies in areas such as labor market policy, public services, structural adjustment packages, and agricultural policy (Sen and Grown 1987; Palmer 1991; Elson 1992 and 1995; UNDP 1995; Deere and Leon 2001). Many of these policies would benefit from more systematic statistical information and documentation regarding unpaid work. Shivakumar's attribution of self-interest to feminists recommending these changes—claiming that "the called-for increases in female participation in policy-making will differentially advantage those who call for such increases"—is far-fetched and even discriminatory, given that it would be difficult to hear a similar charge made to men suggesting changes in statistics and policy. What one reads in Shivakumar's paper is a strong irritation about the spoiling of a neatly-defined, presumably "objective" economic paradigm by what he sees as the "normative" prescriptions of feminism. Although, to his credit, he does present some recommendations "to satisfy the Beijing mandate," his alternatives fall short of the task to be accomplished and, as he points out, do not solve some of the problems analyzed. In any case, we are thankful for his effort to take this project seriously and to bring it to the heart of economic theory.

Concluding Comments

The main argument of this chapter takes us back to the eternal question of what is *value* and what is *valuable* to society. Much has been written about this subject and a discussion of it falls outside of the scope of this chapter. Ultimately, we are left with the basic question of how to measure and evaluate human well-being and how to recognize those who contribute to it. The point repeatedly being made is that current GNP statistics include what is bad for our health—such as the production of food with carcinogenic chemicals—or for the environment—such as the output of polluting factories. Yet, there has been resistance to the measuring of work and production of goods and services that sustain and enhance life. In Nancy Folbre's terms, societies and individuals need to know, among other things, "who pays for the kids?" This requires an effort to evaluate time spent and costs involved.

We also want to know, for example, who contributes to the survival strategies of the poor so that we can design gender-aware and social class-aware policies to overcome poverty. Unpaid work is not unevenly distributed across class and social groups. While affluent households can employ (mostly) women for domestic work, they can also purchase goods and services that poorer households produce at home and without outside help. When lower-income women participate in the paid labor market, either their workload increases or the standards in home-produced goods and childcare need to be lowered (Giménez 1990). There is a significant difference in the total number of hours that women from different income levels and social backgrounds dedicate to domestic work. An empirical study carried out in Barcelona, Spain, showed that the absolute value of domestic work was higher for middle-income households, followed by the lower-income and higher-income categories. However, the value of domestic work in lower-income households represented a higher percentage of total household income, which included social income or the value of public services perceived (Carrasco 1992).

There is more to the challenge of measuring unpaid work since it calls for, in Elizabeth Minnich's terms, "transforming knowledge" or moving beyond the boundaries of conventional paradigms. This includes the rethinking of "mystified concepts," or "ideas, notions, categories, and the like that are so deeply familiar they are rarely questioned" and which result in "partial knowledge" (Minnich 1990). The challenge leads us to question the ways in which we measure well-being and to understand who contributes to it in our communities and in society as a whole. Further, it leads us to question the assumptions behind received knowledge—in this case, those that conceptually link "work" to paid labor time and the market.

Finally, we have seen that the discussion about the difference between paid and unpaid work leads to questions about the extent to which economic rationality assumed to inform market-related behavior is the norm and to what extent human behavior is based on other motives and norms most commonly linked to unpaid work, such as love, compassion, altruism, empathy, individual and collective responsibility, and solidarity. This chapter reinforces the arguments in chapter 3 about the need to construct alternative models other than those based on market-oriented motives of rational economic man.

Paid and Unpaid Labor

1. For a summary of the literature and relevant definitions, see Goldschmidt-Clermont 1982, and Juster and Stafford 1991.
2. UN Statistical Commission 1983. For a more detailed account, see Benería 1982.
3. For further detail, see Benería 1982.
4. See chapter 4 for more detail.
5. There are, of course, exceptions to this trend, such as the phenomenon referred to as the "nanny bubble" since the late 1990s in the United States, representing an increase in employment of immigrant domestic workers among the very rich. If anything, this trend has accelerated in high-income countries, as discussed in chapter 3, particularly as a result of the crisis of care work.
6. Based on data from Canada, Denmark, Holland, Japan, Norway, the United Kingdom and the United States, Juster and Stafford (1991) show that men's unpaid domestic work increased for most countries between the 1960s and the 1980s while women's decreased in larger proportions.
7. Data prepared for the Inaugural Meeting of the National Commission on Philanthropy and Civic Renewal, Washington, D.C., September 1996. Formal volunteering was defined as "specific commitments of time to organizations" and informal volunteering as "less structured arrangements like helping one's neighbors."
8. Ibid.
9. A soup kitchen that I visited in an East Los Angeles church in 1996 was run entirely by Spanish-speaking women and served daily dinner for about 100 men.
10. See chapter 2 for more detail.
11. For more detail, see, for example, Goldschmidt-Clermont 1982 and 1987; Benería 1992; Fraumeni 1998.

12. A variation of the opportunity cost method is the *lifetime income approach* (Fraumeni 1998).

13. The sample of countries used was selected "on the basis of availability and reliability of time-use data" but with variations in the methods of data collection.

14. These strategies may consist of types of paid work outside of the mainstream monetary system, as with some cases in which the creation of a local currency facilitates exchanges. One such case has been developed in Ithaca, New York, where "Ithaca money" is issued locally and used to exchange labor services as well as to purchase from the local stores that accept it. Even though these cases have little weight for the economy as a whole, they can be important at the local level and they provide interesting examples of work not recorded in conventional statistics.

15. Based on my conversation with Barbara Bergmann on this topic, March 14, 1998.

16. I wish to thank a participant in a seminar I gave at Radcliffe's Public Policy Institute on this topic for this point. She mentioned her own experience in using managerial skills learned at home for her market work, and vice versa, to argue that it is often difficult to neatly differentiate between paid and unpaid work in terms of Himmelweit's analysis.

17. For example, some World Bank economists have been critical of the UNDP's efforts to include estimates of unpaid work in its *1995 Human Development Report*. However, to my knowledge, the objections have mostly be voiced in discussions and meetings rather than in a written form.

Chapter Twelve

Female Labor, Regional Crises, and Feminist Responses

Valentine Moghadam

I n an essay that critically evaluated the Keck and Sikkink book on transnational advocacy networks, sociologist Peter Evans emphasized what he called "transnational consumer/labor networks" that target transnational corporations. And in an essay on the disappearance of discussions of inequalities since the 1995 Social Summit, development economist Jacques Baudot argued that only gender inequality was being addressed in international policy circles, "in part because it may be seen as compatible with the basic tenets of the neoliberal creed."[1] Both Evans and Baudot were apparently unaware of the existence of transnational feminist networks and of their decidedly vigorous critique of gender and social inequalities in the global economy.

In this chapter I examine the relationship between the globalization process and the emergence of transnational feminist networks. I argue that the worldwide expansion of a female labor force, the important (albeit exploited) role of female labor in the global economy, and the persistence of social and gender inequalities underpin the rise of a women's movement on a world scale. The global social movement of women is characterized by a set of grievances, claims, and objectives (global feminism), and an effective organizational type (the transnational feminist network). TFNs thus reflect one aspect of the globalization process, while also responding to its dark side.

If female labor incorporation, persistent inequalities, and the hierarchies and crises of the global economy have formed the structural basis of women's mobilizations, the United Nations and its world conferences have played an important role in providing organizational resources. And of course, women's own experiences in the economy, the polity, and the household have provided the impetus for analysis and action. As I demonstrate in this chapter, women's mobilization and collective action have taken the form of increasing participation in trade unions and in transnational feminist networks.

The Feminization of Labor and the Global Economy

Through institutions such as the nation-state and the transnational corporation, the world economy generates capital largely through the exploitation of labor, but it is not indifferent to the gender and ethnicity of that labor. Gender and racial ideologies have been deployed to favor white male workers and exclude others, but they also have been used to integrate and exploit the labor power of women and of members of disadvantaged racial and ethnic groups in the interest of profit making. In the current global environment of open economies, new trade regimes, and competitive export industries, global accumulation relies heavily on the work of women, both waged and unwaged, in formal sectors and in the home, in manufacturing, and in public and private services. Generally speaking, the situation is better or worse for women depending on the type of state and the strength of the economy. Women workers in the welfare states of northern Europe fare best, followed by women in other core economies. In Eastern Europe and the former Soviet Union, the economic status of working women changed dramatically for the worse following the collapse of communism. In much of the developing world, a class of women professionals and workers employed in the public sector and in the private sector has certainly emerged due to rising educational attainment, changing aspirations, economic need, and the demand for relatively cheap lay bor. However, vast numbers of economically active women in the developing world lack formal training, work in the informal sector, have no access to social security, and live in poverty.

Proletarianization and Professionalization: Industry and Services

Let me begin with a definitional note. In my usage, *proletarianization* refers to the formation of a female working class. I distinguish this from the entry of middle-class women into the professions, which I refer to here as *professionalization*.[2] Proletarianization and professionalization coincide with the involvement of working women in trade unions and feminist organizations, including transnational feminist networks that promote women's human rights or that critique neoliberal economic policies for their adverse impact on low-income women.

As world markets expanded in the 1970s, a process of female proletarianization began to take place. In developing countries—and especially in Southeast and East Asia, parts of Latin America and the Caribbean, and Tunisia and Morocco—growing numbers of women were drawn into the labor-intensive and low-wage industries of textiles, garments, sportswear, electronics, and pharmaceuticals that produced for export as well as for the home market. The surge in women's waged employment in developing countries began in the 1970s, following an earlier period of capitalist development and economic growth that was characterized by the displacement of labor and craft work, commercialization of agriculture, and rural-urban migration.[3] Some called the marginalization of women "housewife-ization";[4] others have described it as the initial part of the "U pattern" of female labor-force participation in early modernization.[5]

During the 1970s, it was observed that export-processing zones (EPZs) along the U.S.–Mexico border and in Southeast Asia, established by transnational corporations to take advantage of low labor costs in developing countries, were hiring mainly women. By the early 1980s, it was clear that the new industrialization in what was then called the Third World was drawing heavily on women workers. Many studies by WID specialists and socialist-feminists centered on the role played by the available pool of relatively cheap female labor.[6] Gender ideologies emphasizing the "nimble fingers" of young women workers and their capacity for hard work, especially in the Southeast Asian economies, justified the recruitment of women for unskilled and semi-skilled work in labor-intensive industries at wages lower than men would accept, and in conditions that unions would not permit. In Latin America, women entered the labor force at a time when average wages were falling dramatically. Around the world, women's share of total industrial labor rarely exceeds 30 to 40 percent, but as Ruth Pearson pointed out, the proportion of women workers in export processing factories producing textiles, electronics components, and garments was much higher, "with figures as high as 90% in some cases."[7] An INSTRAW (Institute for Research and Training on Women) study found that exports of manufactures from developing countries were largely comprised of the kinds of products typically produced by female labor, leading Susan Joekes to conclude that industrialization had been "as much *female* led as *export* led."[8]

The process of the feminization of labor continued throughout the recessionary 1980s and into the 1990s, encompassing countries like Bangladesh, which had one of the largest increases in the share of women participating in the labor force—from 5 percent in 1965 to 42 percent in 1995. In 1978 the country had four garment factories; by 1995 it had 2,400. These factories employed 1.2 million workers, 90 percent of whom were women under the age of twenty-five.[9] Female proletarianization continues apace in China's highly globalized and integrated economy, where huge plants producing for the world market employ thousands of women each.[10] In 2000 it was reported that 90 percent of the workers in the 850 EPZs around the world were women—and "in the majority of cases workers' rights and social protection are non-existent in EPZs. Although they work in factories, what EPZ Workers have in common with informal sector workers is that they are unprotected, largely unorganized, female labour."[11]

Feminization occurred also in public services, where throughout the world women's share grew to 30–50 percent—at a time when public-sector wages, like industrial wages, were declining. In Iran, Egypt, and Turkey, women's share of public-service employment (including jobs as teachers and university professors in public schools and state universities, nurses and doctors in state hospitals, and workers and administrators across government agencies) increased during the 1990s. This occurred at a time when salaries had eroded tremendously and more men were gravitating toward the more lucrative and expanding private sector.[12]

As world trade in services has increased and global firms continue to engage in out-sourcing, the involvement of women in various occupations and professions of the service sector has grown. Women around the world have made impressive inroads into professional services such as law, banking, accounting, computing, and architecture; in tourism-related occupations; and in the information services, including offshore airline booking, mail order, credit cards, word-processing for publishers, telephone operators, and all manner of data entry and teleservices. In Barbados, according to one source, some three thousand people, or one in fifty of the country's labor force, were working in informatics in 1997, largely processing airline tickets and insurance forms. Low-cost typesetting is done in China, even by workers who do not understand what they are typing.[13] In India, Bangalore has become a technology hub, where thousands of young women work in offshore customer service centers for such firms as General Electric, British Airways, Amazon.com, and American Express.[14] Women in India represented 30 percent of employees in the computer industry in 2001, and 250,000 jobs were opened for women in the country's mobile phone industry. On the other hand, "many of these jobs are casual or part-time, and of much lower quality than men's."[15] The new technologies have enabled the reorganization of work based on the concept of flexibility.

The world trade in services favors women's labor migration, in contrast to the demand for male manufacturing workers during the earlier periods of industrialization in Europe and the United States.[16] Mexican, Central American, and Caribbean women have migrated to the United States to work as nurses, nannies, or domestics; Argentine women, to Italy to work as nurses; Filipinas and Sri Lankans, to the Middle East to work as waitresses, nurses, nannies, or domestics. Labor shortages in Europe and the growing demand for nurses has led to an out-migration of nurses from Ghana, South Africa, Jamaica, and Trinidad and Tobago.[17] In at least two countries—the Philippines and Sri Lanka—the majority of emigrants have been women.[18] There is also considerable intra-regional female labor migration, such as within Europe (e.g., East and Central Europeans to Western Europe) and Southeast and East Asia (e.g., women from the Philippines to Hong Kong).[19]

During the oil-boom years of the 1970s and afterwards, labor migration in the MENA region involved Palestinians, Egyptians, Jordanians, and Yemenis working in the oil-rich Gulf kingdoms. The remittances sent back by the predominantly male labor migrants allowed households in the capital-poor and labor-sending countries to maintain a relatively good standard of living. For both economic and political reasons, intra-Arab labor migration declined in the 1990s.[20] But this period also saw an increasing number of Moroccan,

Tunisian, and Algerian women migrating alone to work in various occupations in France, Italy, and Spain, among other European countries.

The proletarianization and professionalization of women have cultural repercussions and sometimes entail backlashes and gender conflicts. In some advanced capitalist countries, working women often have encountered serious forms of sexual harassment. In the semiperipheral countries of the Middle East, the increasing participation of women in the labor force was accompanied in the 1980s by subtle or overt pressures on them to conform to religious dictates concerning dress. Hence in Egypt, many professional women came to don modest dress and to cover their heads. In the earlier stage of the Islamist movement, the influx of women in the work force raised fears of competition with men, leading to calls for the redomestication of women, as occurred in Iran immediately after the Islamic revolution. Later, although Islamists in Turkey, Iran, Egypt, Jordan, and Morocco did not call on women to withdraw from the labor force—indeed, among their female adherents are educated and employed women from the lower middle class—they did insist on veiling and on spatial and functional segregation. On the other hand, Islamists in Algeria and Palestine have continued to emphasize female domesticity, for reasons of both ideology/theology and male material interests.

The surge in women's employment is characteristic not only of semi-peripheral countries. In sixteen European countries, the increase in the number of women in the labor force over the period 1983–91 was quite dramatic, whereas it was relatively modest for men. In six countries the number of employed men actually fell over the period, most significantly by 3.4 percent in Belgium. During the 1990s, the Nordic countries, including Finland, had the highest rate of employment among women, with North America following close behind.[21] The feminization of labor, it should be noted, refers to the influx of women into relatively low-paying jobs, but also to the growth of part-time and temporary work among *men*. This trend was especially noticeable in New Zealand, the United Kingdom, and the Netherlands, mainly in retail trade, hotels and catering, banking, and insurance.[22] Indeed, in the Netherlands, men's part-time work in 1992 was as high as 13.4 percent of total male employment, up from 5.5 percent in 1979. These employment trends for European women and men continued through the end of the 1990s.[23] Unemployment rates vary across the European Union, where some countries show very high rates of unemployment among the young. At the start of the new millennium, Spain had the highest unemployment rate for both women and men (15.4 percent), followed by France (10.8 percent). Spain and France also had the highest female unemployment rates (22.7 percent and 12.8 percent respectively) and highest unemployment rates for young women (36.3 percent and 26.3 percent respectively). Other European countries with two-digit unemployment rates were Finland, Ireland, Slovakia, and Poland. Female unemployment rates exceeded men's in the following countries: Belgium, the United States, Iceland, the Netherlands, Finland, Switzerland, France, Denmark, Luxembourg, Germany, Italy, Spain, Greece, Portugal, Czech Republic, Slovakia, Poland, Mexico. Even in Turkey, with a much lower female participation rate, women's unemployment rate was 99 percent of men's. Clearly women have experienced a disadvantaged position in labor markets in the industrial countries.[24]

The Informal Sector, the Income Gap, and Unemployment

At the same time that women entered the formal labor force in record numbers in the core countries, much of the observed increase in female labor-force participation in semi-peripheral countries occurred in the informal sectors of the economy. The extent of the urban informal sector and its links to the formal sector are matters of dispute, and women's involvement in it is rarely captured in the official statistics, but some studies have suggested significant increases in the size of the informal sector and in women's informal economic activities.[25] In Sub-Saharan Africa in the late 1990s, more than one-third of women in nonagricultural activities worked in the urban informal sector. Rates were as high as 65 to 80 percent in Senegal, Benin, Zambia, and Gambia.[26] Rates of urban informal activity among women have become high in parts of Peru, Indonesia, and Iran. Unregistered and small-scale urban enterprises, home-based work, and some self-employment fall into this category, and they include an array of commercial and productive activities. In the urban areas of developing countries, many formal jobs became informalized as employers sought to increase flexibility and lower labor and production costs through subcontracting, as Beneria and Roldan showed in their study of Mexico City and as Cinar revealed for Istanbul and Bursa.[27] Drawing on existing gender ideologies regarding women's roles, their attachment to family, and the perceived lower value of their work, subcontracting arrangements encourage the persistence of home-based work.[28] There is some debate concerning the reasons for women's concentration in such types of work, but some studies suggest that many women accept homebased employment—with its insecurity, low wages, and absence of benefits—as a convenient form of income generation that allows them to carry out domestic responsibilities and care for their children.[29]

The social relations of gender account for the pervasive income gap between men and women workers, a gap that is detrimental to women but lucrative to employers. On average women earn 75 percent of men's wages, with a narrower wage gap in the public sector than in the private sector.[30] Explanations for the gender gap are varied. Some point out that the gender difference in the income gap is based on lower education and intermittent employment among women workers. Others emphasize the role of gender bias. For example, in Ecuador, Jamaica, and the Philippines, women earn less than men despite higher qualifications, a problem that is especially acute in the private sector.[31] Labor-market segmentation along gender lines perpetuates the income gap. Pearson and Mitter found that in the computing and information processing sectors, the majority of high-skilled jobs went to male workers, while women were concentrated in the low-skilled ones.[32] In fact, all of the above factors are true and are consistent. For if "the uneven distribution of rewards has been the necessary pendant of capital accumulation," as Hopkins and Wallerstein argued,[33] then it is the deployment of female labor along the commodity chains of the global economy that guarantees a supply of relatively cheap labor, along with the desired higher profit margins.

Considering the social relations of gender and the function of gender ideologies, it should come as no surprise that despite women's key role in the global economy, the unemployment rates of women in the semiperiphery are very high, as we saw in the previous section in connection with the industrial countries. Global unemployment is partly a function of the nature of neoliberal economic policies, which have entailed massive retrenchment of labor in many semiperipheral countries, in the former socialist countries that underwent marketization, and in the core countries. In many developing countries unemployed women are new entrants to the labor force, who are seeking but not finding jobs. In certain countries where restructuring occurred in enterprises employing large numbers of women, or in export sectors that lost markets, the unemployment rates of women may also reflect job losses by previously employed women. This was the case in Malaysia in the mid–1980s, Viet Nam in the late 1980s, Poland, Bulgaria, and Russia in the early 1990s, and Morocco, Tunisia, and Turkey in the latter part of the 1990s. The Asian financial crisis of the late 1990s entailed further job and income losses for women workers, especially in South Korea, Thailand, and Indonesia. In South Korea, women lost jobs at twice the rate of men, despite the fact that before the crisis, they had been the preferred labor supply with an unemployment rate half that of men.[34]

In some cases, women have experienced job loss as a result of technological advances in the workplace. As has been noted above, many enterprises producing textiles and electronics for export have relied heavily on women workers. And yet as more sophisticated technology is used to produce these goods, women workers have tended to be replaced by men or recruited at a slower pace, as appears to have occurred in the Mexican *maquiladoras*,[35] and in the textiles industries of Spain and Italy. In all regions, high unemployment represents the downside of economic globalization, especially for women workers, who must contend with not only the class biases but also the gender biases of neoliberal economics. The feminization of unemployment, therefore, is as much a characteristic of the global economy as is the feminization of labor.

The analysis thus far may raise questions about the contingency versus permanence of the female labor force, and the possibility that female labor remains a reserve army of labor. Because the mass incorporation of women as proletarians and professionals is a relatively recent phenomenon, it is perhaps too soon to tell definitively.[36] However, I would argue that the incorporation of female labor is indeed a secular trend, due to the structural requirements of the capitalist world-system in the era of globalization, and also due to women's own aspirations. In turn, the contradictions of female labor incorporation have led women workers to join unions and women's organizations.

As part of the employment trends described above, more women have been joining trade unions, and have indeed been more likely than men to join unions, at a time when overall union membership has been in decline. In a number of advanced industrialized countries, such as the United States, Australia, and the Nordic countries, women have been the largest growing union constituency. Many unions, in response, are actively recruiting women workers, establishing women's departments, and appointing women trade unionists to decision-making positions. The growth of women's involvement in paid employment and in national-level unions has resulted in greater interest in women workers by the international trade unions.[37]

The International Confederation of Free Trade Unions (ICFTU) and the Public Services International (PSI) have active women's departments—and now, so does the AFL–CIO of the United States. In March 2002 the ICFTU—where women were 35 percent of members, compared with barely 7 percent when the union was formed about fifty years earlier—launched a three-year campaign called "Unions for Women, Women for Unions." The main theme for 2002 was "women's right to decent work." At the same time, the Executive Board and Women's Committee of the PSI identified pay equity as a priority issue, and launched a two-year campaign around it. For the major unions, the key issues identified by their women members are maternity protection, sexual harassment, balancing work and family life, job security, and decent wages. In addition, the International Labor Organization has determined that organizing women workers, especially in the informal sector, will strengthen unions as well as provide women workers with security and improved working conditions.[38]

Women trade unionists worked with other women's groups during the March 1995 Social Summit and the September 1995 Beijing conference. At the latter, and in recognition of women's growing importance in the global economy, as well as their growing union membership, Objective F of the 1995 Beijing Platform for Action affirmed the unions' important role in regulating and protecting women workers' rights, particularly where women constitute a very vulnerable group, as in export processing zones. Women trade unionists were also involved in the five-year reviews of the Social Summit and the Beijing conference in 2000.

Both the PSI and the ICFTU attend the annual meetings of the UN's Commission on the Status of Women. Their statements usually describe the exploitative employment conditions that many women workers face, the dangers of "free trade," and the need for implementation of ILO labor standards and other conventions on worker rights, human rights, and women's rights. The PSI has a comprehensive website called WomeNet, which contains news and data about working women around the world. The theme of the ICFTU's Seventh Conference, held in May 1999 in Rio de Janeiro, was "Working Women in the 21st Century: Demanding Our Space, Taking Our Place." As mentioned above, the ICFTU took part in the Beijing + 5 meetings and produced a number of policy briefs. According to one report published during the meetings:

> At Beijing + 5, women trade unionists are concentrating on Strategic Objective F: Women and the Economy. Unions believe that government progress in this area has been poor for a number of reasons—the weakness of democratic political institutions and the absence of a vigorous civil society, defense spending and the devastation caused by armed conflicts. Globalization has had a negative impact with more exploitation in the export processing zones, where the majority of workers are women and the growth of low-paid 3D (dirty, dangerous and degrading) jobs. Cuts in public services have also hit women disproportionately. Job losses have forced women to emigrate to find work and so migrant women's needs are increasingly important.[39]

The report noted that although women workers have found traditional union structures unwelcoming, they now constituted "the future of the trade union movement" and were much more likely than men to account for the increases in union membership. As a result, "one of the important lessons of the Women's Summit is that unions must change to incorporate women's enthusiasm and ideas to fight globalization. Women need unions and unions need women."[40]

In many developing countries, women workers face difficulties in unionization, including employer harassment, state repression, and the masculine character of the existing trade unions. Still, increasing female labor force participation in Latin American, Asian, and African countries has placed issues pertaining to women workers on the agendas of trade unions and of women's organizations in those regions. In Guatemala, women workers at an export shirt-making factory won a union contract, the first in a Guatemala *maquiladora*.[41] In Japan, the Asia-Japan Women's Resource Center studies and promotes the rights of women workers throughout East and Southeast Asia and publishes a newsletter called *Resource Materials on Women's Labor in Japan*.[42] In Taiwan the Grassroots Women Workers Centre, established in 1988, engages in various activities, including defense of the rights of immigrant women workers, and publishes a newsletter called *Female Workers in Taiwan*. According to its spring 1994 newsletter, "the Centre intends to provide opportunities for factory women and family subcontractors to reform the male-dominated workers' union, and to develop women workers' unions and workers' movements through the promotion of feminism." Similar activities and goals are shared by the Committee for Asian Women in Hong Kong. One important development came about in 2001, when the Hong Kong Domestic Workers Union was formed as an affiliate of the Hong Kong Confederation of Trade Unions. India's famous Self-Employed Women's Association (SEWA) operates as a trade union and a consciousness-raising feminist organization. A similar organization was formed in Durban, South Africa, in 1994 and is called the Self-Employed Women's Union.

In the Middle East and North Africa, the involvement of women in paid employment has resulted in the politicization of women and of gender issues, but women have also responded by joining unions (though their proportions remain small), forming their own organizations, and engaging in collective action. In Tunisia, the National Commission on Working Women was created in July 1991 within the Tunisian General Federation of Workers. The commission has twenty-seven branches throughout Tunisia, and carries out surveys and studies pertaining to women and the workplace. Israeli Arab women workers ignored by the Histadrut formed the Arab Women Workers Project, and Palestinian women activists in the West Bank and Gaza formed the Palestine Working Women Society. Morocco's Democratic League of Women's Rights organized a Roundtable on the Rights of Workers in 1995; subsequently a committee structure consisting of twelve participating organizations was formed. The group sought to revise the labor code to take into account women's conditions, to include domestic workers in the definition of wage workers and the delineation of their rights and benefits, to set the minimum work age at fifteen, and to provide workers on maternity leave with full salary and a job-back guarantee. In November 1995, some five hundred women textile workers employed by the Manufacture du Maroc factory outside Rabat went on strike for two weeks to protest "repeated violence" against several women employees. This included the arbitrary dismissal of the general secretary of the factory's union of women workers, her subsequent rape by a foreman, and the firing of seventeen women workers who protested the union leader's dismissal and rape. Morocco's Association of Democratic Women, a feminist organization, then set out to "mobilize human rights organizations and all the women's organizations" in defense of the women workers. The incident shows not only the vulnerability of women at the workplace, but the capacity of women workers to fight in defense of their rights, and the ability of the feminist organizations to mobilize support for women workers.

There are other examples of bold action by women trade unionists in the MENA region, some of which have been followed by state repression. In September 2000, thirty-five women affiliated to the Turkish union KESK who wanted to send letters of support to the UN concerning the Women's Global March 2000 were "detained and ill-treated." The following month, some women who wanted to begin a march to Ankara were confronted by police and arrested in Duzce.[43] And since 1998, Iranian working-class and professional women have formed unions of journalists, publishers, lawyers, teachers, and nurses, despite a political climate that is hostile to independent organizing.

Various transnational advocacy networks have emerged to support women workers. Women Working Worldwide, based in Manchester, England, has links with women worker groups in Central America and in South and Southeast Asia. IRENE (International Restructuring Education Network Europe), based in Tilburg, Holland, organizes educational seminars for unions from around the world, and disseminates a newsletter. Mujer a Mujer coordinates women workers' activities across the U.S.–Mexico border.[44] STITCH is a Chicago-based network of U.S. women that supports Central American women organizing in the maquila apparel-for-export industries. Some of its activists are associated with the International Textile, Garment, and Leather Workers Federation, which has a maquila project.[45]

As Gallin has pointed out, trade unions have championed women's rights since their beginnings and have included many charismatic women among their leaders, including Flora Tristan, Louise Michel, Clara Zetkin, Mary "Mother" Jones, Federica Montseny, Marie Nielsen, and Margarethe Faas.[46] However, the labor movement has been dominated by the culture of the male industrial workers, and the culture of unions has been rather masculine and often unfriendly to women workers. Thus in some cases women created their own unions. In Canada, the Federation of Women Teachers' Associations of Ontario is a women-only organization.[47] Denmark produced the Danish Women Workers' Union, KAD.[48] In more recent years, however, and particularly in northern Europe, Italy, Australia, and North America, union membership is taking on a female face.[49] In 2001, Germany's Trade Union Confederation had a female membership of 2.5 million women, or 31 percent of total members. According to the AFL-CIO, whereas U.S. women accounted for 19 percent of union members in 1962, by 1997 fully 39 percent of all union members were women, and they numbered 5.5 million. In 2002, two out of three new members were women, which is no doubt why the AFL-CIO launched its own "Unions for Women, Women for Unions" campaign.[50] U.S. labor organizations such as UNITE (a textile and garment workers' union) and the Hotel and Restaurant Employees "now understand that feminist issues like sweat-shops, comparable worth for women, sexual harassment and education provide the vital pathway toward the expansion and revitalization of their movement."[51]

Since the mid–1980s, women have made their way into positions of power in Australian trade unions at a time when overall union membership began to decline. The numbers of women on the foremost national council, the Australian Council of Trade Unions, rose from zero to one-third; in the mid–1990s in the State of South Australia the three major white-collar unions (teachers, nurses, public servants) were all led by women.[52] In Canada, where 31 percent of women workers (and 38 percent of men workers) were unionized in 1992,[53] women's committees succeeded not only in bringing benefits to women workers but also in bringing "increased energy" to unions such as the Ontario Public Service Employees Union.[54] According to Linda Briskin, "Canada has a strong movement of union women, and a vibrant autonomous women's movement," and these movements have "successfully pres-sured the unions to take up the issues of childcare, abortion, sexual harassment, pay equity, affirmative action and employment equity, etc.—as women's issues and as union issues."[55] According to Rosemary Warskett, Canadian "union feminism" effectively challenged the narrow vision of industrial unionism. "It is now well established in Canada that collective bargaining demands should address the needs of women and other discriminated groups."[56]

In global terms, the highest union density is found in northern Europe—Denmark, Finland, Norway, and Sweden—where women's participation as workers and as union of-ficials is the greatest. In those countries, union density is very high in community, social, and personal services (68–87 percent), in trade, restaurants, and hotels (47–49 percent), and in manufacturing (80–100 percent), in both the public and private sectors. Women are making up an increasing share of union membership, especially in services, with the most impressive figures found in Denmark. In the 1990s Danish women represented 42 and 62 percent of the two main union federations; they were 30 and 39 percent of the delegates to the union Congress and 13 and 41 percent of members of leading committees, as well as 10 and 30 percent of leaders of individual unions.[57] On at least one occasion that I know of, during the 1990s the Danish labor movement sent an all-woman delegation to the annual Congress of the International Labor Organization in Geneva. In Finland during the 1990s women comprised 45 percent of the membership of one of the two labor confederations (SAK); they also constituted about 37.5 percent of delegates to the SAK Congress, and 40 percent of the union council. The proportions of women in union leadership positions also increased in other European countries, as well as in some of the large international unions.

According to an ICFTU report released in June 2000, many unions have organized campaigns against violence and sexual harassment at work. These include Argentina's CGTA, the CDT in the Democratic Republic of Congo, and Malaysia's MTUC. Spanish unions concluded agreements with the government on job security and part-time work. Poland's NSZZ campaigned for better maternity protection within the ILO Convention. India's HMS drew up a detailed Charter of Demands for women workers, while Japan's RENGO campaigned for the strict implementation of the Equal Employment Opportunity Law. The ICFTU maintains that "unions have strengthened relations with NGOs and women's organizations and together they have been effective in putting forward women's views and demands to the government."[58] Gallin reports that "unions have increasingly entered partnerships with women's NGOs, organizing drives and forming alliances to represent informal workers' interests."[59]

Female labor incorporation and trends in women's unionization provide the social basis for women's mobilization on a world scale, but they also have occurred in a context of growing inequalities and economic crises. What follows is a cross-regional review of developments that have adversely affected women, and the ways that TFNs have responded.

Global Inequalities, Regional Crises, and Impacts on Women

As more women were drawn into the processes of economic globalization, they became aware not only of persistent social and gender inequalities but also of the creation of new forms of inequalities and the emergence of periodic economic crises that threaten the well-being of entire communities. Although many economists, particularly those wedded to neoliberalism or globalism, argue that free markets benefit all, others gather convincing empirical data to show that inequalities have been increasing within and across countries. Feminists use the same data to highlight the adverse impacts on women.

According to the UNDP's 1999 *Human Development Report,* while globalization offers great opportunities for human advancement, enriching people's lives, expanding choices, and creating a community based on shared values, markets have been allowed to dominate the process, at the expense of building these shared values and achieving common goals."[60] Market volatility has been behind a number of regional macroeconomic crises, which affect the poor in various ways. Declining labor earnings, unemployment, and inflation combine to reduce household income. Many poor households react to a crisis by postponing preventive or curative health measures, or by reducing the nutritional intake of children, or by withdrawing their children from school.

Sub-Saharan Africa has been in economic decline since the 1970s, and it has the largest proportion of people living on less than $1 a day. Stagnation set in after governments submitted to structural adjustment policies in hopes of attracting foreign investment and loans. Yet the region accounts for only 2 percent of all international trade, less than it did during the last days of colonialism fifty years ago. Although corrupt governments, excessive military spending, armed conflicts, and natural disasters such as drought can explain part of the problem, it is also true that deteriorating terms of trade in the form of steep declines in prices for African commodities are also salient. In countries where socialist-style economies were replaced by deregulated free-market models, farmers and industrialists lost business, workers lost jobs, and many women turned to prostitution—including export prostitution in Europe.

Latin America went through a severe economic recession in the 1980s, and crises erupted again in the 1990s, most notably in Mexico and Argentina in 1995, and Brazil in 1999. According to studies by the Inter-American Development Bank, at the turn of the new century, the wealthiest 10 percent received 40 percent of national incomes, while the poorest 30 percent received just 7.5 percent. One of the reasons is that the vast majority of the working population, and mostly women, work in poor-quality jobs. The crises in Mexico and Argentina imposed severe hardship on the poor, and contributed to the feminization of poverty. In Argentina poverty rose from 16.9 percent in 1993 to 24.8 percent in 1995. Argentina's economy deteriorated further in 2001 and 2002, leading to public riots, the downfall of several governments, and widespread disillusionment with the U.S.-backed free-market policies that were adopted in the 1990s. The IMF prescribed its usual austerity package.[61]

In the 1980s social funds were implemented to help offset the effects of structural adjustment policies (SAPs), but most neglected to improve the income-generating capacity of the poor. The IFIs focused on assisting stabilization and liberalization efforts and generally neglected to help governments protect pro-poor services from public spending cuts. Fiscal strategies to protect pro-poor spending began to take place only during Brazil's devaluation crisis of 1999. Latin America's basic services remain underfunded.[62] As a result, poverty may have increased in Mexico during the 1990s, despite economic growth and NAFTA. At least forty million (or 40 percent) of Mexico's population of 97 million live in poverty, and of that number, seventeen million live in misery.[63] Between 1994 and 1998, the share of the nation's income earned by the 20 percent of wealthiest Mexicans leaped from 49 to 54 percent while the earning of the poorest 40 percent of families fell from 14 to 12 percent.[64] Small wonder that illegal immigration from Mexico to the United States shows no sign of abatement.

During the decade of economic reform, unemployment rose at a rapid rate, according to a 1999 ILO report on Latin America and the Caribbean. The majority of new jobs were in the informal sector, where wages, productivity and social protection are much lower than in the formal sector. The ILO reports that youth unemployment rates usually have been double the national average (and triple for workers aged 15–19), and that women's unemployment rates are between 10–60 percent higher than the rates for men.[65]

The transition to a market economy in Eastern Europe and the former Soviet Union has been associated with increased inequality and social stratification. In the 1990s, living standards fell for a majority of people, unemployment and poverty grew, the distribution of assets and earnings changed radically, and social benefits fell. In particular, the FSU countries saw inequality climb to levels comparable to Latin America.[66] According to research by UNICEF, mortality rates rose considerably, particularly among men in Russia, leaving behind widows who had to cope with unemployment or low wages as household heads. In Central Asia, women were the targets of dramatic job cuts as state-owned companies were sold to the private sector. In many countries of the former socialist world, according to data from the ILO's *Key Indicators of the Labor Market 1999*, female unemployment rates are very high: 12.5 percent in Slovakia; 14.6 percent in Latvia; 20.1 percent in Croatia; 27.4 percent in Bulgaria; 44.5 percent in Macedonia.

Unemployment rates similarly have been very high in the Middle East and North Africa, especially for women: 24 percent in Algeria, Egypt, and Morocco; 14 percent in Syria; 20 percent in Turkey during most of the 1990s.[67] Morocco and Algeria have seen a high rate of impoverishment, a dangerous curtailment of social protection, and a heightened sense of exclusion among the marginalized and the excluded. In 1994, Algeria became unable to service its $26 billion foreign debt, which was consuming 93.4 percent of export earnings, and it had to resort to an IMF and World Bank SAP in exchange for debt relief. The SAP led to a 40 percent devaluation of the dinar, the lifting of subsidies on basic food, and the liberalization of foreign trade. Between 1994 and 1998, 815 public enterprises were dissolved, and Public Economic Enterprises laid off 60 percent of their workers.[68] Although the retrenchments affected mainly men, women's livelihood was adversely affected. More women sought jobs to augment deteriorating household budgets, but gender biases as well as structural economic problems foreclosed employment opportunities. Meanwhile, poverty increased, and government data showed that the percentage of the population living below the poverty line in 1995 was 8.9 percent in the urban areas and 19.3 percent in the rural areas. The poor and vulnerable population, however, was calculated to be 14.7 percent in urban areas and 30.4 percent in rural areas.[69]

Inequalities are wide and the poverty level high in Morocco, too. In 1999 it was estimated that around 20 percent of the population of 30 million lived in poverty, 10 percent in sheer misery, while 30 percent—mostly the young and the elderly—were classified as vulnerable. Around 56 percent of Moroccans were illiterate, and only 18 percent of women could read and write. Unemployment hovers at around 20 percent, though again much higher for women than for men, and the quality of the educational system has fallen markedly. According to Layachi, the socialist government of Abdelrahman Yousoufi was caught "between the pressing problems of his people, on the one hand, and the demands of international institutions which are likely to result in even more hardship, on the other."[70] Or as a Moroccan feminist rhetorically asked at an AWMR annual meeting in July 2000, "How can the state improve the status of women, children, and the poor when international financial institutions are in control?"[71]

Tunisia has done much better in preventing the spread of poverty and has put into place an extensive social welfare system, which may be the only one of its kind in the MENA region. And yet, its trade with Europe may be endangered when the Free Trade Agreement that it signed with the EU comes into effect in 2007. It is estimated that between fifteen hundred and three thousand firms—many of them textiles and garment firms that employ women—will go out of business. The association agreement, which calls for abolishing tariff barriers in Tunisia, could increase imports and trade deficits, and is likely to diminish state revenue from tariffs.[72] This could have an adverse impact on the social welfare programs administered by the state, as well as retrench thousands of women workers.

The Asian financial crisis that swept across South and Southeast Asia exposed the dangers of the global trade economy. The crisis imposed significant costs in Thailand, Indonesia, the Republic of Korea, and to lesser extents, Malaysia and the Philippines. Economic crisis set in when skittish international investors began dumping their Asian holdings, resulting in financial panic, bankruptcy, massive unemployment, and increases in poverty. National governments were unable to stabilize the economic free-fall or cushion the shocks to workers and families. The countries had few policy tools (e.g., social insurance) available to combat poverty directly. (There were limited benefits provided by "provident funds," which are lump-sum benefits for pensioners or disabled workers.) The Republic of Korea did offer unemployment insurance, but its program covered only 22 percent of the labor force and provided only a few months of benefits at a fraction of workers' earnings.[73] Thus, when the Asian economies nosedived, their own safety nets were insufficient to meet the needs of the five million workers thrown out of their jobs or the countless families thrown into poverty. Meanwhile, the IMF response was the traditional austerity regime. As former World Bank chief economist Joseph Stiglitz put it, the IMF demanded reductions in government spending and elimination of subsidies for basic necessities like food and fuel "at the very time when contractionary policies made those subsidies more desperately needed than ever." Moreover, "not only was the IMF not restoring economic confidence in East Asia, it was undermining the region's social fabric."[74] This aggravated the crisis while preventing the affected governments from spending on antipoverty social services and income supports. The IMF later recognized this mistake and reversed its policy.

There is some evidence that women were the special victims of the Asian crisis. Women in these countries, as elsewhere, continue to confront social barriers that crowd them into some industries and occupations, foreclose entry into others, and generally push them onto the margins of economic life. Women are the last hired, the first fired, and the least likely to qualify for benefits provided by their employers or by their governments. Country papers circulated at the January 2000 consultation of the Bangkok-based Committee for Asian Women found that in Hong Kong, the female unemployment rate was as high as 25.8 percent and that women made up a high proportion of irregular workers; that during the crisis in South Korea many married women were made redundant or asked to resign from their jobs; that two thousand Malaysian women were laid off when a world market factory in Penang closed its operations in January 2000; and that even before the crisis, Indonesian women experienced higher rates of unemployment as well as various forms of employment discrimination.[75]

The Republic of Korea was the most industrialized of the affected countries. Prior to the crisis, labor markets were tight, with unemployment at a low 2 percent in 1995 and 1996. But between April 1997 and April 1998, overall employment shrank by 5.1 percent. Women workers suffered the worst of the crisis-induced job losses; employment fell 3.8 percent for men but fully 7.1 percent for women. As jobs became harder to find, both men and women fell out of the labor force, but again, the effect was more pronounced for women. Between spring 1997 and 1998, the participation rate for men in the labor force fell by 0.5 percent, while for women the decline was 2.8 percent.[76]

Younger workers suffered the greatest share of job losses, and younger women suffered more than younger men. Employment rates in the 15-to-19-year-old age bracket fell 8.7 percent for men, but 20.2 percent for women. Unexpectedly, job losses for the 20-to-29-year-old age group were roughly equal: 13.3 percent for men and 13.7 percent for women. Older women also bore a disproportionate share of the job losses. Men between 50 and 59 saw employment rates fall 5.5 percent; for women the same age, employment shrank by 6.6 percent. Employment of men sixty years and older fell negligibly by 0.8 percent, but employment of older women declined 7.5 percent.[77]

In Thailand, 54,000 workers were laid off between January 1997 and February 1998. Slightly more than half were women. But these figures account for only the minority of the work force covered by employer-provided severance benefits and greatly understate the number of layoffs that actually occurred. According to one survey, 60 percent of the workers who lost jobs in Thailand were women over thirty years of age, one quarter of whom had been textile and garment workers.[78]

In Indonesia, during 1998, the garment and textile sector, a major employer of women, was responsible for retrenching 240,000 from paying jobs. Before the crisis, just over 49 percent of Indonesian women were working. By August 1998, this number had increased to more than 56 percent. But this increase was entirely the result of women working as unpaid labor in family-run enterprises. The fraction of women surveyed working at paid employment increased by a statistically insignificant 1 percent, from 36 percent to 37 percent. Meanwhile, job-creation programs by the government, which focused on infrastructure development, benefited men, because women make up only a small fraction of the construction and forestry work forces.[79]

The regional crises briefly described above became the target of criticism from various quarters. Well-known economists such as Joseph Stiglitz and Jeffrey Sachs pointed to misguided policies imposed by the World Bank, the IMF, and the U.S. Treasury, blaming them in particular for exacerbating the "Asian flu" that resulted in job loss and impoverishment. Women trade unionists and feminist economists did the same, while also stressing the class and gender inequalities and the North–South asymmetries that underpin these policy prescriptions.

Transnational Feminist Responses

Along with other groups in the global justice movement, transnational feminist networks have pointed out that decision-making in the institutions of global governance is undemocratic, and that many financial arrangements and trade decisions undermine international agreements on human rights, women's rights, labor protection, and environmental protection. They have been critical of exploitative working conditions, of the declining role of the state in the provision of social services, and of the volatility of global financial markets. In a regional meeting on the Asian crisis held in Manila in 1998, a woman trade unionist from the Philippines asserted: "The Asian crisis is fundamentally an offshoot of globalization." She accused Asian governments of "opening up their countries for further capitalist exploitation and plunder" through policy schemes such as deregulation, privatization, and liberalization. She continued:

> The widely liberalized financial system of the Philippines economy as dictated by the GATT–WTO and APEC and acceded to by the Philippine government, has provided the initial shot that triggered the trouble. With the rise in the prices of basic goods and the contracting of the purchasing power of the peso, women of the working class need to stretch their hours even more to find ways and means to augment their income. Because there are no jobs available and even a meager capital for a small business is very hard to come by, anti-social activities have become increasingly palatable. Prostitution has always been the last option for many Filipino women who need to keep their families afloat. ... As the women and children cope to survive, the government prioritizes to cut down on basic social services among others.[80]

Women activists have long called for a serious consideration of women's labor and of their rights. Research has shown that women's labor is a critical factor in many of the mechanisms that make globalization work, including export manufacturing, trade liberalization, and the promotion of sectors such as tourism and financial services. However, the impact of these mechanisms often has been to undermine or weaken women's social and economic rights. In response, women's groups are insisting that "the economic models that underpin globalization need to be transformed not just to ease women's pain but to give them full respect for the role they can play in a global system of well-being and justice. A global economic system in which women are central must be one in which women enjoy their full human rights."[81] WEDO, for example, is adamant about the need for a major overhaul of economic policy decision-making, and of its democratization: "The accepted view among those in power is that the 'benefits' of globalization need to be more equitably distributed, not that macroeconomic decision-making is in need of transformation."[82] A similar view is shared by DAWN: "The eradication of poverty and unemployment cannot be addressed without a fundamental shift in the thinking and direction of the global political economy and its management."[83] And as WIDE has noted, women worldwide have developed strategies and organized themselves to tackle gender and class oppression, on a local level in finding survival strategies, and on an international level by joining forces to develop strategies to influence policies.[84]

The campaign Fifty Years Is Enough/U.S. Network for Global Economic Justice has issued documents describing how IMF and World Bank policies damage women worldwide. "In over 80 countries around the world, the WB/IMF routinely subjugate the social and economic rights of poor and working people, particularly women, to the pursuit of economic reform. ... These impacts are overwhelmingly negative. Extensive data from around the world show that IMF-imposed austerity and economic reform programs have stripped many women of what meager health and education benefits were once available to them." The group also has developed a critique of trafficking in women—both prostitution and labor migration. In one policy document they wrote: "Not only do women dominate as workers in export industries, but they themselves have become the exports. In Indonesia, for example, women migrants to the Middle East increased from 8,000 in 1979 to over 100,000 in 1999. In the Philippines, women composed more than 60% of the 675,000 documented overseas workers in 1994." The document pointed out that the majority of women migrants were service workers—domestic helpers, entertainers, and related work—subject to harsh conditions and vulnerable to sexual abuse and violence. It continued: "The IMF's undermining labor rights in the name of economic reform is a choice to support and encourage the exploitation of women workers."[85]

Feminists also have recognized that the market gives almost no rewards for care, whether paid or unpaid. In the industrial countries, wages for teaching, domestic service, and other caring work have stagnated, or even fallen. The search for efficiency in the global economy imposes a "market discipline" that is at variance with quality. Cost-minimizing standards drive down quality in schools, hospitals, and child-care centers. However, feminists are quick to stress that this does not mean sending women back to the traditional role of housewife and mother. Nor does it mean that women should continue to be responsible for most unpaid care work or reproductive labor. Instead it means sharing unpaid care services between men and women, reducing men's paid work, increasing their time on family care, and increasing the supply of state-supported care services. For example, the Nordic countries have a long tradition of such approaches, which give public recognition and payment for care, rewarding family commitment but without reinforcing traditional gender roles. Transnational feminist networks often call for the array of social and reproductive rights that are in place in the Nordic countries. This is consistent with their call for the return of the welfarist, developmentalist state.

Given the transnational feminist critique of women's labor conditions, of the volatility and hierarchies of the global economy, and of the adverse impact of neoliberal trade policies, it is not surprising that women's groups of all types were present in Seattle to protest the WTO in late 1999. One group that attended was Feminists for Animal Rights (FAR); they were in Seattle because "WTO dispute panels interpret an animal protection law as nothing more than an unfair trade barrier." FAR was also critical of what it said was the way that the U.S. used the WTO to sabotage animal protection regulations. "When the EU banned the use of artificial growth hormones in beef, both in local production and imports, the U.S. promptly challenged the ban, claiming it put U.S. beef producers at a disadvantage."[86] Other groups present in Seattle were Women in Development Europe (WIDE), the Women's Environment and Development Organization (WEDO), the Women's Division of the United Methodist Church, and Diverse Women for Diversity. All issued position papers on global trade and women's rights. According to one participant, "Women's international organizations and networks participated in numbers in the NGO preparations before the Third Ministerial Meeting of WTO. ... During the preparations the issue of Human Rights and Trade came up forcefully in appeals, declarations, papers, and discussions. The point was made that Human Rights, as they are defined in international and regional conventions, should not be violated by trade agreements, policies, and rules. The International Human Rights Covenants are by far superior to all trade agreements."[87]

The Women's Caucus issued a Declaration that called for transparency, access to the WTO and participation by NGOs, a comprehensive gender, social, and environmental assessment before any new round, and gender and regional balance in all WTO decision-making. (See Declaration, Appendix.) Diverse Women for Diversity issued a Declaration that reiterated their goal of biological and cultural diversity as the foundation of life on earth, as well as self-sufficiency, self-reliance, and solidarity, locally and globally. (See Declaration, Appendix.)

A Gender and Trade Network was formed by the women activists in Seattle, including women representing WIDE, WEDO, DAWN–Caribbean, the Center of Concern, and Fifty Years Is Enough. In their policy documents, they called for democratic decision–making and insisted that all WTO agreements be bound by existing human rights agreements, such as the International Covenant on Economic, Social, and Cultural Rights (1966) and the Convention on the Elimination of All Forms of Discrimination against Women (1979). At the Seattle protests and afterwards, WIDE stressed that no trade agreements should be allowed to contradict the agreements set forth at the UN conferences of the 1990s: UNCED 1992, Human Rights 1993, ICPD 1994, Copenhagen 1995, and Beijing 1995. Similarly, the Women's International Coalition for Economic Justice (WICEJ) issued a "Declaration for Economic Justice and Women's Empowerment" calling for an "enabling environment [that would] favor political, economic, and social policies, institutions and values that promote human rights and social justice for all peoples." It called for "macro-policies designed to defend the rights of women and poor people and protect the environment, rather than expand growth, trade and corporate profits exclusively. ... Redefining economic efficiency to include measuring and valuing women's unpaid as well as paid work. Economic efficiency needs to be reoriented towards the effective realization of human development and human rights rather than growth, trade, and corporate profits."[88]

Feminist networks were similarly present at the protests against the World Bank and the IMF and for debt cancellation in Washington, D.C., in April 2000. It was perhaps not surprising that the Women's International League for Peace and Freedom (WILPF) was present, given its long history in the peace and socialist movements, but the presence of liberal-feminist organizations such as the U.S. Feminist Majority and several U.S. radical-feminist groups confirmed that feminists around the world were making the global economy a priority. For example, in the wake of the Seattle protests, the U.S. radical-feminist news magazine *Off Our Backs* devoted an issue to the critique of global economic policies. The issue included an interview with one of the movement lawyers who defended protesters in Seattle and Washington, D.C., another interview with a leading feminist economist and activist on structural adjustment and other neoliberal economic policies, a report on the abuse of domestic workers, an article on women's union organizing in Honduras, and an article on "neoliberalism at work in Nicaragua." The issue included the following admonition: "As a movement, Western feminism has often been criticized for being less than attentive to poor women's and women of color's lives and concerns. Feminism in the U.S. has received even more criticism for wearing cultural blinders when it comes to global women's issues. ... The fact is that feminists should be the vocal majority in the protests against the WTO, IMF, and World Bank and of globalization in general. Feminists have a responsibility to make this issue a priority."[89]

Much of the new work on trade has been carried out by feminist social scientists active within transnational feminist networks such as DAWN and WIDE (e.g., Gita Sen, Mariama Williams, Brita Neuhold), as well as within WICEJ and Women Working Worldwide (which set up the women's caucus at the first Ministerial Conference of the WTO in Singapore in 1996). As advocates for women, and concerned about social and gender inequalities, they monitor and examine the gendered effects of trade agreements within the NAFTA region and the EU, as well as the impact of WTO rules and agreements on working women in developing countries. There is increasing criticism of the reliance on the market and on trade liberalization. The criticism is that the employment losses and dislocation that often accompany trade liberalization, as well as the consequences of price liberalization and privatization of social services brought about by recent trade agreements, are disproportionately borne by women. It is argued that current trade agreements undermine national development and women's entrepreneurship. Domestic trade liberalization and WTO rules make under-resourced women compete with subsidized food imports, while access to Northern food markets is still limited. The foreign exchange generated by FDI is often used to pay external debt rather than stimulate local production and growth. Trade agreements also undermine commitments made by governments in the 1990s conferences on human rights, the environment, and women's rights. TFNs advocate for the removal of the agricultural sector and trade-related intellectual property rights from the WTO's purview (to ensure food security, protect women small farmers, and prevent "biopiracy"), and for deprivatizauon of public services such as health and education. They insist that the WTO take social and gender issues seriously, that a gender perspective be incorporated into macro-economic policies, and that social clauses be integrated into trade agreements. They call for the participation of women's organizations at regional trade meetings. They endorse the Tobin Tax and support a kind of global Keynesianism.

An example of transnational mobilizing around the issues discussed above is the World March of Women 2000. The initiative, which had been launched two years earlier in Montreal, Canada, by the Fédération des femmes du Québec, culminated in a series of coordinated marches and other actions held around the world to protest poverty and violence against women. Nearly six thousand organizations from 159 countries and territories were represented in the rallies and marches held. It is noteworthy that women activists from countries of the Middle East and North Africa, not usually visible in transnational feminist organizing and mobilizing around economic justice, were involved in the planning and execution of the march. Women trade unionists were also involved; for example, in April 2000, some three thousand trade unionists, including many women workers, marched in Durban, South Africa, in an event organized jointly by the ICFTU and its South African affiliates. The demands included affordable and accessible housing and transportation; protection against all forms of violence; equal rights for women in the workplace and throughout society; an end to structural adjustment programs and cutbacks in social budgets and public services; cancellation of the debt of all Third World countries; making gender issues central to labor policies and programs; and treatment and protection for people with HIV/AIDS.[90]

The initiative's *Advocacy Guide to Women's World Demands* described the world as governed by two forces: neoliberal capitalism and patriarchy, defined as the structural causes of poverty and forms of violence against women.

We live in a world whose dominant economic system, neoliberal capitalism, is fundamentally inhuman. It is a system governed by unbridled competition that strives for privatization, liberalization, and deregulation. It is a system entirely driven by the dictates of the market and where full employment of basic human rights ranks below the laws of the marketplace. The result: the crushing social exclusion of large segments of the population, threatening world peace and the future of the planet...

Neoliberalism and patriarchy feed off each other and reinforce each other in order to maintain the vast majority of women in a situation of cultural inferiority, social devaluation, economic marginalization, "invisibility" of their existence and labour, and the marketing and commercialization of their bodies. All these situations closely resemble apartheid.

The World March of Women proposed concrete measures to combat poverty and incidents of violence against women:

- Implementation of the Tobin Tax on speculative transactions
- An end to structural adjustment policies and to cutbacks in social budgets and public services
- Changes to global governance such as the democratization of the UN (including the Security Council), and the establishment of a World Council for Economic and Financial Security.

These demands were presented to World Bank president James Wolfensohn on 15 October 2000.

Conclusions

In this chapter I have tried to show that women have been incorporated into the global economy as a source of relatively cheap labor, and that the social-gender effects of economic globalization have been mixed. The simultaneous emergence and expansion of formal and informal employment among women should be understood in terms of the cyclical processes and secular trends in capitalist development and expansion, and the necessary unevenness of those processes. At a meso level of analysis, we can understand trends in female employment and unemployment in terms of labor-market stratification, various management strategies to extract surplus-value or increase profitability, and (during the 1980s and 1990s) the depressed status of unions. At the macro level of analysis, the capitalist world-economy is maintained by *gendered* labor, with definitions of skill, allocation of resources, occupational distribution, and modes of remuneration shaped by asymmetrical gender relations. Moreover, gender ideologies define the roles and rights of men and women and the relative value of their labor. But the effects of this incorporation have not been uniformly negative, for there have been unintended consequences of women's economic participation.

In separate writings, Susan Tiano and Seung-Kyung Kim provide detailed accounts of how women workers in the Mexican maquilas and in a South Korean free export zone, respectively, accommodate and resist the dominating forces of global capitalism and patriarchy. Others, such as Helen Safa, have shown that the entry of women into the labor force in such large numbers has important implications for changes in gender relations and ideologies within the household and the larger society, and for women's gender consciousness and activism.[91] The emergence of working-class consciousness and the labor movement during the nineteenth and early twentieth centuries is paralleled by the emergence of gender consciousness and the women's movement in the late twentieth century and into the new century.

Thus the era of globalization has produced at least two significant forms of women's mobilization. First, as we have seen, women workers have been joining trade unions, and unions themselves have become more attentive to women workers' issues and to issues identified as feminist. Second, feminists—in particular those organized in transnational feminist networks—have responded to globalization processes in vocal and visible ways. In national unions, international unions, and feminist organizations, women respond to the opportunities and the constraints of the globalization process, making demands on employers, states, and the international financial and trade institutions.

In the next chapter, we turn to an examination of women's movements and women's organizations, with a focus on some of the organizational features of transnational feminist networks.

Chapter Thirteen

From Structural Adjustment to the Global Trade Agenda

Valentine Moghadam

When women's skills become sources of great profit for a few, while these women themselves remain the most prominent members of the dispossessed, the market system cannot be considered "free." [WIDE, 1995]

Human development means supporting the development of people's potential to lead creative, useful and fulfilling lives. Human development for all is or should be the direct goal of economic growth processes and transforming gender relations is central to the human development of both women and men. As class, caste, race and other social relations of power are embedded in inequalities between nations and interwoven with gender relations so as to pose major barriers, their transformation is key to human development. [Gita Sen, of DAWN, 1995]

Women do not want to be mainstreamed into a polluted stream. We want to clean the stream and transform it into a fresh and flowing body. One that moves in a direction—a world at peace, that respects human rights for all, renders economic justice and provides a sound and healthy environment. [Bella Abzug, of WEDO, 1998]

Transnational feminist networks have joined the global economic justice movement that, in place of free markets, unfettered trade, and economic growth at all costs, calls for human development and regulations on trade and markets. Indeed, they were early

Valentine M. Moghadam, "From Structural Adjustment to the Global Trade Agenda," *Globalizing Women: Transnational Feminist Networks*, pp. 105–141. Copyright © 2005 by Johns Hopkins University Press. Reprinted with permission.

contributors to it, through their critique of structural adjustment in the 1980s and early 1990s. What they bring to the movement is a distinctly feminist perspective that calls for gender justice and economic justice. In this chapter we examine three transnational feminist networks involved in "globalization from below." DAWN, WIDE, and WEDO work together, separately, and in coalition with other women's groups as well as other advocacy networks to critique neoliberal capitalism and to formulate an alternative, feminist economics that takes into account women's productive and reproductive labor, and their economic and reproductive rights. As critics of what they see as the heavy-handedness of the institutions of neoliberal capitalism—multinational corporations, the World Bank, the IMF, and the WTO—they call for democratic economic decision-making and the incorporation of human rights and women's rights considerations into trade agreements. In order to accomplish their goals, they carry out research, attend conferences, publish papers, and take part in UN meetings. They formed women's caucuses at the UN conferences of the 1990s, engaged in line-by-line readings of conference documents, and sought to ensure that gender justice and economic justice issues were not watered down. As can be seen from the above epigraphs, they present a critique and a utopian vision of equality and empowerment, as well as practical recommendations to international bodies on how to achieve more immediate development goals.

Development/Economics for/by Women: An Overview

An expanding network of women researchers and activists from developing countries, with affiliated organizations and individuals from the Caribbean, Latin America, the Pacific, South Asia, Southeast Asia, and Africa, DAWN promotes alternative approaches to economic development and more equitable gender systems. In its own words, DAWN is an "autonomous inter-regional organization of the South which acts as a network and catalyst advocating alternative development processes that emphasize the basic survival needs of the majority of the world's people, particularly Third World women and their children."[1]

DAWN originated in a meeting held in Bangalore, India, in August 1984, when Devaki Jain—"the mother of DAWN"—invited women she knew to discuss structural adjustment, the debt crisis, and poverty, as well as the UN's Decade for Women.[2] An economist and activist, Jain had a vision of Third World women coalescing around a Third World critique of development policies and forming a South–South network. She and others were prominent women from Africa, Asia, Latin America, the Caribbean, and the Pacific who spoke eloquent English, were highly educated, had their own NGOs, and were situated in a socialist-feminist or Marxist-feminist framework. Many of them had lived outside their own countries, were very cosmopolitan, and were known as WID/WAD experts. According to Caren Grown, Jain gathered together "a network of Third World women who could engage in advocacy and activities in Third World areas. Their analyses were reflective of the experiences, critiques, and aspirations of many Third World women."[3] The women met again in 1986 at the World Congress of Sociology in New Delhi, and the network was formally launched under Jain's leadership. After two years, the network moved to Rio de Janeiro, where a secretariat was established and Brazilian sociologist and activist Neuma Aguiar served as coordinator. The secretariat rotated to the Caribbean in 1990 under the leadership of Jamaican political scientist Peggy Antrobus, and then moved to Fiji at the end of 1995, where Claire Slatter, a member of the Fiji Parliament, became the new general coordinator.

Following the initial meeting in Bangalore, the network prepared a platform document which was used as the basis of a series of panels and workshops at the NGO forum at the third UN world conference on women, in Nairobi in 1985. That document was eventually published as *Development, Crises, and Alternative Visions: Third World Women's Perspectives*. It highlighted the impacts of four interconnected and systemic global crises—famine, debt, militarism, and fundamentalism—on poor women of the South, and offered alternative visions. Caren Grown recalls that "DAWN brought together thirty women and a unique analysis of economic policy to Nairobi. It was a very important defining moment for Third World women."[4]

DAWN: Voices of Third World Women

Critical of neoliberal and patriarchal forms of development, DAWN sought to formulate an alternative model of socioeconomic development that would be people centered, holistic, sustainable, empowering of women, and based on an analysis of the issues from the perspective of women in the South. DAWN's analysis incorporated the diversity of regional experiences and related the experiences of women at the micro level of the household and community to an understanding of macroeconomics policy and global trends. From the outset, DAWN adopted feminism and poor women as its political points of departure and analyzed gender and class in the development experience. Discussions revolved around women's potential to solve such structural crises as the food-water-fuel crisis, the balance of payments and debt crises, militarization and violence, and cultural crises, and to formulate alternative visions and strategies. The self-empowerment of women through networks and organizations was regarded as a crucial means by which women could transform societies and international relations. Independence from government control was also stressed: "It was argued that women should not depend on government but develop autonomously through self-organization."[5] The network's utopian vision, now a staple of every publication, was first spelled out in their "manifesto," Development, Crises, and Alternative Visions:

> We want a world where inequality based on class, gender and race is absent from every country, and from the relationships among countries. We want a world where basic needs become basic rights and where poverty and all forms

of violence are eliminated. Each person will have the opportunity to develop her or his full potential and creativity, and values of nurturance and solidarity will characterize human relationships. In such a world women's reproductive role will be redefined: men will be responsible for their sexual behavior, fertility and the well-being of both partners. Child care will be shared by men, women and society as a whole.

We want a world where the massive resources now used in the production of the means of destruction will be diverted to areas where they will help to relieve oppression both inside and outside the home. This technological revolution will eliminate disease and hunger, and give women means for the safe control of their lives, health, sexuality and fertility.

We want a world where all institutions are open to participatory democratic processes, where women share in determining priorities and making decisions. This political environment will provide enabling social conditions that respect women's and men's physical integrity and the security of their persons in every dimension of their lives.[6]

Research on gender and development issues was an important part of DAWN's work from the start, and the network contributed considerably to overall thinking on the subject. Key figures in DAWN such as Gita Sen, Peggy Antrobus, Neuma Aguiar, and Noeleen Heyzer of Singapore (who later became the executive director of UNIFEM) networked with other feminist social scientists and activists to produce telling critiques of structural adjustment. In the wake of the much-discussed UNICEF publication *Adjustment with a Human Face,* they urged the Commonwealth Secretariat in London to convene a commission on women and structural adjustment. Diane Elson, a well-known British socialist-feminist economist who had co-authored papers with Ruth Pearson on the exploitation of female labor in world market factories, joined the commission, which subsequently produced the influential book *Engendering Adjustment for the 1990s.* Latin American members of DAWN produced *Alternatives, Volume 1: The Food, Energy, and Debt Crises in Relation to Women,* and. *Alternatives, Volume 2: Women's Visions and Movements,* both of which were published in 1991. A publication on women and the environment was prepared for the 1992 UINCED conference, while alternative economic frameworks were the foci of publications prepared for the Social Summit in Copenhagen and the Fourth World Conference on Women (FWCW) in Beijing. For the ICPD, at which DAWN actively promoted women's reproductive rights, the network contributed *Population and Reproductive Rights: Feminist Perspectives from the South.* Prominent at the Beijing conference, DAWN's activities took the form of participation in panels and workshops at the NGO forum in Huairo that preceded the conference and, at the official conference, lobbying of government delegates and attendance at working groups formed to remove the brackets from contested paragraphs of the draft Platform of Action.[7]

During the 1990s, DAWN researchers worked separately and in collaboration with WIDE researchers to develop an alternative feminist economic framework. Wendy Harcourt, a founding member of WIDE and a leading officer of the Rome-based Society for International Development (SID), organized seminars and conferences that offered a forum for DAWN presentations on structural adjustment, gender and macroeconomics, reproductive health and rights, and related topics. The forum available to DAWN expanded with the launching of the International Association for Feminist Economics (IAFFE) in 1992, which had its first annual conference in Amsterdam in 1993 and subsequently produced its own journal. In 1995 and 2000, social scientists associated with DAWN (and other feminist networks) contributed to two special issues of the journal *World Development* on gender, economic theory, and macroeconomics.[8] Following its feminist analysis and critique of structural adjustment, DAWN turned its attention to the social and gender effects of globalization, including the new global trade regime. It also developed a website and a newsletter, *DAWN Informs.*

Organizationally, the network emphasized regional activity "in an effort to extend its reach and influence, connect more closely with the priorities of women's and civil society organizations in each region and help strengthen capacity to deal with issues arising from the impacts of globalization."[9] In order to influence debates on global development issues and monitor and mobilize around regional processes, DAWN organized its research and advocacy work around three themes. The theme of the political economy of globalization included collaboration with other advocacy networks toward a critique and transformation of global governance and institutions such as the World Bank, the IMF, and the UN system. The theme of sexual and reproductive rights entailed monitoring the follow-up to the ICPD and the Beijing conference with respect to women's sexual rights, male responsibility, and human and citizen rights. The third theme, on political restructuring and transformation, was meant to analyze "the deepening disorder and crises created by current global economic regimes," produce "a critique of mainstream ideas on governance, accountability, [and] state/civil society," and offer "a political framework for social transformation."[10]

As a network of highly educated and prominent women in developing countries, some of whom have held government or other influential positions, DAWN members and founders have served as resource persons or consultants for UNIFEM, UNFPA, UNDP, ILO, and UNESCO, and are often invited to prepare analyses or position papers for various organizations or publications. One such paper, by Gita Sen and Sonia Correa, was prepared for UNIFEM in preparation for the five-year review of the Beijing Platform for Action, in 2000. Entitled "Gender Justice and Economic Justice: Reflections on the Five Year Reviews of the UN Conferences of the 1990s," the paper concluded that the major challenges remained the wide gap between South and North on economic issues pertaining to trade, investment, and redistribution of wealth, and the difficulty of reaching consensus on gender issues within the global justice movement, in part because of the prominence of Catholic social-justice organizations that did not support sexual rights.[11]

WIDE: Voices of European Women

Like DAWN, the network WIDE was organized in response to concerns about global economic developments. Founded in 1985 immediately after the Nairobi conference, it "took off" in 1990, when it acquired a more stable funding base. Some of the founders and earliest members of WIDE—Helen O'Connell, Wendy Harcourt, and Hilkka Pietila—had been involved in socialist-feminism and the WID/WAD/GAD intellectual movements, where they had come to know the founders of DAWN. Early on, WIDE focused on development cooperation and a feminist critique of foreign aid. Recognition of the links between North and South economic and social processes was heightened by the experience of Thatcherism in Britain, the beginning of cutbacks in social spending in Europe, and the expansion of labor market flexibility. WIDE developed a feminist development agenda that included criticism of neoliberal capitalism, defense of the welfare state, attention to women's unpaid labor, and the EU's relations with Third World partners. The women of WIDE also were inspired by DAWN's broad definition of development and its vision for an alternative form of development, as spelled out in the DAWN manifesto. Thus WIDE's annual conference in May 1995 focused on "Women and Alternative Economics" from a European perspective. Feminist economist Diane Elson, the keynote speaker, discussed strategies for action on issues of property rights, the transformation of markets, and the reform of financial institutions.[12] Like DAWN, WIDE too became involved in the international conferences of the 1990s. In an important accomplishment, its president, Helen O'Connell, was accredited to the official conference in Beijing and presented a statement during the General Exchange of Views, when official governmental delegations read their prepared statements.[13] WIDE had helped to found the Women's Global Alliance for Alternative Economics, and that group also was present at the Beijing conference.

During the 1990s, WIDE developed into a Brussels-based network of European women involved in feminist organizations working on development issues in twelve European countries. Most of the decade was spent on research, lobbying, and advocacy around gender and development issues, with the objective of educating publics, influencing EU policies, and empowering women. In its lobbying and educational efforts, WIDE identified the contradictions and inconsistencies between the EU's stated objectives of aid and development cooperation on the one hand and the adverse effects of structural adjustment on the other. This activity was part of its project of monitoring the Lomé Convention, which since 1975 had been the main form of development cooperation between the EU and seventy African, Caribbean, and Pacific states. At the same time, WIDE sought to influence the debates on women, gender, development, and trade at EU intergovernmental conferences and to monitor the implementation of the Platform for Action of Beijing by the EU and its member states.[14] It produced a wealth of research publications, technical reports, and policy briefs for EU policymakers as well as for its own members.

Individual members of WIDE, as well as the network itself, produced trenchant analyses of gender, development, and economics. The position paper prepared for the Beijing conference, for example, began with an elaboration of the way that the flawed assumptions of neoclassical economic theory guide the wrongheaded policies of neoliberal economics. The inspiration had been Diane Elson's 1991 book *Male Bias in the Development Process*, which defined male-biased development outcomes as those that result in more asymmetry and inequality between men and women. Elson identified the proximate causes as male bias in everyday attitudes and decisions, in theoretical analysis, and in the process of defining and implementing public policy. The key structural factor shaping these attitudes and policies, Elson argued, was the social and economic organization of access to resources and to child care. In adopting this analysis, WIDE feminists began to emphasize women's reproductive activities, pointing out that much of it is unpaid (if it is domestic and based in the home) or underpaid (if it is occupational and within the labor market). They objected to the unspoken assumptions about women's unpaid family labor inscribed in structural adjustment policies. The "success" of structural adjustment policies, they noted, depended on the interdependence between the productive economy and the reproductive economy (also called by some "the care economy"), although neoliberal policy and theory did not acknowledge this. There were other criticisms, too. WIDE pointed out that programs of expenditure cuts were frequently designed in a way that jeopardized human development targets and undermined the ability of women to respond to new price incentives in agriculture and job opportunities in export-oriented manufacturing (in that women had to compensate with their labor-time for cuts in social sectors). Their recommendation was that all programs for macroeconomic policy reform should include not only targets for monetary aggregates and policy instruments for achieving them but also targets for human development aggregates and policy instruments for delivering them. Moreover, the relation between the policy instruments and human development targets had to be analyzed in gender-disaggregated terms that recognized the inputs of unpaid labor as well as paid labor.

Many WIDE documents, including its newsletter, exemplified the feminist political economy or socialist-feminist approach. For example, WIDE challenged "the laissez-faire dogma that markets are free, equally open to everyone, democratic, and fair."[15] The network believed that in order to achieve economic parity and stability for most women, cooperative and more socialist avenues of economics had to be explored. And WIDE activists spoke of how women must "reclaim the market in a global system where every part of life—even a person's kidney—is increasingly peddled as a commodity, and which sees people as consumers rather than citizens."[16] With its concerns for poor women, low-wage women workers in export sectors, and unpaid caregivers in the context of social cutbacks, WIDE was critical of the neoliberal macroeconomic policy that "prioritizes the economy over humanity, market rights and freedoms over human rights and freedoms." and adopts "an instrumental approach to women's enormous contribution to the development process," wherein "women are presented as a means or an instrument to be used towards a goal of curbing poverty, rather than full human beings who have rights." They pointed out that the process of economic liberalization has differential implications for women and men; "women are forced into situations where they have to work for exploitative wages in over-crowded and deregulated labour-markets; the cutting back of public expenditure and accompanying privatization of public services has increased demands on women's time, income, and energy while, at the same time reducing women's access to essential social-infrastructure." Their position was that "the EU's policy on development co-operation should start from a commitment to promoting and protecting woman's rights and to combating gender-based inequalities. The EU should prioritize: implementation of the Beijing Declaration and Platform for Action; implementation of the 1995 EU Gender Resolution; coherence in all EU policies; and recognizing the reinforcing relationship between gender equality and sustainable development."[17]

WEDO: Bela Abzug's Vision

The feminist network WEDO was founded about five years after DAWN and WIDE, taking over the activities of the Women's Foreign Policy Council and the Women USA Fund. But under the charismatic leadership of the late Bella Abzug, and with an expert on gender and development as its executive director (Susan Davis), WEDO soon developed into an "international advocacy network that works to achieve a healthy and peaceful planet, with social, political, economic and environmental justice for all through the empowerment of women, in all their diversity, and their equal participation with men in decision-making from grassroots to global arenas."[18]

Like DAWN and WIDE, WEDO was intensely involved in the UN conferences of the 1990s. WEDO came to prominence in 1992 at UNCED in Rio de Janeiro, where it was active in showing the links among the state of the environment, economic policy, and women's well-being. Since then, the network has been involved in campaigns against bioengineering and patents on life forms, and a campaign to show the link between environmental concerns and breast cancer. During much of the 1990s, WEDO's politics combined radical feminism and eco-feminism, a reflection of the influence of one of its leading members and officers, Vandana Shiva, the well-known Indian physicist and eco-feminist who is also active in the global justice movement, and of course the influence of Bella Abzug herself, as in the following statements:

> The challenges to women's goal of a peaceful, healthy and equitable planet remain formidable, but the progress we have made in WEDO's nine years of existence gives us the confidence and hope that women, working together can transform Mother Earth.[19]
>
> As we contemplate this, the bloodiest century of human history, which dawned at Sarajevo with an incident that launched a world war ... and it is ending in Sarajevo with brutal murders of children, women and men, mass rape and violence spurred on by age-old ethnic rivalries, greed, the genocide of the

civilian population of Bosnia, Herzegovnia, Somalia, and the wars of Rwandas and Chechnyas of the world, is it not time to admit that the present dominance, style and conduct of male leadership has been a disaster?[20]

In my heart I believe that women will change the nature of power rather than power change the nature of women.[21]

For we are the Old Ones, the New Breed, the Natives, who came first but lasted, indigenous to an utterly different dimension. We are the girlchild in Zambia, the grandmother in Burma, the woman in El Salvador and Afghanistan, Finland and Fiji. We are the whale-song and rainforest, the deep wave rising huge to shatter glass power on the shore.[22]

We are poised on the edge of the millennium—ruin behind us, no map before us, the taste of fear sharp on our tongues. Yet we will leap. The exercise of imagining is an act of creation. The act of creation is an exercise of will. All this is political. And possible. Believe it … We are the women who will transform the world.[23]

Bella Abzug attended the 1995 Beijing conference, although at that time she was ailing and wheelchair-bound, and she was honored by the UNDP for her life's work in the women's movement. She was clearly one of the few American feminists admired and loved by Third World feminists, as many women from developing countries would approach her and ask to have their pictures taken with her.[24]

After Abzug died in 1998, WEDO dedicated an issue of their newsletter to recollections, quotes, and memories of Bella. Vandana Shiva, member of the WEDO board of directors, said: "We will, together, continue to build on Bella's dreams and visions."[25] Building on that vision, WEDO in 1999 took a strong position against the war in Kosovo and the NATO bombing of Yugoslavia. At the seventh session of the UN's Commission on Sustainable Development, the women's caucus organized by WEDO issued a statement that criticized neoliberal economic policies for inducing poverty and environmental degradation and called for a realization of the promises made at the Earth Summit. But it also called for "an end to the production and consumption of the products of the world's most entrenched and destructive industry—the arms industry." Otherwise, the statement continued, "there can be no lasting peace and no healthy planet. It is not sufficient to aim to eradicate poverty; we must eradicate the causes of war."[26] An article in a 1999 issue of its newsletter, *WEDO News & Views,* was entitled "Bombs Are Good for Business, for Some," and asserted that "NATO's war machinery is built on its plunder of the rest of the world, the environment and women."[27]

WEDO continued to critique economic policies and practices for their adverse effects on the environment and on the lives of women, children, and the poor. It worked within and outside the UN system to "challenge … the hegemonic and undemocratic IFIs and … the fundamentalist dogma of the free market."[28] WEDO led the Women's Caucus at the

March 1995 Social Summit in Copenhagen and became known for its vigorous critique of economic policy as well as its stance on environmental issues. One of its board members described WEDO as having a "holistic strategy ... which links feminist issues—health, gender violence, reproductive rights, empowerment—to a larger economic and political context."[29] The priority issues were: environmental health and bio-safety—focusing on environmental links to breast cancer, persistent organic pollutants, and the global anti-nuclear campaign; global environmental and economic justice—advocacy at the UN Commission on Sustainable Development, World Trade Organization, and the World Bank, and organizing around the Earth Charter and expanded microcredit for women; and gender justice—monitoring and advocacy at the UN forums around the commitments made to women at the Cairo conference and the Beijing conference, focusing on empowerment.[30]

TFNs actively engage with intergovernmental bodies, such as the UN, the OECD, the European Union, and the World Bank. All three networks considered in this chapter were involved in the myriad activities prior to, during, and following the UN conferences of the 1990s, as well as the five-year reviews of the ICPD, the Social Summit, and the Beijing conference in 1999 and 2000, and the Financing for Development Conference in Mexico in March 2002. They have partnered with each other, with other feminist organizations, and with human rights, labor, environmental, and economic justice groups around a number of campaigns and issues, such as preventing the Multilateral Agreement on Investment, protesting the World Trade Organization's rules, and ending the Third World debt. They supported the World March of Women, the worldwide protest against capitalism and patriarchy in 2000 that began as an initiative of feminists in Quebec, Canada. Their global advocacy work has involved partnerships with other organizations and networks to reform international institutions and to ensure that governments live up to the commitments that they made at the international conferences of the 1990s.

Participation in the UN-sponsored international conferences was a priority for the TFNs during the 1990s, although a debate emerged in 2002 as to the efficacy of such participation. TFNs have participated in other conferences as well, such as those organized by the Association for Women in Development, or AWID (renamed the Association for Women's Rights in Development) and by the Society for International Development. Participation in these conferences is often made possible by support from UNIFEM and European foundations such as Germany's Heinrich Böll Foundation and the Friedrich Ebert Stiftung. Conference participation is regarded as a way to lobby government delegations, take part in the drafting of documents, engage in policy dialogues, influence policy-making, and disseminate the analyses and values of the TFNs. This is also done through their newsletters and websites, which serve as tools to inform women, both North and South, about events, conferences, NGO workshops, politics, and debates. WIDE's newsletter, in addition, contains news about the European "national platforms" (member groups) and developments in Eastern Europe. *DAWN Informs* frequently includes articles addressing political or economic questions. And *WEDO News & Views* provides both information and perspectives on issues.

Global Activities: Influencing the UN Conferences of the 1990s

An examination of aims, activities, and projects of transnational feminist networks shows the ways in which they work simultaneously at local, national, regional, and global levels. Individual members are often local activists who use that experience to conceptualize the links with national and global developments. Much of WIDE's published work, for example, has focused on the local, national, and global economies, analyzed through the lens of gender and class oppression. The TFN organizational structure, moreover, is one that usually mobilizes members on a national or regional basis. Manuals, technical reports, and conceptual publications produced by WIDE and DAWN complement the global analyses with country or community-level examples. While the three TFNs examined here work closely with each other and with other transnational feminist networks, WIDE also has formal links with European-based TANs such as EURODAD (the European Network on Debt and Development) and EUROSTEP (European Solidarity towards Equal Participation of People). Together they have produced studies on gender and structural adjustment and on the institutions of the European Union. All three TFNs examined here were also deeply involved with the UN conferences of the 1990s.

The International Conference on Population and Development (ICPD), Cairo, September 1994

Transnational feminists who participated in the ICPD knew from the preparatory meetings that the draft document's language on women's reproductive rights would be challenged by delegations representing the Vatican and a number of conservative Latin American and Muslim countries. They were thus prepared to do battle, and they went to Cairo with some advantages. WIDE had been accredited to the European Preparatory Committee as an NGO involved with planning the ICPD. Feminists working at the MacArthur Foundation who were sympathetic to TFNs "influenced Cairo" in that during the planning stages they had met with UNFPA Executive Director Nafis Sadik to ask that the process be opened up to the women's NGOs. Another factor that helped influence the process was that Bella Abzug of WEDO and Adrienne Germaine of the International Women's Health Coalition (later with HERA) were part of the U.S. delegation.[31] At the ICPD, WEDO was responsible for facilitating the Women's Caucus, as it had done during the two-year preparatory period, and provided line-by-line amendments to the ICPD proposed program of action. The purpose was to encourage the official delegates to "invest in women's empowerment and social development as an alternative to population 'control' strategies."[32] Women's empowerment would entail educating girls, providing access to user-friendly family planning services, promoting reproductive health and safe motherhood, and preventing child and maternal deaths—which in turn were regarded as essential components of sexual and reproductive rights. Negotiations slowed down due to the controversy surrounding not only abortion "but also the Vatican and Muslim delegations' objections to the draft document's definitions of 'reproductive rights' and their relationship to the family, to sex education, and to family-planning services for teenagers."[33] Eventually, a compromise was struck between governments, international organizations, and NGOs.

The controversy surrounding abortion, sex outside marriage, and the family dominated the news, but the ICPD provided a forum for other issues as well. For example, WEDO launched its cancer prevention campaign and set up a public forum on the need for international action to prevent environmentally induced cancers and other health hazards. Margarita Penón Arias, president of the Arias Foundation for Peace and Human Progress, spoke at the WEDO forum held during the ICPD in Cairo:

> Chlorinated pesticides, though often restricted or not registered in the manufacturing countries, are frequently used in developing countries for cotton and banana production and in the fight against malaria. Annual pesticide use in my region reaches levels equivalent to four kilograms (8.8 pounds) per person. In my own country of Costa Rica pesticide application is six times the average use in the rest of the developing world and more than double that in the industrialized countries.
>
> It is indeed frightening that the use of such pesticides continues in my part of the world, especially when we consider that the incidence of breast cancer in developing countries has been rising for the past two decades. Even more frightening, the effects of these toxins will linger for generations. Decades of use means that residues persist in our soils, thereby allowing for their introduction in the food chain. This has added implications for women. As the traditional handlers and preparers of food, the transmission of these toxic chemicals through the food chain increases women's exposure to these venomous substances, even if they do not live in an area of direct application.[34]

The World Summit for Social Development (the Social Summit), Copenhagen, March 1995

As part of the European regional preparations for the March 1995 Social Summit, WIDE was invited to attend the ECE High Level Conference in Vienna in October 1994, where it helped create the NGO document and draft the conference room paper. WIDE's main lobbying purpose was "to document the responsibility of the ECE region towards the rest of the world, not only through aid relations, but also through trade relations and countries' participation in the International Financial Institutions."[35] DAWN produced a document that criticized liberalization policies and proposed "a threefold strategy of reclaiming the state (for the benefit of the majority), challenging the market (to social responsibility), and building the institutions for strengthening civil society."[36]

WEDO and other TFNs lobbied governments to deal seriously with "growing inequities and poverty that affects women in greater numbers than men," as Bella Abzug asserted. Specifically, WEDO organized and facilitated the women's caucus for the Social Summit, whose agenda criticized "the fundamental structures shaping the global economy" and called for concrete actions by governments and international institutions to reduce poverty at least 50 percent by the year 2005.[37] A workshop entitled "Globalization of the Economy and Economic Justice," which was attended by over one hundred women, was co-sponsored by WEDO, along with NAC CANADA (National Action Committee on the Status of Women) and Alt-WID US. The group circulated a discussion paper entitled "Wealth of Nations, Poverty of Women," which identified a common ground between economic restructuring in the industrial economies, the economies in transition in Eastern and Central Europe, and the structural adjustment programs that the World Bank and International Monetary Fund impose upon the debtor countries of the South. They argued:

> These various forms of economic restructuring are being driven by a corporate agenda and a simplistic view of the merits of free market capitalism. These policies have a cumulative effect on increasing the gap between the rich and poor both within nations and between nations.
>
> When these macro-economic policies are evaluated through their experience of women, their negative impact on the quality of life of women and children, and on the functioning of local communities becomes clear. A disproportionate amount of the human cost of global economic ideology is being borne by women. Governments and corporations are using women's labour, energy, time and sexuality to sustain this agenda of corporate growth.[38]

The women's caucus produced a comprehensive gender analysis of the summit document to ensure informed dialogue on the women's agenda between activists and delegates, and convened the caucus's opening meeting. Daily caucus sessions at the Social Summit developed strategies and tactics on ways to push the women's action agenda forward. The caucus was very critical of neoliberal economic policies and their impact on women and saw the final summit document as providing some relief from the negative impacts of structural adjustment by calling for debt relief—including debt cancellation—to free funds for social problems. They urged the World Bank and IMF to make social development a primary policy focus and to help slow excessive military spending. They reaffirmed the ICPD principles of women's empowerment for social development, and they endorsed the

20:20 formula by which 20 percent of development aid and 20 percent of national budgets would go to social programs.[39]

Two key documents—"Amendments to the Draft Declaration: Background Note Presented to the Chairman" and "Draft Definition of Core Terms of the Summit"—were produced by the women's caucus. Here they noted that "some of the terms proposed by governments in the Social Summit documents ... did not reflect previous negotiations and agreements about the interrelationships between poverty, economic equity, environmental conservation, human rights and gender equality."[40] In addition to working with the women's caucus, WIDE, DAWN, and WEDO jointly drafted the Copenhagen Alternative Declaration, with "wide-ranging criticisms of a neo-capitalist system that favours giant corporations and gender inequalities," which was signed by over six hundred NGOs.[41]

Jointly with other NGOs and Danish women's groups, WEDO launched the 180 Days/180 Ways Women's Action Campaign on 8 March 1995. The brainchild of both WEDO and Peggy Teagle, a co-chair of the Canadian NGO organizing committee for the Social Summit, the campaign was a kind of countdown to the September Beijing conference. Over the course of the 180 days, "more than five hundred national and international organizations and countless local groups in over eighty countries actively worked to build support for the empowerment of women," which WEDO termed "a pledge for gender justice."[42] At the same time, WEDO developed a "gopher" on the internet via the Institute for Global Communication, to open up the UN process to greater public involvement and to make Women's Caucus documents available worldwide almost simultaneously with their distribution at UN meetings.[43] (The UN later developed its own extensive website, WomenWatch.)

The Fourth World Conference on Women, Beijing, September 1995

As part of the preparatory work, the UN's regional commissions convened regional meetings to produce country reports and preliminary regional plans of action indicating how the status of women had changed since 1985 and in comparison to men over the same period of time. WIDE asked to work directly with the NGO committee that helped generate a paper for the European committee, and they helped produce a draft platform of action with other NGOs in New York. Keen to ensure that the Beijing Platform was not weaker than the Cairo declaration, WIDE joined a monitoring group made up of several European NGOs, including EUROSTEP.[44] Concern about the role of the Vatican delegation at the ICPD led TFNs to lobby European and other sympathetic governments to hold fast to an agenda that would promote women's reproductive health and rights. WIDE presented the Spanish contingent with a briefing that outlined the important themes to have emerged from Cairo: the girl child, gender, sustainable development, gender equity and equality, and reproductive health.[45] As a result of this monitoring and lobbying, the EU as a whole, and the Spanish delegation in particular, played a prominent role in Beijing in the defense of these issues.[46]

Some of the activities that WIDE sponsored at the Beijing conference included a workshop, organized with Women's Alliance for Development Alternatives (Alt–WID), entitled "Women in a Global Economic Restructuring: Making Links—Identifying Strategies" and a roundtable on "Women's Alliance for Economic Alternatives." The TFN was accredited to send a delegation of five members to lobby the national delegations.[47] For its part, WEDO was active at both the NGO forum, where it held presentations, and at the official conference, where it lobbied officials, facilitated the Women's Linkage Caucus, and joined the UNIFEM panel on economic restructuring. At the NGO forum, WEDO joined eighty women's organizations to create nine days of programs and workshops on the environment and development issues from a gender perspective. WEDO also celebrated the September 6 International Day of Action for Women's Equality, the culmination of the worldwide 180 days/180 ways Women's Action Campaign. And like WIDE—whose finances at the time were such that it extended grants enabling women's groups from developing countries to attend the Beijing conference[48]—WEDO also helped fund more than one hundred women's organizations from developing countries.[49]

During the Beijing conference, an international network of women (including Gita Sen, Peggy Antrobus, and Caren Grown) formed the "Women's Eyes on the World Bank Campaign" to monitor the World Bank's performance and to place women as essential actors within the World Bank machinery. Objectives were to increase the participation of grassroots women in the Bank's economic policy-making and to institutionalize a gender perspective in Bank policies and programs. A petition signed by nearly a thousand activists was presented to World Bank president Wolfensohn, after which the monitoring group was formalized. Laura Frade of Mexico became the coordinator of the Women's Eyes/Latin America Campaign, and she kept tabs on those World Bank projects in Latin America that dealt with health, education, environment, and social development. DAWN also became actively involved in processes and initiatives aimed at achieving policy changes, such as the World Bank's Structural Adjustment Participatory Review Initiative (SAPRI), and the External Gender Consultative Group.

Post-Beijing Activities

Having been active in all the UN conferences of the 1990s, DAWN, WIDE, and WEDO were ready for the five-year reviews, especially those of the ICPD, the Social Summit, and the Beijing conference.[50] At Cairo + 5 they had the opportunity to voice concerns and suggestions about implementation of the ICPD recommendations, also known as the Cairo agenda, which they felt were being thwarted by uncooperative governments and by the Vatican. WIDE pioneered work on gender and trade, and this became a major preoccupation of transnational feminist research and lobbying. At the WSSD + 5, the women's caucus, of which WEDO was a leading member, clashed with the U.S. and the EU on macroeconomic and global governance issues such as debt cancellation, the currency transaction tax (also known as the Tobin Tax), which had been endorsed by TFNs, and trade-related intellectual property, or TRIPs, in relation to essential medicines.

A major focus of WIDE has been to maintain the integrity of the broad development agenda agreed to in the 1990s and to argue that the new global trade agenda should not undermine the recommendations of the 1990 UN conferences, such as human rights commitments and especially the commitment to women's equality. As WIDE explained in its newsletter, "Economic and social policies and programmes should not decrease women's social and economic security or make women more vulnerable to violence, exploitation, and coercion and less able to escape from it. [They should not] eliminate or diminish women's access to basic services like health care and education, violations of women's human rights. Economic and social policies must promote cooperation, peace and community development in both the North and South, instead of competition, war, and social disintegration."[51]

Working on Women and Trade

WIDE's work on women and trade began with a conference in May 1996, after which it produced a conceptual paper on the European Union trade agreements with Asia and promoted economic literacy among its members and constituents through workshops and primers. The network decided to focus on alternative economics and trade and to continue to lobby the European Union on trade policy and developmental aid. There was consensus on the need for WIDE to work with trade unions, NGOs, academics, activists, fair trade organizations, groups focusing on transnational companies and financial institutions, and groups working on the trafficking of women.[52] WIDE's 1997 annual meeting, held in Finland, was attended by some 130 participants from twenty countries. The focus was on globalization, the role of international financial institutions, and impacts on women. Country reports on Russia, the Nordic welfare states, and India showed how economic globalization had affected women. According to the conference report, entitled Trade Traps and Gender Gaps: Women Unveiling the Market, "the globalization of markets has unleashed the forces of deregulation of national financial and labour markets, accelerating the onslaught of inequality, poverty, social disintegration and environmental degradation. These negative effects of the global market will only further be exacerbated by current attempts on the part of transnational corporations and their political supporters to modify and improve rules for the operation of the market on their own terms." The report highlighted "the lack of transparency and accountability in economic life in all levels, ... the lack of accountability to citizens of global economic structures," contrasting these with "the accountability which is built into the locally based economic and trading initiatives of which examples were presented during the conference."[53]

In its work on gender and global trade, WIDE has insisted on "coherence" or consistency of regional and international policies and agreements. That is, new agreements should not ignore, subvert, or supersede previous agreements, particularly those having to do with women's rights, human rights, and labor rights. WIDE argues that agreements made at UNCED, Vienna, Cairo, Copenhagen, and Beijing are at risk of being undermined by trade agreements and the new power of the WTO; that governments are placing less emphasis on implementing the programs that came out of UN conferences and more on implementing WTO rules; and that the global trade regime harms women workers and entrepreneurs. Its annual conference in May 2003 was devoted to an analysis of the global trade regime from feminist and human rights perspectives, a critique of the "fundamentalism of the market," and an elaboration of an alternative model based on "the absolute priority of human rights instruments."[54]

EU enlargement—to include twelve new countries, most of them part of the former Soviet bloc—has been another focus of WIDE's attention since the late 1990s, and the network has sought to work with East European women's networks to formulate expectations and demands regarding the enlargement process from a women's rights perspective. This came to fruition at the May 2000 general meeting, when a group of women associated with KARAT, the Warsaw-based network of East and Central European feminists, was invited to take part.[55] In a 2002 briefing paper on women's rights and gender equality in the European Union, WIDE called on the EU to fulfill its commitment to gender mainstreaming; to reassess economic policy from a gender perspective; to ensure gender equality in labor markets in transition and implementation and enforcement of equal opportunity legislation; and to "transform the enlarged European Union into a regional and global actor for women's rights and gender equality."[56]

When WEDO turned its attention to global trade in the late 1990s, its gender agenda for the WTO had three objectives: to mandate inclusion of women and gender in economic decision-making and governance; to strengthen women's capacity to attain economic equity; and to prevent TNC exploitation of women's indigenous knowledge and plant genetic resources. Like other TFNs, WEDO used intergovernmental political structures, especially the UN, to promote these concerns. For example, its 1998 publication *Women Transform the Mainstream* was published in collaboration with the United Nations Department of Economic and Social Affairs. It consists of eighteen case studies of women activists challenging industry and government for clean water and gender equality in sustainable development.

The main foci of WEDO's work are environmental health and sustainable development, approached through monitoring implementation of major global agreements and ensuring the integration of gender issues, and "engendering" governance at both national and global levels. In 2000 it began a "50/50 campaign" to achieve parity in women's political representation. Its own research on this subject led it to argue that "the quota system combined with proportional representation creates a critical mass of women previously underrepresented on party lists, government bodies, and parliament."[57] WEDO also produces feminist analyses of the global economy and U.S. economic processes and priorities. In a report prepared in collaboration with about a dozen U.S. women's organizations, WEDO noted that despite the unprecedented period of economic growth in the United States, too many women and children—particularly minority and rural women—continued to live in poverty. What had changed was that more women were working than ever before, but they were working for low pay, in insecure jobs where they did not earn enough to adequately support their families. Government policies had not only failed to address this issue, but some policy decisions had actually exacerbated the situation, according to the 2000 report *Women's Equality: An Unfinished Agenda*. According to Executive Director June Zeitlin, "the failure to apply a gender lens in our own domestic economy is magnified many times over when the U.S. promotes these macroeconomic policies in the World Trade Organization and elsewhere in the world."[58] WEDO participated at the Seattle protests against the WTO in late 1999, and members carried placards reading: "Women Want a Gender Agenda at the WTO." Its March 2000 newsletter, *WEDO News & Views,* contained a number of articles on global trade and on the WTO. The organization also prepared a primer, *A Gender Agenda for the World Trade Organization,* which it posted on its website.

Working on Environmental Health

On environmental health issues, WEDO has specific positions, objectives, and campaigns, regarding cancer and the environment and bioengineering and patenting. These link up with some of the major concerns of the antiglobalization movement, the global environmental movement, and the women's health movement. A key activity in WEDO's bioengineering and patenting project was to prevent patents of life forms for private profit at the cost of sustainability, especially in Europe and the United States, where "corporations push to patent genes, human cells, body parts and organs, and all or parts of plants." The TFN also opposed genetically altered seeds.[59] With respect to women's health, following the 1994 ICPD, WEDO organized a series of nationwide workshops and conferences made up of women's health activists, cancer survivors, scientists, doctors, and ecologists. The conferences explored environmental factors in the breast cancer epidemic, such as pesticides, organo-chlorides, and other toxins; radiation from the military and other sources; and low-level electromagnetic fields.[60] Working with Greenpeace to organize the U.S.-based program, WEDO helped start up similar programs in the Netherlands and Brazil. Later, it helped to sponsor and run the Global Action Plan to Eradicate Breast Cancer, an activist agenda launched in Kingston, Ontario, in July 1997.[61] The campaigns were inspired by Bella Abzug's vision: "[Our job] is to do for breast cancer what happened to AIDS in the 1980's— to put breast cancer on the center stage. We need to internationalize the research agenda and network a movement committed to change, not guided by profit. Like AIDS activists, we need to stand up and take charge. We must take on the nuclear industry, the chemical industry, the makers and users of pesticides and organo-chlorides, and other potential sources of poison in our breasts and bodies. And most particularly we must demand action from our governments to legislate, regulate, and discipline transnational corporations and this out-of-control global economy."[62]

One role that WEDO has assumed is that of monitoring countries' behavior on gender, development, and the environment. In the newsletters, WEDO makes brief reports on various countries' progress and regression in the three areas. News items and articles include critiques of corporate capitalism, the commercialization and industrialization of all agricultural and food production, the genetic manipulation of food, and the privatization of health services.[63] It has published a guide called *Mapping Progress: Assessing Implementation of the Beijing Platform*, which has detailed reports on the gains and losses women have made worldwide. Another monitoring report—*Risks, Rights, and Reforms: A Fifty-Country Survey Assessing Government Actions Five Years after the International Conference on Population and Development*—charted the challenges to progress in the areas of women's reproductive health and rights as a result of conservative backlashes as well as economically driven health sector reforms. The 1999 study concluded that the goals of Cairo and Beijing were "linked to the eradication of poverty and the elimination of unsustainable patterns of production and consumption."[64] A 2002 study analyzed the extent to which international financial institutions had involved women in their decision-making processes, and highlighted the fact that fully 100 percent of the board of directors of the IMF and 92 percent at the World Bank were men. The results of the study were reiterated in the UNDP's *Human Development Report 2002*.[65]

The Financing for Development Conference, Monterrey, Mexico, March 2002

As part of their preparations for participation in the Financing for Development Conference, WEDO, DAWN, and WIDE—along with their partners WICEJ, the International Gender and Trade Network, and other economic justice NGOs—issued reports, policy briefs, and working papers on the FfD process, as well as on substantive issues such as gender and macroeconomics, gender and trade policy, the feminization of poverty, gender budgets, and the impact of economic liberalization on women farmers, entrepreneurs, and wage workers. Their newsletters were devoted to exploration of those issues, and policy papers were posted on their websites.

They attended regional preparatory meetings and deliberated over the draft "consensus document." They joined with other NGOs to endorse the objectives of the September 2000 Millennium Summit, which included the goal to halve the percentage of people living in absolute poverty by the year 2015. They criticized the United States for its lead in having removed references to the Tobin Tax from the draft consensus document and urged governments to reintroduce it. (This did not occur.) Many of the TFN activities in connection with the FfD conference were commissioned or funded by UNIFEM. A WEDO program officer conceded that "preparing for the FfD conference has been very difficult, because the issues are so technical." But she explained why TFNs were involved in the FfD conference:

> Our objective in the process is to make sure that at the country level they engender poverty eradication. Women are the world's poorest; they are poor in resource allocation, in income, in capabilities. The sexual division of labor perpetuates this. We want to raise consciousness. We'll also need to monitor implementation in the follow-up process. This is why the network is so important. For example, we may support a gender budget initiative in a particular country if opposition to it arises. WEDO can act as catalyst and coordinator, but the real work is done at the country level. So we are helping to build a global women's caucus that can support the local women's initiatives.
>
> The U.S. has been unbelievably horrible throughout the process. We have to do a lot of work here in the U.S. and lobby our government. We'll do this with the Center of Concern, Women's Edge, and Interaction, over issues such as ODA [overseas development assistance].[66]

Following the Monterrey conference, all the TFNs that had participated in the process roundly criticized the final consensus document, arguing that it did not include the necessary commitments from industrialized countries to eradicate poverty. They rejected the document's affirmation of the neoliberal model of globalization as the strategy for reducing poverty, which they argued impeded the ability of states to carry out socioeconomic development objectives. According to the statement by the women's caucus, "the Monterrey Consensus promotes the market as a game in which players are rewarded when they create an environment favorable to the private sector in both North and South. ... For women, who are 51 percent of the world's population and the majority of the poorest, there can be no such consensus. ... We demand that our governments hold firm to the commitments they have made in UN conferences and their follow-up processes in Rio, Vienna, Cairo, Copenhagen, Beijing, Istanbul, and Durban, for the realization of an equitable, people-centered and gender-sensitive sustainability."[67] In a post-Monterrey bulletin that also discussed issues relevant to the World Summit on Sustainable Development (held in August 2002 in South Africa), WIDE criticized "the ongoing trends at the government and corporate level to dismantle and combat socially and ecologically oriented regulations against further ruthless exploitation of human beings, in particular women's work and knowledge, and of the earth's wealth."[68]

Working in the UN system has preoccupied TFNs, but some feminists have expressed misgivings about it. Just as some feminists (and socialists) have argued against working within state systems to effect change, some global feminists point out that the UN is an intergovernmental system wherein many international agreements yield minimal results. One problem is that states are free to honor or ignore many of the conventions and declarations they sign, particularly in "soft" areas such as human rights, women's rights, the environment, and labor rights. Another problem is that the UN's international conferences tend to be dominated by the core countries, and thus agreements on "hard" issues such as development, finance, and trade do nothing to undermine the interests of the core or challenge the inequalities of the world-system. Thus, grassroots organizing and mobilizing is a more effective strategy, critics argue.

Others, however, stress the difficulty of organizing and mobilizing in many repressive environments and the importance of the UN as a forum for lobbying and advocacy work. After all, it is at the UN that the issues of ethnic cleansing, child labor, sex tourism, market reforms, and rape at wartime have been raised. Given the increasing importance of problematic institutions and policies at the global level, social movement organizations and advocacy networks have no choice but to engage with multilateral organizations. The UN in particular provides a platform as well as a sympathetic environment for critics of global inequalities and injustices. As WEDO board member Rosalind Petchesky stated, "We need democratic, accountable institutions of global governance in the face of globalization and enfeebled, complicit national governments. In this respect, the UN system *is all we have*. Thus we must work *both* inside and outside the system, and that means being more strategic about how we divide our time and members to make our presence felt in a wider range of international forums."[69] Petchesky also highlighted the need for democratization of global governance and the role of women's organizations in such an endeavor: "Our participation in WSSD+5 and Beijing+5 has pointed the way to a strategic agenda for progressive social movements, including women's movements. Such an agenda for those working transnationally over the next decade involves pressing for democratization of the IFIs to make them fully part of and accountable to the UN system and all its member states, and making civil society, especially women's groups, an integral part of that system."[70]

Criticism of participation in UN international conferences became especially vocal after the disappointments of the Monterrey conference on financing for development. It was at this time, too, that questions were raised about the utility of another world conference on women, and the Association for Women's Rights in Development (AWID) initiated a discussion on the matter. It is likely, however, that global feminists will continue to work within the UN system and participate in its conferences, "as these provide opportunities for wider and more effective feminist lobbying and advocacy," especially on economic issues.[71]

Organizational Structures

As discussed in chapter 4, TFNs are committed to democratic, participatory, and nonhierarchical forms of organizing, mobilizing, and decision-making. Consensus building and equality of representation across geographic regions are also major goals. For these reasons, DAWN has a rotating secretariat and its research programs are distributed across the regions. Similarly, its publications reflect considerable consultation and consensus building. That this is a principled position of the network is clear from the preamble to its manifesto, *Development, Crises, and Alternative Visions*, which was produced in a collaborative and participatory manner. The preamble describes how the book was written through "extensive debate and discussion with researchers, activists, and policy makers." It was felt that by adopting an open and flexible process that also drew on varied experiences, the group would be better able to come to a common perspective and objective. *Development, Crises, and Alternative Visions* was drafted by Gita Sen, then at the New School for Social Research in New York City, and her graduate assistant Caren Grown. Meetings were held in each of the regions represented by DAWN members, where draft chapters were critically analyzed. The book was first self-produced and subsequently published by Monthly Review Press in New York. In keeping with the initial book-writing process, DAWN developed an organizational structure intended to be participatory, democratic, and nonhierarchical. For example, in the late 1990s, Gita Sen headed the research project on globalization; her approach to globalization, however, had been criticized within DAWN, and she had been asked to rewrite it.[72]

DAWN: Participation through Networking

The organizational structure of DAWN includes a rotating secretariat led by a general coordinator. There are regional coordinators for the Caribbean, Latin America, Francophone Africa, Anglophone Africa, Southeast Asia, and South Asia. Research coordinators are chosen for projects on the political economy of globalization (Gita Sen, India), social reproduction (Sonia Correa, Brazil), sustainable livelihoods (Vivienne Wee, Singapore), political restructuring/social transformation (Viviene Taylor, South Africa). Focal points are in East Africa, Central Africa, North Africa, and South Africa. Research focal points are sexual and reproductive rights (in Africa and the Pacific), and globalization (in Africa, Latin America, Pacific). Another part of the organizational structure is the "DAWN Founding Members"— in 1999 these were Neuma Aguiar, Peggy Antrobus, Hameeda Hussain (Bangladesh), and Devaki Jain.

Like other TFNs, DAWN has some paid positions, while many assignments are carried out by volunteer labor. Caren Grown was a paid employee of DAWN during 1984–87; the general coordinator also receives a stipend. Members, officers, and researchers are recruited through or from various networks. For example, Sonia Correa was recruited from SOS Mujeres to work on preparations for the ICPD.[73] Members of DAWN can be active in other networks. As such, DAWN is a network of networks.

A controversial position taken by DAWN after the network was officially launched was that only Third World women living in Third World countries could become members. This reflected and reinforced its collective identity as a network of Third World feminists and a South–South organization. The goal was to develop a feminist perspective from the developing world and to cultivate organizational and analytical leadership among women from developing countries. This principled position extends to practical matters such as subscriptions to the newsletter, *DAWN Informs;* the newsletter is free to members based in the South, and in 2002 it cost $20 for members and friends in the North. DAWN is linked to a number of other Third World feminist networks such as CAFRA (Caribbean), AAWORD (Africa), Indian women's organizations, ISIS (Chile and Philippines), Asian–Pacific Resource and Research Center for Women (ARROW), HERA, and women's organizations in Brazil, Mexico, and other Latin American countries. These links take the form of joint research projects, policy statements, and panel presentations.

Like other TFNs as well as many TANs, DAWN is not a mass organization. Its strength lies in its gendered political and economic analysis and its broad network of highly educated and well-connected members rather than in its grassroots ties. On the other hand, individual members may be founders of NGOs working at the local level. According to one of its publications, DAWN "counts on the participation of 4,500 women throughout the Third World."

As we saw in chapter 4, TFNs can count on connections, including friends and supporters in influential positions, to sustain their efforts. For example, UNIFEM's executive director, Noeleen Heyzer, is a founding member of DAWN who supports the work of TFNs. UNIFEM funded many of the activities related to the post-Beijing reviews and the financing for development conference. Catherine McKey of the Ford Foundation approved the first grant to DAWN that launched the organization, allowing them to gather at Nairobi and to produce the book. The Brazil office of the Ford Foundation was also supportive, as was the MacArthur Foundation later, when DAWN friends Car en Grown and Leni Silverstein and founding member Carmen Barrosco ran program areas. DAWN has also counted on funding from bilateral donor organizations, especially those of the Nordic countries, which are seen as less ideological and more flexible.

Although DAWN's research and advocacy themes are shared throughout the network, each region may have its own priorities. For example, Latin America focuses on social reproduction, including reproductive rights and health, and sexuality.[74] The focus of South Africa seems to be political restructuring and social transformation, while Southeast Asia takes up issues such as public financing and tax reform. Members of DAWN–SEA are part of the Freedom from Debt Coalition (FDC), which seeks a tax reform package for the redistribution of wealth toward social and gender opportunities and equity.[75] DAWN–Caribbean is especially active and in 1999 developed a new agenda, a new steering committee, and a new coordinator. It was decided that research activities would be undertaken by "multi-ethnic, multi-lingual research teams coordinated by Research Focal Points" on trade liberalization, women's budgets, privatization of social services, communication strategies, and political restructuring and social transformation. This reactivation "signals the launch of another regional effort to strengthen women's leadership in work on defining alternatives to secure and sustain the livelihoods of Caribbean people in this age of globalization."[76]

WIDE: Targeting the EU in Brussels

WIDE is a European-based network that currently includes nine national platforms, each of which is itself a network of women's groups, or "national platforms." The first national platform established was in Ireland, and a more recent addition was Austria, which has become among the most active of the national platforms. The others are Spain, France, Belgium (with two platforms, one French and the other Flemish), Great Britain, Switzerland, Finland, and Denmark. Each has its own program of work but shares information with the Brussels office; the latter also schedules the annual conference and the general assembly. At the May 1995 general assembly in Brussels, for example, each national platform presented a report on its activities and its plans for the Beijing conference. The general assembly was chaired by the president, had a financial report by the treasurer, and a report by the coordinator of the Brussels office. The same procedure took place at the general assembly in May 2000.[77] The conference—also known as the consultation—that precedes the general assembly is an important part of WIDE activities and outreach; each has a specific theme and guest speakers, and EU officials are invited to attend and to participate in various ways. In May 2002, the conference theme was "Europe Moving to the Right: Where Lie the Alternatives for Transnational Feminism?" Speakers addressed the question in terms of the gendered nature of neoliberalism, militarism, and xenophobia; the impact on development cooperation; and responses by social justice movements. Marianne Ericksson, Swedish member of the European Parliament, noted that women's rights could be diluted in the draft Convention on the Future of Europe, "as even liberal MEPs are not committed to making sure that they are incorporated into the treaty."[78]

In the first few years of existence WIDE was based in Dublin but in 1993 moved its office to Brussels, so that it could carry out more effectively its lobby and advocacy work within the European Union, European Parliament, the Council of Ministers, and delegations of member states. WIDE also cooperates with and coordinates its activities with other networks in Europe, such as Protestant and Catholic agencies, EURODAD, and EUROSTEP. WIDE is part of the Global Alliance for Alternative Development, which also includes DAWN and Alt–WID. The focus of the Global Alliance is alternative economics—an effort to interrogate economic theory from a feminist and gender perspective.

European donor and development agencies were keen to fund women's projects in the 1990s, and WIDE benefited from their largesse. Despite its well-known critiques of neoliberal economic policies, WIDE's funding came principally from the EU, and in the mid–1990s it was invited by the Dutch government to submit an application for a large grant. As its reputation spread, WIDE was invited to take part in and prepare position papers for the EU Committee on Women's Rights, the UNDP Human Development Report 1995, the

OECD/DAC/WID group, and the preparatory conferences for the Social Summit and the Beijing conference. WIDE continues to receive funding from the EU, from the foreign affairs or development ministries of European countries (e.g., SIDA of Sweden and FINNIDA of Sweden), from large NGOs operating in the Netherlands, Belgium, and Britain, and from such U.S. foundations as Ford and MacArthur. In 2003, the Brussels office had a staff of four multilingual employees, but much of WIDE's work was done by volunteers, as well as occasionally outsourced for the preparation of technical papers.[79]

WIDE's leadership, the central office, and the national platforms have been attentive to organizational tensions. In her remarks at the general assembly in Brussels in May 1995, then president Helen O'Connell mentioned two tensions in the organization's structure. One was the tension arising from the need to have a good working relationship with EU officials, and being able to express criticism of EU policies. The other tension was that between having a central office and being a network. At the time, the tension was resolved through information exchange among the national platforms and between the national platforms and the WIDE office in Brussels. In 2000, political and financial considerations alike led WIDE to move away from the Brussels-centered direction it had been taking and to rely on a more active role on the part of the national platforms.[80] At the same time, WIDE began to collaborate with women's organizations from those Central and East European countries that were to join the European Union. At the May 2000 annual meeting, WIDE and representatives of KARAT, the coalition of Central and East European women's organizations, agreed on principles of EU enlargement that would include attention to women's rights, while also discussing the possibility of joining WIDE as national platforms in the future.

For most of the 1990s, WIDE grew as a transnational network, but funding shortages after 1998 forced a restructuring. The number of original national platforms dropped from twelve to nine, a sign of the difficulties in maintaining a far-reaching network, as well as the limited life span of many local activist groups without adequate resources. In 2000, WIDE reduced the size of the staff in the Brussels central office, hoped to reactivate some of the national platforms, and introduced a new tier of individual, dues-paying members. Several of the platforms, such as Austria, France, and Spain, took on active roles, but the central office continued to predominate.

An advantage of WIDE's location in Brussels is its access to EU officials and members of the European Parliament; moreover, its organizational structure, scope of representation, and caliber of its research products have conferred a legitimacy and respect that reinforce this access. For example, the 2000 annual meeting was attended by a representative of the European Commission's Development Group on Trade and MEPs from Belgium, Denmark, and Germany (mostly Greens or Social Democrats). Two MEPs participated at WIDE's October 2002 conference on the rightward shift of European political parties. In EU and EP circles, WIDE is well known for its work on gender, development, and trade, and for its extensive links with Southern NGOs. The network is frequently asked to prepare papers ("green, white, and position papers" in EU parlance) and is consulted by MEPs.

WEDO: Lobbying through Networks

Unlike the other TFNs, WEDO is more international than transnational in its organizational structure. It is a U.S.-based feminist advocacy network that includes activist women from developing countries among its board of directors. It is not a membership organization. For most of the 1990s WEDO's executive director was the energetic Susan Davis, who was succeeded by June Zeitlin in 1999. The board of directors has included well-known activists and scholars such as Jocelyn Dow of Guyana, Wangari Maathai of Kenya, and Vandana Shiva of India. At WEDO's comfortable offices in midtown New York, salaried staff members lead programs on environmental health, gender justice, economic and social justice, and gender and governance; WEDO also has a communications director and a coordinator for global networking. Three senior advisors—from Denmark, the Netherlands, and Kenya—are consulted frequently, though they are not on staff. There are also student interns from local universities. Each WEDO program has partners in the global South, as well as a key contact known as a focal point. Weekly staff meetings help the program officers share information, exchange ideas, and coordinate their work.

Nadia Johnson, program officer for economic and social justice, described WEDO's strategies to disseminate views and influence decision-making, and pointed to the crisscrossing nature of networks. She also described the process leading up to the WTO's ministerial meeting in Doha, Qatar, in November 2001 and the UN's conference on financing for development in Monterrey, Mexico, in March 2002.[81] External funding, largely from UNIFEM, enabled women from the global South—"especially women from our own networks in Uganda, Nepal, and Central and Eastern Europe"—to attend the prepcoms for the financing for development conference. "Workshops were convened to bring together women at the grassroots level working on related issues, such as land reform and sustainable development. They included our partners who were involved in Beijing and Beijing+5, as well as focal points and coordinators in the region." Some of these women were involved in other networks, and Johnson pointed out that a common goal is to "spread the networks, let them trickle up and trickle down." Like other TFNs, WEDO has "friends in high places," including a member of the Danish delegation to the Doha ministerial meeting, Janice Goodson Feorde, who is a WEDO senior adviser. In another example of the intersecting nature of feminist networks, Janice Feorde is also a member of the Danish women's organization KULU, which is an organizational member of WIDE. As Johnson stated, "Having more women in delegations is a good strategy."

WEDO works closely with DAWN and WIDE, with whom the network has produced joint papers. Johnson explained that the groups "share the same goal: economic justice for women. We are part of the economic justice movement." Johnson also maintains contacts with the International Gender and Trade Network and the Center of Concern (Maria Riley, Mariama Williams); the Women's International Coalition for Economic Justice (Carol Barton, New York); and the Association for Women's Rights in Development, or AWID, which had become more of an activist feminist network since Canada's Joanna Kerr had been elected president. "At the February prepcom [for the Financing for Development Conference] we had a women's consultation. Mariama was there, and so were we. Mariama was asked to come up with the women's advocacy paper and recommendations. I moderate the LISTERV. The importance of the latter for information exchange should not be underestimated."[82]

Funding from UNIFEM, the UNDP, the Ford Foundation, Finnish groups, and others— "the Nordic region is very giving"—sustain WEDO's operations, but these resources are limited. WEDO finds that financial constraints affect its ability to reach out to more partners, constituents, and policy-makers:

> We have limited resources, both human and financial. Here at WEDO I'm the only staff person working on economic and social justice. We need more staffing, more capacity. We need quarterly newsletters, economic literacy training, more research, more computers. There's a lot of work to be done.
>
> It's always hard to maintain a network, to keep the information-sharing and the dialogue going. One has to cultivate relationships within a network and work to keep them. Keeping the network coherent and cohesive is equally important. One way I do that is, for example, I might send an e-mail to Helen, our focal point in Uganda, to see if she is interested in pursuing a particular idea or initiative. But we could use more funds to develop joint initiatives.[83]

Achievements and Limitations

Taking on the major institutions of global capitalism is a daunting project for any social movement, but especially for feminist groups, who have less political leverage and relatively fewer resources than other social movement organizations or transnational advocacy networks. For example, although individual DAWN members (e.g., Gita Sen, Peggy Antrobus, Sonia Correa, Gigi Francisco) are well connected and are active in major international initiatives and prominent in international gender-and-development circles, the network is not always as visible. Gita Sen noted that at the Millennial Round of the WTO in Seattle, "there was a huge global mobilization by civil society. Every union, every NGO working on development was there. But women should have been present in larger numbers to press for our concerns. We haven't developed enough organizations that can work at that level. DAWN, for example, is just a network. We don't have a big, dedicated staff or equipment."[84]

Yet TFNs working on economic justice issues have had some successes that need to be acknowledged. WIDE's research on the trade links between Europe and Latin America culminated in a publication on gender and trade indicators that became a lobbying tool and then a teaching tool, used, for example, at the Institute of Social Studies in The Hague. The instrument was subsequently adopted by the European Union.[85] Referring to DAWN, Caren Grown maintained that it "has been an important catalyst in raising economic issues in the global women's movement." The very emergence of the TFN, she continued, was "a great achievement," in that "for the first time, Third World women took an independent stand and said, We have our own issues and voices, and we can interpret our own reality.' They [DAWN] were the only ones then, they were the first." As feminists with political experience from developing countries, the women of DAWN offered a unique perspective. Moreover, the timing was right for the emergence and spread of TFNs, for shortly afterwards, the communications revolution helped them expand.

As TFNs expanded, a number of international and multilateral organizations took note, adopted some of their concepts, and responded to some of their critiques. Years of feminist analyses and collective action have led some international institutions to adopt a gender perspective, and in this respect the work of TFNs such as DAWN and WIDE has had a positive impact. The United Nations and many of its specialized agencies, funds, and programs now prioritize women and gender issues in their publications, projects, and policies, and this has helped to legitimize women's activities and demands both nationally and globally. In 1995, the UNDP's Human Development Report Office produced its annual *Human Development Report* with a focus on gender equality and inequality. As a complement to its well-known human development index (HDI), it produced two new indices, the gender empowerment measure (GEM) and the gender development index (GDI). Since then, every global HDR ranks countries according to HDI as well as GDI and GEM. This has served as a model for the national human development reports, which are produced by teams of social scientists within the developing countries.

The World Bank has responded in some measure to women's demands. For example, in 1994, Minh Chau Nguyen of the World Bank embarked on a tour of a number of countries to promote the World Bank's new policies on integrating women into planning and projects, including a policy paper entitled "Enhancing Women's Involvement in Economic Development," and to respond to criticisms by women's groups.[86] Thereafter the World Bank produced a flurry of publications on gender and development.

Following the 1995 Beijing conference, the World Bank responded to worldwide criticism, especially from women's groups, by adopting new policy priorities—at least in principle. The Bank declared that it would assist "member countries in their efforts to bring about the fuller integration of women into all stages of the development process and improvement in their economic situation." There were four major objectives: (1) to enhance women's roles in productive and social activities, (2) to facilitate women's access to productive resources, (3) to reduce women's social, legal, and economic constraints, and (4) to strengthen institutions responsible for promoting women's economic and social participation. The Women in Development Unit of the Social Programs and Sustainable Development Division was given the primary responsibility for ensuring the integration of gender considerations in Bank lending programs. Each regional department was assigned a gender specialist working full time on operations. In addition, the World Bank established the External Gender Consultative Group (EGCG), shortly after the Beijing conference. The EGCG convenes in Washington, and it held its first annual meeting in 1996, with Gita Sen of DAWN as its chairperson and other noted feminist researchers and activists as members. Its work plan and the priorities include commentary on the Policy Research Report on Gender and Development, feedback and monitoring of participatory processes for development of gender sector strategy, and feedback on gender in the World Bank's annual publication, *World Development Report*. The EGCG was also promised a key role in the preparation of a gender-focused *World Development Report*.

Some feminists have raised questions about co-optation while others regard the World Bank's new approach as paying lip service to gender issues.[87] It is not yet clear how effective or influential the World Bank policy shift and the gender specialists are. The newly formed Gender Sector Board was put on an equal footing with health, education, finance, energy, poverty, and civil society, at least formally. But one concern was that the sector boards, which were meant to support the operational programs, had little money themselves, and weaker staffing. A major criticism is that the World Bank's cognitive framework, which is neoclassical economics, leads it to make "the business case for gender equity" rather than pursue gender justice and economic justice.[88]

Nonetheless, the developments described above provide an apposite example of how a transnational social movement—in this case, the transnational women's movement—can compel a powerful international institution to address issues of accountability and participation. According to Zenebeworke Tadesse, a founder of AAWORD (and a board member of the Women's Learning Partnership for Development, Rights, and Peace) who hails from Ethiopia, "transnational women's groups have demystified the idea that women's issues are narrow [e.g., solely reproductive]; they have shown how gender matters in macroeconomic issues, in trade and in finance. It is an accomplishment that the World Bank's president announced that gender justice is a worthy goal."[89]

At the same time, the scholar-activists within TFNs are cognizant of the radical nature of their critique and the lack of will, so to speak, on the part of governments and multilateral organizations to effect the sort of changes that global feminists seek. As Zene Tadesse put it, "Macroeconomic issues are sacrosanct. Governments don't necessarily pay attention [to us], as they have bought into the neoliberal doctrine." She feels that real change could occur as women enter political and policy arenas, although she adds, "Unfortunately, the legislatures lack capacity on issues of economics and public investments." What is needed, then, is "more advocacy and coalition-building; we need to democratize decision-making; and we need to raise questions about how budgets are formed and resources allocated. We need both rights/legal reforms and public expenditures." This "critical realist" approach to the state recognizes limits to the progressive agenda, given the nature of the state, and to state capacity in an era of globalization. As a result, collective action by the women's movement and women's organizations, in tandem with other organizations, could be effective in achieving common social justice goals. "It was important for women to define the issues. But it is important to work with men, too, in broader coalitions. We have transcended the fear of working in mixed groups. We can now work with men without the fear that they will dominate us or without losing the edge that women bring to the table."[90]

There are other challenges. "Women activists have to bridge the gap and transcend the divide" between their formulations about economic justice and gender justice and the understanding and implementation "on the ground." They have to learn how to "translate these formulations in a way that makes sense to the average woman."[91]

Conclusions

Economic globalization has created a more integrated, but still unequal, global economy, along with the growing power of institutions such as the World Bank, the IMF, and the WTO. The state still matters, but economic policies—whether structural adjustment policies or the global trade agenda—increasingly have been adopted for the "international community" as a whole. At the same time, a worldwide consensus on gender equality has emerged, encouraged by the United Nations and some of its specialized agencies, such as UNIFEM, UNFPA, and the UNDP. For that reason, transnational feminist networks dedicated to economic policy issues on behalf of poor and working-class women have focused their energies largely on multilateral organizations, international conferences, and global agreements. In so doing, they have contributed to the making of global civil society or the transnational public sphere—that site of civic engagement and connectedness, and of collective action and solidarity that is outside the state, market, and family, and beyond nationalist constraints. As such, DAWN, WIDE, and WEDO are manifestations of "globalization from below," reacting to the inequalities and injustices of "globalization from above."

The transnational feminist networks examined in this chapter see themselves as part of the global social movement of women, the global justice movement, and global civil society, and they have contributed to the global social movement infrastructure. A key strategy is to work closely with UN and other multilateral bodies, as many transnational advocacy networks do, to influence policy. But their practical engagement with international organizations and the world of policy-making is framed by their more ambitious goals of fundamental social change: reinventing globalization and replacing the current neoliberal model with a model grounded in social justice, human rights, and gender equality; the return of the welfarist, development state that is accountable to its citizens, including women citizens; and the transformation of gender relations from patriarchal to egalitarian.

As we have seen, DAWN, WIDE, and WEDO share many values and goals, and often collaborate on research, advocacy, and lobbying at the regional and global levels. They may differ organizationally—for example, DAWN is less of a professionalized, formal organization than are WIDE and WEDO, and WIDE works at the national and regional levels more than does WEDO—but all three are comprised of politically astute and strategic-minded women with perspectives on the global economy as well as on their national economies. As Caren Grown remarked: "The women in DAWN have very clear ideas about what their governments ought to be doing. They have positions on labor standards, trade, intellectual property rights, and other issues."[92] And they understand the connections between economic justice and other issues pertaining to women. As a Nadia Johnson of WEDO noted: "Globalization has become a major issue, and it has galvanized women. That's why there has been a lot of work done around economic justice issues. Economic policies have become important, to feminist researchers and to funders. There is also recognition of how economic issues impact violence against women."[93]

Chapter Fourteen

Women Miners, Human Rights and Poverty

Ingrid Macdonald[1]

Introduction: Women's Rights as Human Rights[1]

All people—women, men, girls and boys—possess certain inalienable human rights that provide them with universal claims on society. These rights are expressed within international human rights instruments such as the Universal Declaration of Human Rights 1948 (UDHR), the International Covenant of Civil and Political Rights 1966 (ICCPR) and the International Covenant of Economic, Social and Cultural Rights 1963 (ICESCR). There are also numerous other important human rights instruments.[2] For example, the International Labour Organization (ILO) Declaration on Fundamental Principles and Rights at Work represents the universal core labour standards which all ILO member nations are bound to promote and realize. These include the 'elimination of discrimination in respect of employment and occupation' which is a right enjoyed by both female and male workers. There are also eight 'core' ILO Conventions on labour rights, which seek to prohibit forced and child labour and protect the rights of freedom of association, collective bargaining, the right to organize, equal opportunity and equal

---

1   I would like to thank Joanna Kyriakakis who assisted with research for and drafting of this chapter while undertaking an internship at Oxfam Community Aid Abroad. Joanna is undertaking a Doctor of Juridicial Science degree in International Law at Monash University, Australia.

2   See MacDonald and Ross, 2003

treatment for men and women workers and workers with family responsibilities and the rights of indigenous and tribal peoples.[3]

The rights expressed under the international human rights system are universal, inalienable, interdependent, indivisible, and complementary. This means that it is necessary to protect and promote a person's civil, political, social, economic and cultural rights, and what are commonly called their collective rights, to enable them to enjoy full human dignity. It also means that these rights transcend national borders, economic paradigms and political structures, and some of them are more legally binding than others. For example, the prohibition on torture is a preeminent norm of international law whereas the right to social security is not (see Higgins, 1994: 19, for the validity of prohibition as a requirement of customary international law and Schacter, 1991: 85, for the binding nature of the UDHR).

Notwithstanding this on-going debate, rights are guaranteed to all human beings 'without distinction of any kind, such as race, colour, sex, language, religion, political or other opinion, national or social origin, property, birth or other status' (UDHR 1948: art. 2). Women are therefore entitled to the same protection and promotion of their human rights as men. The Vienna Declaration of 1993 provides, '[t]he human rights of women and of the girl-child are an inalienable, integral and indivisible part of universal human rights'[4], and Article 14 of the Fourth World Conference on Women 1995 ('the Beijing Declaration') declares that 'women's rights are human rights.'[5] Further, positive government action and policies are anticipated and obligatory to ensure women's rights are enjoyed without discrimination. For example, Article 2(2) of the ICCPR provides that State parties must 'take the necessary steps ... to adopt such legislative or other measures as may be necessary to give effect to the rights recognized' in the Covenant. Similar obligations toward the adoption of national legislation and measures to ensure the actualization of human rights standards for women are required by most human rights instruments.[6]

---

3   There are eight 'core' ILO Conventions on labour rights, namely Convention 29 (forced labour), 87 (freedom of association and protection of the rights to organize), 98 (right to organize and collective bargaining), 100 (equal opportunities and equal treatment for men and women workers: workers with family responsibilities), together with ILO Conventions 182 and 190 (child labour) and 169 (the rights of indigenous and tribal people). Available at www.ilo.org.

4   Text available in *Human Rights Law Journal*, 1993, pp. 352–70.

5   The Beijing Declaration and Platform for Action, op. cit, 'Mission Statement,' para 1 Available at: http://www.un.org/womenwatch/daw/beijing/platform/plat.1.htm [Accessed November 4, 2002].

6   See for example, the *Convention on the Elimination of All forms of Discrimination Against Women*, which is framed by the obligations of State Parties to take positive measures to address the inequalities and discrimination faced by women; see also ILO convention 111: *Discrimination (Employment and Occupation) Convention*, 1958, article 1, which obligates member states to take positive action and amend national legislation in order to promote and achieve equal opportunity and treatment in respect of employment and occupation with a view to eliminating any discrimination. This Convention has been ratified in Australia with the Human Rights and Equal Opportunity Act (Cth) 1986.

The specific right of women to work and to work free of discrimination is also enshrined in a number of human rights instruments, such as Article 11 of the Convention On the Elimination of All Forms of Discrimination Against Women (CEDAW) (UNDFW, 1979), Article 26 of the Beijing Declaration, Article 23 of the Universal Declaration of Human Rights, and is implicit particularly in ILO Convention 111—*Discrimination (Employment and Occupation) Convention, 1958.*

However, in practice the duty to ensure women's human rights, including workers rights, is often far removed from the reality of implementation, application and enforcement, including in respect of the disadvantages suffered by women and children involved in small and large scale mining.

The Barriers to Realizing Women's Rights

Women are the most discriminated against, the most vulnerable and least empowered members of many societies, including those with rich mining, oil and gas resource endowments. It is therefore not surprising that women comprise 70 per cent of the world's poor and this proportion is growing. Throughout the world, women work longer hours for less pay than men employed in similar positions, and they are grossly under-represented in private sector management and political positions, leading the United Nations Development Group to comment that women represent the 'world's largest excluded group' (UNDP, 1993: 25).

Women comprising 70 per cent of the world's poor is not a 'natural occurrence' or the result of biological differences between men and women. There are many different illegitimate social, political, economic, civil and cultural barriers that perpetuate systems of discrimination, oppression and the abuse of women's rights. As a result, the benefits of economic development are not distributed equally, and progress towards equality between men and women does not take place naturally. It can therefore not be assumed that women automatically benefit from economic and industrial development efforts, especially in respect of mining projects.

In India, for example, considering both market and non-market work (such as domestic care and subsistence farming), women work an average day 117 per cent that of men's, while in Indonesia it is 109 per cent and in the Philippines 121 per cent (UNDR, 2004: Table 28). In contrast, in both developed and developing countries women's wages are well below those enjoyed by their male counterparts, with the ratio in most east and south Asian countries near to or less than half that of men's (UNDR, 2004: Tables 24, 25). There is no country within the world where women earn the same as men (Seager, 2003).

Women also comprise the vast majority of the world's unpaid informal and subsistence agricultural workforce. In those countries where data is available, the United Nations Development Group reports that women invariably allocate the greatest portion of their time to non-market activities (such as domestic care and subsistence agriculture) in contrast to men whose time is predominately allocated to market, and hence income generating, activities. For example, in Indonesia, women allocated 65 per cent of their time to non-market activities and 35 per cent to market activities, in contrast to men who allocated 14 per cent and 86 per cent respectively. In the Philippines the figures show an allocation between non-market and market activities at 71 per cent and 29 per cent for women, and 16 per cent and 84 per cent for men, and in India at 65 per cent and 35 per cent for women, and 8 per cent and 92 per cent for men (UNDR, 2004: Table 28). Yet much of the work of women, such as child-care, household responsibilities and daily food and water provision, has no value within the current neo-liberal system of economic development. This system, based on 'gender neutral' economic theories, places primary value on paid labour (Hunt, 1996: 25–6). As women are often not active or only partially active within the paid labour force, especially in relation to male dominated activities such as mining, their non-paid labour is not valued. In addition, underemployment is often not acknowledged in statistical data and hence considered in policy. As a result, economic development, has often served to marginalize the roles and responsibilities of women and exclude them from any benefits of such development. The Director-General of the International Labour Organization in his 2003 report on work and poverty acknowledges that 'far too much of women's work is still uncounted and undervalued' (ILO, 2003: art. 6). Further:

> The distinction between the public and private spheres operates to make the work and needs of women invisible. Economic visibility depends on working in the public sphere and unpaid work in the home or community is categorized as unproductive, unoccupied and economically inactive.
>
> Charseworth et al., 1991: 614

Throughout the world women also continue to suffer persistent and systematic human rights abuses for no other reason than they are women.[7] In the workplace, home, health system, the public domain and in conflict situations, women are subjected to violence, abuse and discrimination that is often sanctioned or ignored by judicial and political institutions. Examples include sexual assault, domestic violence, forced prostitution and lack of access and control over reproductive and employment choices.

Given the considerable barriers to the actualization of women's rights, there are key international human rights instruments dealings exclusively with removing the barriers to women's rights and empowerment. CEDAW (UNDFW, 1979) has been declared and adopted so as to address directly the disparities between men and women as regards their access and enjoyment of human rights, and the persistence of practices and attitudes that hamper the actualization of women's rights. The Beijing Platform for Action of 1995 is also specifically concerned with women's rights and empowerment. Such instruments are built

---

7   Human Rights Watch, Women's Human Rights. Available at: http://www.hrw.org/women/index.php [Accessed November 4, 2002]

upon the recognition that despite the existence of human rights instruments extensive discrimination against women continues and inequality persists (UNDFW, 1979: preamble). The protection and promotion of women's rights is fundamental to poverty alleviation and development.

Kofi Annan in the United Nations 1998 Annual Report states:

> The rights-based approach to development describes situations not simply in terms of human needs, or of developmental requirements, but in terms of society's obligation to respond to the inalienable rights of individuals. It empowers people to demand justice as a right, not as charity ...[8]

The rights based approach to development recognizes that there can be no real solution to poverty, without respect for, understanding and promotion of human rights, particularly the rights of traditionally marginalized groups, such as women and girls, ethnic minorities and indigenous peoples. As such, it recognizes that economic poverty is not a natural state or phenomenon, but results from the direct denial, violation and abuse of the human rights of men, women, girls and boys, by entities that have more access to power, or through systems that are based on injustice, inequality and discrimination.

Human rights and human development operate in a symbiotic relationship, with the achievement of one based upon the other. This idea was encompassed by the United Nations Development Programme (UNDP) in their Human Development Report 2000, where it stated that 'human development is essential for realizing human rights, and human rights are essential for full human development' (UNDP, 2000). The UNDP also asserts that '... [h]uman rights and sustainable human development are interdependent and mutually reinforcing.'[9]

Given the majority of the of the world's poor are women, the promotion of women's rights, gender equality and the empowerment of women are essential prerequisites to achieving sustainable people-centred development and combating poverty. Recognized under the 1986 Declaration on the Rights to Development[10], the active, free and meaningful participation of all people, including women in development, including their active, free and meaningful participation in the workforce, is fundamental to addressing the well-being of the society as a whole. Article 16 of the Beijing Declaration provides:

> Eradication of poverty based upon sustained economic growth, social development, environmental protection and social justice requires the involvement of

---

8   United Nations, *Striking a Better Balance*, vol 3, Annex 6: 143.

9   United Nations Development Programme, 1998, *Integrating Human Rights with Sustainable Human Development: A UNDP Policy Document*, January.

10   Adopted by the General Assembly of the United Nations, GA Res 41/128 of 4 December 1986, preamble.

women in economic and social development, equal opportunities and the full and equal participation of women and men as agents and beneficiaries of people-centred sustainable development. As such, promoting the right of women to work is fundamental for ensuring that development benefits flow to all members of the community equitably, and actualize goals to alleviate poverty.

The Large Scale Mining Companies and Feminization of Poverty

Globally, the push towards a free-market system has resulted in the increasing impact of mining companies' activities on the world's poorest and most vulnerable people, including women and children. Recent figures show that as a result of the increasingly rapid and unfettered movement of international capital, the revenues of five of the world's largest transnational companies add up to more than double the combined Gross Domestic Profit of the poorest 100 countries (Utting, 2002).

This process of economic globalization is being driven by transnational companies, wealthy governments and multilateral financial institutions including the International Monetary Fund, World Trade Organization, World Bank Group and Asian Development Bank. The resulting economic liberalization, market deregulation, privatization of industries and services has meant that, as stated in a recent Oxfam America briefing paper (Langman, 2003: 6):

> Foreign direct investment (FDI) ... has become such an important part of global development strategies that it has replaced foreign aid as the main source of external capital for many developing countries. Today, FDI amounts to about 60 per cent of the international capital flowing into developing countries each year and is nearly ten times larger than official development assistance. In contrast, in the late 1980s, the amounts of annual aid and FDI in developing countries were roughly the same.
>
> UNCTAD, 2002

It has also enabled a rapidly growing mining industry, dominated by transnational corporations, to expand into some of the world's most remote communities, including those within the Asia Pacific (Langman, 2003: 5–16).

Governments, multilateral financial institutions and companies justify the promotion of large scale mining in poor countries in the name of economic development and reducing poverty. Yet despite decades of economic liberalization, deregulation and privatization easing the way for such activity, inequality between and within countries has increased.[11] The Human Development Report 2004 reports that the previous decade saw an unprecedented backward slide in development outcomes for many nations with the result that in 46 countries people are poorer and in 26 countries more people go hungry than a decade ago (UNHDR, 2004: 128).

This backward development slide appears to be even more pronounced in resource rich countries. The World Bank's recent Extractive Industries Review found that:

> Data on real per capita gross domestic product (GDP) reveal that developing countries with few natural resources grew two or three times faster than resource-rich countries over the period 1960–2000. Of 45 countries that did not manage to sustain economic growth during this time, all but six were heavily dependent on extractive industries, and a majority of them also experienced violent conflict and civil strife in the 1990s.
>
> World Bank, 2004

Otherwise known as the 'resource curse,' numerous studies have shown that many of the world's most resource-rich countries are also the world's poorest in economic terms (Ross, 2001: 7). Oil, gas and mining industries are important to more than 50 developing countries, which are home to 3.5 billion people. Yet more than 1.5 billion of these people live on less than $2 US per day. Moreover, 12 of the world's 25 most mineral-dependent states, and six of the world's most oil-dependent states, are classified by the World Bank as 'highly indebted poor countries' with the world's worst human development statistics (Ross, 2001: 7).

Despite enormous funds being generated through resource extraction, these funds have largely not been used to combat poverty. Instead, the revenues generated by extraction have often been embezzled by corrupt elites, spent on military armaments by authoritarian regimes, or have even fuelled regional instability through groups warring over control of the revenue streams from resource extraction (Ross, 2001; Global Witness, 1999; Hafild, 2003). Many of the people within these countries remain impoverished and their rights undermined due to corruption and economic mismanagement, which has severe impacts on the majority of the poor: women and children.

---

11   UNDP (2001) states that: 'The income gap between the richest one-fifth of the world's people and the poorest one-fifth measured on average national income per head, increased from 30 to 1 in 1960 to 74 to 1 in 1997.'

The increasing global power and influence of transnational companies, and their impact on development and poverty means that they, alongside governments, must be responsible for upholding human rights, including the rights of women workers. As UN Secretary General Kofi Annan has noted:

> The fragility of globalization ... poses a direct challenge to the self-interest of the corporate sector, and a central part of the solution is the need ... to accept the obligations—and not merely the opportunities—of global citizenship.[12]

Traditionally, governments have had the primary responsibility for ensuring that mining companies do not violate people's rights, including the protection of the rights of women mine workers. This reflects the power historically wielded by the state, both individually and collectively through institutions like the United Nations. Yet, rights and duties under international law are slowly being extended to non-state actors and individuals. Thus far, individuals have been found legally responsible for war crimes, crimes against humanity and other gross human rights abuses.[13] The UN Universal Declaration of Human Rights also codifies not only the moral responsibility of companies to uphold rights of those affected by their activities, but is increasingly seen implying their legal liability as 'organs of society' to respect, promote and secure human rights.[14]

The UN Sub-Commission on the Promotion and Protection of Human Rights also recently adopted the Norms of the Responsibilities of Transnational Corporations and Other Business Enterprises with Regards to Human Rights ('UN Norms').[15] The UN Norms codify company duties regarding human rights, and were drafted by independent human rights experts elected from different regions by the UN Commission on Human Rights. The

---

12   Address of Kofi Annan, Secretary General of the United Nations, to the World Economic Forum, Davos, Switzerland, 28 January 2001, available at www.weforum.org.

13   See cases concerning: *Trial of Major War Criminals Before the International Military Tribunal Nuremberg*, 1947; *Statute of the International Criminal Tribunal for the Former Yugoslavia*, UN Doc S/Res/827, 1993; *Statute of the International Tribunal for Rwanda*, SC Res 955, 49 UN SCOR (3452nd meeting), UN Doc S/Res/955, 1994; and the requirements of the *Rome Statute of the International Criminal Court*, 37 ILM 999, opened for signature 17 July 1998.

14   *Universal Declaration of Human Rights*, (1948), op cit, preamble: Renowned international legal scholar Professor Louis Henkin states that: '... [e]very individual and every organ of society excludes no one, no company, no cyberspace. The Universal Declaration applies to them all.'

15   United Nations Norms on Responsibilities of Transnational Corporations and other Business Enterprises with regard to Human Rights (with commentary); E/CN.4/Sub 2/2003/38/Rev.2 (2203); UNESC CHR, Sub Commission on the Promotion and Protection of Human Rights, 55th session agenda item 4.

UN Norms include the rights of women workers and would be applicable to the mining industry, including protections covering freedom of association and collective bargaining, a safe and healthy working environment, prohibitions on child and forced labour and the right to a living wage.

Oxfam Community Aid Abroad's Focus on Women and Mining

Oxfam Community Aid Abroad[16] focuses on women and mining issues based on decades of work with local community women and men impacted by mining in the Asia Pacific. In the past few decades, the Australian mining industry has increased its activities in economically developing countries in the Asia–Pacific. Australian mining operations are therefore increasingly impacting on poor and vulnerable community women and men—the same women and men that Oxfam Community Aid Abroad has worked with for over 50 years. Many of these local women and men complained, and continue to complain, of human rights abuses and environmental degradation caused by, or on behalf of, Australian mining companies. These people often have no institution that they can access for fair and equitable redress, so companies have been able to disregard their concerns. As a result, Oxfam Community Aid Abroad established the position of the Mining Ombudsman in 2000. The primary objective of the project is to demonstrate the need and feasibility of the Australian Federal government formally establishing such a broad based industry mechanism within Australia.

The Mining Ombudsman is invited by local community women and men impacted by the activities of Australian listed mining companies to investigate their grievances and attempt to secure resolution or redress from the company concerned. There are cases currently in Peru, Papua New Guinea, the Philippines, Indonesia and Fiji.[17]

Through the Ombudsman, we have found that the grievances of community women and men affected by such mining activities often constitute denial of their basic human rights—especially to free, prior and informed consent; to self-determination, land, and a livelihood. These grievances are often industry-wide, arising at every stage of the project cycle. Indigenous peoples are particularly vulnerable in part because they are usually the poorest, most marginalized groups in society, and because of the particular damage that can

---

16   Oxfam Community Aid Abroad is an independent, secular, non-government development agency and the Australian member of the Oxfam International confederation. The agency undertakes long-term development projects, provides humanitarian responses during disaster and conflict, and advocates for policy and practice changes to promote human rights, justice, gender equality and women's empowerment in 30 countries across Asia, Africa, the Pacific, Central America and Indigenous Australia.

17   See Oxfam Community Aid Abroad Mining Campaign at www.oxfam.org.au/campaigns/mining and the *Mining Ombudsman Annual Reports 2001, 2002, 2003*, and *2004* for further information.

result from loss or damage to the lands, waterways, flora, fauna and sacred sites with which they have a longstanding spiritual, often custodial relationship.

In June 2002, we convened the *Tunnel Vision: Women, Mining and Communities* workshop in Melbourne. The first of its kind in Australia, the workshop brought together speakers from Indigenous Australia and the Asia Pacific speaking on the impacts of mining on women living in local communities. It found that women had overwhelmingly been excluded from the benefits of mining, and bore the brunt of its negative social and environmental impacts.[18] Issues raised echoed the grievances voiced by women from communities who have brought their complaints to the Mining Ombudsman. These grievances include:

1. Companies entering into negotiations only with men, making women neither party to the negotiations, nor beneficiaries of royalties or compensation payments, even in matrilineal societies where women are the culturally recognized landowners. As a result, women are often stripped of their traditional means of acquiring status and wealth.
2. Companies not recognising the religious and spiritual connections of indigenous women to their environments and land, especially when they are displaced by mining activities.
3. Women generally have little or no control over and access to any of the benefits of mining developments, especially money and employment. They therefore become more dependent on men who are more likely to be able to access and control these benefits through being recognized by the mining companies and being the ones who are paid the benefits or receiving work at the mine.
4. The traditional roles and responsibilities of women are marginalized as the community becomes more dependent on the cash based economy created by mine development.
5. The workload of women increases as men work in a cash economy created by mining operations, and women bear increased responsibility for the household and food provision through traditional means. This workload can be further exacerbated if there is environmental pollution or contamination of land or water sources. It is the women who bear the responsibility of finding alternative food sources, walking further distances to access clean drinking water and caring for the sick children or family members.
6. Women become more at risk of impoverishment, particularly in women-headed households. This is particularly the case where women are abandoned by their husbands.
7. Women bear both the physical and mental strain of mine development, especially when it involves resettlement. This is especially evident in increased levels of domestic violence.
8. Women suffer from an increased risk of vulnerability to HIV/AIDS and other STD infections, family violence, and sexual abuse—often fuelled by alcohol abuse and/or a transient male workforce or the need to find money to feed their families.
9. Women suffer active and often brutal discrimination in the workplace.

---

18 A copy of the report containing the papers presented by the speakers is available from the Oxfam Australia website www.oxfam.org.au/campaigns/mining.

These gender impacts represent the denial of the basic human rights of women from local communities affected by mining and women engaged in the mining industry.

The Exclusion of Women from Large Scale Mining

Large scale mining has high levels of productivity with low levels of employment, due to it being based largely on mechanized processes requiring specialized technical skills. It is also increasingly associated with foreign corporate management by large transnational companies facilitated through privatization, deregulation and liberalization as already discussed. Women are represented in very small numbers within the large scale mining industry. For example, women comprise only 8–14 per cent of the Australian mining industry workforce, of which only 2–20 per cent are within the professional technical divisions of the industry.[19]

We can speculate on any number of factors that lead to the exclusion of women from large scale mining which include not least the male dominated nature of the extractive industries. In a report to the Australian Institute of Mining and Metallurgy 'Women and Mining' taskforce in November 1998, it was found that some of the main reasons why women were discouraged from becoming involved in the mining industry were the remoteness of mine locations, the male dominated 'old boys' culture and inadequate site infrastructure (Pattenden, 1998). Further, first hand accounts from women and women's representative bodies in communities impacted by large scale mining projects are available which identify a number of recurrent themes in women's exclusion from the large scale mining sector, or brutal discrimination when they are employed. For example, see the papers presented in the *Tunnel Vision* report, direct testimonials collected through the Mining Ombudsman work and the reports of the International Women and Mining Network (RIMM, 2000).

The exclusion of women from the large scale industry is contrary to the rights of women and reduces what, if any, development benefits may flow to communities from mining and is also contrary to the rights of women.

Exclusion from Decision-Making

The exclusion of women from engagement with large scale mining projects begins at the first interaction between the mining company and the local people. In the *Tunnel Vision* workshop speakers discussed the experiences of women from Indigenous Australian, Papua New Guinean, Indonesian, Philippines and Indian communities who were systematically excluded from dialogue pertaining to mining project developments. It was pointed out that predominantly male company heads and politicians tend not to recognize women and

19   Jessica Horsley, *Women in Mining—The Statistics* on behalf of the Women in Mining Working Group for AusIMM available at www.aussimm.com/women/women.asp.

issues pertaining to women, and too readily accept the demands by community men that women need not be consulted, often despite national laws requiring that women participate in negotiations.

Yet, under the UN Convention on the Elimination of All Forms of Discrimination Against Women (CEDAW) women have a right to engage equally in decision-making affecting them. In the event of a discrepancy between traditional law and the convention regarding this entitlement, the latter must prevail (UNDFW, 1979, articles 2f and 5). This right of participation also arises pursuant to the 1986 Declaration on the Right to Development which provides that every person is entitled to 'participate in, contribute to, and enjoy economic, social, cultural and political development, in which all human rights and fundamental freedoms can be fully realized,' (UNDFW, 1979, article 1) and as discussed, is essential for achieving sustainable development and combating poverty.

Women's exclusion is often compounded by cultural constraints and stereotypes regarding the appropriate roles of men and women. Speakers within the Tunnel Vision workshop reflected an array of experiences as to women's exclusion from the large scale sector. As a result the women missed out on the economic benefits of mining whilst bearing the burden of many of the negative social and environmental impacts, thus intensifying their impoverishment and disadvantage. In the Indian example, high levels of illiteracy amongst women, lack of technical skills and the social stigma associated with women's participation in the paid work force were cited as among the key factors operating to exclude women from employment in large scale mining, which is increasingly technology dependent. The commencement of large scale mining in areas such as Indonesia and Papua New Guinea, operated to supplant the traditional power base of women and their centrality in land ownership and economic production, largely through the exclusion of women in the dialogue process and involvement in the subsequent cash economy. Men, who often dominate the pre-project negotiations with mining companies, if such negotiations occur, largely assume the primary entitlement to the work that flows from those projects.

Hostile Work Hours

The work environment within the extractive industry is hostile to women. In its advocacy, the Construction, Forestry, Mining and Energy Union in Australia have attempted to draw attention to concerns over long working hours in the mining industry and the impact of such hours on families. One claim regarding the average hours of work in the Australian gold mining industry is 3,000 hours per person per year, which represents 60 hours per week. It was proposed that this represents world's best practice (Colley, 2003).

A recent Western Australian review into extended working hours across different industries, in the context of Australia wide data, found that the Mining Industry has the highest average weekly hours across all sectors considered (Hartley et al., 2004). In 2003 the average hours per week in the mining sector in Western Australia was 48.4. Results from research in the United Kingdom similarly show the mining industry to be characterized by pervasive long working hours, ranking the mining industry second after agriculture in terms of numbers of employees working above 48 hours and 60 hours per week (Kodz et al., 2003: Figures 5.15 and 5.17).

An industry wide culture of long working hours impacts in particularly onerous ways upon women and serves to marginalize and exclude women from full participation. As already discussed, women are largely responsible for child care and other domestic responsibilities, as a result, women's participation in jobs that require long work hours is hampered by their responsibilities to family and home, or they may be excluded automatically on the basis of a perceived inability to participate to the full extent demanded by the culture of the workplace (Hartley et al., 2004: 32–33). In this Western Australian study, the view emerged that:

> [E]xtended working hours is part of a male work culture … with particular consequences for women since women's capacity to work extended hours is more constrained given that women continue to be the primary care giver. While working extended hours may be viewed as mandatory to career advancement by both men and women, it remains an expectation that women are less able to meet due to their family responsibilities. Thus, women are disadvantaged when working within a pervasive work culture wherein it is perceived that there is a correlation between long working hours and commitment and professionalism (footnotes omitted).

A recent United Kingdom study (Kodz et al., 2003) into long working hours suggests that women are marginalized in certain industries by both systemic long working hours and by the active promotion of that culture by male colleagues for the purpose of excluding women, for example by 'working long hours, holding late meetings, or using after work socialising for discussing work issues, and criticising female staff for leaving "early"' (ibid: 207). Women working in male dominated industries reported a heightened experience of pressure to work long hours, and a strong disinclination to engage in what is perceived as 'presenteeism,' a male work characteristic. Women also suffer greater negative impacts upon their health and general well-being as a result of employment involving longer work hours than men (ibid: 241–2).

Yet the obligations upon ILO member states under Convention 156: *Workers with Family Responsibilities* demands that governments address women's exclusion from the formal mining sector as a result of hostile work cultures. For example, Convention 156 requires each Member state to, so far as possible, enable persons with family responsibilities to exercise their right to engage equitably in employment, and to minimize conflict between employment obligations and family commitments (ILO, 1981: article 3.1). More broadly, ILO Convention 111: *Discrimination (Employment and Occupation) Convention, 1958* requires member states to take positive measures to address discrimination affecting access to employment and occupation, with discrimination encompassing 'any distinction, exclusion or preference made on the basis of ... sex ... which has the effect of nullifying or impairing equality of opportunity or treatment in employment or occupation'(ILO, 1981: article 1.1a).

Fly In/Fly Out Operations

Another element identified as being hostile to women is the predominance of 'fly-in' and 'fly-out' operations ('FIFO') in the mining industry. As mining often occurs in remote locations, employees are literally flown in for intense work shifts and then flown out for rest. For much the same reasons as apply to long working hours generally, this mode of operation and employment is especially hostile to women employees, especially those with family and child care responsibilities.

In it's joint submission to the Western Australian Review Panel on extended working hours, the Chamber of Minerals and Energy of Western Australia (CME) and the Australian Mines and Metals Association (AMMA) reported that amongst their members two thirds of employees worked 12 hour shifts, the most common work roster arrangement was 2 weeks on/1 week off, and half of the sites surveyed operated on a FIFO basis (Hartley et al., 2004: 10). The overall roster pattern within the mining industry in Western Australia shows that up to 76 per cent of workers work on this basis.

Negative impacts of FIFO employment arrangements are disproportionately suffered by women. Women are subjected to increased risks of sexual and other violence, marital stress and breakdown, and infections such as HIV, due to the separation of families and the health risks associated with make shift mining communities that are more isolated, attract an influx of male workers, and often do not include easy access to health and educational resources.

The ILO (2003) reports an above-average risk of HIV infection for workers in traveling and itinerant occupations, due to the worker's separation from their families and the availability of alcohol and sex along travel routes. Women as a category are themselves more vulnerable to infection due to their sexual and economic subordination to men which can prevent women from having the power to negotiate safe sex, and can expose them to greater risks of sexual violence and harassment at work.

Some mining companies have equal employment opportunity or formal diversity policies that purport to protect the rights of women workers (Hall, 2003). However, in discussions with women workers engaged in the mining industry, both professional and non-professional, they state that where these policies exist they do not always significantly improve their work environment. Further, the 'Women in Mining' Taskforce report contained various quotes including: 'EEO is a term coined by Human Resources Departments who may wish it to exist for technical departments who do not (female, 26–35)' (Pattenden, 1998: 25). Also:

> I've had a few situations where I have seriously considered taking some (companies) to the Equal Opportunity Tribunal, but I know that as soon as I do that I won't get another job in the mining industry. The mining industry is so small in Australia—in fact, the whole worldwide mining industry—is so small that you do something like that and everybody knows about it and everybody remembers it. And you're finished. You can never expect to work in the industry again (female, 40s).
>
> Pattenden, 1998: 29

Depression and frustration are common complaints of women mine workers who can become professionally and socially isolated in the mining industry. The 'Women in Mining' Taskforce report found, in respect of Australia, 'that harassment and discrimination remain a significant problem within the minerals industry across professions' (Pattenden, 1998: 26, 31). As stated in the Preamble of CEDAW, the negative effect of discrimination upon the actualization of women's rights will undermine development efforts and the well-being of society as a whole:

> Discrimination against women violates the principles of equality of rights and respect for human dignity, is an obstacle to the participation of women, on equal terms with men, in the political, social, economic and cultural life of their countries, hampers the growth of the prosperity of society and the family and makes more difficult the full development of the potentialities of women in the service of their country and of humanity...
>
> UNDFW, 1979, preamble

What is also evident is that women generally have higher levels of employment in areas such as catering, cleaning, food supply and other types of low skilled work (RIMM, 2000). The statistics emerging from the most recent United Nations Human Development Report bears this out, showing that across both developed and developing nations, the percentage of women in the services sector continues to be substantially higher, and in the industries sector substantially lower, relative to men. For example in the Philippines women make up 172 per cent of the services industry comparative to men. In Thailand, it is 119 per cent (UNDP, 2004, table 27, pp. 229–232). Women employed in these types of roles are more vulnerable given that companies can claim that it is not them that employs them but the contractor, and so they are not therefore responsible for the conditions under which these women work. These types of contract roles are characterized by low pay, high pressure, long overtime at short notice and shift work, casual and short-term contracts based on supply of the good or service to the company with limited to no employment protection (RIMM, 2000). In the Mining Ombudsman Case Study on the Vatukoula Gold Mine (Macdonald, 2004), the problems encountered by women workers at the Vatukoula Gold mine in Fiji are described as:

> Currently, women who work at the mine are engaged in tasks such as administration, cleaning and supervising. A good majority of women are also engaged as hand pickers—a task which requires them to sort by hand the good from the bad ore before it is taken through the gold processing machinery ... Where a private contractor employs women as hand-pickers, their situation is even more vulnerable. Although contrary to the employment legislation in Fiji, women claim to work for a period of three or four years as casual workers without a written contract. Should they fall pregnant, they are automatically dismissed from their work.
>
> Bale-Tuinamola, 2003

The promotion of the idea of a flexible workforce within large scale mining risks what limited rights women do enjoy in the workplace being slowly eroded and inequalities exacerbated. Increased levels of contract labour and resistance to fundamental core labour standards such as the right of collective bargaining and the guarantee of a living wage[20] has severe impacts on vulnerable workers such as unskilled women working in supply chains (Oxfam International, 2004). Not only does this undermine the human rights of women workers, it reduces any development benefits that they and their families may receive.

---

20 A living wage is intended to provide female and male employees with a minimum wage that not only provides themselves and their families with adequate shelter, food, clothing, education, healthcare and transport, but also includes a reasonable amount of discretionary income.

The Problems for Women Engaged in Small Scale Mining

In a 1999 report, the ILO found that female participation in the mining sector becomes more and more pronounced the smaller the scale of the activity. It also predicts that this will be an increasing trend into the future.

Women's higher representation in smaller scale mining has important implications when we consider the problems particular to small scale and traditional mining. It also begs the question, why are women working in the small scale informal mining sector but largely excluded from the large scale formalized mining industry?

Some of the problems inherent in the small scale mining sector that are briefly detailed below are more fully discussed in the ILO (1999) report, the World Bank Extractive Industry Review *Striking a Better Balance* report (World Bank, 2004) and the Conference Report from the II International Conference on Women and Mining 2000 (RIMM, 2000). These problems involve basic labour rights violations such as the denial of the right to freedom of association and collective bargaining, adequate health and safety protections and the right to a fair wage, they also involve other human rights violations such as the denial of the right to fresh water, a healthy environment and to live free of violence. Such problems include:

1. The small scale and traditional mining sectors are largely unregulated. This means that women workers in this sector are more susceptible to significant risks to health and safety, with the likelihood of work site accidents largely increased and the employment of dangerous practices more widespread. The ILO reported that the dangerous conditions particular to the small scale sector results in a workplace fatality rate of up to 90 times that experienced in mining operations in industrialized countries. As women are often engaged in the processing of raw materials, including sieving and washing materials, unsafe practices occur such as undertaking those tasks from home or polluting watercourses that are used for domestic purposes, which places families at greater risks from silicosis and mercury poisoning. With women principally responsible for the care of families and the sick, this places the greatest burden on women. Women are further impacted by a lack of regulation, as they are more susceptible to sexual violence and exploitation, which are also a problem in the small scale mining sector.

2. Small scale and traditional mining is often subordinated to large scale mining, and miners in those sectors are placed at risk of dispossession of their land and mining rights by the commencement of large scale mining operations. This has led in cases to the subsequent illegality of small scale and traditional mining, the failure by governments to recognize traditional mining rights and the resultant risk of forcible eviction and violence against traditional and small scale miners by security forces. Examples abound throughout Indonesia, the Philippines, Africa and Latin America and some are documented within the Mining Ombudsman work, including the Indo Muro Kencana case and Kelian case from Indonesia (Macdonald and Ross, 2003). Further, when large scale mining comes to regions with established small scale and traditional mining, it is often the women who are the first to lose their jobs and who do not obtain employment

within the large scale mining industry and therefore lose their source of independence and livelihood—this situation is particularly difficult for female headed households.

3. Small scale and traditional miners are also often stuck in a cycle of poverty, where they are only able to access less productive lands, receive less than the real value of their product and are largely unrepresented or serviced by unions to address these problems.

4. The ILO have also identified women's need to bring children with them to a mining site as a factor contributing to the problem of child labour in mining, as often the only alternative, leaving the child unattended at home, is considered a worse outcome. This problem is not just confined to small scale mining but also large-scale mining.

5. The health issues for makeshift communities surrounding small scale mining are also more acute than in other areas, which are not suffering influxes of migrant workers, shortages of basic resources and the like. Again, this burden is felt most heavily by women, who have responsibility for the domestic and care activities.

The Way Forward: Addressing the Gender Inequity of Mining— What Can We All Do?

In order to address the disadvantage of women engaged in and impacted by the small and large scale mining sectors, a prerequisite is the recognition of women as key stakeholders in the management and development of natural resources, and economic actors in their own right. It should also be remembered that workers in small and large scale mining are also often women living in communities impacted by mining. As such, they are detrimentally impacted when there is environmental pollution, social problems, human rights abuses and illnesses that affect local communities—all of which are human rights infringements.

Basic minimums that should be committed to and actualized by governments and companies, include the right to collective bargaining, abolition of child labour, non-discrimination and equal opportunities and the right to a basic living wage. These are important protections for women that should apply to all types of mining, traditional, small scale, large scale and service industries. Protecting and promoting the rights of women is fundamental to achieving sustainable development and combating poverty.

In order to promote gender equality and women's empowerment, gender must be main-streamed into all stages of the project cycle from planning and design to implementation, monitoring and evaluation and in the workplace. This means that women's perspectives, needs and interests must be considered in all planning and programming, and women must participate in all activities as decision-makers and beneficiaries.

As a result, companies, small and large, must provide not only policy commitments, but a work environment where women can work free of discrimination and harassment. Governments are legally required to ensure this occurs. These policies must be monitored and enforced to ensure compliance and they must be applied down supply chains in order to protect female contract workers. The education of all workers, male and female, is also fundamental for securing change. If women have complaints concerning male colleagues, they must have the ability to access a safe, confidential and independent mechanism to seek redress. Retaliation against complainants by work colleagues can not be allowed under any circumstances.

Overall, women's rights must be respected and promoted by all of us in all of our activities. The promotion of women's rights and gender equality is fundamental to combating economic poverty and sustainable development. This is something that each and every one of us can do something about in our own sphere of influence, with the first starting point being recognition that oppression and discrimination of any kind—even that which is argued for under the guise of culture, including a workplace culture—is unacceptable.

Unless we actively ensure that the rights of women are promoted, including the rights of women workers, economic poverty will only get worse—for in the end, what is the benefit of mining if it does not benefit women, who comprise half of the world's population and the majority of the poor?

References

Bale-Tuinamoala, Laisa, 2003. 'The Impact of Mining on Women in Fiji,' *Voices for Change 2003*, Fiji Women's Rights Movement, Madang, Papua New Guinea, August 2003.

Charseworth, H, Chinkin, C. and Wright, S., 1991. 'Feminist Approaches to International Law,' *American Journal of International Law*, vol. 85, pp. 613–614.

Colley, Peter, 2003. *CFMEU Mineworkers: Partner or Production Factor*, Speech Presented at the Sustainable Development Conference, Brisbane, Australia, November 2003, available at http://www.cfmeu.asn.au/minmg-energy/policy/Colley_MCA2003a.pdf [28 June 2004] :10.

Global Witness, 1999. *A Crude Awakening*, at http://www.globalwitness.org, The Conflict Diamond Campaign.

Hall, Brigette, 2003. *The WIMNet Diversity Questionnaire—Summary of Responses to Date*, available at www.ausimm.com.au/women/women/asp.

Hartley, L., Creed, H, Gilroy, P. and Todd, D., 2004. *Extended Working Hours Review*, Final report to the West Australian Government, Perth.

Higgins, Rosalyn, 1994. *Problems and Processes: International Law and How We Use It*, Clarendon Press, Oxford, p. 19.

Horsley, Jessica, 2004. *Women in Mining—The Statistics*, on behalf of the Women In Mining Working Group for AusIMM available at www.aussimm.com/women/women.asp.

Human Rights Watch, 2002. *Women's Human Rights*, Available at: http://mvw.hrw.org/woman/index.php [accessed November 4, 2002].

Hunt, J., 1996. 'Situating Women's Development Needs Within the Human Rights Framework,' in G. Moon (ed), *Making Her Rights a Reality: Women's Human Rights and Development*, Community Aid Abroad, Melbourne, pp. 25–26.

International Covenant on Civil and Political Rights (ICCPR) 1967, adopted 16 December 1966, entered into force 23 March 1976, G.A. Res. 2200A (XXI), UNDoc. A/6316, 999 UNTS 171, reprinted in 6 ILM 368. article 2.

International Covenant on Economic, Social and Cultural Rights (ICESCR) 1967, adopted 16 December 1966, entered into force 3 January 1976, G.A. Res. 2200A (XXI), UN Doc. A/6316 (1966), 993 UNTS 3, reprinted in 6 ILM 360.

International Labour Organization (ILO), 1958. *Convention 111: Discrimination (Employment and Occupation) Convention*, article 1.

International Labour Organization (ILO), 1981. *Convention 156: Workers with Family Responsibilities*, article 3.1.

International Labour Organization (ILO), 1998. *Declaration on Fundamental Principles and Rights at Work*, article 2.

International Labour Organization (ILO), 1998. *Declaration on Fundamental Principles and Rights at Work*, article 2 (d).

International Labour Organization (ILO), 1999. *Social and Labour Issues in Small Scale Mines*, International Labour Office, Geneva, available at http://www.ilo.org/public/english/dialogue/sector/te [accessed 28 June 2004].

International Labour Organization (ILO), 2003. *Report of the Director-General: Working Out of Poverty*, ILO, Geneva, pp. 95–96.

Kodz, J., Davis, S., Lain, D., Strebler, M., Rick, J., Bates, P., Cummings, J., Meager, N., 2003. *Working Long Hours: A Review of the Literature*, United Kingdom Department of Trade and Industry, Employment Relations Series no. 16, available at http://www.dti.gov.uk/er/emar/errs16vol1.pdf.

Langman, J., 2003. *Investing in Destruction: The Impacts of a WTO Investment Agreement on Extractive Industries in Developing Countries*, Oxfam America and Make Trade Fair, June, p. 6.

Macdonald, I., 2004. *Mining Ombudsman Case Report: Vatukoula Gold Mine*, Oxfam Community Aid Abroad, available at www.oxfam.org.au/campaigns/mining.

Macdonald, I. and Ross, B., 2003. *Oxfam Community Aid Abroad Mining Ombudsman Annual Report*, Oxfam Community Aid Abroad, available at www.oxfam.org.au/campaigns/mining.

Oxfam International, 2004. *Trading Away Our Rights: Women Working in Global Supply Chains*, Make Trade Fair and Oxfam International.

Pattenden, Catherine, 1998. *Women and Mining*, A report to the 'Women and Mining' Taskforce: The Australasian Institute of Mining and Metallurgy, November, available at www.aussimm.com.au/women/women.asp.

RIMM, 2000. II International Conference: International Network 'Women and Mining,' 16 September 2000, Bolivia, available at www.iwmn.net.

Ross, M., 2001. *Extractive Sectors and the Poor*, Oxfam America, p. 7.

Schachter, Oscar, 1991. *International Law in Theory and Practice*, Martinus Nijhoff, Dordrecht, Netherlands, p. 85.

Seager, Joni, 2003. *The Atlas of Women: An Economic, Social and Political Survey*, The Women's Press, London.

UNCTAD, 2002. *Least Developed Countries Report 2002: Escaping the Poverty Trap*, United Nations, New York, p. 12.

UNDAW, 1995. *The Beijing Declaration and Platform for Action*, Fourth World Conference on Women, Beijing,

UNDAW, 1995. *The Beijing Declaration and Platform for Action Mission Statement*, Available at: http://www.un.org/womenwatch/daw/beijmg/platform/plat.1.htm [accessed November 4, 2002].

UNDFW, 1979. *The International Convention on the Elimination of All Forms of Discrimination Against Women*, United National Development Fund for Women, available at: http://www.unifem.org [accessed November 4, 2002].

UNDP, 1993. *Human Development Report*, Oxford University Press, New York.

UNDP, 2000. *Human Development Report*, New York, Oxford: University Press.

UNDP, 2001. *Human Development Report*, New York, Oxford: University Press.

UNDP, 2004. *Human Development Report*, New York, Oxford: University Press.

UNESC CHR, Sub Commission on the Promotion and Protection of Human Rights, 2003. *55th Session Agenda*, item 4.

UNHCHR, 1993. 'Vienna Declaration and Programme of Action,' United Nations World Conference on Human Rights, Vienna, *Human Rights Law Journal*, 352: 18.

United Nations Development Programme, 1998. *Integrating Human Rights with Sustainable Human Development. A UNDP Policy Document*, January.

United Nations, 2003. *Norms on Responsibilities of Transnational Corporations and other Business Enterprises with regard to Human Rights (with commentary)*, E/CN.4/Sub.2/2003/38/Rev.2 (2203).

United Nations, *Striking a Better Balance*, vol. 3, Annex 6: 143. *Universal Declaration of Human Rights*, 1948. Adopted 10 December 1948, G.A. Res. 217A (III), UN Doc. A/810, at 71, article 2.

Utting, P., 2002. *Regulating Business via Multi-stakeholder Initiatives: A Preliminary Assessment*, UN Research Institute for Sustainable Development, available at www.unrisd.org.

World Bank, 2004. *Striking a Better Balance: The World Bank Group and Extractive Industries*, vol. 1: Ch.2, available at www.eireview.org.

CPSIA information can be obtained
at www.ICGtesting.com
Printed in the USA
LVOW03s1959060916

503467LV00004B/6/P